Literature and Revolution

REINVENTIONS OF THE PARIS COMMUNE

Edited by
Kristin Ross

Available titles in the series:
Carolyn J. Eichner, *The Paris Commune: A Brief History*
Owen Holland, *Literature and Revolution: British Responses to the Paris Commune of 1871*

Literature and Revolution

*British Responses to
the Paris Commune of 1871*

Owen Holland

RUTGERS UNIVERSITY PRESS
NEW BRUNSWICK, CAMDEN, AND NEWARK,
NEW JERSEY, AND LONDON

978-1-9788-2193-4 (paperback)
978-1-9788-2985-5 (cloth)
978-1-9788-2194-1 (epub)
978-1-9788-2195-8 (mobi)
978-1-9788-2196-5 (pdf)

Cataloging-in-publication-data is available from the Library of Congress
LCCN 2021025114

A British Cataloging-in-Publication record for this book is available from the British Library.

Copyright © 2022 by Owen Holland

All rights reserved

No part of this book may be reproduced or utilized in any form or by any means, electronic or mechanical, or by any information storage and retrieval system, without written permission from the publisher. Please contact Rutgers University Press, 106 Somerset Street, New Brunswick, NJ 08901. The only exception to this prohibition is "fair use" as defined by U.S. copyright law.

References to internet websites (URLs) were accurate at the time of writing. Neither the author nor Rutgers University Press is responsible for URLs that may have expired or changed since the manuscript was prepared.

∞ The paper used in this publication meets the requirements of the American National Standard for Information Sciences—Permanence of Paper for Printed Library Materials, ANSI Z39.48-1992.

www.rutgersuniversitypress.org

Manufactured in the United States of America

Contents

Preface   vii

1. Introduction: A Commune in Literature   1
2. Refugees, Renegades, and Misrepresentation: Edward Bulwer Lytton and Eliza Lynn Linton   19
3. Dangerous Sympathies: Mary Elizabeth Braddon, Anne Thackeray Ritchie, and Margaret Oliphant   47
4. "Dreams of the Coming Revolution": George Gissing's *Workers in the Dawn*   79
5. Revolution and *Ressentiment*: Henry James's *The Princess Casamassima*   98
6. The Uses of Tragedy: Alfred Austin's *The Human Tragedy* and William Morris's *The Pilgrims of Hope*   119
7. "It Had to Come Back": H. G. Wells's *When the Sleeper Wakes*   142
8. Conclusion: Looking without Seeing   168

Acknowledgments   183
Notes   185
Bibliography   221
Index   241

Preface

It has been observed that trees are a difficult subject for human observation and study for the simple reason that the duration of a typical tree's life so greatly exceeds that of most people. The same might be said of revolutions. Much as a revolutionary "moment" is undoubtedly the effect of a particular historical conjuncture and set of material circumstances—a national defeat in war, for instance, or an exorbitant rise in the price of bread—revolutions are also processes that unfold across extended periods of time, and the temporal determination of such a process can be hard to predict, to fathom, and retrospectively to narrate. As Raymond Williams put it in *The Long Revolution* (1961), the subject of his book was hard to define because "its uneven action is taking place over so long a period that it is almost impossible not to get lost in its exceptionally complicated process."[1] The rather more circumscribed aim of this book is to examine the influence of one very short-lived revolutionary "moment" that took place in Paris between March and May 1871 on the literary and cultural life of another country.

In the wake of the Franco-Prussian War of 1870–1871, which had been concluded by armistice on 28 January 1871 and which had involved a lengthy and punishing siege of Paris, the republican government of Adolphe Thiers became increasingly worried about political mobilization among the Parisian working class. On 18 March, the government's attempt to seize and confiscate the cannon of the National Guard in Montmartre spurred the people of Paris into action, triggering a popular insurrection that saw women fraternize with soldiers of the regular army, two of whose generals, Thomas and Lecomte, were captured and executed following a breakdown in military discipline. After mass demonstrations converged on the Hôtel de Ville, the government fled for Versailles, and Paris was presided over for ten days by the Central Committee of the National

Guard until the Commune was proclaimed on 28 March, after municipal elections had been conducted two days beforehand.

The Commune represented an alternative nucleus of political authority that posed a direct challenge to the national government in Versailles. During its two-month existence, it took a number of radical steps, including the separation of church and state and the abolition of the death penalty, and it passed various measures in support of the Parisian working class; all political representatives were paid at the rate of an ordinary worker, and their mandates were immediately revocable. In this sense, the Commune was both radically democratic and incipiently socialist. Far more significant, however, was the very fact of the Commune's existence. On the occasion of its one hundredth anniversary, the historian Eugene Schulkind wrote that until the advent of the Commune, "most workers of Paris, as in the rest of France, appear to have consciously or unconsciously accepted the assumption that working people were not equipped to be legislators."[2] Confined within the compass of a single city, the Commune can nonetheless stake a strong claim to be recognized as the first working-class government of the radical Left, animated by a revolutionary vision of internationalism, solidarity, and economic justice. After the government at Versailles had regrouped, it reacted to the Commune by brutally suppressing it during the *semaine sanglante* (Bloody Week) of 21–28 May. As the British artist and socialist Walter Crane wrote two decades later in a poem, "In Memory of the Commune of Paris," the Commune was "Maligned, betrayed, short-lived to act and teach."[3] Nevertheless, its impact was felt across much of Europe for the decades to come. As one of its earliest British historians observed, for a movement of major "historical importance," the Paris Commune was "compact almost beyond precedent," but he nonetheless regarded it as one of "the most remarkable events of modern times."[4] When Oscar Wilde visited Paris in 1883, over a decade after the Commune's fall, Robert Sherard reported Wilde's comment, on passing the ruins of the Tuileries Palace, which had been destroyed during the Bloody Week, that each "little blackened stone" was, to him, "a chapter in the Bible of Democracy."[5]

Britain is separated from France by little more than a short stretch of water, but political disturbances in France have often proved to be a source of acute anxiety on both sides of La Manche. The *longue durée* of Britain's political development is, as Perry Anderson has written, defined by the historical complications consequent upon the eventual defeat and failure of its own "bourgeois revolution."[6] This has meant that British responses to European, and particularly French, revolutionary upheavals have always been particularly fraught with internal as well as external significance. This book is, first and foremost, a work of literary criticism. Yet, as Anderson has argued elsewhere, the discipline of literary criticism enjoys (or once enjoyed) a "peculiar status" in English cultural life as a "displaced home of the totality," partly as "a symptom of the vacuum at the centre of the culture."[7] So while this book is primarily a literary study of certain British authors who responded, in different ways, to the political event of the Paris Commune, it also covers a period in which certain assumptions were formed—about the relationship of literature to society and politics, the integral connection between "culture" and "civilization," and the nature of the masses' access to such cultural goods—that would go on to undergird the professional discipline of literary criticism when it emerged and began to consolidate its institutional status during the early decades of the twentieth century.[8]

If Anderson's claim about the discipline of literary criticism is taken seriously, one might also extend its logic backward and consider whether the absence in nineteenth-century Britain of any academic discipline or intellectual formation capable of supplying a general theory of the social totality might therefore be perceived to place a special burden on cultural commentators and literary figures like novelists and poets to act as keepers of the social and political peace. One discipline that might have undertaken such work was sociology, and the closest equivalent to sociology in Victorian Britain was a French import, practiced by the Positivist disciples of the philosopher Auguste Comte. These figures, notably Frederic Harrison and Edward Spencer Beesly, were generally sympathetic to the Commune and featured among its earliest British defenders—a fact that did not endear them to many of their contemporaries. On Anderson's terms, then, a study such as this one would need to accentuate the intellectual significance of the *cultural* response to an event like the Paris Commune, partly for lack of any other sustained response, notwithstanding the ubiquitous denunciations of the popular press. The difficult task of suturing the psychic wounds that had been inflicted on bourgeois subjectivity by the Commune's challenge to the ruling social order, albeit at one remove, fell instead to a heterogeneous group of novelists and literary figures who responded, in the main, by reasserting the sanctity of the cultural realm as a space of privilege while identifying the Communards themselves with a nihilistic desire for destruction. As the later chapters of this book demonstrate, novelists including George Gissing, Henry James, and H. G. Wells all responded to the Commune by mobilizing a Nietzschean ideologeme of *ressentiment* that contained the threat of social revolution by reducing its determining impetus to little more than a politics of envy.

The emergence of the Commune in the wake of the Franco-Prussian War disturbed the established order of rival nation-states in proposing a vision of international, working-class solidarity that cut across national boundaries. Its suppression resonated far beyond the particular locality of Paris, and after its defeat, an influx of political refugees led London to become an "asylum of the defeated."[9] At the same time, the Franco-Prussian War sparked imperial anxieties about the threat of invasion, in which European powers figured as potential sources of domination.[10] In the wake of this traumatic shock to the ruling social order and its predominant mode of social and economic organization, a wide range of British writers responded to these contradictory pressures toward integration and disintegration, seeking to represent the Commune to a British reading public that consumed accounts of the conflict in newspaper reportage, commentary in journals, diaries, historical fiction, and poetry.

In a period of renewed crisis of pan-European identity, it is an apt moment to revisit episodes in the history of the Continent during which anxieties about social stability and fragmentation have loomed large. The brutal suppression of the Commune—which the British poet Algernon Charles Swinburne supported with the assertion that the Communards should be shot down "wherever met like dogs"—exemplifies what Jacques Rancière has characterized as "hatred of democracy" on the part of ruling elites.[11] Cultural critics played an important role in elaborating the terms of this response in Britain. For some, the Commune represented a dangerous (and potentially contagious) threat to civilization, while others heralded the dawn of a new liberty. Although the contemporary moment is animated by very different tensions, this book alludes, in terms that remain largely unspoken, to a longer history of British anxiety about Europe by focusing on the way in which such anxieties have been culturally produced, particularly during periods of political instability both within and beyond the nation's borders.

The book examines three different kinds of material: newspaper and periodical commentary (including the wide array of images relating to the Commune that circulated in periodicals such as the *Illustrated London News* and the *Graphic*); poetic responses to the Commune; and the numerous historical and other novels that take the Commune as their backdrop, both explicitly and implicitly. A large number of novelists fictionalized the Commune, or aspects of its aftermath, including Edward Bulwer Lytton, Eliza Lynn Linton, Mary Elizabeth Braddon, Anne Thackeray Ritchie, George Gissing, and Henry James. Margaret Oliphant and H. G. Wells, meanwhile, responded more obliquely to the anxieties engendered by the Commune through the medium of spectral allegory and dystopian science fiction, respectively. The Commune also met with a more positive response, particularly among Britain's emerging fin-de-siècle socialist movement. In socialist periodicals such as *Commonweal* and *To-day*, a number of poets—most notably William Morris—elaborated a poetics of martyrdom with reference to the Communards, as part of a wider culture of celebrating and commemorating the Commune. This book interweaves close reading of these works with a more expansive account of the Commune's place in the intellectual landscape of late-Victorian Britain, drawing on the writings of Victorian thinkers including John Ruskin, Matthew Arnold, Frederic Harrison, and George Bernard Shaw. The book explores how different writers appealed to and created different publics, contributing to wider cultural debates about the meaning of the Commune. Almost all of the writers discussed in this book used the traumatic experience of the Commune to orientate themselves in relation to contemporary developments in Britain. As time passed, writers responded not only to the event itself, as mediated by the initial reports, but also to intervening fictions and representations. While the book follows a roughly chronological sequence, it also traces the cumulative effect of changing representations of the Commune, which tracked domestic anxieties engendered by the 1880s socialist revival and the "Woman Question."

The historiography of the Commune is both well established and current, but there is a relative dearth of material that investigates cultural and literary responses to the Commune in Britain. Compared to the widespread critical literature on British responses to the French revolutions of 1789 and 1848, cultural responses to the revolution of 1871 have been relatively (though not entirely) overlooked, despite the wide array of primary material that would allow such a narrative to be reconstructed. This book attempts to make good on that lack, while also extending and revising critical understandings of the Commune by accentuating the transnational aspect of its afterlife in Britain. In the French context, the historiography of the Commune is strongly identified with the work of historians such as Eugene Schulkind, Stewart Edwards, Jacques Rougerie, Alain Dalotel, Robert Tombs, Gay L. Gullickson, Martin Phillip Johnson, Carolyn Eichner, and John M. Merriman.[12] Their work has detailed the events of the Commune and offered different interpretations of the reasons underlying its emergence. Kristin Ross, Peter Starr, Colette E. Wilson, Philip M. Katz, and J. Michelle Coghlan have surveyed the Commune's cultural afterlives in France and the United States, with Starr, Wilson and Coghlan focusing particularly on the politics of cultural memory.[13] With regard to its reception in Britain, Matthew Beaumont situates responses to the Commune within a broader trend of anti-communism and cacotopianism, placing particular emphasis on the genre of reactionary "future histories" as one kind of fin-de-siècle ideology of social dreaming.[14] Beaumont also cogently argues that "if the Commune was a non-event in England, it was nonetheless a decisive non-event," a point echoed by Scott McCracken, who notes in his work on the literary afterlives of the Commune that it was often paradoxically "represented through a discourse of its non-representation."[15] Other scholars, notably Albert Boime, Gonzalo J. Sánchez, John Milner, Bertrand Tillier, and Adrian Rifkin, have recovered the Commune's place in art history and visual culture, while Julia Nicholls's recent monograph has made a significant contribution to understanding the intellectual history of its partisans and fellow travelers.[16] Building on these works, as well as the suggestive insights offered in Kristin Ross's *Communal Luxury: The Political Imaginary of the Paris Commune* (2015), the present book extends this growing body of research to encompass the literary landscape of late-Victorian Britain, showing how discussions of the Commune functioned as a screen for the projection of hopes and fears, serving as a warning for some and an example to others, as well as a sounding board for the cultural production of anxiety about revolution during the closing decades of the nineteenth century.

Literature and Revolution

CHAPTER 1

Introduction

A COMMUNE IN LITERATURE

In an admiring obituary for Alfred Tennyson, published in the *New Review* in November 1892, Edmund Gosse suggests that some of his contemporaries mourned the passing not only of an esteemed poet laureate but of an entire epoch in English literature. In doing so, Gosse allows himself a revealing reference to (relatively) recent history when he writes: "What I dread, what I have long dreaded, is the eruption of a sort of Commune in literature. At no period could the danger of such an outbreak of rebellion against tradition be so great as during the reaction which must follow the death of our most illustrious writer."[1] Brief though Gosse's reference to the Paris Commune of 1871 is, it suggests the way in which this acute and localized episode of class struggle, which triggered a much broader crisis of bourgeois confidence across most of Europe, continued to haunt his ruminations on the literary landscape of late-Victorian Britain two decades after the event itself. In imagining the potential crisis of cultural authority following Tennyson's death, Gosse's mind, it seems, turned instinctively to the Commune. Yet even as Gosse declaratively announces the termination of an entire literary epoch, he also unknowingly preempts the opening of another in his anticipation of a later current of conservative modernism.[2] While the anti-communism of T. S. Eliot and Ezra Pound would fasten on the specter of the Bolshevik Revolution, Gosse's tilt toward reaction was more muted in being less shaken by the turn of world-historical events.

In Gosse's attempt to summarize the cultural zeitgeist surrounding Tennyson's death, he suggests that some people might think "we have no poet left so venerable, or so perfect in ripeness of the long-drawn years of craftsmanship," and, straining toward the superlative, he adds that some might even imagine "poetry is dead amongst us." Such a view, he quickly qualifies, "is scarcely generous and not a little ridiculous."[3] In listing some living poets whom Tennyson favored with correspondence, Gosse includes Rudyard Kipling and William

Watson (on whose posthumous reputation fate can hardly be said to have smiled kindly) among those who would be likely to keep the flame of culture burning. But Gosse also calls readers' attention to the rather more alarming presence of the "multitude so stirred into an excited curiosity about a great poet," whom he observed hovering on the edges of Tennyson's funeral in Westminster Abbey, and he frets in rather more genuine terms that this multitude will "presently crave . . . a little more excitement still over another poet," which will not be satisfied because "We have not, and shall not have for a generation at least, such another sacrifice to offer to the monster."[4] The mere attendance of the "multitude" at Tennyson's funeral should not be taken to suggest their conversion to "a love of fine literature," Gosse warns, because "fine literature—however scandalous it may sound in the ears of this generation to say it—is for the few."[5] The knack for reading and appreciating "fine literature," Gosse suggests, is less a matter of volition than of inherited taste and innate capacity for discrimination of value. Such a knack would thus always prove beyond the reach of the demogorgon that had unsurreptitiously intruded itself on Tennyson's literary lying-in-state. In a roughly contemporaneous 1891 *Contemporary Review* article titled "The Influence of Democracy on Literature," Gosse's humble protestation that he seeks to do no more than "tap the intellectual barometer cheerfully" is rather belied by his later statement that "whatever the form of government, literature has always been aristocratic, or at least oligarchic."[6] While it is not wholly to be regretted, in Gosse's view, the influence of democracy on literature is generally to the bad, not least because its "essence . . . is marked by the destruction of those very ramparts which protected and inspired the old intellectual free States."[7]

Paris under the Commune, according to one contemporary British eyewitness, was "like Rome after the barbarians had overrun it."[8] In Gosse's cultural imaginary, these latter-day barbarians continued to muster at the gates, motivating his own self-presentation as gatekeeper and guardian of the sacred groves of Parnassus, and it is particularly telling that, as late as 1892, he could still look to the Commune as a touchstone for this latter-day barbarianism. The Commune's suppression resonated far beyond the particular locality of Paris, and as Karl Marx commented about the Commune in his first draft of *The Civil War in France* (1871), "Whatever . . . its fate at Paris, it will make its way around the world."[9] For Marx, along with many other partisans of the socialist movement, the Commune lived on as a talismanic symbol, heralding the consolidation of a sense of collective identity and purpose and providing a focal point for rituals of collective memory and celebration. The Commune made its way, as Marx predicted, into the political writings of several of the most significant radical writers of fin-de-siècle Britain, at the same time as the Commune's surviving militants were scattered in exile from the Jura region in Switzerland all the way to the antipodes in the French territory of New Caledonia. Jürgen Osterhammel records that "more than 3,800 insurgents were sent in nineteen convoys of ships to the Pacific archipelago of New Caledonia, a colony under French rule since 1853" and points out that "the deportation was conceived as a means of 'civilizing' both the indigenous kanaks and the Communard revolutionaries, and that was the spirit in which it was carried out."[10] Meanwhile, around "1,500 adult male Communards..., accompanied by at least 600 wives and 1,200 children," sought refuge in London, a fact that generated both media interest and more practical efforts to organize solidarity.[11]

The aim of this book is to demonstrate how the Commune also made its way into the literary culture of Britain during the years between 1871 and the first decade of the twentieth century. Unlike the exiles, many other Communards did not escape the ferocity of the Versailles reprisals, and as Eric Hobsbawm has observed, "This brief, brutal—and for the time uncharacteristic—unleashing of blind terror by respectable society reflected a fundamental problem of the politics of bourgeois society: that of its democratization."[12] The "blind terror" soon subsided into patterns of rhetorical and discursive containment, sometimes no less brutal, only differently so. Gosse's remarks attest that the problem of democratization proved especially pronounced in the realm of fin-de-siècle Britain's cultural life, and the effects of this impasse were exacerbated by the advent of the Commune. As Priscilla Parkhurst Ferguson has commented with reference to French responses to the Commune, the sheer "virulence of the condemnation of the Commune by most writers of the time flows from the fear of what abolition of hierarchy would do to the very conception of literature and the literary."[13] That this was also true, from a distance, for many British writers is one of the principal arguments that will be unfolded in later chapters of this book.

Gosse's seemingly incidental remarks are, in this respect, simply the tip of an iceberg, and he was by no means alone in his discomfort. George Moore, who spent much of the 1870s in Paris training to be an artist, studiously avoids any reference to the Commune in his Rousseauian memoir *Confessions of a Young Man* (1886), but he does record that he returned from Paris to London convinced that "art is the direct antithesis to democracy," while professing a Nietzschean disdain for "the mass."[14] In *On the Genealogy of Morals* (1887), Friedrich Nietzsche—who numbered Gosse and Moore among his earliest Anglophone readers—characterized "modern democracy, anarchy... and especially the hankering for *la commune*" as an "immense *afterclap*," which he identified with "the most primitive form of society."[15] For Nietzsche, the Commune represented a form of atavistic regression that posed an existential threat to his aristocratic conception of individualism. False reports about the burning of the Louvre seriously disturbed his mood and confirmed his predisposition to view events through the "sole focus" of culture.[16] As Jacques Rancière has observed, in a different but related context, such a "denunciation of 'democratic individualism' is simply the hatred of equality by which a dominant intelligentsia lets it be known that it is the elite entitled to rule over the blind herd."[17] British responses to the Commune were similarly marked, in some quarters, by a "hatred of equality," and Eleanor Marx later recalled, in an 1893 letter, "the condition of perfectly frantic fury of the whole middle class against the Commune" to the point where "it was proposed—quite seriously—that the Communards who had taken refuge in England should be handed over to the doctors and the hospitals for purposes of vivisection."[18]

In Britain, the Commune also evoked longer-standing fears about the Continental specter of revolution, not least because the Communards' seizure of power represented an embryonic alternative to the bourgeois social order. As late as 1892, Gosse could still turn to the Commune as a byword for this threat, which he invokes by way of a displacement into the realm of culture in general, and literature in particular, held at one remove from the real politics of the actual Parisian Communards, many of whom were, as Kristin Ross has shown, deeply motivated by the idea that culture itself might be radically democratized without the kind of loss or attenuation imagined in Gosse's fearful prophecy of "a sort of Commune in literature." In Ross's words, the Communards' ideal of communal luxury "entails transforming the aesthetic coordinates of the entire community" in line with the demand that beauty be allowed to "flourish in spaces shared in common and not just in special privatized preserves."[19] Such a demand, according to Ross, "means reconfiguring art to be fully integrated into everyday life."[20] These ideas were shared by a number of the Commune's defenders in Britain, from the revolutionary socialist William Morris to the exiled Russian anarchist Peter Kropotkin. One of the important insights of Ross's book has to do with her extension of the Commune's temporal horizon in order to examine "a kind of afterlife that does not exactly *come after* but . . . is part and parcel of the event itself: . . . a life beyond life."[21] This book is, in part, similarly concerned with the *prolongation* of the Commune in the writings of its British partisans and celebrants (discussed at more length in chapter 6), but it also devotes significant attention to those who sought to contain and disavow its memory; what Ross refers to as the "continuation of the combat by other means" was a two-sided affair, and this book is equally concerned to investigate the responses of those British writers who found various literary strategies with which to attempt the stabilization of bourgeois subjectivity in the wake of the traumatic shock of a revolutionary event.[22] Attending to these multiple patterns of response to the Commune confirms the intensity of the struggle between the consciously pro- and anti-Communard writers, but it also reveals the existence of a kind of ideological no-man's-land, in between and sometimes adjacent to the main fronts, and several of the writers who will be discussed in this book occupied a portion of this terrain.

Against the Communard imaginary of communal luxury and the democratization of cultural life, Gosse performs a rearguard action in defense of an elitist conception of tradition, canonicity, and exclusivity. He envisages the prospect of a "Commune in literature" as a threat to standards of taste, bearing within it a leveling impulse that would sacrifice high culture on the altar of social revolution. In his 1891 article "The Influence of Democracy on Literature," Gosse is even more forthright in identifying "communism" (or "democracy pushed to an impossible extremity") with the attempt to "prevent intellectual capacity of every kind from developing, for fear of the ascendency which it would exercise."[23] In his Tennyson obituary, meanwhile, he does not explicitly mention the politics of the Commune but instead relies on an unspoken conception of literary and cultural production as a field of political struggle, in which both the Commune's partisans and its enemies might play opposing roles. It is telling, however, that Gosse dramatizes these apprehensions with passing reference to the Commune, an event that Marx characterized as "the first revolution in which the working class was openly acknowledged as the only class capable of social initiative."[24] In a brief aside in Gosse's 1891 essay, he momentarily entertains this alarming possibility, applying it to the sphere of cultural production, writing: "It may be that we are still under the oligarchic tradition, and that a social revolution, introducing a sudden breach in our habits, and perhaps paralysing the profession of letters for a few years, would be followed by a new literature of a decidedly democratic class."[25] Although he immediately abandons this speculative thought to return to his antidemocratic tirade, Gosse here briefly recognizes that social forces and relations of production animate the very creative and aesthetic endeavors of the literary coteries whose praises he sings. He also acknowledges that a social revolution might alter and democratize these conditions. Gosse soon represses this thought, consigning it to the "spectral mirror of the future," but if one were given to bold statement, one might say that he unwittingly discloses the political unconscious of the fin de siècle's entire bourgeois literary profession.[26]

In Karl Marx's midcentury essay *The Class Struggles in France: 1848 to 1850* (1850), he observes that "the degree to which the continental revolutions have repercussions on England is also the thermometer by which one can measure how far they really challenge bourgeois conditions of life, rather than affecting only its political formations."[27] Marx was principally concerned with the prospective economic effects of an earlier period of class struggle, but this statement is no less applicable to the potential cultural and ideological repercussions of the events of 1871. The Commune certainly provoked outrage and dismay in London's literary circles. Among those whom Gosse would later esteem as likely inheritors of Tennyson's poetic mantle, Algernon Charles Swinburne's response to the Commune is especially notable for its extremity. Gosse edited the 1918 edition of Swinburne's letters for William Heinemann and dated their friendship from "the beginning of 1871," meaning that the first flowering of their literary relationship, which had an importantly formative influence on the young Gosse, coincided with the period of the Commune.[28] Swinburne's knee-jerk response to the Commune was intransigent and authoritarian. In a letter to William Michael Rossetti, he comments, "I may say to you as frankly as I would say to [Victor] Hugo that so far from objecting to the infliction of death on the incendiaries of the Louvre I should wish to have them proclaimed (to use a phrase of his own) not merely 'hors la loi' but 'hors l'humanité,' and a law passed throughout the world authorising any citizen of any nation to take their lives with impunity and assurance of national thanks—to shoot them down wherever met like dogs."[29] Swinburne invokes humanity, here, in order to rationalize the taking of human life in the name of culture. It would be hard to find a more unmitigated expression of class hatred that, for Swinburne, apparently overrides the Communard insurgents' claims to even the most basic human dignity. That he dated this letter 1 June 1871, several days after the Versaillais soldiers had committed widespread atrocities in retaking Paris from the Communards, only heightens the effect of Swinburne's unabashed disclosure of these protoauthoritarian reflexes.

Swinburne articulates his anti-Communard sentiment in terms of a claim to cultural universalism, continuing as follows: "A political crime is a national crime and punishable only by the nation sinned against; France alone has the right to punish the shedding of French blood by putting to death on that charge a Bonaparte or a Thiers, a Rigault or a Gallifet; but it is the whole world's right and duty to take vengeance on men who should strike at the whole world such a blow as to inflict an everlasting incurable wound by the attempted destruction of Rome, Venice, Paris, London—of the Vatican, Ducal Palace, Louvre, or Museum."[30] Although the Louvre had been badly damaged during the Bloody Week, reports that it had been deliberately burned down were, in fact, false, and it has long been a source of historiographical controversy as to whether the Communards or the Versaillais should bear the brunt of responsibility for the destruction of Paris during the fierce, street-by-street fighting of the Commune's last days.[31] As the historian Gay L. Gullickson writes, "Virtually everyone has taken sides in telling its story."[32] Notwithstanding this uncertainty, Swinburne's mobilization of a cultural universalism ("the whole world's right and duty") in the name of "vengeance" against the revolutionary militants of the Commune reveals a dark underside to the world republic of letters, whose central locus Pascale Casanova situates in Paris: "the capital of the literary world, the city endowed with the greatest literary prestige on earth."[33] For Swinburne, an aggressively curatorial ideal of cultural preservation reduces the Communards to a kind of bare life that could be readily and unthinkingly taken ("hors l'humanité").[34]

In this respect, Swinburne's response closely (though unknowingly) mirrors that of the French poet, critic, and aesthete Théophile Gautier, whose *Tableaux de Siège: Paris 1870–1871* (1871) contains a number of scathing reflections on the Communards and whose aestheticism was an important influence on

Swinburne's poetry. In the chapter "The Venus of Milo," Gautier tracks the movements of the ancient Greek statue (held by the Louvre and since attributed to Alexandros of Antioch) during the two sieges of Paris. He observes that Venus was about to be "restored in her radiant beauty to her pedestal" after the lifting of the Prussian siege,

> when came the Commune with its host of barbarians, come, not from the Cimmerian fogs, but sprung up from the Paris pavements like the foul fermentation of subterranean filth. The aesthetics of these fierce sectaries and their contempt for the ideal are well known. In their hands the goddess, had they discovered her, would have run great risk; they would have sold her or broken her up as being a proof of human genius offensive to levelling stupidity. Is not the aristocracy of masterpieces that which most offends envious mediocrity? It is quite natural that the ugly should hate the beautiful.[35]

Gautier's choice of terms ("levelling stupidity," "envious mediocrity") already anticipates the Nietzschean ideologeme of *ressentiment* that, as will become apparent elsewhere in this book, was a persistent keynote of the literary response to the Commune in Britain, from Henry James to H. G. Wells and from George Gissing to Mary Elizabeth Braddon.

As with Swinburne, Gautier also deliberately emphasizes the specifically cultural and aesthetic dimension of his repudiation of the Communards, whose "levelling stupidity," in Gautier's conception of such activity, can only involve a kind of cultural vandalism associated with willful destruction and iconoclasm. If the Communards, for Swinburne and Gautier, were latter-day "barbarians" inside the gates of the capital of the nineteenth century, they were also trespassing in the capital of "the universal republic of letters," which, in Pascale Casanova's formulation, has "neither borders nor boundaries" but exists as "a universal homeland exempt from all professions of patriotism, a kingdom of literature set up in opposition to the ordinary laws of states, a transnational realm whose sole imperatives are those of art and literature."[36] Yet, as Swinburne's and Gautier's responses to the Commune surely indicate, the price of admission to this eminently bourgeois republic could be very high indeed. As Marx sardonically commented in *The Civil War in France*, "The bourgeoisie of the whole world, which looks complacently upon the wholesale massacre after the battle, is convulsed by horror at the desecration of brick and mortar!"[37] Not to be outdone, Edmond de Goncourt, in his journal entry for 31 May 1871, articulates the logic of this deeply compromised position with startling clarity in his justification of the massacre of the Communards: "All is well. There has been neither compromise nor conciliation. The solution has been brutal, imposed by sheer force of arms. The solution has saved everyone from the dangers of cowardly compromise."[38] In the case of Gautier and Swinburne, their decision to proclaim themselves as self-appointed guardians of the aesthetic, *against* the social revolution of the

Commune, does not treat politics as simply incompatible with the aesthetic (as some versions of aestheticism would have it); instead, they more actively disclaim the prospect of a politics that might upend the social and economic dispensation that valorizes that very aestheticism. Even as the aestheticist pose adopted by Gautier and later Swinburne revolved around the shock tactics of "épater le bourgeois," their fierce condemnation of the Commune represents an essential willingness to close ranks against a more fearsome enemy.

In Casanova's account, nineteenth-century Paris was able to combine "two sets of apparently antithetical properties, in a curious way bringing together all the historical conceptions of freedom," existing as a symbol of revolution, identified with "the overthrow of the monarchy" and "the invention of the rights of man" during the late eighteenth century, but also as "the capital of letters, the arts, luxurious living, and fashion."[39] Paris was thus both "the arbiter of good taste" and "the source of political democracy," and Casanova's account emphasizes the congruence and general compatibility of these only "apparently antithetical properties."[40] Indeed, the very fact that "the image of Paris was bound up with the memory of the French Revolution and the uprisings of 1830, 1848, and 1870–71" constituted a major share of the city's "symbolic capital," according to Casanova, and the repeated literary transcriptions of the city's revolutionary history created a "unique configuration" that allowed the myth of an "idealized city" to emerge in which "artistic freedom could be proclaimed and lived."[41] Yet the outbreak of the Commune provoked a vicious form of reaction on the part of some of the most budding cosmopolitan citizens of this world republic, so much so that it might lead one to question whether the Commune can be quite so neatly integrated into a sequence of revolutionary upheavals in which the cultural arbiters of "good taste" find themselves lined up on the same side as the revolutionaries fighting for "political democracy." The antithetical aspects of the antithesis were sometimes rather more pronounced than Casanova allows, and each break in the sequence of revolutions represents a moment of properly ideological rupture in which literary and cultural figures were not merely neutral observers but sometimes found themselves on opposing sides of the barricades (figuratively speaking). It is an important contention of this book that the choices made by such figures reveal something significant not only about the particularities of the cultural response to the Commune in Britain but also about the way in which these figures conceived of literature's relationship to the prospect of social revolution (both past and future) and the way in which self-consciously literary endeavors might unconsciously work to mobilize or contain such possibilities.

Elsewhere in late-Victorian Britain's literary and artistic milieus, the Communard exiles who began to arrive in London in large numbers were met with a rather more compassionate response, and some of them were extended different kinds of material and intellectual solidarity. The network of friends who had constituted the Pre-Raphaelite Brotherhood during the late 1840s and 1850s and who, in doing so, cultivated an environment of "'bohemian' tolerance," stand out in this respect.[42] Dante Gabriel Rossetti, for example, wrote to William Bell Scott on 2 October 1871 and mentioned that he had responded (via Sidney Colvin) to a notice in the *Pall Mall Gazette* in order to subscribe to a "Communalist Benevolent Society," adding that the Communards "seem really, poor fellows, to be helping each other in a very sad plight."[43] He also endeavored to use his connections to support individual Communards. On 16 December 1871, he wrote a letter to John Lucas Tupper, an old friend from the early days of the Pre-Raphaelite movement, in order to seek employment for the Blanquist refugee Émile Leverdays, about whom he said, "[his] chief (and I believe very high) attainments are as an anatomical draughtsmen."[44] Tupper had worked as a draughtsman at St Guy's Hospital during the 1860s, and it appears that he successfully secured a position for Leverdays, whose 1890 obituary in Henry Maret's French newspaper *Le Radical* describes Leverdays—"l'auteur d'une *Histoire des assemblées parlantes* [1883]"—as having been attached during his latter days to "l'Academie de médecine de Londres en qualité de dessinateur d'anatomie."[45] Rossetti's brother William, meanwhile, notes in his *Diary* entry for 8 April 1873 that he "gave to Guérant (the French Officer who got mixed up in the affairs of the Commune) a few of Gabriel's books to bind," adding that "Guérant does not seem sanguine as to getting back to France at any early date: he is already obtaining some modicum of employment in book-binding."[46] Dante had written to the painter and fellow Pre-Raphaelite Ford Madox Brown from Kelmscott Manor on 30 January 1873 to inquire about an unnamed "book-binding Communist," likely to be Guérant, and Brown, whose daughter Lucy married William Rossetti in 1874, played an important role in securing support and employment for exiled Communards.[47]

For much of the 1870s, Communard refugees rubbed shoulders with various literary and political luminaries at the bohemian gatherings that took place at Brown's London residence at 37 Fitzroy Square.[48] The Irish MP Justin McCarthy records in his *Reminiscences* that he met Swinburne "for the first time" at Fitzroy Square—Swinburne's view of the Communards had presumably mellowed by this point—as well as the novelist Eliza Lynn Linton, whose novel *Joshua Davidson: Christian and Communist* (1872) offers one of the most undeniably and uncharacteristically sympathetic depictions of the Commune available in the popular fiction of the period.[49] Brown engaged the ex-Communard Jules Andrieu as the French and Latin tutor for his son Oliver, and according to William Holman Hunt, it appears likely that Andrieu, along with his wife and son, lodged at Fitzroy Square, where Brown frequently "gave receptions, brilliant in the celebrity of the guests": "Perhaps it was his French spirit of comradeship, or his sympathy for all revolutionists, that had made him follow with great concern the fortunes of the communists in Paris. When they were driven out, hearing of a refugee in London, he invited him, his wife, and his son to take up their quarters in his home; accordingly the three formed part of the circle, and Brown organised lectures and sold tickets to individuals of advanced ideas eager to applaud the leader in the last Parisian revolt."[50] Andrieu, it seems, played quite a central role in the social life of the bohemian circle that gathered at Fitzroy Square, and he took advantage of the relatively stable income provided by his employment to work on a retrospective account of the Commune, titled *Notes pour Servir à l'Histoire de la Commune de Paris en 1871*. An early version of Andrieu's *Notes* appeared in the *Fortnightly Review*, a magazine that had been founded by Anthony Trollope in 1865, along with the English Positivists Frederic Harrison and Edward Spencer Beesly, who were among the Commune's vanishingly small number of British defenders during the 1870s.[51] For Andrieu, the Commune was the result of the "firm conviction that the present political and social systems are false, and that gradual reforms and ameliorations therein can at best be like local remedies which in the long run aggravate the disease."[52]

The socialist illustrator Walter Crane recalled in his autobiographical memoir *An Artist's Reminiscences* (1907) that several Communard artists found refuge in Britain. These included "M. Gueraud, a remarkably tasteful and skilful mounter of drawings," and the sculptor Jules Dalou, whom Crane recalled meeting at the Palace Green residence of the painter and aristocratic radical George Howard.[53] Other former Communards found a variety of British publishers willing to provide a platform for their commemorative valorizations of the Commune. Gustave Paul Cluseret, who had served as the Commune's Delegate for War and who found refuge in Geneva after the Commune's defeat, published an article, "The Paris Commune of 1871: Its Origin, Legitimacy, Tendency, and Aim," in *Fraser's Magazine*, edited by James Anthony Froude, in March 1873. Cluseret used the article to argue that the Commune "was, undoubtedly, one of the most important dramas enacted in the nineteenth century, both for the ferocity displayed by the victors, and for the principles proclaimed in the face of the Governments of Europe by the vanquished."[54] Between April and September 1879, Paschal Grousset published a six-part article, "How the Paris Commune Made the Republic," in Edmund Yates's *Time*, in which he described the Commune as "the central event of the century."[55] Elsewhere in the periodical press, the Communard novelist Jules Vallès reviewed Victor Hugo's *Quatrevingt-Treize* (1874) for William Minto's *Examiner* in March 1874, commenting that Hugo's novelistic rendering of the revolutionary events of 1793 "gives the preference to those who have fallen struggling and whose memory is unjustly sullied," adding that "[Hugo] was full of that thought when, after the defeat of May, 1871, he vouchsafed his protection to the fugitives."[56] Félix Régamey, meanwhile, was employed as an illustrator for the *Illustrated London News*, while portions of a translation of Louise Michel's play *The Strike* were published in the Socialist League's *Commonweal* journal in 1891 after the League's anarchist faction had seized control of the organization.[57] Some Communards also founded their own publications in exile: Eugène Vermersch established a short-lived London daily, *L'Avenir*, which appeared for thirty-two issues between October and November 1872, in which some of Paul Verlaine's poetry appeared, while Jean Baptiste Clément published a single issue of a projected new journal, *La Voix de Peuple*, in November 1871.[58]

More comprehensive works also appeared: the illustrator George Montbard published a blisteringly satirical critique of British imperialism, *The Case of John Bull in Egypt, The Transvaal, Venezuela and Elsewhere* (1896), while Prosper-Olivier Lissagaray's *History of the Paris Commune of 1871* was published by Reeves and Turner in 1886 in a translation by Eleanor Marx (to whom Lissagaray had been briefly engaged). Marx played a very active role in the socialist revival that took place in Britain during the 1880s and was a member of the Socialist League. In 1885, the third issue of the League's *Commonweal* journal, then edited by William Morris (another erstwhile Pre-Raphaelite), hosted Édouard Vaillant's retrospective article "Vive la Commune!," in which Vaillant proclaimed that the Commune's defeat "is but momentary, and for the delay the triumph will be but so much the greater, the more assured," adding that "it is not in Paris and France alone, but in all Europe, and even America, that the Socialistic idea is agitating the masses and the workers."[59] Vaillant had returned to Paris after the general amnesty of 1880 and, at the time of writing, was an elected member of the Paris Municipal Council; he asserted that the "assault upon the old society" remained a live political project for which he drew support and succor from allies in Britain and elsewhere outside France.[60] Writing in the pages of the same journal four years later, in a letter to the chairman of a commemorative meeting celebrating the anniversary of the Commune, Morris echoed Vaillant's stance in his comment that "we . . . celebrate [the Communards'] defeat as the herald of the victory which is to be, and as a preparation for it," adding: "If there were any amongst the defenders of the Commune who did not understand that its ultimate aim, its reason for existence, was the abolition of class society, its enemies at least understood it well—and wrote their endorsement in the blood of 30,000 men slain."[61]

Morris, like Brown and Rossetti, had first risen to public attention as part of the Pre-Raphaelite Brotherhood during the 1850s, yet, with his entry into the socialist movement during the 1880s, Morris went much further than any of his former artistic collaborators and cothinkers in substantiating a properly *political* understanding of the Commune's legacy. During the 1870s, however, there is no evidence to suggest that Morris showed much of an interest in the Commune, unlike some of the other Pre-Raphaelites previously named. During the 1880s, by contrast, Morris played a crucial role in building a network of socialist agitators and educators who actively celebrated the Commune's memory in poetry and prose, discussed at more length in chapter 6. The fact that the Commune found a number of politically and ideologically committed supporters in Britain doubtless incentivized its opponents to continue the work of sullying its name and tarnishing its legacy. As Julia Nicholls has put it, "In the weeks, months, and years that followed [1871], the war against the Commune did not dissipate, but merely changed form."[62] Both the Commune's partisans and its enemies showed an "acute awareness," as Kristin Ross observes, "of the battle over the Commune's memory that had begun to rage even as the Bloody Week was ending."[63] In Britain, this battle continued well into the first decade of the twentieth century, and popular fiction was an important site in this struggle over representation and ideas.

The incipient anticommunism espoused by the Commune's detractors constituted a kind of ambient ideological background noise for much of the period. The Commune represented a moment of acute crisis in the formation of European cultural identity; even for a self-professed radical like Swinburne, whose cosmopolitan republicanism had, until that point, occupied one of the outermost flanks of acceptable political discourse in Britain, the Commune forced matters to a head. It revealed in stark terms a line of fracture that many observers would have preferred to ignore but that some were prepared to acknowledge. The cultural critic Matthew Arnold commented in a letter to his mother, dated 20 March 1871, "There is no way by which France can make the rest of Europe so alarmed and uneasy as by a socialistic and red republic. It is a perpetual flag to the proletaire class everywhere—the class which makes all governments uneasy."[64] By 31 May, when the Commune's defeat was already assured, Arnold was even more certain about the lasting significance of its legacy: "The Paris convulsion is an explosion of that fixed resolve of the working class to count for something and *live*, which is destined to make itself so much felt in the coming time, and to disturb so much which dreamed it would last for ever."[65] Thomas Carlyle wrote in similar terms to his brother John that the advent of the Commune constituted a "tremendous Proclamation to the Upper classes in all countries" from the "poorest classes in Paris" that "*our* condition ... is still unimproved, more intolerable, from year to year and from revolution to revolution."[66] The Commune, as Arnold and Carlyle recognized, dealt a near-fatal blow to the bourgeoisie's capacity falsely to eternalize the contingent set of social and economic relations that allow it to secure its grip on political power. Although the Commune ultimately went down to defeat, it supplied living proof that an alternative was possible. Another of Victorian Britain's most forthright cultural commentators, John Ruskin, saw the "fighting in Paris" during the Commune as the "Inauguration" of the "*Real* war in Europe," not between nations but between

INTRODUCTION

classes: between "Capitalists," whom he named as the "guilty Thieves of Europe, the real sources of all deadly war in it," and "the workman, such as these have made him."[67] Writing in November 1872, George Eliot was similarly struck by "the tremendous European change which is being prepared by the new attitude of Common Labour," adding: "The centre of gravity is slowly changing and will not pause because people of taste object to the disturbance of their habits."[68] The future Conservative prime minister Lord Salisbury, meanwhile, wrote anonymously in the *Quarterly Review* that the Commune was "the preface to a controversy which will thrust what we call politics into the background, in favour of a social conflict the most critical and most embittered that has yet shaken the fabric of civilisation."[69]

When set against Arnold's and Ruskin's intellectually probing responses, Swinburne's knee-jerk hostility to the Commune offers a metonymic instance of a reaction that had a much larger footprint in the historical fiction of the period, a genre that achieved a "phenomenal new popularity in Britain" at the time.[70] The basic maneuver, observable in much of the popular historical fiction that deals with the Commune, involves a reduction of the Communards' political aspirations to a purely destructive, even infernal, character. Such a position is detectable in the work of a diverse array of writers, and the following group of novels, some of which are discussed at more length in chapters 2 and 3 of this book, offers a representative rather than exhaustive sample. The historical fictions and sentimental romances of the Commune include Edward Bulwer Lytton's *The Parisians* (1872–1874), Alexandra Orr's *The Twins of Saint Marcel* (1872), Maria M. Grant's *Lescar, the Universalist* (1874), Matilda Betham-Edwards's *Brother Gabriel* (1878), Charles Quentin's *Through the Storm* (1880), Mrs. John Waters's *A Young Girl's Adventures in Paris during the Commune* (1881), Leith Derwent's *King Lazarus* (1881), Mary Elizabeth Braddon's *Under the Red Flag* (1883), Anne Thackeray Ritchie's *Mrs Dymond* (1885), William Westall's *Her Two Millions* (1887), George Alfred Henty's *A Woman of the Commune* (1895), Francis Henry Gribble's *The Red Spell* (1895), Herbert Hayens's *Paris at Bay* (1897), John Oxenham's *Under the Iron Flail* (1902), and William Barry's *The Dayspring* (1903). A number of American writers also wrote Commune novels that were published in Britain, including James F. Cobb's *Workman and Soldier* (1880), Henry F. Keenan's *Trajan: The History of a Sentimental Young Man* (1885), Edward King's *The Red Terror* (1895), Robert W. Chambers's *The Red Republic* (1895), and Eugene C. Savidge's *The American in Paris* (1896). These novels together constitute a hybridization of historical romance fiction and the novel of the recent past.[71] Of the novels just listed, only Bulwer's *The Parisians* and Chambers's *The Red Republic* appear in Jonathan Nield's contemporary survey of the historical novel, along with the Chatto and Windus translation of Émile Zola's *The Downfall* and Paul and Victor Marguerite's tetralogy *Une Epoque*, though there is somewhat better coverage in Ernest Baker's *Guide to Historical Fiction* (1914).[72]

In some cases, notably those of Henty, Hayens, and King, the historical motivations of the narrative clearly shade off into a form of juvenile adventure fiction, confirming Peter Keating's observation that it became "increasingly difficult to distinguish in any clear-cut way between an historical and an adventure novel" during the late-Victorian period.[73] Keating also notes that France continued to be regarded as the "main threat" to British national security in much late-Victorian historical fiction, adding that the 1889 centenary of the French Revolution sparked a tendency to explore "every possible aspect of France's revolutionary past," including the way in which French history saw "a similar pattern repeated over again."[74] As the preceding group of novels attests, 1871 proved to be as much of a catalyst for such exploration as 1889, even as it was regarded in some quarters as simply the latest iteration of a preestablished pattern of revolutionary recurrence. In the group of historical romance fictions of the Commune, where one finds a proliferation of winningly formulaic chapter titles such as "Through Flames to the Rescue," "Paris on Fire," and "The Swelling of the Red Flood," the Commune appears over and over again, and "each return is a resurrection," as one of John Oxenham's characters puts it in a moment of unwitting metacommentary on this fairly homogeneous group of novels.[75] Resurrection, of course, brings with it the attendant threat of reanimation and remobilization, meaning that the threat must be contained. Taken together, then, these novels attest to a pattern of neurotic repetition, in which the relentless restaging of the Commune's defeat constitutes an attempt to suture the psychic wounds inflicted by the Communards' ultimately unsuccessful challenge to the ruling order of bourgeois property relations. It is no coincidence that many of the novels included in the preceding list (notably those by Bulwer, Westall, Henty, and Oxenham) are organized around an inheritance plot of one sort or another or a story line in which the transfer of an estate features significantly.[76]

But if these novels sanctify the prevailing dispensation of property relations, they frequently do so by way of an appeal to the workings of a divine order. Peter Brooks has observed that the "enormous narrative production of the nineteenth century may suggest an anxiety at the loss of providential plots," which went together with "its foregrounding of the historical narrative as par excellence the necessary mode of explanation and understanding."[77] Yet many of the previously named novelists, who, in turning to the Commune also turned to history, made this turn precisely in order to reveal a providential plot at work within the historical process itself. At the conclusion of Bulwer's *The Parisians*, for example, the narrator exclaims, in reflecting on the Commune's defeat, that the "government of a divine Thought . . . enforces upon every unclouded reason the distinction between Providence and chance."[78] Likewise, a particularly contrived turn in the plot of James F. Cobb's *Workman and Soldier* leads one of the characters to "[pour] out his heart in gratitude to that loving Father, who had so providentially ordered the course of events," while Charles Glyn, the first-person narrator of John Oxenham's *Under the Iron Flail*, feels secure in the knowledge that the Communard "desperadoes who held Paris in their grip" are "foredoomed by the gods to destruction."[79] In making such appeals to providence and divine omniscience, these writers inscribe the open contingency of the revolutionary episode into narrative containers and carefully (albeit formulaically) ordained plots that retroactively render the revolution's defeat (and, by extension, *revolution's* defeat) a historical inevitability. For these writers, there was, in short, a special providence in the fall of the Commune, and their efforts in retrospectively fictionalizing the historical event formed part of a more or less crude attempt to discover a providential schema at work within the historical process, conceived in teleological terms as a closed totality, rather than an open field of human struggle and agency. Many of the popular novels of the Commune thus reveal the ideological work of fiction in retroactively constructing the "necessity" of the Commune's defeat.

If narrative, as Fredric Jameson suggests, is a socially symbolic act, then the political unconscious of these novels is not far to seek, at least insofar as it discloses the basic contours of a nascent anticommunist imaginary. As Jameson writes, "It is in detecting the traces of [the] uninterrupted narrative [of class struggle], in restoring to the surface of the text the repressed and buried reality of this fundamental history, that the doctrine of the political unconscious finds its function and its necessity."[80] These traces take a variety of forms in the literature of the late-Victorian period discussed in this book, from outright and surface-level reaction in the popular fiction and historical romances to much subtler accommodations with the reality principle in novels that treat the Commune more indirectly and obliquely and that were far less certain about the utility of the category of providence. This latter group includes George Gissing's *Workers in the Dawn* (1880), Henry James's *The Princess Casamassima* (1886), and H. G. Wells's *When the Sleeper Wakes* (1899). These novels provide the focus for the later chapters of this book. In markedly different ways, they render the very thought of social revolution beyond the pale of a properly cultural sensibility, and they construe its successful realization as either undesirable or ultimately impossible or both. In the popular fiction that deals explicitly with the Commune, meanwhile, the political content of the texts is more easily detectable, as it were, on the "surface," and the narrative vignettes drawn from the Commune's last days often correspond quite directly to contemporaneous, explicitly anti-Communard historical writing. However, all of the texts discussed in this book might be said to constitute, in Jameson's sense, "vital episodes in [the] single vast unfinished plot"—with all of its twists and turns, the perpetual myth of its obsolescence, and its rhythms of repetition and return—that he shows to be at work in *The Political Unconscious*.[81]

The weight of the Commune's defeat led those writers most concerned to valorize and celebrate its legacy to construct a poetics of martyrdom (discussed in chapter 6), but the very fact of this historical defeat allowed those who were rather more ambivalent about or openly hostile toward the Commune, and the prospect of social revolution that it represented, to develop literary strategies that elaborate and reinscribe the terms of that defeat in a variety of ways. Across a range of generic modes—from the historical adventure romance of Henty to the early English naturalism of Gissing and from the sentimental melodramas of Braddon and Ritchie to the "high," protomodernist realism of James and the "prophetic" fiction of Wells—a large number of British (and American) writers used the historical experience of the Commune to explore the contours and contexts of revolutionary sentiment, entertained in various forms, only for it to be subsequently disavowed and contained.

One of the later historical romances, *The Dayspring* (1903), was written by the Catholic priest and educator William Francis Barry, whose narrator offers a remarkably candid (and moralizing) account of the reasons for dwelling at some length on the depiction of Emile Vaillant, one the novel's fictionalized (and entirely fictional) Communards:

> It is necessary that we should know his thought, for it lives on despite the terrible reproach of a Red Shrove Tuesday. Vaillant saw in our proud palaces only the labour which had reared their height, the taxes which had defrayed their magnificence, the people as a foundation of animated concrete above which soared these Egyptian pyramids. He would not have kindled a lucifer-match to singe their marbles. But over their downfall expect not from such a man the tears of sensibility or the lament of dilettantism. This was the view which he took; this, it must be said, is the view taken by others, who never heard his name but who have drunk deeply of the same spirit.[82]

The fictional Emile Vaillant, unlike many of the historical Communards who make cameo appearances in Barry's novel, is a uniquely sensitive figure who is not predisposed to incendiarism and destructive violence—and this, of course, both generates and legitimizes the narrator's generally sympathetic treatment of him—yet Vaillant also chooses to adopt an almost militantly utilitarian position with regard to the cultural "treasures" of bourgeois high culture. He cannot bring himself to destroy the "proud palaces" of the class enemy, but neither does he lament their destruction at the hands of his coconspirators and comrades. In short, he lacks the kind of cultural "sensibility" that Barry's narrator ostentatiously displays in the insistent use of the possessive first-person plural pronoun, with which the narrator invites readers to enter into an imagined community that can be safely held apart from the Communards, even as their actions are laid open to a sympathetic effort at understanding. The very fact that Vaillaint's thought "lives on" motivates this effort, even as its ultimate aim is clearly one of containment and neutralization rather than reanimation.

Gaston Mortemar, the Communard protagonist of Mary Elizabeth Braddon's *Under the Red Flag* (1883), adopts a similarly utilitarian position with regard to bourgeois high culture, proclaiming his view that "in the age that is coming there will be no carved oak sideboards worth twenty thousand francs, no Gobelins tapestries, no Sèvres porcelain. There will be a bit of beef in every man's *pot-au-feu*, a roof over every man's head, food and shelter, light and air, and cleanliness and comfort."[83] Braddon depicts Gaston's leveling vision as one that excludes the very possibility of luxury, thereby occluding the more radical Communard proposition that "senseless luxury," in Kristin Ross's words, "would be replaced by communal luxury, or equality in abundance."[84] Gaston's imaginative horizons, as Braddon constructs them, extend no further than what the narrator of William Morris's utopian romance *News from Nowhere* (1890) would describe as "a dull level of utilitarian comfort."[85] Gaston's aspirations are not without value, but they appear in an unfavorable light when explicitly set against the edicts of high-cultural connoisseurship in the way that Braddon outlines here. Rather confusingly, and seemingly without any apparent sense of contradiction, Braddon's narrator later catches Gaston in a moment of reverie, dreaming of "universal peace, liberty, art for art's sake, and all the impossibilities of the socialist's Utopia."[86] It is a symptomatic confusion that the novel never resolves or expands upon: Braddon's Communard protagonist espouses an ideal of art for art's sake at the same time as his aesthetic outlook involves the exclusion of some kinds of artistic production, at least insofar as he envisages a future in which there will be "no Gobelins tapestries, no Sèvres porcelain." In Braddon's novel, then, Gaston occupies an ostensibly impossible position as both revolutionary philistine *and* aesthete, anticipating the far fuller iteration of this contradiction in Henry James's *The Princess Casamassima* (1886), which is discussed at more length in chapter 5.

In different ways and in markedly different registers, Braddon and Barry (and James) articulate a conservative position that was very widely dispersed across many of the British responses to the Commune, whereby the shell-shocked reaction to the military destruction wrought on Paris during the Bloody Week becomes elevated into a more wholesale repudiation of the Communards' alleged or imputed philistinism, which, in turn, provides a rationale for rejecting their revolutionary project *tout court*. Out of this spurious concatenation of social revolution and leveling philistinism, it is possible to detect the emergence of an anticommunist structure of feeling that animated the cultural outlook of a surprisingly large number of late-Victorian Britain's leading literary personnel— from the very top of the profession's "strongly individualised summits" (to purloin Edmund Gosse's phraseology) to the "broad and featureless residuum" below.[87] There can be no suggestion that this heterogeneous pattern of responses constituted a unified or coherent class strategy; on the contrary, the very variousness and the diffuse nature of the responses elicited by the Commune in

Britain is a testament to its far-reaching influence across a variety of literary forms, genres, and stylistic modalities.

Skeptical readers of this book may fret that its singularity of focus commits what might appear, to contemporary critical standards and tastes, as a kind of Lukácsian heresy insofar as it pays attention to what Georg Lukács once described, in a chapter titled "The Ideology of Modernism," as "the social or artistic significance of subject-matter" and "content."[88] It is to be hoped that such readers can allay any potential anxieties on this account if they simultaneously recall Theodor Adorno's observation that artistic form itself is subject to historical determination. Since this process of historical determination can hardly be said to take place in a vacuum, it is—unsurprisingly enough—important to attend to the stuff of history that makes such determination possible. As Adorno observes in his exploratory essay "Towards a Theory of the Artwork," "The historical moment is constitutive of artworks; authentic works are those that surrender themselves to the historical substance of their age without reservation and without the presumption of being superior to it. They are the self-unconscious historiography of their epoch; this, not least of all, establishes their relation to knowledge."[89] Many of the writers discussed in this book, with some partial exceptions, approached the "historical substance of their age"—as it manifested itself in the Commune—with more than just a "presumption" of superiority; they sought, through the medium of their writing, to achieve a position of elevation from which the event could be both retrospectively narrated and judged. In this respect, artistic failure went together with the "self-unconscious historiography of [the] epoch." What follows, then, is not a study of "content," in the naïve sense, but a contribution toward the critique of the historical determination of literary form, organized, in this particular instance, around a study of the most significant episode in the nineteenth century's history of class struggle—the Paris Commune—and its literary afterlives in Britain.

CHAPTER 2

Refugees, Renegades, and Misrepresentation

EDWARD BULWER LYTTON AND ELIZA LYNN LINTON

"History," according to Thomas Carlyle, is "a distillation of Rumour."[1] Carlyle elaborated this maxim in his three-volume study *The French Revolution: A History* (1837) with reference to Stanislas-Marie Maillard's role in storming the Bastille on 5 October 1789. Carlyle construed Maillard as the leader of a band of Dionysian maenads, whipped up into an ecstatic frenzy of "Rascality" and "Sansculottism."[2] Carlyle's formulation has the effect of partly diminishing Maillard's historical stature as a commander of the Bastille volunteers: he *would* be a "remarkable" figure, Carlyle observes, "if fame were not an accident, and History a distillation of Rumour."[3] Carlyle here implicitly suggests the difficulty of attaining any secure epistemological footing on which to pass retrospective judgment about world-historical events and actors. British responses to the French Revolution, among which Carlyle's *History* features prominently, have been widely studied, and it need hardly be pointed out that observers in Britain looked across the Channel with varying degrees of both apprehension and enthusiasm during the immediate aftermath of the Revolution and the period of the Napoleonic Wars that followed.[4] With particular reference to Carlyle, George Levine writes that Carlyle's framing of the historical events works largely by "suggestion, synthesis, compression (and often reiteration)," adding that he tended "to transform fact into symbol."[5] Carlyle's *History*, Levine continues, was both "a sermon and a prophecy, of which the events it describes are the crucial exempla."[6] For Chris Vanden Bossche, meanwhile, Carlyle sets forth "a sequence of symbolic episodes through which the narrator, and the reader, discover the meaning of their own era," organized around an attempt to "reenclose the forces set loose by the revolution."[7] Some thirty-four years after the first publication of Carlyle's study, British responses to the Commune of 1871 were similarly concerned to parse the symbolic meaning of the revolution and its potential consequences in Britain. Carlyle himself wrote gloomily in his journal about "the horrid insurrectionary puddle now going on in Paris" and admitted to his brother John that he was "much in the dark about the real meaning of all these quaisi-infernal Bedlamisms," while other, younger observers fretted about the circulation of rumor and the potential for the conversion of such rumors into accepted historical fact.[8]

In an article in the *Bee-hive*, dated 25 March 1871, the Positivist and Communard sympathizer Edward Spencer Beesly condemned what he saw as a "conspiracy of misrepresentation" in the English press, asserting that "our newspapers are *not* to be believed."[9] By contrast, in an unsigned article titled "The Commune of Paris," published in the *Edinburgh Review* during October of the same year, William Stigand commented that the alleged "atrocities of the Commune," which he enumerates in his article, "were sufficiently diabolical without calling in the aid of fiction."[10] Mindful of the way in which the insurgents of the June 1848 revolution had been misrepresented but nonetheless determined to censure the Communards, Stigand acknowledged that some of the stories circulating in Paris at the time of the Commune's suppression were "inventions" that "served to exasperate the minds of the people, and intensify the thirst for vengeance, which was already insatiable enough."[11] Yet there was no need for such "inventions," or fictions, Stigand implies, because the unembellished truth was sufficient to condemn the Communards out of hand. Taking up a more defensive position, the Positivist Frederic Harrison criticized such misrepresentations of the Communards in his article "The Fall of the Commune," published in the *Fortnightly Review* in August. Harrison was forthright in his condemnation of falsifications circulating in the press. Unlike Stigand, Harrison, along with other Positivists including Beesly, publicly defended the Commune in periodicals such as the *Fortnightly Review*. As Harrison put it, "no one reading the French newspapers of that time [May 1871] . . . can fail to see that they are filled from beginning to end with unadulterated fiction. It is not news which they give us, but wilful lying."[12] The "so-called reporters," Harrison continued, "are simply romancists" who "evolve [their stories] from their own inner consciousness," as might an author of fiction.[13] The Positivists' complaints included false reports of the death of the pro-Communard artist Gustave Courbet, underreporting of working-class support for the Commune, and circumstantial accounts of Communards spreading petroleum on rags in order to fire public buildings.

Stigand, Harrison, and Beesly differently attest to the way in which the ideological polarization precipitated by the Commune simultaneously blurred the boundary between fact and fiction. In the immediate aftermath of the Commune's suppression, responses to the event in Britain were marked by an acknowledgment that the epistemological ground for condemnation or commemoration was itself unstable and fraught with contention. The early cultural reception of the Commune in Britain opened up the problem of representation in such a way that "calling in the aid of fiction," to borrow Stigand's words, became crucial in some quarters to the mediation and containment of the threat that the Commune had posed—and might continue to pose—to the bourgeois social order. This climate of repressive distortion lasted many years; as the socialist illustrator and artist Walter Crane put it in 1907, "The Commune, its ideals and its acts, were entirely misunderstood, or misrepresented in the English press, and it is only recently, after the lapse of years, that its true aims ... are beginning to be apprehended as an attempt to establish a true civic Commonwealth, on a basis of collective service and ownership."[14] In the intervening period, a large number of authors resurrected the Commune in fiction, only to kill it off, time and time again. Its numerous returns in the work of relatively minor popular authors, including Mary Elizabeth Braddon, Anne Thackeray Ritchie, George Alfred Henty, and others, suggest that it registered as a disturbance; the compulsive repetition suggests the existence of a trauma. Such narratives evoked longer-standing fears about the Continental "specter" of revolution, and writers responded with narrative strategies that sought to contain this threat. Among the earliest to do so was the novelist and radical-Whig-turned-Tory-peer Edward Bulwer Lytton.

Revolution from Below:
Edward Bulwer Lytton's *The Parisians*

Kristin Ross has suggested in her account of the Commune's political imaginary that the origins of the Commune lay in the "popular reunions at the end of the [Second] Empire, the various associations and committees they spawned, and the 'buzzing hives' that were the revolutionary clubs of the Siege" during the Franco-Prussian War.[15] Bulwer, despite being the very antithesis of a Communard, would have concurred with this statement, at least insofar as his reconstruction of the period leading up to the Commune between 1869 and 1871 provides one of the earliest instances of the anti-Communard strategy of retroactive containment through fictional representation. Bulwer's biographer Leslie Mitchell points out that his attitude to France was marked by "a basic fear and distrust" as a result of the Revolution of 1789, sentiments that can only have been heightened by the advent of the Commune.[16] Mitchell adds: "At the end of his life, Lytton saw the world as a dangerous place. Visiting Paris, shortly after the revolution which had brought the Commune to power, was a determining experience."[17] In Bulwer's unfinished novel *The Parisians*, first serialized in *Blackwood's Magazine* between October 1872 and January 1874, he depicts the Parisian political underground of the late 1860s and early 1870s—where Ross and others locate the Commune's originary moment—as a sensationalized contrast to the bourgeois world of salons and soirées. Juliette Atkinson sees *The Parisians* as one of "a number of novels [that] interpreted what they saw as France's decline as a consequence of the social and literary corruption of the Second Empire."[18] In a prefatory note to the novel, Bulwer's son, Robert, who wrote under the pen name Owen Meredith, commented that *The Parisians* belongs to a "special group" among his father's many novels, "distinctly apart from all the other works" in being distinguished by "moral purpose" and "expostulation against what seemed to him the perilous popularity of certain social and political theories," thus offering "a warning against the influence of certain intellectual tendencies upon individual character and national life."[19] Although Meredith does not make it explicit, it is clear that he had the "social and political theories" of the Parisian Communards uppermost in mind.

The idea of the underground, as both a figurative space of potential political sedition and a literal, physical network of catacombs that ran beneath the city, occupies an important place in popular understandings of Paris's history as a city of revolution, and this concatenation of fears about the city's political and physical undergrounds is writ large in Bulwer's novel. In Walter Benjamin's survey of the "mythological topography of the city" in *The Arcades Project*, he gives an account of the extent of the Parisian catacombs: "Paris is built over a system of caverns from which the din of Métro and railroad mounts to the surface, and in which every passing omnibus or truck sets up a prolonged echo. And this great technological system of tunnels and thoroughfares interconnects with the ancient vaults, the limestone quarries, the grottoes and catacombs which, since the early Middle Ages, have time and again been reentered and traversed."[20] During the nineteenth century, the existence of such spaces haunted the bourgeois political imaginary and began to intersect with anxieties about working-class organization and revolutionary upheaval. As Benjamin attests elsewhere in the *Arcades*, these anxieties took on particular significance during the Commune. In Convolute C, "Ancient Paris, Catacombs, Demolitions, Decline of Paris," Benjamin quotes an extract from Georges Laronze's *Histoire de la Commune de Paris 1871* (1928), in which Laronze records that, during 1871, the "method of treachery then in fashion" was the "subterranean method."[21] Another of Benjamin's gathered fragments, collected in Convolute k, "The Commune," and drawn from an exhibition titled "La Commune de Paris" held in the Municipal Offices of Saint-Denis, strikingly illuminates the subterranean aspects of the Commune's political topography. Benjamin records in one of his notes: "After the taking of Paris [by the Versaillais], *L'Illustration* published a drawing entitled *Chasse à l'homme dans les catacombs* (Manhunt in the Catacombs). In fact, the catacombs were searched one day for fugitives. Those found were shot."[22] The catacombs here provide a scene of climactic class violence, as the repressed are forced to return to the underground space from whence they came, only to be hunted down like animals caught in a trap.

During the Commune's last days, some of its defeated partisans were rumored to have sought refuge in Paris's subterranean network of tunnels and ossuaries, in a stark reminder of the fact that the city's literal and figurative undergrounds would sometimes blend into one. According to David L. Pike, "The Catacombes and carrières were a metonymy for the Revolution, whether the writer was Republican or Royalist, whether he or she supported the Restoration, the July Revolution of 1830, the July Monarchy of Louis-Philippe, the insurrection of 1848, the Second Empire, the Commune, or the Third Republic."[23] Bulwer's comparable implication in the "nineteenth-century obsession with the subterranean," and the related culture of "fervid literary speculation," is most readily associated with his earlier text *The Coming Race* (1871), which belongs to a nexus of speculative fictions that differently allegorize the class politics of underground space, including William Delisle Hay's *Three Hundred Years Hence* (1881) and H. G. Wells's *The Time Machine* (1895) and *When the Sleeper Wakes* (1899), along with E. M. Forster's short story "The Machine Stops" (1909).[24] In Bulwer's case, the anxieties on display in *The Coming Race*, discussed by a number of critics, are made all the more explicit in his exploration of the Commune's repercussions in his subsequent (and unfinished) novel, *The Parisians*, offering a faint echo of Carlyle's figuration of the French Revolution as "a descent into hell."[25]

In *The Parisians*, Bulwer introduces this spatial politics of the city by contriving a reason for his aristocratic protagonists to gain illicit entry into the radical political underground of Paris during the twilight of the Second Empire. The chief protagonist, Alain de Rochebriant, belongs to the French nobility, and his Legitimist political sympathies lie with the unkinged Bourbon dynasty. One of his English acquaintances, Graham Vane, has come to Paris in search of the elusive Louise Duval, the illegitimate daughter of his deceased uncle. In the course of his search, Vane finds his way into the Café Jean Jacques, which, as the name might lead one to suppose, is not simply a venue for billiards and dominoes, initial appearances notwithstanding (figure 2.1).

This part of the novel is set during the year 1869, well before the emergence of the Commune, yet Vane gradually discovers "that the *café* had a *quasi*-political character" (1:220). The conversation in the café assumes "a strain of philosophy far above the vulgar squabbles of ordinary party politicians,—a philosophy which took for its fundamental principles the destruction of religion and of private property" (1:221). The narrator condescendingly refers to those who frequent the café as "philosophers" and "sages," noting that they "appeared for the most part to belong to the class of *ouvriers* and artisans. Some of them were foreigners—Belgian, German, English" (1:221). The transnational character of this working-class club is no coincidence, however, as it just so happens that Graham Vane has inadvertently stumbled upon the meeting place of the Parisian section of the International Workingmen's Association—an organization that, he is later informed, "had its origins in England" (1:222). The real object of Vane's attention is not the club, as such, but one of its leading members, M. Lebeau, whom Vane believes to possess information about the whereabouts of Louise Duval.

The persona of "M. Lebeau" is, as Vane has been informed by a Parisian detective, a disguise for the disgraced aristocrat Victor de Mauleon, a renegade

Figure 2.1. Sydney Hall, illustration for Edward Bulwer Lytton, *The Parisians*, 4 vols. (London: W. Blackwood, [1873]), 2:70, f.p. Library Special Collections, Charles E. Young Research Library, UCLA.

against the status quo of the Second Empire. De Mauleon's involvement with the political underground, in the person of M. Lebeau, piques Vane's interest, and it becomes apparent that De Mauleon has infiltrated the Parisian section of the International, not because of any sympathy with the cause of the *ouvriers* but simply in order to stir up trouble for the emperor Napoleon III, whose claim to power he does not regard as legitimate because of his own monarchist loyalties. As De Mauleon cynically puts it to the young poet Gustave Rameau, "I desire to overthrow the Empire: in order to do that, it is not enough to have on my side the educated men, I must have the canaille—the canaille of Paris and the manufacturing towns. But I use the canaille for my purpose—I don't mean to enthrone it" (2:13). The narrator describes him as "one of those plotters of revolutions not uncommon in democracies, ancient and modern, who invoke popular agencies with the less scruple because they have a supreme contempt for the populace" (1:269).

Ross begins her account of the Commune's political imaginary not with the symbolically significant date of 18 March but with the popular "reunions and the clubs that created and instilled the idea—well before the fact—of a social commune."[26] Bulwer's narrative similarly begins with the fictive re-creation of such a space, his representation of which is significant precisely because he does *not* depict the Café Jean Jacques as a space of autonomous, working-class self-organization. Rather, the chief mover turns out to be a disguised aristocrat, allowing Bulwer to imply that the real agents of the historical process are those with whom the narrator repeatedly makes clear his class affiliation—namely, the very aristocrats who yearn for the restoration of the old, Bourbon monarchical order. In book 5, chapters 5 and 6, readers are granted privileged access to a secret meeting of the International's Parisian committee, which takes place in the salon of a dilapidated house near Montmartre, situated in "one of the few courts which preserve the *cachet* of the *moyen âge* untouched by the ruthless spirit of improvement which, during the Second Empire, had so altered the face of Paris" (1:266). The "defaced coat of arms, surmounted with a ducal coronet, over the doorway," indicates that the house probably belongs to De Mauleon (1:266–267). The committee consists of two Parisians "of the upper section of the middle class," one of whom, Gaspard le Noy, is a surgeon, and the other, Felix Ruvigny, a man of science (1:271). Three foreigners—a Pole (Thaddeus Loubisky), an Italian follower of Mazzini (Leonardo Raselli), and a Belgian *ouvrier* (Jan Vanderstegen)—enter via a secret trapdoor in order to avoid detection by the police (figure 2.2).

The number is made up to eight with the appearance of a Parisian *ouvrier*, Armand Monnier, and the young poet Gustave Rameau. The presiding figure at this meeting, however, is the aristocrat Victor de Mauleon, disguised as M. Lebeau. The function of this cloak-and-dagger plot is to deprive the working-class *ouvriers* and artisans of any agency in setting afoot the events of the Commune. In fictionalizing the period immediately preceding the Commune's emergence,

Figure 2.2. Sydney Hall, illustration for Edward Bulwer Lytton, *The Parisians*, 4 vols. (London: W. Blackwood, [1873]), 2:167, f.p. Library Special Collections, Charles E. Young Research Library, UCLA.

imagining a narrative of its causation, Bulwer reveals his concern to disavow the role played by the International during the final years of the Second Empire. He does so by attributing the International's perceived influence, as well as its tight-knit organization, to the cynical machinations of a scheming, monarchist aristocrat—the kind of figure whom Marx would have described as a feudal socialist "[waving] the proletarian alms-bag in front for a banner."[27]

The First International and the Conspiracy Plot

De Mauleon's infiltration of the International and the descriptions of the various secretive meetings which he initiates situate Bulwer's novel as a precursor to the fin-de-siècle conspiracy narratives familiar from the work of Henry James, Joseph Conrad, and G. K. Chesterton, while modulating the anxieties about secret societies in the context of Italian unification that featured in Wilkie Collins's *The Woman in White* (1859) and Benjamin Disraeli's *Lothair* (1870).[28] Another likely source for Bulwer's unease about the International can be traced to the discussions of the Commune that took place in British periodicals, including the *Edinburgh Review* and the *Quarterly Review*, shortly after the Commune's demise during May 1871. William Stigand commented in the *Edinburgh Review*: "The powerful organisation of the International, and the part it has played in the insurrection of the Commune, is the most striking feature of the times in which we live; and there never has existed, perhaps, since the origin of civilisation, a society as to whose character and working it is so important to come to a just understanding."[29] Stigand continues that "it counts millions of members scattered all over the world" and comments: "We have been assured by a high authority that its numbers in Great Britain amount to 350,000 and on the Continent they are reckoned by millions."[30] Edmond de Goncourt was similarly perturbed and fretted in his journal entry for 12 April 1871 that "the idea of the motherland is dying" because "the International's doctrines of indifference to nationality have penetrated the masses."[31] Mary Elizabeth Braddon's short novel *Under the Red Flag* (1883) plays on the same fears, as Braddon's narrator characterizes the "International Society" as "that fatal association which had sown the seeds of anarchy all over Europe," and several other contemporaneous popular fictions make similar references.[32] The English Liberal politician and journalist of Huguenot descent Henry Labouchère—well-known to scholars of the Victorian period for his role in passing the homophobic Criminal Law Amendment Act of 1885—voiced similar concerns in his diary of the Prussian siege of Paris, which was serialized in the Liberal *Daily News*. In his diary entry for 7 February 1871, Labouchère reports the opinion of an "informant" that "a large number of Ultra-Radicals will be elected in Paris" in the forthcoming election because "the Moderates are split up into small cliques, and each clique insists upon its own candidates being supported, whereas the Internationale commands 60,000 votes, which will all be cast for the list adopted by the heads of that society."[33] While Labouchère's estimate of the International's forces is more modest than that of Stigand's, he concurs with Stigand in presenting an image of a tightly disciplined organization, capable of commanding a majority in electoral contests owing to internecine squabbles among opponents.

In *The Parisians*, De Mauleon's address to the small committee of the Parisian section of the International, which he convenes, clearly plays on these fears, as he asserts that the organization commands "the confidence of thousands now latent in unwatched homes and harmless callings, but who . . . will, like the buried dragon's teeth, spring up into armed men" at the merest signal from the International (1:273). In the characters of Victor de Mauleon and Graham Vane, Bulwer partly allays such fears by fantasizing an aristocratic penetration of a sensationalized forum of proletarian conspiracy, rendering it available for the consumption of a bourgeois readership. In doing so, Bulwer inaugurates a narrative trope of vampish, aristocratic curiosity in the activities of working-class revolutionaries to which Henry James would return, in a far more nuanced and sophisticated fashion, in *The Princess Casamassima* (discussed in chapter 5). In James's novel, the intentions and sympathies of the eponymous princess are much more inscrutable and ironic than those of Bulwer's gaggle of Legitimists, whose charmed life of soirées, *bals champêtres*, and trips to the opera, depicted in the early sections of *The Parisians*, is interrupted in book 10 by the outbreak of the Franco-Prussian War, whereupon the gathered field of blue-blooded nobles proceed to distinguish themselves in action. For example, Enguerrand de Vandemar, who is Alain de Rochebriant's cousin, dies in battle against the Prussians, in spite of the fact that his Legitimism means that he has no loyalty to Napoleon III.

In the same month as Stigand's *Edinburgh Review* article appeared, Lord Salisbury anonymously published a similar article in the *Quarterly Review*, titled "The Commune and the Internationale." Salisbury claimed that "the cause of the Internationale and the cause of the Commune were one," adding, for good measure, "The movements of the Paris socialists, as of the whole Internationale, were governed by a Committee sitting in London."[34] He traced this fear of cross-Channel contamination to the various International Exhibitions of the 1860s, which created the possibility for fraternization between artisans and workers of different nations.[35] Salisbury's discussion of the International reflected what Matthew Beaumont has referred to as "the first stirrings of a cacotopian impulse" in the social imaginary of the middle and upper classes.[36] It is thus particularly appropriate that the introductory chapter of *The Parisians* establishes that the narrator is, in fact, that same "adventurous discoverer of a land without a sun" familiar to readers of Bulwer's 1871 novel *The Coming Race*, since this text is another important cacotopian narrative (1:v).[37] *The Coming Race* plays on fears of underground subversion and concludes with a prophecy about a time when the subterranean "people [the Vril-ya] calmly developing, in regions excluded from our sight," will "emerge into sunlight our inevitable destroyers."[38] This description, as Beaumont comments, "implicitly associates the coming race with the industrial miners past whom the narrator must climb in order to return to the surface of the earth," but they might be read as a figure for the proletariat more generally.[39] David Pike similarly draws out the political resonance of such underground spaces, commenting: "In the practice of revolution and conspiracy, subterranean spaces functioned no differently than barricaded districts above or other secret meeting places. In the common fantasy of an apocalyptic blast from below, however, ... the fragmented space would be unified to express the power of opposition through a single, determinant figure or event capable of overturning a social order projected onto the vertical topography of the city."[40] In *The Coming Race*, Bulwer's anxiety about an "apocalyptic blast from below" is technologically mediated in the form of Vril, the imagined energy source that sustains the advanced underground civilization of the eponymous coming race, the Vril-ya. In *The Parisians*, by contrast, Bulwer's anxiety about working-class upheaval and social disintegration, exemplified in the closing paragraphs of *The Coming Race*, emerges fully fledged into the sunny, embellished boulevards and salons of Second Empire Paris, shifting the narrative ground from dystopian fantasy to novelistic realism. Braddon, another novelist of the Commune, similarly invokes "the French equation between underground space and revolution" in *Under the Red Flag*.[41] After the proclamation of the Commune on 18 March, Braddon's narrator proclaims: "Hideous faces, which in peaceful times lurk in the hidden depths of a city, showed themselves in the open day, at every street corner, irony on the lip and menace in the eye."[42] In Braddon's later novel *One Life, One Love* (1890), she characterizes the Communard exile and murderer Claude Morel as having the "temper of men who surge up out of the paving-stones and gutters of every great city in the time of revolution, and who do evil for evil's sake."[43]

In *The Parisians*, Victor de Mauleon's centrality to the political events of the novel, and that of his doppelganger M. Lebeau, reveals a fairly crude narrative strategy on Bulwer's part, by which he sought to contain and recuperate the threat of working-class political agency with reference to the scheming and wire-pulling of a disillusioned aristocrat, whose own political ambitions have been frustrated by the Second Empire. Contrary to Stigand's confident proclamation, however, Bulwer can only achieve this precisely by "calling in the aid of fiction." It is as if a specimen of the Dilettante Aristocracy that Carlyle had bemoaned in *Past and Present* (1843) were suddenly to step up and fulfill the heroic destiny that Carlyle imagines for him. De Mauleon's command of the radical Parisian *ouvriers* is such that when a working-class demonstration takes place in response to Napoleon III's plebiscite of 8 May 1870, De Mauleon quickly appears on the scene, in the guise of Lebeau, to call it to a halt because he deems it to be premature. The radical artisan Armand Monnier readily obeys Lebeau's instruction to evacuate the barricade, having already made clear, "I don't think the class I belong to would stir an inch unless we had a leader of another class" (2:38). Yet while De Mauleon moves among the Parisian political underground with duplicitous ease, Bulwer also makes clear that he simultaneously harbors anxieties about the physical space beneath the city:

> I miss the dear Paris of old,—the streets associated with my *beaux jours* are no more.... In the twists and curves of the old Paris one was relieved from the pain of seeing how far one had to go from one spot to another,—each tortuous street had a separate idiosyncrasy; what picturesque diversities, what interesting recollections,—all swept away! *Mon Dieu*! and what for,—miles of florid *façades* . . . and the consciousness that if you venture to grumble underground railways, like concealed volcanoes, can burst forth on you at any moment with an eruption of bayonets and muskets. (1:109)

De Mauleon strikingly aligns his nostalgic tirade against Haussmann's embellishment of Paris with an anxiety about turmoil underground in the form of "an eruption of bayonets and muskets," revealing his true relation to the novel's political topography as one of fear and apprehension. For Bulwer, such fears were triggered by the advent of the Commune, which Marx celebrated in *The Civil War in France* (1871) as "essentially a working-class government, ... the political form at last discovered under which to work out the economical emancipation of labour."[44] The complicated machinations of Bulwer's conspiracy plot work to discursively contain such a possibility. Yet the preceding passage also reveals the extent to which the protagonists of *The Parisians*, in their hostility to the Commune, occupy a peculiarly untimely and outmoded position. As the narrator comments, Alain de Rochebriant's "chivalrous sentiments of loyalty to an exiled dynasty ... disqualified the man for the age he lived in" (1:28). Similarly, De Mauleon's candid admission that he is, in fact, deeply ill at ease with the movement of the city's subterranean forces, even as he penetrates the novel's political underground, reveals the worm in the bud of Bulwer's "moral purpose" in writing the novel: he is only capable of condemning the Commune in terms of a vanished world of paternalistic, feudal hierarchy. Yet Bulwer is no "critical realist" in the Balzacian sense, meaning that his ideological investments in the ancien régime ultimately prove to be too insecure and outmoded for the novel to gain any real aesthetic or political traction.[45]

Unfinished Business: The Legitimism of Bulwer Lytton and Matthew Arnold

Leslie Mitchell conjectures that Bulwer's last three novels—*The Coming Race*, *The Parisians*, and *Kenelm Chillingly*—were "all overtly didactic in intention" and that Bulwer "claimed to stand on an eminence from which he could see into the far distance," thereby offering to guide English society away from the turmoil of Continental political upheaval.[46] In this respect, however, it is surely significant that Bulwer left *The Parisians* unfinished. In setting out to write a novel of contemporary history, Bulwer in fact appears to have found himself overtaken by that history and powerless to complete, or satisfactorily resolve, the task at hand. In leaving *The Parisians* unfinished at his death, Bulwer was thus unable successfully to conclude his narrative strategy of containment. He invokes the threat of proletarian insurrection as early as book 1, chapter 8, but the narrative breaks off before the emergence of the Commune during March 1871, and chapters 14 and 15 of book 12 are both incomplete. The novel instead concludes with an "Envoi" in which the narrator comments: "The intelligent reader will perceive that the story I relate is virtually closed with the preceding chapter; though I rejoice to think that what may be called its plot does not find its denouement amidst the crimes and the frenzy of the Guerre des Communeaux" (2:353). A note added by the author's son establishes that the "Envoi" "was written before the completion of the novel," and it is here that Bulwer's narrator attempts to read into the history of the Commune, which is not narrated in the novel, a providential schema that "[evinces] the government of a divine Thought which evolves out of the discords of one age the harmonies of another, and, in the world within us as in the world without, enforces upon every unclouded reason the distinction between Providence and chance" (2:354). Directly after these comments from Bulwer's narrator, the stories of the chief characters are resolved in the form of a document "translated from the letter of Frederic Lemercier to Graham Vane, dated June——, a month after the defeat of the Communists" (2:354). The narrator's professed contentment at the fact that the plot's denouement precedes the events of the Commune is thus complicated, and made to seem somewhat premature, by the fact that the characters' stories are concluded from a position that postdates the Commune's suppression.

Bulwer leaves his readers with a gap between the unfinished chapters of book 12 and the "Envoi," the space between which, had it been filled, would have necessitated at least some attempt on Bulwer's part to reckon with the conclusion of the Prussian siege of Paris and the establishment of the Commune that followed in its wake. In the final completed chapter of *The Parisians*, book 12, chapter 13, Edgar Ferrier—a relative latecomer to the smorgasbord of relentlessly flat characters—looks forward to a time when the people of Paris will "dismiss the traitors who have usurped the government, proclaim the Commune and the rights of labour." Ferrier is described as "the sole member of his political party among the group which he thus addressed; but such was the terror which the Communists already began to inspire among the bourgeoisie that no one volunteered a reply" (2:344). Shortly after Ferrier's statement, the narrative breaks off. The Commune's presence in Bulwer's novel, then, is registered negatively; its appearance is, in fact, a nonappearance, an absence. It is possible that the bare fact of mortality simply intervened at an inapposite moment, before Bulwer could draw his novel to a close. But one might also speculate as to whether Bulwer's attempt to work through the profound social trauma of a proletarian insurrection and seizure of power finally dissipated the otherwise prolific novelistic energies of a writer whose span of life extended all the way back to the Napoleonic Wars at the other end of the century and whose first novel, *Falkland*, had been published in 1827. Bulwer's response to the revolutionary year of 1848 had been characterized by a brusque self-assurance in the capacity of conservatism to stave off the threat of communism. In one of a number of "Letters to John Bull, Esq.," first published during 1851, Bulwer proclaimed that the "principle" of "property in land . . . has saved France from Paris and Lyons, and stayed the Communism engendered in urban populations, by the votes of proprietors in land."[47] By 1871, he had become rather less confident about the enduring force of this "principle."

One of the few critics to have devoted sustained attention to Bulwer suggests that he failed to complete *The Parisians* because of "a sort of failure of nerve," ridden with doubts about the providential security of modern civilization and the unruly forces that were sapping its energy from within.[48] Bulwer's narrator attempts to forestall such fears in the "Envoi," but his remarks appear perfunctory at best in view of the striking absence of any direct attempt to confront the reality of the Commune and the brutality of its suppression. In this sense, the sudden cessation of Bulwer's novel mirrors the abrupt conclusion of William Stigand's article in the *Edinburgh Review*. In his final paragraph, Stigand acknowledges that "the horrors of the closing scenes of the Commune were so great as to be both painful to the memory and not suitable for detailed description; while the political and moral lessons to be drawn from them are not of such interest as those which are to be drawn from a consideration of its origin and of its earlier phases."[49] What was Stigand trying to avoid? The historian John M. Merriman has estimated the number of Communards killed or summarily executed during the Bloody Week at around fifteen thousand; he adds that a further ten thousand prisoners were tried and either executed after trial, imprisoned, or exiled to New Caledonia. In Merriman's words, this "murderous, systematic state repression . . . helped unleash the demons of the twentieth century."[50] Robert Tombs, who suggests that the number of Communard dead may have been greatly exaggerated and that the fantasy of violence may have exceeded the reality, nevertheless considers the Bloody Week to be "a terrible atrocity, surely the worst single episode of civil violence in Western Europe during the nineteenth century."[51] Those contemporary commentators who were concerned to denounce the Communards' seizure of power had simultaneously to reckon with the bloodletting unleashed by the Party of Order to ensure the Commune's defeat. One contemporary report in the *Graphic* suggests that many Communard prisoners were "shot immediately on being captured," noting that the "immediate execution of prisoners without any investigation, or even the slightest attempt at a trial, is certainly unprecedented—more especially in the case of women and children."[52] The conclusion of Stigand's article, however, draws a delicate veil of silence over Adolphe Thiers's bloodthirsty feast of vengeance. (Thiers, the chief executive of the French government at Versailles, gave the order that the Commune should be brutally suppressed.) It is small wonder, then, that Stigand does not seek to draw any "political and moral lessons" from the Bloody Week. Finding himself unable to justify the brutality used in the suppression of the Commune but simultaneously unwilling to defend the Communards because of his alignment with the dominant social order, Stigand instead succumbs to a repressive double bind and consequent silence. Bulwer encountered the same problem in completing *The Parisians*: the "Envoi" declares its faith in providence, while drawing a veil over the brutality of the Bloody Week, which, if confronted, would fatally undermine the "*providential decorum*" of the fiction—a dilemma that none of the providentially minded novelists of the Commune were quite able to resolve.[53]

The effects of this double bind were far-reaching. Even as quintessentially balanced and sagacious a commentator as Matthew Arnold, the self-styled "Liberal of the future," briefly entertained a fantasy of total obliteration with regard to the Commune.[54] Writing to his mother, Mary Penrose Arnold, on 20 March 1871, just days after the proclamation of the Commune, Arnold commented: "What news from Paris! One hardly knows what to wish, except that the present generation of Frenchmen may pass clean away as soon as possible and be replaced by a better one."[55] Such an unguarded comment is particularly telling because of the unspoken fantasy of anticommunist violence that it entertains, however obliquely. In commenting on Arnold's oscillations between Hellenism and Hebraism, Chris Baldick observes: "After earning a reputation in the late 1860s with *Culture and Anarchy* . . . as an irresponsible opponent of English sobriety, Arnold appears to have reverted to Hebraic rectitude in 1871, under the shock of the Paris Commune and the Prussian victory over France."[56] Some of Arnold's contemporaries shared his willingness to indulge in a fantasy of violence. In James F. Cobb's *Workman and Soldier* (1880), for example, the anticommunism of the protagonist's mother takes an openly authoritarian form in her assertion that "I would rather see any despot on the throne than be ruled by the mob."[57] The bluff narrator of John Oxenham's *Under the Iron Flail* (1902) adopts a similarly outspoken stance in his wish to see the total obliteration of Paris. After the Communards take power in the city, he confesses to feelings of "trepidation . . . lest the fiery whirl should come our way" and elaborates that "had the power been given me at that moment I doubt not that I would have blotted the whole seething city out of existence, as one kicks to pieces the thoughtless fire that may kindle the bush."[58] Oxenham (the pen name of William Arthur Dunkerley) here discloses in a far more direct fashion than Arnold the unveiled identification of bourgeois desire for the restoration of order with an authoritarian fantasy of totalizing violence: Charles Glyn, Oxenham's comfortably bourgeois narrator, imagines the city's evisceration by his own hand in order to prevent it from falling into the dirtier and hornier hands of the Communards. As William Morris would have recognized, Oxenham's narrator regards the Communards as "no mere political opponents, but 'enemies of society,'" hence his willingness to fantasize identification with the Versaillais "riot of blood and cruelty" that "quite literally has no parallel in modern times."[59]

In January 1869, Arnold had been elected to membership of a club called the Literary Club, to which Bulwer Lytton (and Salisbury) also belonged, and Arnold visited Bulwer at Knebworth during May 1869, suggesting a certain degree of fellow feeling between the two men. Bulwer certainly professed admiration for Arnold's social criticism, particularly *Culture and Anarchy*, and readers of *The Parisians* might well have detected an allusion to Arnold in Victor de Mauleon's account of his motivation in opposing the Second Empire of Napoleon III.

De Mauleon explains his scorn for the plebiscite of 8 May 1870 by suggesting that "the Empire is doomed—doomed, because it is hostile to the free play of intellect. Any Government that gives absolute preponderance to the many is hostile to intellect, for intellect is necessarily confined to the few" (2:15). Bulwer here echoes Arnold's well-known celebration of the disinterested, free play of the intellect in his 1864 essay "The Function of Criticism," where Arnold argues: "The mass of mankind will never have any ardent zeal for seeing things as they are; very inadequate ideas will always satisfy them."[60] Arnold, in turn, also appears to have sympathized with the Legitimist political affinities of Bulwer's protagonists, sharing their distaste for the politics of Napoleon III's Second Empire and the Third Republic that succeeded it. In another letter to his mother written from the Athenaeum on 28 March 1871, Arnold commented: "Paris does not make me so angry as it does many people, because I do not think well enough of Thiers and the French upper class generally to think it very important they should win; what is certain is that all the seriousness, clearmindedness, and settled purpose is hitherto on the side of the Reds. I suspect they will win, and we shall see for a time the three or four chief cities of France Socialistic Free Cities, in an attitude independent and hostile to the more backward and conservative country."[61] The prediction proved unfounded, but Arnold's comments provide a useful reminder of the unpredictability of this unfolding historical conjuncture as it appeared to those who lived through it. Arnold not only looked forward in anticipation of the Commune's defeat but also speculated about the potential consequences of its victory.

Although it is now very difficult to look back at the Commune, and representations of the Commune, without the burdensome knowledge of its violent suppression, it is important to recall that for its contemporaries, such as Arnold, the possibility of its triumph and consolidation was a serious prospect. This, in turn, can help make sense of the precise nature of the subsequent responses to its defeat. If Arnold's curt dismissal of the Philistine Adolphe Thiers is relatively familiar (and Arnoldian), it is all the more surprising that Arnold elsewhere proved willing to throw in his lot with the quintessential Barbarian, the Comte du Chambord. By 11 June, Arnold wrote to his mother again, this time from his office in the education department, welcoming the victory of the Versaillais by signing off his letter as follows: "What a blessing that things are really getting quiet again in France; I cannot but think the Comte du Chambord their best chance. He would wound fewer *vanities* than any one else, and that is a great thing in France."[62] The Comte du Chambord was the last legatee of the Bourbon Restoration, which held power between 1814 and 1830. Chambord, known to his supporters as Henri V, was the grandson of the ultra-Royalist Charles X, who had abdicated during the July revolution of 1830, clearing the path for the election to the throne of his cousin Louis Philippe, the Duke of Orléans, who was forced to abdicate, in his turn, during the revolution of 1848. Chambord had lived in exile at Holyrood, and subsequently in Austria, and it seems that Arnold was willing to nail his own colors to the Legitimist mast of the House of Bourbon.

Arnold did not publicly air his Legitimist sympathies, confining them to the margins of a private letter to his mother, but this letter nonetheless reveals the sometimes deeply reactionary politics that underwrote Arnold's public avowals of disinterested curiosity, sweetness, and light. In fact, his letter bears out Raymond Williams's identification of the affinity between Bulwer's *The Coming Race* and Arnold's *Culture and Anarchy*. Williams characterizes *The Coming Race* as a "projection of the idealized social attitudes of an aristocracy, now generalized and distanced from the realities of rent and production by the technological determinism of Vril," the miraculous energy source of the subterranean race of Vril-ya.[63] Williams adds that "there are moments when Vril can almost be compared with Culture," in Arnold's iteration of that ideal, because, in Bulwer's novel, "Arnold's spiritual aristocracy, his spiritual force beyond all classes, has been magically achieved, without the prolonged effort that Arnold described, by the properties of Vril."[64] In this similitude, Williams sees a desire on the parts of both Bulwer and Arnold for a "civilizing transformation, beyond the terms of a restless, struggling society of classes."[65] For all the utopian aspiration of that desired "civilizing transformation," its terms were distinctly conformist and conservative, as the foregoing discussion of Bulwer's and Arnold's contemporaneous responses to the Commune should make clear.

Arnold's declared preference for the restoration of the House of Bourbon did not come to pass, as Thiers went on to establish the Third Republic, which, as Kristin Ross comments, was "re-founded and re-stabilized on the corpses of the Communards," inaugurating "a deeply conservative integralist sequence retrenching around national identity in the wake of the Commune."[66] While Arnold's views on the matter of post-1871 French politics were thus hardly prescient, his sympathy with the Legitimist position taken by the majority of Bulwer's protagonists in *The Parisians* suggests one way in which the Commune evoked fears that stretched back to the other end of the century. In *The Parisians*, the narrator's overtly partial commentary on contemporary historical events is, as suggested earlier, designed to eulogize the virtues of the ancien régime. Indeed, the De Vandemars, the De Rochebriants, and the De Mauleons of Bulwer's novel all constitute fictive branches of Henri V's extended family, hence their uniformly Legitimist political sympathies, and they comport themselves with all the "high spirit, choice manners, and distinguished bearing" of Arnold's aristocratic Barbarians.[67] Lord Lytton's narrator informs readers, at one point, that despite "all the efforts of the democrats to establish equality and fraternity, it is among aristocrats that equality and fraternity are most to be found" (1:247). This realization gradually dawns on Alain de Rochebriant as he enters the Parisian society of his cousins Raoul and Enguerrand de Vandemar. The novel is thus partly a story of De Rochebriant's acculturation, from provincial

Brittany to suavely sophisticated Paris—a trajectory of which Arnold would doubtless have approved. De Rochebriant's development, in turn, establishes an ideological counterpoint to the perceived threat of the International, as he becomes part of a cosmopolitan network of blue-blooded aristocrats, who hold fast to an ideal of noblesse oblige and a chivalric code of honor. In the case of Bulwer, then, the anxieties about cultural democratization precipitated by the Commune take the form of an extreme identification with the (ancien) ancien régime, but the very untimeliness of that identification (notwithstanding the continued presence of monarchists in the French Assembly during the early years of the Third Republic) ultimately leads him into a quite literal narrative dead end.

Shades of Red: The "Communism" of John Ruskin and Eliza Lynn Linton's *Joshua Davidson*

In Bulwer's and Arnold's shared concern to defend the virtues of an outmoded ideal of nobility, their responses to the Commune echo the seventh letter of John Ruskin's *Fors Clavigera*, titled "Charitas" and dated July 1871, in which Ruskin responds to the Commune's suppression by drawing a distinction between communists of the "old school," among whom he numbers himself, and communists of the "new school," such as the Parisian Communards.[68] Ruskin opens this letter addressed to the workmen and laborers of Great Britain by proclaiming himself "a Communist of the old school—reddest also of the red."[69] After directing some generally patronizing comments toward the "baby Communists" of the new school and offering some remarks on the ideal of labor outlined in Thomas More's *Utopia* (1516), Ruskin draws a further subdivision within the ranks of the old school, with reference to the color spectrum: "we old Reds fall into two classes, differing, not indeed in colour of redness, but in depth of tint of it—one class being, as it were, only of a delicately pink, peach-blossom, or dog-rose redness; but the other, to which I myself do partly, and desire wholly, to belong, as I told you, reddest of the red—that is to say, full crimson, or even dark crimson, passing into that deep colour of the blood which made the Spaniards call it blue, and which the Greeks call ΦΟΙΝΙΚΣΟζ."[70] Ruskin's rhetorical sleight of hand prepares the way for his assertion in a later letter, repeated in the first chapter of *Praeterita* (1885), that he was also "a violent Tory of the old school."[71]

Like Arnold—and, before him, Carlyle—Ruskin drew inferences from the events in Paris that allowed him to make prophetic predictions about the future of British and European politics: "The guilty Thieves of Europe, the real sources of all deadly war in it, are the Capitalists.... The *Real* war in Europe, of which this fighting in Paris is the Inauguration, is between these and the workman, such as these have made him. They have kept him poor, ignorant, and sinful, that they might, without his knowledge, gather for themselves the produce of his toil. At last, a dim insight into the fact of this dawns on him; and such as they have made him he meets them, and *will* meet."[72] Crucially, Ruskin construed the suppression of the Commune as an "Inauguration," rather than a culmination, a herald of things to come, rather than a defeat without hope of redemption or renewal, thus establishing a discursive and rhetorical pattern that would also animate the political writings of fin-de-siècle socialists such as William Morris and Ernest Belfort Bax (discussed in chapters 6 and 7). In a wide-ranging discussion of *Fors Clavigera*, Judith Stoddart neatly captures the contradictory nature of Ruskin's response to the Commune, commenting that the Communards' "cross-cultural brotherhood of the working classes posed a clear threat to the patriarchal state [Ruskin] advocated in *Fors Clavigera*," while also noting that his "language of paternal inheritance has surprising affinities... with the antiestablishment slogans of the Communards."[73] At this juncture, it is important to note the way in which Ruskin grounds his idiosyncratic profession of a communist faith with references to Christian morality. In searching for a definition of "what Communism is," he ultimately falls back on scripture, citing the text from Saint Paul's Second Epistle to the Thessalonians (3.10), in order to declare that "it means that everybody must work in common, and do common or simple work for his dinner."[74] As this passage makes clear, Ruskin's engagement with the Commune, as Stoddart explains, incorporates both "factual accounts culled from the newspapers" and "a biblical vision."[75]

Ruskin's sympathy with aspects of the Communards' demands, even as he sternly rebukes their strategy, puts him markedly at odds with Bulwer's narrator and protagonists and places him far closer to the protagonist of Eliza Lynn Linton's 1872 novel *The True History of Joshua Davidson, Christian and Communist*. In contrast to the confident aristocrats of *The Parisians*, whose interests are defined in stark antagonism to those of the Communards, Joshua Davidson seeks out the Commune in solidarity and comradeship. The bulk of Linton's narrative is set in London and is predominantly concerned to expose the moral hypocrisy of the established church. Linton traces Davidson's somewhat strained attempt to embody Christian principles concerning the negation of private property and the brotherhood of man, while preaching a gospel "show[ing] how Christ and his apostles were Communists, and how they preached the same doctrines which the Commune of Paris strove to embody."[76] As an artisan—indeed, a carpenter—Davidson has obvious antecedents in the eponymous protagonists of Charles Kingsley's *Alton Locke, Tailor and Poet* (1850) and George Eliot's *Felix Holt, the Radical* (1866). Davidson's attempt to found and run a night school for the poor clearly echoes the ideal of education that Felix Holt seeks to bring to the Sproxton miners in Eliot's novel, as well as Alton Locke's autodidactic commitment to self-cultivation under the tutelage of the Chartist bookseller Sandy

Mackaye. However, whereas Kingsley's and Eliot's narratives end with the symbolic repudiation of the consequences of Locke's and Holt's earlier radicalism, there is no such symbolic resolution and repudiation in Linton's narrative.

On the contrary, Davidson's participation in the Commune serves to intensify his troubles. During the Commune, Davidson's companion Mary—after Mary Magdalen—is shot as a *pétroleuse*. On his return from Paris, Davidson and his comrades struggle to find work and meet with rejection from fellow workers. While Joshua "did not justify all the actions of all the men at the head of affairs during the short reign of the Commune in Paris . . . he warmly defended the cardinal points of their creed, as the logical outcome of Christianity in politics" (263). As a consequence, "Ordinary men thinking ordinary thoughts shrank from him in moral horror. He stood before them as the embodiment of murder and rapine, the representative of social destruction and the godless license of anarchy. He was a Communist: and that to most men and women of the day, means one wilfully and willingly guilty of every crime under heaven" (261–262). The first three editions of Linton's novel were published anonymously, though the fact that it went through so many editions so quickly is an indication of its considerable popularity. Linton added a preface to the 1873 third edition, signed by the narrator as "John," who figures as a loyal disciple—John the Evangelist to Joshua's Christ—and author of a new, communist gospel. This resonance lends extra weight to the striking confusion with which John concludes his "true history" of Joshua Davidson's life, which ends with Joshua's sacrificial death. Joshua is trampled under the feet of a congregation whose passions have been aroused by a conservative clergyman, Vicar Grand, who agrees to debate Joshua and who uses the opportunity to denounce Joshua's allegedly blasphemous comparison between Christ and the Parisian Communards.

Linton's narrator, like Bulwer's, is unashamedly partisan in his view of proletarian self-organization, but his partisanship is born of solidarity, rather than aristocratic disdain and contempt. Linton's sympathetic depiction of the Communards closely mirrors a pamphlet published by her ex-husband, William James Linton, the Chartist wood engraver from whom she had amicably separated in 1867 and who subsequently moved to Hamden, Connecticut, in the United States. Several months after the Commune's defeat, he published a pamphlet, *The Paris Commune*, subtitled "An Answer to the Calumnies of the *New York Tribune*," in which he defended the Communards' actions and attributes to Thiers "the infamy—Napoleon out-Napoleoned—of raising an ignorantly fanatical army" to suppress the Commune.[77] In *Joshua Davidson*, the narrator, John, follows W. J. Linton in blaming Thiers for the Communards' execution of the hostage archbishop of Paris, in reprisal for the Versaillais's treatment of Communard prisoners (248). Echoing the journalistic interventions of Positivist writers, including Beesly and Harrison, John also questions mainstream misrepresentation of the Commune's last days: "The guns of our forts were silent; the men were fighting in the streets, desperate, conquered, but not craven. The Versaillists were pouring in like wolves let loose; Paris was drenched with blood, and in flames. And then the cry of the *pétroleuses* went up like the fire that shot against the sky. What mattered it that it was a lie? It gave the Party of Order another reason, if they had wanted any, to excuse their lust of blood. It was their saturnalia, and they did not stint themselves" (254). John questions the veracity of sensational stories about incendiary female Communards setting the city alight and firmly identifies the Versaillais and "the Party of Order" as the people primarily responsible for the atrocities of the Bloody Week.

It is also possible that Joshua's justification of his Communard sympathies with reference to Christian ethical principles is directly indebted to W. J. Linton's pamphlet, which avers in conclusion: "Our business, our hope, is no longer isolation, but association and devotion to humanity. The Christian theory of *Right* is a problem worked out and demonstrated. We have no new phase of it to learn. But we have to learn the new gospel of *Communion*, the *Duty* of fellowship."[78] Linton's appropriation of Christian rhetoric pointed in the direction of "universal republicanism," in keeping with the position he had advocated since the last days of the Chartist movement.[79] Eliza took her ex-husband's assumption that the "Christian theory of *Right*" would attribute "Honor to the defeated Commune" as the starting point for a fictional exploration of Christianity's communist foundations, worked through with reference to the historical example of the Commune. As Linton explained in her preface to the sixth edition of *Joshua Davidson*, published in her own name in 1874, "pure Christianity, as taught by Him whom men call God and Saviour, leads us inevitably to Communism," and she added, "Now I come forward in my own person, prepared to take the full consequences of what I have written as Joshua's friend 'John.'"[80] This conviction, according to Linton, motivated her decision to carry her hero "to the only modern scene where the central ideas were the rights of humanity against scientific arrangements, the raising of the low, the protection of the weak, the abasement of iniquity in high places, and the glorious liberty of this new Gospel preached to the poor."[81] Choosing such a scene also allowed Linton to launch a polemical assault on the hypocrisy of "the respectable, the well-endowed, and the conservative Christians of to-day," who have "no right to deny" that "what [Christ] was in the days of Herod He would be analogically in the reign of Victoria and under the rule of Napoleon."[82] As Jan-Melissa Schramm puts it, Linton "combines a pertinent insistence on physical embodiment ... and the idea of the Incarnation as an acted life," which, in Joshua's case, leads him to take up a partisan and revolutionary position in support of the Commune.[83] In asking her readers to choose between either "Christianity and Communism, or the maintenance of the present condition of things as natural and fitting," Linton offers a stark choice, and her readers could hardly rest secure in the knowledge that the Parisian events depicted in her narrative had taken place at a safe distance because thousands of Communard exiles had since arrived in London in search of asylum.[84]

Linton had a precedent for Joshua's return to London in the real-life migration of thousands of Communard refugees who crossed the Channel to seek refuge in Britain (predominantly London) in the wake of the Commune's defeat. In an article on "political refugees" published in Walter Besant's *London in the Nineteenth Century*, the radical journalist Adolphe Smith described London as "the asylum of the defeated."[85] Smith, who is best known for his collaboration with the photographer John Thomson to produce *Street Life in London* (1877), had served as a medic in Paris during the Commune. The presence of the refugees encouraged networks of mutual aid and solidarity to form, some of which had an educational focus. The Positivist School at Chapel Street, run by Harrison and Beesly, provided English-language classes for Communard refugees, in addition to its wider project of popularizing the ideas of Auguste Comte and his "religion of humanity" in Britain.[86] These projects demonstrate the way in which some Communard exiles and their supporters carved out precarious spaces of cultural autonomy in the relatively hospitable climate of Victorian London. Smith's comments about London as a haven for political refugees had been true at least since Bonaparte's coup of 1851, and he recorded that many among the recent influx of Communard refugees had sought lodgings "between the Tottenham Court Road and Newman Street, and as far north as Fitzroy Square."[87] Smith recollected that "any refugee who could prove that he had fought for the Paris Commune was able to obtain a meal for twopence" and noted the support of the British Positivists for this instance of "political charity."[88]

In this respect, the conclusion of Anne Thackeray Ritchie's *Mrs Dymond* (1885), a later novel of the Commune that similarly sees a Communard partisan travel to Britain in search of refuge, recalls and rewrites the ending of Linton's *The True History of Joshua Davidson*. But Max Du Parc is no Joshua Davidson. He is unlike Linton's protagonist insofar as Ritchie takes great pains to establish the moderate tenor of Max's political radicalism, which could certainly not be mistaken for any kind of revolutionary communism (either of Davidson's variety or Marx's). Having established Max's respectability and moral uprightness, Ritchie grants him refuge in Britain, "although his name was on the list of those attainted."[89] Max's profession as an engraver is no small matter here, as it helps him to "make his way in the London world" under the patronage of a network of upper-class art connoisseurs, including a "Mr Vivian, that good friend of art and liberty"—a possible allusion to Ford Madox Brown—although the narrator cannot be certain "if it was Sir Frederick, or Sir George, or Sir John to whom Mr Vivian in turn introduced Du Parc on his arrival, and who received him with cordial deeds and words of help and recommendation."[90] Much as Gaston Mortemar turns his talents as a writer to literary success at the end of Braddon's *Under the Red Flag*, Max's profession as an engraver offers a route to redemption in exile.

Max's efforts meet with some success: "His admirable etching of Mrs Vivian and her two daughters first brought him to notice and repute: it was followed by the publication of that etching already mentioned of a beautiful young woman gazing at a statue"—a possible allusion to James Tissot's etchings *In Full Sunlight* (1881) and *The Portico of the National Gallery* (1878), though the dates are the wrong way around.[91] Before long, he has "more money than he knew what to do with."[92] Ritchie hereby reveals at the conclusion of her novel that Max is something of composite figure. One possible model is Louis Marvy, an "old friend" of Ritchie's father, whom she describes in her reminiscences of Ruskin as "a very charming and gentle person," noting that Marvy was "an engraver by profession" and that "he had ... been mixed up in some of the revolutionary episodes of 1848."[93] Max, however, is a Communard, not a *quarante-huitard*, and in this regard, he more closely resembles those Communard exiles who fled to Britain and who found work as artists, often with the patronage of erstwhile Pre-Raphaelites like Ford Madox Brown and Dante Gabriel Rossetti. The sculptor Jules Dalou, for example, spent eight years in Britain in the wake of the Commune, and his work came to be so well regarded that he was commissioned by Queen Victoria to produce a monument in her private chapel at Windsor dedicated to five of her grandchildren who had died in infancy.[94] Dalou also enjoyed the aristocratic patronage of George Howard, the 9th Earl of Carlisle, whose wife, Rosalind, held radical socialist views, and Howard introduced Dalou to a number of collectors who moved in the same liberal aristocratic circles.[95] Tissot is another possible candidate, as is the graphic artist Félix Régamey, who not only found refuge in Britain but continued his work as an artist for the *Illustrated London News*, supplying images that were engraved and reproduced in the newspaper.[96] During the Commune, Régamey had worked as the *Illustrated London News*' special artist in Paris, and on 20 May, he contributed a remarkable image of a female Communard militant, rifle in hand, with her husband in soldier's uniform by her side, marching and cradling a baby (figure 2.3). The caption that accompanies the engraving reads, simply, "Vive la Commune!"[97] The visual language of sympathy with the revolutionary cause in this image is plain to see, as Régamey appropriates a sentimental familial motif for the purpose of celebrating the Communard insurgency, at the same time as he inverts traditional gender roles.

After Régamey traveled to Britain, he enjoyed the support of the painter and sculptor Alphonse Legros.[98] He also continued to work for the *Illustrated London News*, and on 6 January 1872, an image appeared in the newspaper under his signature that depicts a group of Communard exiles relaxing in a club room near Leicester Square (figure 2.4). One former Communard fries sardines over an open fire, while others smoke and read various French newspapers, and in an

Figure 2.3. Felix Régamey, "Vive La Commune," *Illustrated London News*, 20 May 1871, 492. Mary Evans Picture Library.

allusive nod to Régamey's earlier image, a mother and father nurse and feed a child at a table around which numerous other exiles are gathered in conversation. Defeated and seeking asylum, the Communards, in Régamey's image, nonetheless maintain shared, collective spaces, in which politics, care, and sociality go together with the smell of pan-fried fish. Another of Régamey's illustrations showed scenes of poverty and deprivation (figure 2.5).

Over an extended period, from the time of the uprising through to its aftermath, Régamey put into circulation in the British press images that invite sympathy for the Communards, both at the moment of their militant insurrection

Figure 2.4. Felix Régamey, "A Communist Club-Room Near Leicester Square," *Illustrated London News*, 6 January 1872, 2. Mary Evans Picture Library.

Figure 2.5. Felix Régamey, "French Communists in London," *Illustrated London News*, 8 June 1872, 560. Mary Evans Picture Library.

and in the wake of the Commune's suppression and defeat, when its scattered participants were forced to eke out an existence in poverty and exile. In Ritchie's choice to make her male, French protagonist both a Communard sympathizer and an artist and engraver, she signaled an acknowledgment of the presence of several such refugees in Britain, some of whom attained public notoriety. At the same time, however, Ritchie's narrative of the Commune carefully contains and curtails the kind of imaginative (and political) sympathy that might be extended to such figures by ensuring Max's eventual isolation and total separation from his erstwhile comrades after his exile in Britain. As chapter 3 will explore, Ritchie demonstrates that the path of redemption is open to penitent individuals, such as Max, but the sentimentally liberal embrace of forgiveness effectively erases any possibility of continuing political commitment, at least within the narrative horizon of Ritchie's novel.

Joshua Davidson, by contrast, meets with no such welcome at the conclusion of Linton's narrative, as he is instead harangued by the English workmen, whom he tries to convert, with the charge of having "burnt Paris" and "murdered innocent men," as well as having "insulted God and religion" (264–265). Linton's narrator finds some consolation in the fact that "the same things were said of the early Christians as have been said of him, of the Communists, and of all reformers of all times" (275). But the novel ends on a note of deep irresolution, as John is plunged into confusion and doubt in response to Joshua's death at the hands of the "Christian Party of Order": "Like Joshua in early days, my heart burns within me and my mind is unpiloted and unanchored.... Everywhere I see the sifting of competition, and nowhere Christian protection of weakness; everywhere dogma adored, and nowhere Christ realised. And again I ask, Which is true—modern society in its class strife and consequent elimination of its weaker elements, or the brotherhood and communism taught by the Jewish carpenter of Nazareth? Who will answer me?—who will make the dark thing clear?" (275, 278–279). John's three unanswered questions bring Linton's narrative into dialogue with an earlier generation of "social problem" novels that sought spiritual resolutions to the reality of class antagonism. In Linton's novel, the Paris Commune acts as the narrative's focal point, painfully reopening the "Condition of England" question that Thomas Carlyle had addressed in his 1840 essay *Chartism* and that Kingsley and Eliot subsequently explored in *Alton Locke* and *Felix Holt*, as did Elizabeth Gaskell, Benjamin Disraeli, Charles Dickens, and others. When Carlyle first broached the question, the threat posed by the specter of French revolutionary upheaval featured prominently among his concerns, and he warned his readers not to assume that revolution could never occur in England simply because "England is not France." Carlyle's reference to the "struggle that divides the upper and lower in society over Europe" offers a timely reminder that the so-called Condition of England question was, from the outset, not conceived within a strictly national paradigm.[99] Rather, Carlyle explicitly framed it in a transnational, cross-border context.

The "Condition of England" novels are sometimes characterized as fictions of resolution, rather than revolution.[100] These texts divert attention away from the problem of social and class antagonism through forms of spurious narrative closure or containment. In her discussion of *Mary Barton* and *Felix Holt*, Carolyn Lesjak points to a "series of displacements involving ever-wider spheres: from production to the domestic sphere of consumption, from the domestic sphere to the national sphere, and finally from the national sphere to the imperial sphere, with each move ensuring a symbolic resolution of conflict."[101] Linton's *Joshua Davidson* inverts this process, such that the brutal realities of class conflict that Joshua and his cothinkers experience in Paris during the Commune are transpositioned into Britain. Joshua's return from abroad—following the migration of thousands of Communard refugees—forestalls the kind of narrative closure identified with the device of the emigration plot, familiar from *Mary Barton* and *Alton Locke*. Neither can the sphere of consumption displace the sphere of production, as the emphasis falls on the failure of Joshua and his comrades to find work, after their involvement with the Commune. Linton's narrative instead foregrounds the way in which the Commune reopened longer-standing anxieties about class antagonism and social reform in Britain that had been attendant on earlier episodes of political turmoil both at home and abroad. For Kingsley's and

Eliot's artisan radicals, Alton Locke and Felix Holt, a quietist interpretation of Christian morality becomes a tempering influence on their radicalism. No such holding maneuver was possible for Linton, who instead presents Joshua Davidson's death, and his unabashed solidarity with the Parisian Communards, as an unresolved—and possibly irresolvable—challenge to the ruling social order. As with Bulwer's and Stigand's responses to the Commune, Linton's novel ends with silence—the silence of an unanswered question. Numerous other writers would try to speak into this silence as the decades wore on, but the keynote of these early responses to the Commune during the 1870s was a sort of stunned muteness, seen most clearly in the writings of Bulwer and Stigand, mixed with more radical and complicated efforts toward recognition and understanding, as seen in the work of Ruskin and Linton. In the body of texts considered in this chapter, the competing impulses of apprehensive revulsion and solidaristic fellow feeling both found a hearing. As chapter 3 will consider, these seemingly contradictory impulses came uncomfortably together in the later novels of Mary Elizabeth Braddon and Anne Thackeray Ritchie and collided with their more forthright attempts to reckon with the gender panic provoked by the Commune.

CHAPTER 3

Dangerous Sympathies

MARY ELIZABETH BRADDON, ANNE THACKERAY RITCHIE, AND MARGARET OLIPHANT

The story of how the Commune came into being on 18 March 1871 has been told many times over, but the role played by the working-class women of Paris can be briefly revisited here because of its relevance to the way in which several British novelists would later fictionally reconstruct the role of women during the Commune. After the humiliating defeat of the French army by Prussian forces in January 1871 and the subsequent dissolution of the Government of National Defense on 13 February, Adolphe Thiers, the new head of state, ordered that the 250 cannon belonging to the Parisian National Guard be confiscated. Generals Lecomte, Paturel, and Susbielle led brigades of soldiers into the working-class neighborhoods of the Buttes Chaumont, Belleville, and Montmartre but were met with widespread popular resistance. In Prosper-Olivier Lissagaray's retelling of these events, he records: "As in our great days, the women were the first to act."[1] The women of Paris fraternized with the soldiers, successfully encouraging them to disobey orders, and as Louise Michel later put it, "Entre nous et l'armée, les femmes se jettent sur les canons, les mitrailleuses; les soldats restent immobiles"; when the soldiers refused to follow General Lecomte's order to fire on the people, "La Révolution était faite."[2] This was just one of many instances when women played a decisive part during the Communard insurrection. Carolyn J. Eichner notes that the Commune was a "short-lived overthrow of the patriarchal status quo" that "served as an incubator for embryonic feminist socialisms," adding that "feminist socialists played central intellectual and popular roles as journalists, organizers, orators, protestors, nurses, cooks, and fighters."[3] Eichner's work, along with that of Gay Gullickson, has contributed to an important critical reevaluation of the Commune, foregrounding the role played by women during the revolution and noting the way in which existing pro- and anti-Communard historiography either "ignores women" or depicts them as "wild, evil, and unnatural, most frequently citing them as the *pétroleuses*, the mythical women blamed for burning Paris."[4] For Gullickson, the Commune was "a defining moment for Western conceptualizations of gender, not least because it gave birth to the powerful, evil, and imaginary *pétroleuses* (female incendiaries) who were accused of setting fire to Paris during the semaine sanglante."[5] The gender panic provoked by the specter of revolutionary Communard women was an important bellwether of reaction in British responses to the Commune. At the same time, gender ideology was a significant vector for the transmission of Communard ideas into Britain, which allowed a number of novelists, notably Mary Elizabeth Braddon and Anne Thackeray Ritchie, to negotiate the contours of a dangerous sympathy with the Commune. Their writings on the Commune form the chief focus of this chapter.

The Emergence of the *Pétroleuse*

The story of the Communards' seizure of the cannon circulated in the British press in the immediate aftermath of 18 March, offering images of women, and a model of political activism, that ran counter to the dominant patriarchal constructions of Victorian femininity. In an article likely to have been written by Laurence Oliphant, the diplomat and mystic who was then special correspondent for the *Times* in Paris, the author reports "mixing with a gloomy group of women and National Guards out of uniform"; in listening to their conversation, he "overheard them indignantly denouncing their chiefs, the Government, M. Thiers, and the world in general."[6] After the government soldiers refused to fire on the National Guard troops, Oliphant observes that "the wild enthusiasm of the shouts of fraternization, the waving of the upturned muskets, the bold reckless women laughing and exciting the men against their officers, all combined to produce a sensation of perplexity not unmingled with alarm at the strange and unexpected turn things were taking."[7] Oliphant's alarm, and his giddy sensation at bearing witness to the outbreak of social revolution, stems, at least in part, from the challenge to dominant gender roles posed by the "bold reckless women" who rallied to the defense of the National Guard cannon. Oliphant vacated Paris shortly thereafter (but returned later in the year), as did other British foreign correspondents, including the future poet laureate Alfred Austin, who was foreign affairs correspondent for the *Standard*, and Henry Vizetelly, who worked as a correspondent for the *Illustrated London News* and who regarded the Commune as a "régime of folly."[8] The *Standard*'s special correspondent, who remained in Paris, professed himself "very thankful for not having the ladies of [his] family in Paris."[9] Meanwhile, in the July number of the *Englishwoman's Domestic Magazine*—a journal established by Samuel Orchart Beeton in 1856 and aimed at a predominantly upper-class female readership—the author of the regular fashion column, "Our Paris Letter," declared: "It is shocking to think what a dreadful *rôle* women played during the last days of the struggle between the Commune and the army. There were troops of them enlisted under a *générale* of their own sex. Their mission was chiefly to throw incendiary matter in houses and public buildings. To denominate these fearful viragos a new word has been coined. They were called *pétroleuses* from the petroleum they made use of."[10] Isabella Beeton, who assisted her husband in editing the magazine, had decided to report on Paris fashion shows in 1860, and Beeton's decision, as Elisabeth Jay suggests, "could be seen as extending the traditional territory of the female Paris correspondent into a more public sphere."[11] Faced with the outbreak of social revolution in 1871, however, this particular correspondent makes a determined effort to disavow and condemn women's active public involvement in the defense of the Commune.

The writer is especially disturbed by the fact that "neatly dressed" women who possess the "respectable appearance" of "worthy housewives" might, in fact, harbor revolutionary desires and that they might use the cloak of motherhood as a disguise for the prosecution of acts of political violence, concealing their "deadly petroleum" within a "*boite au lait,*" as if they were simply traveling "to fetch the milk for the morning meal."[12] The cause for concern hovers around the fact that a fluid associated with mothering and nurture is replaced with a liquid of incendiary potential, the immiscibility of the fluids suggesting the unnatural mixing of gender roles. Mary Elizabeth Braddon plays on this lactic anxiety in her novel *Under the Red Flag* (1883), in which the *pétroleuse* Suzon Michel, a "creature [who] had unsexed herself," also happens to be the proprietor of a *crèmerie*.[13] Elsewhere in the same issue of the *Englishwoman's Domestic Magazine*, another writer laments: "Amongst the leading features of the revolutionary struggles in France, the saddest and most astonishing are those in which masses of women bearing a mild and inoffensive character suddenly acquire fierce and sanguinary tastes."[14] As Gay Gullickson astutely comments, "it is relatively accurate to say that for many nineteenth-century observers, women's crimes [during the Commune] were crimes *against* femininity, not *of* femininity, whereas men's crimes were crimes *of* masculinity."[15] The outbreak of the Commune, and the widely reported participation of women in the revolution, disturbed the image of Second Empire Paris as a space of idealized gentility and high fashion and briefly reestablished the city's preeminence as a site of revolutionary politics, even if, ultimately, the "catastrophe of 1871 and ... the politics of the Third Republic drastically undermined the revolutionary vocation of Paris."[16] Anne Thackeray Ritchie neatly captures the disorientating nature of this momentary resurgence in her 1885 novel *Mrs Dymond*, in which the emergence of the Commune leads one of the novel's upper-class characters to exclaim: "How the red has come into fashion; how much it is worn."[17] Mademoiselle Fayard can only comprehend the outbreak of revolution in terms of a preexisting language of fashion.

The gendered dimension of this political resurgence proved especially troubling for those commentators and cultural ideologues, like the Beetons, whose publishing activities relied on the cultivation of an image of female domesticity.

One can observe a similar process of selective reconstruction of the Commune's legacy at work in George Eliot's *Impressions of Theophrastus Such* (1879), which briefly engages with the incendiary imagination inspired by the figure of the *pétroleuse*. In her last work, Eliot presents a series of essays on a wide variety of topics unified by the voice of the eponymous narrator, whose impressions the essays are designed to convey. In a terse allusion to the Commune, Theophrastus is principally concerned with the gender panic it provoked, as the ubiquitous figure of the dangerously unsexed female *pétroleuse* flickers briefly into view in the midst of a wider diatribe on the debasement of society's moral currency:

> I confess that sometimes when I see a certain style of young lady, who checks our tender admiration with rouge and henna and all the blazonry of an extravagant expenditure, with slang and bold *brusquerie* intended to signify her emancipated view of things, and with cynical mockery which she mistakes for penetration, I am sorely tempted to hiss out "*Pétroleuse!*" It is a small matter to have our palaces set aflame compared with the misery of having our sense of a noble womanhood, which is the inspiration of a purifying shame, the promise of life-penetrating affection, stained and blotted out by images of repulsiveness.[18]

Eliot here dilates on the theme of "noble womanhood," taking for granted that the figure of the *pétroleuse* would signify to her readers a byword for incendiarism and destruction, irrespective of whether such claims were grounded in truth or otherwise. Such "images of repulsiveness" circulated widely in mainstream periodicals during the Commune and its immediate aftermath. For instance, Arthur Boyd Houghton's engraving "The Commune or Death—The Women of Montmartre" appeared in the *Graphic* on 10 June 1871, depicting a group of female Communards waving flags and shouting raucously in front of a residential building recently set ablaze; one of the assembled group of women holds aloft a lighted torch, suggesting possible culpability for the burning building left behind in the group's wake (figure 3.1).[19]

In a similar vein, the first English edition of Bertall's *Les Communeux 1871, Types–Caractères–Costumes* (1871) was published in 1873, with specially commissioned text purportedly written by an English eyewitness, and included an image of "a pair of pétroleuses" as "an embodiment of what all the World believed in, and feared at the Moment" of the Commune (figure 3.2).[20]

In Eliot's text, Theophrastus ironizes the sensationalization of the *pétroleuse* on display in these images by suggesting that quotidian transgressions against manners and social conventions should be considered *worse* than the burning of palaces, yet this ironic stance hardly conveys sympathy for the archetypal female

DANGEROUS SYMPATHIES

Figure 3.1. Arthur Boyd Houghton, "The Commune or Death—The Women of Montmartre," *Graphic*, 10 June 1871, 541. Mary Evans Picture Library.

Communard, whom Theophrastus clearly regards with a feeling bordering on contempt. The "style of young lady" invoked by Theophrastus is an antithesis to Eliot's fictional heroines (Maggie Tulliver, Esther Lyon, and Dorothea Brooke, if not quite Gwendolen Harleth), whose moral composure and spiritual maturity would doubtless meet with Theophrastus's ready approbation. In this sense,

Figure 3.2. Bertall, "A Pair of Pétroleuses," in *The Communists of Paris 1871: Types–Physiognomies–Characters* (London: Buckingham, 1873), image no. 39. McCormick Library of Special Collection, Northwestern University Library.

Eliot connives with reactionary representations of the Commune's partisans, at least insofar as she proves willing to put such images to work for the purposes of moralized social commentary in *Impressions of Theophrastus Such*.

As time passed and the historical event receded from view, novelists who sought to fictionalize the Commune responded not only to the event itself, as mediated by the initial reports and fuller historical accounts, but also to intervening fictions and representations. In the wake of Eliza Lynn Linton's favorable representation of the Commune in *The True History of Joshua Davidson*, various novelists replied during the 1870s and 1880s with narratives of recuperation and containment in which the cultural politics of gender loomed large as a focus of anxiety. In this regard, Braddon's *Under the Red Flag* (1883), which includes the memorable figure of the milkmaid-turned-*pétroleuse*, and Ritchie's *Mrs Dymond* (1885) belong among a wider group of comparable fictions of the Commune that blend melodramatic romance narratives with sensational plots of political intrigue revolving around the fall of the Commune. These novels include *The Twins of Saint-Marcel* (1872) by Alexandra Orr (née Leighton, and the sister of the painter Frederic Leighton), Maria M. Grant's three-decker *Lescar, the Universalist* (1874), Matilda Betham-Edwards's three-decker *Brother Gabriel* (1878), and Mrs. John Waters's slight novella *A Young Girl's Adventures in Paris during the Commune* (1881). While these novels broadly confirm Peter Keating's observation that much of the period's historical fiction placed itself "abjectly at the service of dominant late Victorian domestic and imperial ideologies," it is also possible to detect in these narratives a more complex undercurrent of dangerous sympathy for the Commune, which it is the purpose of this chapter to explore.[21]

Braddon's *Under the Red Flag* and Ritchie's *Mrs Dymond* are, in many ways, the most accomplished of this group of historical romance fictions, though the novels, as a group, if not quite a subgenre, share a number of common characteristics. They often feature male protagonists who initially sympathize with the Commune but later recoil in horror from the revolution's sensationally depicted excesses. The political trajectories of these protagonists run conterminously with romance plots in which English (and sometimes Irish) heroines bear witness to the Commune, while leading their (usually French) lovers away from political involvement toward a more pliable ideal of familial responsibility, rendering their earlier identification with the Commune a matter of sympathetic narrative interest but one that is ultimately recuperated within a paradigm of bourgeois domesticity. In Alexandra Orr's *The Twins of Saint-Marcel*, the earliest example of this group of novels, Aurée Castel, the protagonist and first-person narrator, quite consciously describes the book as a "domestic tale," set against various unspecified "regular histories," in order to excuse herself in not looking too closely at "the disturbed state of our political world inside Paris."[22] Orr's invocation of the category of the "domestic," here, serves as a means of warding off the more troubling demands of politics, and this kind of evasive maneuver is a staple feature of these texts. Taken together, these novels constitute an attempt to solidify the British cultural response to the Commune around a novelistic strategy of sympathetic disavowal, while also demonstrating the extent to which gender politics acted as a crucial vector by which the Commune insinuated itself into British cultural life at the fin de siècle.

"Vengeance Belongs to God": Mary Elizabeth Braddon's *Under the Red Flag*

Braddon's short novel *Under the Red Flag* first appeared on 5 November 1883 and took up the entire issue of the *Mistletoe Bough*, a Christmas annual that Braddon had founded in 1878. Braddon recorded in her diary entry for 22 November 1883 that she received 27,300 copies of the *Mistletoe Bough*, of which she had sold 25,689 by late November, suggesting its considerable popularity.[23] Braddon was, by this point, a well-established popular novelist best known for melodrama and sensation fiction after she had achieved considerable success with her 1862 novel *Lady Audley's Secret*. One of her biographers, Robert Lee Wolff, suggests that during the late 1870s and early 1880s, Braddon became something of a "crypto-radical" and records that she was a careful student of Zola.[24] *Under the Red Flag* was republished as the title story of *Under the Red Flag and Other Tales* in 1886 and, according to Wolff, Braddon was "prepared to present the ideas of revolutionaries as fairly as she could" until "revulsion set in, and in the Commune she could see nothing but evil," suggesting the severe limits of her attenuated crypto-radicalism.[25] In this respect, Braddon's *Under the Red Flag* typifies the orientation that characterizes the novels discussed in this chapter, in which it is possible to observe writers extending a limited kind of imaginative sympathy to an individual of vacillating revolutionary sensibility but who ultimately quails before the prospect of thoroughgoing social revolution.

The story—prodigiously researched by Braddon—takes its name from a fictional communist newspaper, *Le Drapeau Rouge* (or *The Red Flag*), for which Braddon's French protagonist, the journalist and aspiring novelist Gaston Mortemar, is "the most popular among its contributors" (113). Gaston is also "an enthusiastic believer in Communism and the International" (144) and is said to have "friends here, there, and everywhere among the extreme Republican party" (112). He supports both Henri Rochefort, a member of the Government of National Defense and the editor in chief of the *Mot d'Ordre*, and Gustave Flourens, "the hot headed enthusiast who just at this time was in command of five battalions of the National Guard, the beloved of Belleville and Ménilmontant" (112). Gaston's *The Red Flag*, meanwhile, "lauded Blanqui and the Blanquists" (112) and rivals Félix Pyat's paper, *Le Combat*, as well as Blanqui's *Patrie en Danger*. After the fall of the Second Empire and the declaration of the Republic on 4 September 1870, Gaston's paper calls on "the supreme sovereign people . . . to arise in their might, and steer the tempest-driven ship to a safe harbour—the smooth roadstead of Communism, Collectivism, Karl Marxism, what you will" (113). The somewhat miscellaneous trio of isms, along with the sardonic exclamation with which the narrator concludes this survey of *The Red Flag*'s political orientation, raises some doubts. It is not clear, for example, whether the obvious incoherence in Gaston's apparent support for both Blanqui and Marx is a result of Braddon's confusion or Gaston's. Nevertheless, Braddon invites her readers to identify with a male protagonist whose ideological predilections are certainly beyond the pale of bourgeois respectability, at the same time as the narrator's skeptical commentary inserts a measure of distance between the protagonist's political convictions and the projected omniscient voice of bourgeois common sense.

Matters are helped, as far as the narrator is concerned, in that Gaston's paper is suppressed shortly after the establishment of the Commune because of his opposition to the arrest of the archbishop, which had "disturbed Gaston Mortemar's faith in the men who ruled Paris" (145). From this point on, Gaston is a "marked man" (145), despite his initial sympathies with the Commune, which enables Braddon to narrate the Commune's rise and fall while ensuring that her protagonist follows a trajectory of rupture with and eventual disavowal of the revolutionary forces, thus securing his own narrowly individual exculpation. Gaston stands apart from both the various historical Communards who feature in the novel and from "the mob" (85, 97) whom the narrator frequently invokes. In addition to Flourens, the narrator singles out Raoul Rigault, Théophile Ferré, Emile Eudes, and Jean-Baptiste Sérizier from among the Communard "masters of Paris" and castigates them for wanting to "establish a reign of ignominy and terror" (143). Gaston, meanwhile, appears as something of a weak-willed straw in the wind, "steeped to the lips in the fever of politics, . . . blown hither and thither, his soul tossed and agitated by every breath of the public whirlwind" (112). The one stands apart from the many, but Braddon's individuation of a single Communard sympathizer, whom the novel ultimately presents as a victim of his own misguided enthusiasm, proffers the possibility of a narrative arc of "redemption." The novel's key spokesperson for this position is Gaston's lover, Kathleen O'Hara, who encourages Gaston in his journalistic endeavors but who adopts a resolutely reactionary position with regard to the mobilized Parisian working class of Belleville and Ménilmontant, whom she describes as "steeped in crime, misery, hatred—a seething mass, fermenting in the corruption of idleness and sin—ready to arise like a poison cloud, and spread death and ruin over the city" (116). Gaston, for his part, reassures Kathleen that he preaches "Communism, not Revolution," in response to her anxiety that he is "urging the people to act as they acted in '93" (118–119). Kathleen is, in this respect, a straightforward vector for the transmission of the narrator's (and Braddon's) self-evidently anti-Communard sentiments into the heart and mind of the novel's Communard protagonist, allowing Braddon to stage the drama of Gaston's disillusionment with the Commune under the auspices of a sentimental romance plot.

Kathleen is one of two orphaned Irish sisters who were raised in a convent in Bruges before their escape to Paris during the final years of the Second Empire;

once in Paris, Kathleen's sister, Rose, finds work making artificial flowers. Rose, the elder of the two sisters, becomes engaged to Philip Durand, a promising journeyman cabinet maker who belongs to a workers' syndicate, while Kathleen becomes engaged to Gaston, after Gaston abandons his brief flirtation with Suzon Michel, the proprietor of a *crèmerie*. Gaston's decision to spurn Suzon plays a decisive role in turning her into a vengeful *pétroleuse*, but she ultimately comes to play an important part in the novel's providential arc of redemption. Gaston's disillusionment with the Communards' anticlericalism, particularly their decision to pillage a Dominican monastery at Arcueil at which he had received part of his education, leads him to join his erstwhile teachers the monks, with whom he is arrested and eventually shot. Much of the latter part of the narrative is then taken up with Kathleen's search for the Communard Sérizier, whom she believes to be responsible for Gaston's murder and whom she eventually discovers and promptly reports to the authorities. The narrator characterizes her determined search across Paris as a kind of "pilgrimage" (191) and her subsequent discovery of Gaston, miraculously alive and in the care of a suitably penitent and reformed Suzon Michel, is nothing less than a "revelation" (266). Braddon blends the melodrama of Kathleen's search for Sérizier with a providential narrative schema that ultimately reunites her with the lover whom she had presumed to be dead. In her hunt for Sérizier, meanwhile, she "felt as if she were the spirit of vengeance" (250), reassured by her sister's words: "Vengeance belongs to God. . . . And with Him it is not vengeance, but justice" (234).

Braddon's maneuver can be stated bluntly: where Bulwer failed, Braddon succeeds in establishing a providential plot that identifies a recalibrated version of the Versaillais suppression of the Commune with the dispensation of divine justice, while also supplying a provisional answer to the question posed by Eliza Lynn Linton at the conclusion of *Joshua Davidson*. Whereas Linton had allowed the question of Joshua's support for the Commune to remain troublingly, challengingly open, Braddon sutures the psychic wounds that such a challenge posed to the bourgeoisie by recuperating the Christological character of Linton's narrative in a more conservative iteration of Christian eschatology: Braddon's Communard protagonist, Gaston Mortemar, repudiates his political sympathy for the Commune, gets shot for his troubles, and dies only to be resurrected as a successful novelist, a "man with place and name in the ranks of literature" (278) whose life unfolds against a backdrop of "perfect and holy calm" (279), as well as "industry, honour and domestic love" (278). Braddon even presents the former *pétroleuse* Suzon Michel condemning herself in her own words in the final chapter, titled "Atonement." Shortly before she is exiled to Cayenne, she informs Philip Durand, "I was a devil in those days of the barricades" (273). The "unsexed" *pétroleuse* becomes a penitent who acts as a kind of deus ex machina, negating the Commune's destabilization of bourgeois gender relations at the same time as she selflessly facilitates the happy resolution of the novel's romance plot.

In constructing this plot, Braddon was partly indebted to some contemporaneous novelists of the Commune, who were more in tune with Braddon's orientation than Linton's. Braddon borrowed the device of the resurrection plot, for example, from Alexandra Orr's *The Twins of Saint Marcel* and Mrs. John Waters's *A Young Girl's Adventures in Paris during the Commune*. In Waters's short novella, the female protagonist's aunt is overjoyed when she discovers that "the friend [she] thought dead," Alphonse Gaspard, is "still living."[26] In Orr's novel, meanwhile, the narrator Aurée Castel's lover, Emile, a non-Communard soldier who had served with the Garde Mobile during the Franco-Prussian War and is presumed dead, returns in the novel's concluding pages in a "moment of life from the dead."[27] Orr, like Braddon and numerous other novelists of the Commune, also holds fast to a providential schema in narrating the fall of the Commune, which the narrator regards as nothing less than an "emanation from the infernal regions."[28] After the Communards' defeat, Aurée poses the question, "Oh, my country! what can save you?" at which point her sister, Cerise, takes over the narration for the first time in the novel to supply an answer to Aurée's question: "Nothing but the knowledge of the gospel of peace—nothing but the removal of her blind ignorance by the spreading of the Book of God."[29]

There are several other pertinent examples of a providential worldview in later historical romances of the Commune, espoused either by characters or narrators. For instance, the female protagonist of G. A. Henty's *A Woman of the Commune* (1896) proclaims, without a hint of irony, her "old-fashioned" (and antifeminist) view that "a woman's mission is to cheer and brighten her husband's home, to be a good wife and a good mother, and to be content with the position God has assigned to her as being her right and proper one."[30] Similarly, in the American writer Edward King's *The Red Terror* (1895), the young protagonist, Frank Corners, trusts to "Providence" in hoping that a letter signed by the Communard General Dombrowski will allow him to pass through the Communard lines in order to save his grandfather and his brother, Grandpa Drubal and little Will, who are imprisoned in La Roquette.[31] It is hardly the case that these fictions of the Commune offer what Thomas Vargish would characterize as a "richly various, particularized, diverse" iteration of the providential aesthetic, which he detects in the work of several major Victorian novelists (notably Charles Dickens, Charlotte Brontë, and George Eliot), but they certainly offer up a stubbornly didactic kind of "moral content" that is quite revealing about the perceived vocation of much popular fiction during the closing decades of the nineteenth century, which went together with a profoundly conservative political orientation.[32] In this respect, these novels bear out Vargish's claim that "even during the 1870s and eighties, when the possibility of a literature devoid of moral didacticism became the fashionable critical topic, the intensity of the debate suggests the strength and persistence of the earlier tradition" of moral didacticism.[33] In Braddon's novel, this politically conservative and aesthetically traditionalist mind-set ultimately crowds out any suggestion of crypto-radicalism and occludes the muted expression of imaginative sympathy for Gaston's Communard sentiments.

In confronting the Commune, Braddon selects two areas for particular emphasis. First, she repeatedly calls attention to the Communards' anticlericalism as a counterpoint to the providential schema of Kathleen's and Gaston's story, and second, she accentuates the Communards' cultural philistinism. Her focus on Communard anticlericalism is observable in her selection of an episode, drawn from contemporary historical accounts, about an alleged Communard attack on Dominican monks for extended fictional reworking, which drives home her narrator's antipathy to the politics of the Commune. In Kathleen's search for Sérizier, she passes through the Avenue d'Italie and hears how "those harmless Dominican Fathers were hunted down, slaughtered like sheep in the shambles" (188). Earlier chapters in the novel devote considerable attention to the arrest of the "guiltless monks" (149), Sérizier's drunkenness, his hatred of the priests with "a passion that almost touched on lunacy" (154), and his order to shoot the monks (159, 163–164). In Braddon's narration of this episode, Sérizier is present at the "*battue*" and takes an active role, crying out, "Fire, fire upon them!" (164). Braddon appears to have based this section of the novel on a markedly similar episode dealing with "Les Dominicans d'Arcueil" drawn from the first volume of the "notoriously anti-Communard" Maxime Du Camp's *Les Convulsions de Paris* (1878–1880).[34] Du Camp presents Sérizier as taking a leading role in the execution of the monks, though Sérizier himself denied this.[35] Du Camp's four-volume book blends memoir and reminiscence, but, according to Colette E. Wilson, he was a generally "unreliable witness and self-interested manipulator of facts and events" whose "writing style, based on storytelling techniques," made it all the easier for him to "[blur] the distinctions between the fictional and the real."[36] Du Camp's style would thus certainly have lent itself well to Braddon's more straightforwardly fictional appropriations, but his unreliability also simultaneously undermines any residual claims that Braddon's novel might have made to historical verisimilitude or *facticity* and accentuates the avowedly ideological character of her narrative.

Braddon's recourse to Du Camp partly validates Hayden White's Barthesian view that "'realism' in the nineteenth-century novel and 'objectivity' in nineteenth-century historiography . . . developed *pied-à-pied*."[37] Yet Braddon's evident reliance on Du Camp does not simply disclose their shared "dependency on a specifically narrative mode of discourse," as White would put it, because Braddon *chose* her source extremely carefully.[38] She did not, for example, give any heed to the countervailing account offered in Lissagaray's *Histoire de la Commune de 1871* (1876), which is also organized around a "narrative mode of discourse" but in which Lissagaray describes Sérizier's trial as "premeditated," on the basis that Sérizier "was not even in the Avenue" at the time the monks were shot, and adds: "The only witness called against him said, 'I do not affirm anything myself; I have heard it said.'"[39] Hearsay and rumor, it seems, constituted evidence enough for the execution of detained Communards. In this sense, Braddon's and Du Camp's mutual implication in the writing of history as fiction, and the importation of fiction into history, cannot be reduced to a purely *discursive* project because their ideological intent was quite specifically designed to prop up the very *material* realities that the Communards had set themselves against.

Partly because the contemporary historiography of the Commune was so fraught an arena of ideological contestation, Alexandra Orr finds it necessary to assert in her preface that her novel is "so entirely 'founded upon facts,' that the story has merely been introduced to connect real incidents with the history of the time."[40] She records having consulted, for her "history," the conservative theater critic Francisque Sarcey's diary of the Prussian siege of Paris—as Arnold Bennett later would—along with various unspecified newspapers of 1870-1871; she also claims to have observed at first hand many of the "incidents here related" and to have relied on "letters and journals, written on the spot and at the time" by several "relatives and intimate friends."[41] Orr's concern with *facticity*, which is a more appropriate word than *verisimilitude* in this context, intrudes directly into her novel as well, in that she appends a number of single-word footnotes to her narration of the Commune, in which she reassures her readers that they are, indeed, in the presence of "Facts."[42] Braddon's narrator, meanwhile, decries the Communards' "hearsay," "wild stories," and "foul fictions" concerning "priestly crime," which were, according to the narrator, "invented to stimulate the populace to carnage and spoliation" (183). Although keen to burst the Communards' supposed "bubbles of foul imagining" (183), Braddon's narrator proves rather less keen to interrogate the ideological fictions propagated by the Versaillais, again revealing the deeply conservative ideological investment of her narrative enterprise and attesting to the historiographical double standard at work in her novel.

Braddon's second important area of intervention involved an attempt to reinforce a view of the Communards as cultural philistines. In a nod to Ruskin, Braddon's narrator expresses considerable admiration for Philip Durand's artisanal talents as a cabinet maker, but the function of this admiration is to put forward a view that such talents would inevitably suffer, and be frustrated, were the Communards ever successfully to realize their political ideals. Kathleen, again, is the novel's chief spokesperson for this view. As the narrator puts it, "It seemed to Kathleen as if a world, in which there were no rich people to buy works of art, no beautiful women clad in satin and velvet, no splendid carriages drawn by thoroughbred horses, no palace windows shining across the dusk with the yellow light of myriad wax-candles, . . . would be rather a dreary world to live in, albeit there was bread for all, and a kind of holy poverty, as of some severe monastic order, reigning everywhere" (119). Kathleen (and Gaston) can only conceive of communism as a leveling downward, bound up with a political project that would bring to birth a world dreadfully shorn of beauty. Mindful, as was

Ruskin, of potential working-class support for the Commune in Britain, Braddon counterposes Gaston's "fervid" (121) political speeches to the sturdy, moderate handicraft of Philip Durand, who embodies Ruskinian principles insofar as "the mind of the artist informed the hand of the craftsman" (110).[43] Philip takes great pleasure in performing his work "beside the hearth, while Rose stood by and watched the slow careful work—the chiselling of a feather, the rounding of a peach, the minute touches that marked the scales of a fish," and they carefully guard their store of "little capital" during the siege and the Commune (111). Philip, unlike Gaston, plays no part in the Commune. Yet Gaston, after his resurrection and rebirth, comes to resemble Philip at least insofar as he begins to perfect the art of writing *as a craft*. As a hack journalist, Gaston had been "the drudge of literature," and his "faculties [were] the slaves of a tyrannical master, whose name is To-day" (91). Yet when he eventually brings to fruition the "dim idea of a novel" that he had "nursed" (91) during his days as a journalist, it transpires that he quickly "obtained a more brilliant success than any book that had appeared since Madame Bovary," and this happy eventuality (which leads Wolff to detect an allusion to Zola) releases him "forever from the tread-mill routine of a third-rate newspaper" (278).[44]

Gaston's literary success reveals something important about Braddon's conception of the novelist's vocation in a period of political upheaval. Gaston's time as a radical journalist threatens a model of writing as propaganda, demonstrating the capacity of print to spread revolutionary opinions and to sway public opinion in the way feared by Kathleen. Jules Vallès's unabashedly pro-Communard autobiographical novel *L'Insurgé* (1882–1883)—the third book in his *Jacques Vingtras* trilogy, commenced during his exile in London—was one version of this threat, and it attracted some generally hostile notice in Britain.[45] Part of the animosity attached to the fact that, as Priscilla Parkhurst Ferguson puts it, Vallès "embraced his notoriety as a political journalist and scorned the very notion of the man of letters who placed himself beyond the everyday and the political."[46] For Ferguson, Vallès espoused a "conception of a lived revolution and a communal literature" that was at odds with Gaston's apotheosis as a successful literary novelist, as imagined by Braddon.[47] In this sense, one might think that *Under the Red Flag*'s redemptive ending allows Braddon metaphorically to invite her reborn protagonist to join her, as it were, on her own ground (at least as she imagined it). Gaston opens up a deposit box in "the central bank of literature" (to borrow Pascale Casanova's phrase), which the Communards ultimately failed to appropriate and socialize.[48] Yet the price of entry to this world republic of letters necessitates a prior relinquishment, on Gaston's part, of his revolutionary commitment. In the last chapter of *Under the Red Flag*, Braddon celebrates the fact that Gaston's entry into "the ranks of literature" meant that he was "free to write what he liked, and [was] secure of publisher and public" (278), yet that "freedom" is carefully circumscribed insofar as it preemptively excludes the possibility that Gaston might continue to write *as a Communard*, after the manner of Vallès.

"Red Comes into Fashion": Anne Thackeray Ritchie's *Mrs Dymond*

By the time Anne Thackeray Ritchie came to publish *Mrs Dymond* (1885), Paris had long been a mainstay in both her personal life, since she had spent much of her childhood there, and her literary endeavors.[49] Ritchie's approach to the world republic of letters was heavily overdetermined by the fact of her father's preeminent status as one of its most notable citizens. Unlike Braddon, meanwhile, Ritchie's novel of the Commune goes much further in negotiating the terrain of dangerous sympathy for the Communards' revolutionary uprising. *Mrs Dymond* is, in many ways, the most fully fledged example of the group of late-Victorian historical romance fictions that deal with the Commune, and along with Braddon's *Under the Red Flag*, it offers fruitful ground for an examination of the gendered aspects of the Commune's afterlife in Britain. *Mrs Dymond* was Ritchie's last novel, after which she turned her attention primarily to biography and memoir. Ritchie's critics have tended to regard the novel as her most successful. Winifred Gérin, for example, comments that *Mrs Dymond* is "undoubtedly the best-written of Anny's novels, the least dispersed, the most concentrated in interest."[50] First serialized in *Macmillan's Magazine* between March and December 1885, *Mrs Dymond* is a well-wrought drama of "family entanglements" (204), and much of the plot centers around Susanna Holcombe's marriage to the significantly older Colonel Dymond, her frosty reception at the hands of the colonel's relatives, and her dogged struggle to assert herself in the face of this hostility. The entirety of book 4 is set in Paris "in that disastrous year of 1871, when all voices were telling of changes and death, and trouble" (400). The Commune, for Ritchie, serves as both a conveniently recent historical backdrop for the action of her concluding chapters and a more unsettling means of equating her protagonist's emotional deliverance with a revolutionary threat to the bourgeois social order.

Whereas Braddon had relied on careful (though hardly impartial) historical research, Ritchie's preoccupation with the Commune, and her decision to incorporate it into the later chapters of *Mrs Dymond*, stems in part from her own firsthand experience in Paris during March 1871. She arrived in the French capital shortly before the outbreak of the Commune in search of her cousin Charlotte Ritchie. On arrival, she was confronted with the first stirrings of the revolution, and the hurried notes in her *Journal* for that month suggest a mind that was both perturbed and fascinated in equal measure. Her entry for 18 March reads: "News of a Revolution[;] murder of the generals[;] people *acting* it in the streets as they described it all."[51] On 21 March, she records that she saw a barricade on the Rue Pigalle and "met [hurrying crowds of] figures [who looked] like [they had come straight out of] the French Revolution" and notes that she "rushed across fire [of guns] with Charlotte."[52] Much to Ritchie's consternation, her cousin decided to remain in Paris, leaving her with no other option than to return home "by Newhaven [via Le Havre] . . . —Horribly frightened now it was all over."[53] After her return from Paris to Freshwater on the Isle of Wight, Ritchie continued to dwell on the Commune, and she wrote to Charlotte on 17 April: "Even here in this peaceful place the Revolution seems passing & repassing. As long as I live I shall not forget the strange *thrill* in the air though thank God I saw no horrors."[54] Ritchie's presence in Paris during the early days of the Communard insurgency clearly registered an indelible impression on her imagination, but her conscious decision to store away the events she witnessed in her mind's eye for the purpose of writing a novel reveals an important aspect of Ritchie's immediate response to the Commune. If Ritchie initially thrilled to the possibility of social revolution, this moment of enthusiastic trepidation (more akin to revolutionary tourism than ideological valorization) soon passed into the more complicated and contradictory terrain of novelistic representation.

That Ritchie directly incorporated some of her own Parisian experiences into *Mrs Dymond* is clear enough from a simple comparison of certain passages of the novel with relevant portions of her *Journal* entries for 1871. For instance, her entry for 14 March records that she came "to Paris with Alice Probyn & Cook's tourists . . . from [Le] Havre."[55] In *Mrs Dymond*, meanwhile, the narrator comments that Susanna "had come across by chance with a party of Cook's tourists availing themselves of the escort of the great circumnavigator of our days" (401–402). During an episode of fighting, Susanna and Madame Du Parc set out in an attempt to find luncheon and provisions for a journey out of Paris, and "as they were crossing the Rue St Honoré Madame said 'Ah!' in a peculiar voice, and a couple of bullets whistle by," recalling Ritchie's own rush through gunfire with her cousin Charlotte (471). Somewhat earlier in the novel, shortly after the establishment of the Commune, Susannah and Madame Du Parc observe a group of revolutionaries from the window of their apartment:

> Up the centre of the street came a mad-looking, dancing procession. A great red flag was borne ahead by a man in a blouse and a scarlet Phrygian cap. Then followed a wild bacchanalian crew, headed by a dishevelled woman also crowned with the cap of liberty, and dressed entirely in red from head to foot, followed by some others dancing, clapping their hands, and beating time to a drum and tambourine; half a dozen men, with pistols in their belts, with huge boots, and a scarlet figure, carrying a second flag, wound up the procession. The whole band swept on like some grim vision; it was there, it was gone, the window closed up, the street was empty again. (457)

Ritchie's presentation of this band of Communards deploys a number of reactionary tropes, including the suggestion of mental instability and drunkenness implied by the air of "wild bacchanalian" revelry. The "grim vision ... ominous of past terror, of new disaster," hardly invites sympathy or enthusiasm on the reader's part (457–458). On the contrary, the scene figures two middle-class women watching the first stirrings of the Commune from an elevated, spectatorial position that belies their sense of apprehension and mounting horror.[56]

The narrator's attitude toward the revolution, and the revolutionaries, appears to be one of simple condemnation, but this ostensibly reactionary position must be weighed against a more complicated articulation of sympathy, mediated through the radical political commitments of Susanna's French lover, Max Du Parc, who dresses "in an old velvet coat, shabby enough for any Communist" (447). As with Braddon's focus on Gaston Mortemar's shifting Communard sympathies, Ritchie offers a window into the world of the Communards, humanizing some of the revolution's supporters, while simultaneously drawing back in horror from the alleged excess of violence associated with the revolution's last days—violence that leads some of those very same supporters to reassess and, ultimately, to relinquish their support for the Commune. Ritchie imagines the Commune, at its climax, as a "wild saturnalia of the streets, where dishevelled women were dancing round the flames, and men, yelling and drunken, were howling out that the last day had come" (508). These "dishevelled women" and "drunken" men are never individuated, nor are their political motivations given any serious consideration; they simply exist as part of an agglomerated mass against which the temperate good sense of the bourgeois protagonists can be all the more clearly delineated.

Ritchie's representation of the women who took part in the uprising is similarly revealing. Ritchie's narrator describes a group of "women assembling in the streets and doorways ... uttering fiercer, vaguer threats of vengeance [than their male companions] against tyrants, against Versailles, and the police, and, indeed, before many hours had passed the first of their unhappy victims was being hunted to his death along the Rue des Martyrs" (486–487). Ritchie's Communards stalk the streets of Paris like Furies seeking revenge. In this respect, her depiction of these female Communards, like Braddon's representation of Communard women with "streaming locks of tangled hair, which were hideously suggestive of Medusa's snaky tresses" (158), closely follows the discourse of "mob horror" that would have been familiar to Victorian readers of Dickens's *A Tale of Two Cities* (1859).[57] Dickens's novel, set during the French Revolution of 1789–1795, presents the grotesque figure of Madame Defarge plotting a violent form of revenge against her aristocratic oppressors, and her footsteps echo stridently in the clamoring of Braddon's and Ritchie's *pétroleuses*. Versions of the same "infuriated mob" and "seething crowd," presiding over "a wicked, cruel, godless power," shout and scream through the pages of Waters's *A Young Girl's Adventures in Paris during the Commune* and Orr's *The Twins of Saint Marcel* as well.[58]

It is all the more remarkable, then, that Ritchie's writing has been construed in some quarters as a form of "revolutionary" practice. Carol Hanbery MacKay regards Ritchie, along with the photographer Julia Margaret Cameron, the theosophist and women's rights activist Annie Besant, and the feminist and novelist Elizabeth Robins, as one of a group of "covert revolutionaries" associated with a "boundary-crossing" cultural politics that she likens to a "'velvet revolution,' . . . acknowledging that they pushed boundaries with an uncanny awareness of the subtle implications of their transgressions," thereby "rewriting the social scripts assigned to them."[59] MacKay's choice of metaphor is oddly evocative of Carolyn Eichner's characterization of three Communard activists—Elisabeth Dmitrieff, André Léo, and Paule Mink—who form the chief subject of her book-length study of Communard women. Eichner writes that by "pushing gender and class boundaries, they literally made revolution. And through their radical acts and ideas, they challenged existing gendered systems."[60] It would be too much of a stretch to construe Ritchie, let alone Braddon, as a Communard or a revolutionary in the sense invoked by Eichner; clearly, she was not. Yet Ritchie, in particular, shared with the Communards a desire to challenge "existing gendered systems," albeit in a far more muted way, and this submerged cultural politics surfaces in a pronounced manner in her novel of the Commune. MacKay develops her discussion of creative negativity in Ritchie's writings with a focus on her biographical studies in *A Book of Sibyls* (1883) and her introductions to her father's novels, but it is potentially productive, for an understanding of both Ritchie's creative oeuvre and British responses to the Commune, to consider *Mrs Dymond* as part of the same cultural project whereby Ritchie "used strategies . . . to negate the effects of stifling containment and to stage [her] own rebellions as a kind of loyal opposition" to the ruling-class status quo.[61] In brushing up against the historical reality of a defeated revolution, as *Mrs Dymond* does, Ritchie's oppositional stance reaches a kind of limit point, inviting closer scrutiny of the contradictions that arise from her position of "loyal opposition," to use MacKay's aptly chosen phrase.

It is possible, for example, to find a quietly rebellious critique of Victorian gender politics at work in Ritchie's presentation of Susanna's self-assertion in love after her husband's death, as she forges a new relationship of tenderness and genuine affection with Max Du Parc, the son of her mother's French landlady. In her depiction of Susanna's marriage to Colonel Dymond, Ritchie occasionally sounds notes reminiscent of the contemporaneous "new woman" fiction of Olive Schreiner and Mona Caird, whose critiques of the constraints of bourgeois marriage were more sustained and more forthright than is the case in *Mrs Dymond*.[62] Ritchie's narrator describes Susanna's attitude toward her marriage in the following terms: "She was not insincere, but she was not outspoken, she did not say all she felt, she put a force and a constraint upon herself, crushed her own natural instincts, lived as she thought he expected her to live, was silent where she could not agree, obliged herself to think as he did, and suffered under this mental suicide" (231). Susanna's self-denying ordinances recall George Eliot's Dorothea Brooke as much as they anticipate Mona Caird's Viola Sedley. Ritchie also presents Susanna as a strangely bifurcated figure, and this doubled selfhood, both externally perceived and internally felt, emerges as a consequence of her marriage: "There were two Susannas some people used to think, one young and girlish, with a sweet voice and smile, with a glad and ready response for those who loved her; the other Susanna was Mrs Dymond, stately, reserved, unexceptionable, but scarcely charming any more" (225–226). Susanna's bifurcated sense of self is, in part, a response to the stifling conditions imposed on her by the social and familial expectations of Victorian patriarchal ideology, but Ritchie also unmistakably presents the choices facing Susanna as being enmeshed and entwined with the social revolution of the Commune, which poses an equally challenging threat to her sense of self. Susanna travels to Paris, after her mother falls ill, and her growing realization of her affection for Max emerges conterminously with the "tragic, distorted days" of the Commune, during which period Susanna "had been living this double life" (499). Ritchie brings Susanna's quest for self-realization into a relation of uncomfortable proximity (uncomfortable, that is, for the narrator) with the political events of the Commune such that the trajectory of the female bildungsroman, which structures the novel's dominant romance plot, unavoidably collides with a social and political narrative of revolutionary upheaval and conspiracy.

The novel's pattern of doubling—with regard both to Susanna's dual sense of self and to the generic fusion of the bildungsroman with a plot of political intrigue—is also rendered geographically, as the setting is divided almost equally between Coniston in the Lake District and Paris. After Susanna's arrival in Paris, her mother's death and funeral precipitate the first of many collisions between the personal and the political, as her mother's funeral takes place concurrently with the funeral of a dead Communard: "The end of his funeral eulogium was being pronounced—his last words had been '*Vive la Commune!*' said a man in black tail-coat and a red sash, and suddenly all the people round about took up the cry" (480). These cries reach Susanna's ears as she "stood by her mother's grave" and "heard them cheering," such that her private grief becomes embroiled with a public display of political commemoration for a deceased revolutionary martyr (480). The collision of plots is further complicated by the fact that Max, an engraver by trade, professes sympathy with the political "cause" of the novel's Parisian revolutionaries. Echoing Braddon's presentation of Gaston Mortemar, Ritchie delineates Max's radical commitments early in the novel. After his father's death, Max is "bound to an engraver" under the patronage of his godfather and family friend, Monsieur Caron, "a paper manufacturer in the neighbourhood, with an establishment near Paris, a man of some note, a philanthropist and benevolent experimentalist, belonging to any number of isms and prisms of fancy" (180). Together they collaborate in producing a history of socialism, a "publication for the people, a book to be illustrated by Max, with lithographs and wood-blocks and engravings and cheap carbon reprints of photographs, on the cheapest paper, to be published at the lowest price" (184). Caron's mass-circulation publishing principles are hardly Ruskinian, but his paternalistic understanding of socialism as a "divine theory by which the rich and the good and the capable were to teach their secrets to the poor and the dull and the incapable, to show them how to be self-respecting and respected by others" (184) could have been copied directly from Ruskin's discussion of the Commune in *Fors Clavigera*.

Ritchie first met Ruskin as a child in her father's drawing room, but she came to know him well after her visit to Coniston in 1876; and the Coniston setting of the early part of *Mrs Dymond* undoubtedly owes something to Ritchie's acquaintanceship with Ruskin.[63] In 1892, she published *Records of Tennyson, Ruskin and Browning*, a volume of reminiscences in which she describes Ruskin as "a man [who] lent out his mind to help others," and she demonstrates a wide and conversant knowledge of his writings, including *Fors Clavigera*.[64] Given her evident regard for Ruskin, it is hardly surprising that one hears Ruskin's "miraculous voice" discreetly suffusing Ritchie's fictionalization of the Commune, nor that her construction of events accords with the basic pattern of response that Ruskin had first outlined in the seventh letter of *Fors*, which mingles compassionate human understanding with diffident political condemnation.[65] Caron, in particular, echoes the duality of Ruskin's response in *Fors*. Like Ruskin, he acts as a sympathetic interpreter of the Communards' motivations, explaining to Susanna: "They are only asking for justice, for happiness. They ask rudely, in loud voices, because when they ask politely they are not listened to" (463). Yet like Ruskin, he also turns to condemn the Commune for its violence, which he regards as "tyranny" and "monstrous wickedness" (503), again echoing the discourse of Dickensian mob horror familiar from the narratives of Braddon, Orr, and others.

In contrast to the sensationalized repudiation of the Commune's anticlericalism in the novels of Orr and Braddon, Ritchie portrays Max as a fierce critic of the hypocrisies of the Catholic Church. Max and Caron also move in radical circles, and during the last days of the Second Empire, they are shown to be acquainted with Jaroslav Dombrowski, the Polish military officer and radical republican who fought and died as one of the Commune's leading generals. Dombrowski does not appear directly in *Mrs Dymond*, as he does in Edward King's *The Red Terror* (1895), but Caron's political friends discuss the fact that the Polish revolutionary "had been sent on some mission . . . of vital importance to the cause" (350).[66] Having revealed Max's proximity to such a historical figure, Ritchie's narrator swiftly establishes a measure of distance with the assertion that "Max himself had little faith in these mysterious expeditions and conspiracies. He was ready to do his part, even to go on missions if needs be . . . but he had no fancy for plots and secret societies" (350-351). To avoid any semblance of doubt about Max's fundamental decency and, ultimately, his fitness as Susanna's suitor, Ritchie's narrator adds that "it may as well be explained at once, that, although he lived in the company of schemers and plotters, he himself belonged to no secret societies" (351). Again reminiscent of Gaston Mortemar, Ritchie presents Max as a figure who is both a part of and yet, crucially, *apart from* the Communards' political movement. After the establishment of the Commune, Caron's philanthropic brand of utopian socialism wins Max's mentor a measure of influence among the Communard militants, but he is ultimately shot by a "huge, half-drunken Communist" after interceding on behalf of a gendarme in an attempt to prevent a summary execution (506). The news of Caron's death strains to breaking point Max's belief in the Commune, where he occupies "some subordinate place . . . in the Ministère de la Marine," but his mentor's influence continues to assert itself:

> In his first natural fury and heart-rent grief at his old friend's death, Du Parc's impulse had been to wash his hands of the whole thing . . . and to come away with the rest; then came the remembrance of that life-long lesson of forbearance and tenacity; that strange sense—which some men call honour only— awoke; the strange sense of secret duty that keeps men at their guns, faithfully fighting for an unworthy cause in the front of an overwhelming force. Was it also some feeling of honest trust in himself which impelled Caron's disciple to stand to his post? He remained, protesting, shrewdly and intelligently using every chance for right. (507-508)

Ritchie's exploration of Max's grief at his mentor's death is carefully calibrated to draw an ideological cordon sanitaire around the "unworthy cause" of the Commune, while simultaneously valorizing the "sense of secret duty" and "honest trust" that animated some of its partisans, personified here in the figure of Max Du Parc.

In Ritchie's treatment of Max, she brings her readers far closer to reaching a sympathetic understanding of the motivations of those who fought for the Commune than does Bulwer Lytton's *The Parisians* or Braddon's *Under the Red Flag* (or, indeed, many of the historical romances of the Commune that appeared during the 1880s and 1890s), but Ritchie's presentation of those motivations, as individuated in Max, remains circumscribed and made to seem distinctly moderate and restrained. Max joins the Commune partly as a result of Caron's deep and lasting influence on his political outlook but also as "one more pair of arms to help keep order in the chaos, one more recruit on the side of justice and of law" (419). Much like George Eliot's Felix Holt, who leaps to the head of the rioters in Treby Magna in an unsuccessful attempt to prevent serious damage, Max joins the fighting out of a predisposition to maintain order, rather than a thoroughgoing commitment to see through the revolution. Ritchie here shares the dilemma faced by an earlier generation of historical novelists, including Dickens, Flaubert, and Tolstoy, whom Brian Hamnett describes as being "caught between reaction and social revolution," while working in plain view of "an abyss ... into which all the political gains of constitutional liberty irredeemably collapse."[67] Unable to resolve this dilemma with an endorsement of the claims of social revolution, but equally unwilling to sanction "the cold-blooded revenge of the Versaillais" (511), Ritchie instead responds in the manner of earlier liberal writers by humanizing the individual revolutionary at the same time as she preemptively negates the legitimacy of his revolutionary commitment in fashioning a narrative that renders the revolution a source of disenchantment and regret.

The most readily available means of achieving this separation between the individual and his political commitment runs through the already firmly established counterclaims of the novel's romance plot. It is thus hardly surprising to discover that Max offers his clearest expression of the reason for his involvement with the Commune to Susanna, after she implores him to leave Paris on the grounds that "these Communists are no fit associates" for him, to which Max replies by saying: "It is true I am only one man in a stupid crowd; but if I go with that crowd I may hope perhaps to lead it in some measure, or to help at least to lead it" (449). The parallel with the eponymous protagonist of *Felix Holt* is unmistakable, and Max's decision to remain at his post bears fruit, on the narrator's terms, insofar as he proves able to prevent a group of Communard incendiaries from setting fire to the Ministère de la Marine by locking them in a garret, an incident that, as Ritchie's narrator remarks, is "curiously like" an episode recounted in Du Camp's "eloquent and terrible volumes" (506–507).[68] In selecting such an incident for special treatment, both Du Camp and Ritchie differently assert a model of individual heroism that preserves the fiction of bourgeois subjecthood in the face of the threatening presence of collective proletarian agency. Ritchie, like Braddon, relies on Du Camp's reactionary narrativization of the Commune. It is notable, though, that Ritchie selects an episode in which her protagonist frustrates a group of Communards in their allegedly bloodthirsty designs, whereas Braddon opted to depict the bloodletting in full flow.

Far more so than the novels of Braddon and Orr, *Mrs Dymond* offers a careful negotiation of a dangerous sympathy by which Max's active participation in the Commune is rendered both humanly comprehensible and politically understandable. At the same time, the cathexis of Susanna's affections, as they transfer from Colonel Dymond to Max, is complicatedly bound up with Ritchie's complex articulation of sympathy for Max's secular radicalism and with the political fate of the Commune. As Esther Schwartz-McKinzie astutely puts it, "the novel implicitly equates Susanna's release from her mould, and her gradual sexual awakening, with revolution."[69] Schwartz-McKinzie construes Ritchie's presentation of the Commune as a "backdrop" for Susanna's self-development, but one might equally bring it into the foreground and notice the way in which the revolutionary situation precipitates a breakdown in codes of bourgeois social etiquette that makes possible Susanna's first public affirmation of her love for Max.[70] During the last days of the Commune, as Susanna is about to leave Paris in search of safety on a train bound for Rouen, she utters the following words to Max:

> "I—I can't leave you in this horrible place," she said passionately. "How *can* I say good-bye?" and as she spoke she burst into uncontrollable tears.
> He took her in his arms, then and there, before them all—who cared?—who had time to speculate upon their relations? (496)

Ritchie allows her heroine this cloyingly sentimental yet daringly public expression of love for a Communard because Max's revolutionary commitment has already been neutralized (in a broadly Ruskinian manner). Ritchie thus articulates the novel's moderate feminist challenge to patriarchal gender relations in conjunction with a disavowal of the revolutionary politics of the Commune: the radical claims of the novel's gender politics, such as they are, ultimately rely on the preservation of the status quo. This moment in the novel represents the climactic sublimation of Max's political commitment—and, along with it, the novel's exploration of the political issues it examines—into the romance plot, which culminates in Max's eventual exile in Britain. In this respect, Ritchie's narrative strategy of sympathetic disavowal presents one of the most sophisticated means of domesticating the threat posed by the Commune encountered in this chapter.

Spectral Allegory:
Margaret Oliphant's *A Beleaguered City*

An altogether stranger and more spectrally Gothic mediation of the Commune is to be found in the popular novelist Margaret Oliphant's *A Beleaguered City* (1880). Oliphant became a close friend of Ritchie after they met during an Alpine holiday in Switzerland in 1875. According to Winifred Gérin, "The friendship with Mrs Oliphant might be said to mark a turning-point in Anny's career," and they were undoubtedly brought closer by the unhappy circumstance of shared grief: Ritchie happened to be staying with Oliphant when news reached her that her sister Minny had miscarried and died in childbirth in November 1875.[71] Oliphant's brother Frank had died in July 1875, and she had suffered the loss of her first husband in 1859 as well as four of her children in infancy. In December 1871, several months after the suppression of the Commune, Oliphant had made an extended visit to France, spending some time in Paris with her namesake,

Laurence Oliphant, during which period she "took a drive... to see what the capital looked like after the cruel suppression of the Commune."[72] Just under a decade later, she published *A Beleaguered City*, a novella that draws on aspects of this experience and that bears some affinities with Braddon's and Ritchie's slightly later narratives of the Commune even as it occupies a markedly different stylistic and generic terrain. It takes its place in the tradition of Victorian ghost stories, alongside those of Sheridan Le Fanu and Charlotte Riddell, while Oliphant herself thought of *A Beleaguered City* as "the one little thing among [her] productions that is worth remembering."[73]

Oliphant borrowed the title of her novella from Henry Wadsworth Longfellow's 1839 poem of that name, in which a spectral host besieges the city of Prague, but it is telling that Braddon also refers to Paris on multiple occasions in *Under the Red Flag* as "a beleaguered city" (122, 137, 140), as does John Oxenham.[74] Drawing on Oliphant's experience of visiting Paris in the wake of the Commune's defeat, her spectral tale of the unseen figures the Commune as a context that is both there and not there, briefly registered by way of misprision, hovering momentarily in view only to flicker away again like the novella's great multitude of spirits. That she was undoubtedly aware of this context, however, is confirmed in an article she contributed to *Blackwood's Magazine* in October 1878, titled "Three Days in Paris," which addresses the opening of that year's Great Exhibition and which appeared a few months before an abridged version of *A Beleaguered City* was first published in the *New Quarterly Magazine* in January 1879. In her first paragraph, Oliphant takes note of the city's history of violent conflict and civil war, commenting that "no more tragic place... is in the world—Massacres of St. Bartholomew, Massacres of September, Reigns of Terror—associations more appalling than those which surround any capital in Europe form the common thread of her story. Nor is it necessary even to go back upon history, when we know that the traces of blood and warfare are scarcely yet wiped out of those very streets."[75] Without explicitly mentioning the Commune, Oliphant signals her awareness of its uncanny persistence, even as she simultaneously occludes the reality of bitter class antagonism associated with it by asserting Paris's universality, which "sweeps everybody into it..., is for all classes... [and] involves everybody with a vague kind of brotherhood, sympathy, and friendliness."[76] In the article's penultimate paragraph, meanwhile, it becomes clear that Oliphant regards Paris as a haunted city. In commenting on the replacement of gas by electric light in the streets, she observes that it "sheds a kind of ghastly atmosphere of light all about, a weird unnatural illumination, out of harmony with every tone and tint of nature, in which passers-by seem to glide like ghosts."[77] Oliphant adds that the electric "light of Hades" brings with it a "charnel-house phosphorescence," silently reminding her readers, in her concluding paragraphs, that the political conflict on which she had remarked in a seemingly offhand manner at the beginning of the article came at the cost of many thousands of deaths.[78] In her later *Memoir of the Life of Laurence Oliphant*, recalling her visit to Paris in December 1871, Oliphant found recourse to similar language, describing the city as "but a ghost of her bright and careless self in [those] days" when "terrible tokens" of the wreckage of the Commune were still visible in the streets.[79] Oliphant took a tour of the ruins in late 1871, but the "ghosts" of the Commune would continue to haunt her and would subsequently migrate to the provincial city of Semur in the Haute Bourgogne, which she visited immediately after her trip to Paris in 1871 and which provides the ostensible setting of *A Beleaguered City*.

Oliphant's novella relates the evacuation of the residents of Semur as they gradually realize that their city has been occupied by the spirits of the dead. This "miraculous occupation" supplies Semur's inhabitants with a chance to reflect on the course of their own lives, stunned as they are into a kind of mortal dread and terror by the shocking appearance of a "terrible placard" that fills up the "whole *façade*" of the city's cathedral, suggesting the first of many parallels to the historical events of the Commune.[80] During the Commune, public space became visibly politicized, as Kristin Ross notes, by the "immediate publication of all the Commune's decisions, and proclamations, largely in the form of *affiches*."[81] In Ritchie's *Mrs Dymond*, Susanna similarly observes "various placards and appeals of the day . . . fluttering" around the newspaper kiosks after the outbreak of the Commune (471–472). In the beleaguered city of Semur, by contrast, the "terrible placard" is an emanation of "NOUS AUTRES MORTS," who present an injunction to the city's living inhabitants: "Go! leave this place to us who know the true signification of life" (Oliphant, *Beleaguered City*, 54–55). In Oliphant's radically reworked iteration of the resurrection plot, the "pregnant phrase, *la vraie signification de la vie*" (61), haunts Semur's living inhabitants and causes them to question their religious, scientific, and social presuppositions. The city's mayor, Martin Dupin, narrates his decision to flee Semur, describing how he felt: "I was only hurried out, hastened by something which I could not define—a sense that I must go" (64); his words call to mind the bourgeois flight to Versailles after the proclamation of the Commune. As he and his family enter the street, they encounter "a stream of possessions similar to [their] own" (64), suggesting a generalized sense of displacement and dislocation on the part of the city's wealthier residents. In Oliphant's tale of the unseen, the Commune flickers into view at moments like this as a suggested context that is available, as it were, only negatively, as little more than "a mist, a silence, a darkness" (84).

Oliphant divides the novella into ten chapters, the majority of which are narrated from the viewpoint of Martin Dupin, but Oliphant also includes four other narrators—the radical and visionary Paul Lecamus, the conservative M. de Bois-Sombre, Madame Dupin de la Clairière (the mayor's wife), and Madame Veuve Dupin (his mother)—whose memories of the "miraculous occupation" are interspersed with the mayor's own recollection of events. Dupin, meanwhile, considers it his "duty so to arrange and edit the different accounts of the mystery, as to present one coherent and trustworthy chronicle to the world" (19–20). In this respect, the novella dramatizes the problem of competing interpretations in the face of a profoundly divisive and unfathomable event that one character likens to a "revolution" (135), alluding to the proliferation of eyewitness accounts that appeared after the Commune, each staking a different claim to narrative authority. The multiplicity of narrators also attests to the uncanny veracity of the spectral presence in Semur, even though at no point in the story does a single ghost actually appear; their presence is simply felt, much as the repressed memory of several thousand slaughtered Communards must have haunted the bourgeois imaginary during the early decades of the Third Republic. Unlike Henry James's masterful reworking of the ghost story genre in *The Turn of the Screw* (1898), which foregrounds the potential psychological instability of the story's principal character, a young governess, thereby calling into question the reliability of her narrative (notoriously so), the multiplicity of different narrative perspectives in Oliphant's novella assures readers that this is, in fact, a *real* ghost story. But the diverse perspectives that the different narrators bring to bear are also particularly instructive in what they reveal about the residents' projections of the meaning of their ghostly visitation and the serious interpretative differences that arise. As Esther Schor puts it in a suggestive reading of the novella, "the encroachment of the Unseen on the Seen causes an interpretive crisis" for the residents of Semur, adding that Oliphant's "haunted interpreters enact our task as readers by confronting an uninterpreted 'text'" while simultaneously interrogating Oliphant's own "authority as an interpreter of literature."[82]

Dupin and his wife disagree about the significance of the events they witness. When his wife urges sympathy, Dupin angrily accuses her of wanting to "go over to [their] enemies" in an act of "love" for "these dead tyrants" who have overtaken their city (107). Dupin instead prefers militaristic mobilization, and when news of the events travels outside Semur, Dupin learns that "some spread reports of internal division" among residents, noting: "It was said that there had been fighting in Semur, and that we were divided into two factions, one of which had gained mastery, and driven out the other" (99). To the outside world, the ghostly occupation appears much like a civil conflict, in a manner that is clearly reminiscent of the Commune. As Dupin struggles to make sense of his expulsion from the city, he vaguely recalls a biblical narrative: "There is a story somewhere which I recollect dimly of an ancient city which its assailants did not touch, but only marched round and round till the walls fell, and they could enter. Whether this was a story of classic times or out of our own remote history, I could not recollect. But I thought of it many times while we made our way like a procession of ghosts, round and round, straining our ears to hear what those voices were which sounded above us, in tones that were familiar, yet so strange" (104). Dupin here betrays his distinct lack of scriptural knowledge, confirming his status as a secular-minded republican mayor, who prefers to keep the conservative religious party of his city at arm's length. Yet the fact that his mind turns repeatedly to the story of Joshua's assault on Jericho reveals an intriguing intertext for Oliphant's novella. In *The Civil War in France* (1871), Marx also invokes the biblical story of Jericho in order to satirize the "riotous mobs of swells"—a prototype for the party of order—that began to mobilize against the Commune in the days following 18 March and that marched on the Place Vendôme on 22 March.[83] The "silly coxcombs," according to Marx, "expected that the mere exhibition of their 'respectability' would have the same effect upon the revolution of Paris as Joshua's trumpets upon the wall of Jericho."[84] Like these Parisian reactionaries, Dupin imagines "we were like an army suddenly formed, but without arms, without any knowledge of how to fight" (83) and finds himself suggesting that "we should blow trumpets at some time to be fixed, which was a thing the ancients had done in the strange tale which had taken possession of me" (104). The conservative M. de Bois-Sombre is most keen to support Dupin in this interpretation of events, regretting the "forcible expulsion of which [they] had been the objects" and likening the displaced residents to "soldiers campaigning without a commissariat" (176). In this respect, the expelled residents of Semur appear as ciphers for the Versaillais, willfully miscomprehending the nature of the events and readily mobilizing for a violent response; yet the ghostly adversaries are far too immaterial for that, and such efforts are soon frustrated.

Dupin's narration, however, also admits a more troubling and radically destabilizing possibility of identification *with* the perceived enemy, as he likens those whom he leads to a "procession of ghosts," thus mirroring the very "spirits" (148) who occupy the city. Dupin struggles to keep at bay this prospect of radical recognition of and identification with the occupying forces, as urged on him by his wife, and he never fully explores this possibility in any of his own narrative fragments. That possibility is, instead, incorporated into the chronicle of events in the narrative of Paul Lecamus, whose interpretation of the ghostly visitation differs markedly from that of the mayor. Lecamus relates his awareness of the spectral presence, early in his narrative fragment, with reference to "the sensation as of a multitude in the air," which leads him to recall that "I have lived in Paris, and once passed into England, and walked about the London streets. But never, it seemed to me, never was I aware of so many, of so great a multitude" (134–135). No sooner has Lecamus conjured the image of an urban crowd, disembodied and ethereal as it is, than his mind turns to thinking about the scene in provincial Semur as a "revolution which was happening before [his] eyes" (135). The spirits of the dead ("NOUS AUTRES MORTS") who spectrally occupy Semur, bringing with them a message of "desire and longing, yet hope and gladness" (142), represent both the "other dead" of Semur *and* the othered dead of the Commune, whose lives had borne witness to a traumatic shock for the bourgeois social order and whose bodies were unceremoniously flung into mass graves but who reappear, in Oliphant's narrative, as a reincarnation of a badly exorcized specter.

Dupin frames Lecamus's narrative by voicing skepticism about its teller, having made clear that he regards Lecamus as "something of a visionary" (24) and a "dreamer of dreams—one who holds a great many impracticable and foolish opinions" (25). M. de Bois-Sombre, meanwhile, regards him as "a hare-brained enthusiast" (174). Yet it becomes equally clear that Lecamus, who is allowed to enter into and remain in the city during the ghostly occupation, possesses a greater claim than the mayor to act as an interpreter on behalf of the "other dead" and to share their message with the world outside the city. During the time in which he was "alone with the unseen," Lecamus records that there was "pleasure in all the city" (144), and he adds, addressing Dupin: "You have been made to believe that all was darkness in Semur . . . but within, soon after you were gone, there arose a sweet and wonderful light—a light that was neither of the sun nor of the moon" (140). In some important respects, Lecamus's narrative mirrors the account of those, like Marx, who sought to vindicate the Commune. As Marx put it in *The Civil War in France*, "After the exodus of the 'better class of people,' the Paris of the working class reappeared, heroic, self-sacrificing, enthusiastic in the sentiment of its herculean task! No cadavers in the morgue, no insecurity in the streets. Paris was never more quiet within."[85] In this respect, Lecamus's narration of his time in Semur also accords remarkably well with Henri Lefebvre's description of the Commune as a "fête révolutionnaire," organized around the working class's reoccupation of a city from which it had been expelled.[86]

In particular, Lecamus notes that the unseen ghostly occupants of Semur seek to transmit their message through song: "They sang going in bands about the streets. . . . And as they sang there was joy and expectation everywhere" (142). Hearing this music, Lecamus deems it to be "more beautiful" than any of the music originating in the mortal world of the seen, and adds: "The singers were called forth, those who were best instructed . . . , to take the place of the warders on the walls; and all, as they went along sang that song: 'Our brothers have forgotten; but when we speak, they will hear'" (144). One might compare Lissagaray's account of the concerts, organized by the Commune's Federation of Artists, that were given in the Tuileries on the eve of the Bloody Week (see figure 3.3). He records that three orchestras played "in the galleries" and that "Mozart, Meyerbeer, Rossini, the great works of art have driven away the musical obscenities of the Empire," while "a monster concert" was later "given for the benefit of the widows and orphans of the Commune," even as the "Versaillais shells burst" two hundreds yards away in the Place de la Concorde.[87] The narrator of Clara Quin's *Through the Storm* (1880), a rare example of a pro-Communard romance novel, echoes Lissagaray even more directly, commenting that "in the midst of all this, Paris was calm, even gay. The theatres and concert-rooms were open; the drama was much purer, the music more refined than it had ever been

Figure 3.3. "Concert for the Wounded at the Tuileries," *Illustrated London News*, 20 May 1871, 500. Mary Evans Picture Library.

under the Empire; . . . and, in the face of all its difficulties, this new social life had much beauty."[88] In *A Beleaguered City*, Lecamus records the ghosts' "beseeching" song as follows: "We have come out of the unseen . . . for love of you; believe us, believe us! Love brings us back to earth; believe us believe us!" (144–145); but he explains that it went sadly unheard by the living citizens of Semur. He thus finds himself in the unique situation of being the only living person in a position to interpret the song's message, which he explains as follows: "(If you take my opinion, they know pain as well as joy, M. le Maire, Those who are in Semur. . . . They hope like us, and desire, and are mistaken; but do no wrong. This is my opinion. I am no more than other men, that you should accept it without support; but I have lived among them, and this is what I think.) They were taken by surprise; they did not understand it any more than we understand when we have put forth all our strength and fail" (145–146). Lecamus offers an interpretation grounded in radical understanding and recognition, seeking to persuade the mayor of the visitors' benign intentions, while also sympathizing with the failure of their song to communicate its desired message and the subsequent failure of the "embassies" that were "sent out" from Semur (147).

In making this decentering gesture of spectral solidarity, Lecamus finds that "the unseen became to [him] as the seen" (147) and that he "stood in [the] city like a ghost" (139). In acting as a sympathetic interpreter of the ghostly occupiers, Oliphant implies, Lecamus also exposes himself to a form of radical resubjectivization that brings him into proximity with the social being of those whose message he had sought to convey. It is thus fitting that Lecamus ultimately passes over into the world of the unseen and becomes a "dead man" (243) who melts away into the realm of the spirits with whom he had lived. In this sense, Oliphant offers a more acute exploration of the crisis of bourgeois subjectivity with which other novelists of the Commune confront their protagonists.

For example, Susanna Dymond, during the Prussian siege of Paris, comes to realize that "in all these strange days and stirring episodes [she] seemed to herself but one among the thousands who were facing the crisis of their fate, a part of all the rest" (Ritchie, *Mrs Dymond*, 418). Ritchie offers a momentary glimpse of the possibility that Susanna might become *part of* the masses, blending her eponymous protagonist into the otherwise indistinguishable body of the general populace. Susanna hovers on the brink of what Georg Lukács would characterize as a form of historical typicality. Although Lukács does not refer to the Commune in his major work *The Historical Novel* (1962), his remarks on the manner in which Walter Scott and Leo Tolstoy "created characters in whom personal and social-historical fates closely conjoin" are instructive in this context.[89] Lukács notes the way in which the "minor aristocrats" who appear in Scott's and Tolstoy's historical novels express "certain important and general aspects of popular experience ... directly in [their] personal lives," adding that "if the historical novelist can succeed in creating characters and destinies in which the important social-human contents, problems, movements, etc., of an epoch appear directly, then he can present history 'from below,' from the standpoint of popular life."[90] As parsed by Fredric Jameson, "The historical novel as a genre cannot exist without [the] dimension of collectivity, which marks the drama of the incorporation of individual characters into a greater totality, and can alone certify the presence of History as such."[91] Susanna momentarily apprehends the possibility that her own story might be "a part of all the rest," that her individual experience might, in a sense, be typical of a greater sociohistorical whole at a moment of intense political crisis; but the outbreak of the Commune ultimately frustrates any further exploration of this possibility, and the dominant, recuperative romance plot soon reasserts itself with Susanna's declaration to Max that the "Communists are no fit associates" for him (Ritchie, *Mrs Dymond*, 449).

Many popular novels of the Commune follow a similar pattern, mobilizing the claims of a romance plot against those of political involvement. In Francis Henry Gribble's *The Red Spell*, for instance, Elise Rollin frequently laments the fact that her lover, Ernest Durand, sides with the Commune, opining: "If the Commune were finished, he would be mine and mine only."[92] Gribble, however, modulates the recuperative conclusion, typical of sentimental romances of the Commune, by denying Elise her wish: like Max Du Parc, Ernest Durand becomes disillusioned with the Communards, but he nonetheless chooses "to die with them all the same," joining one of the final skirmishes in Père La Chaise.[93] Oliphant's novella offers a still more challenging exploration of this terrain of dangerous sympathy. Although *A Beleaguered City* is better characterized as a spectral allegory or a supernatural romance (rather than a historical one), Oliphant went further than Ritchie in exploring the contours of bourgeois resubjectivization in the face of a traumatically debstabilizing revolutionary event, allowing Lecamus to act as the spokesperson for the "mysterious visitors" (122). Lecamus's narrative seeks to preserve fidelity to the revolutionary event of their visitation, even as Dupin assures himself that Lecamus is "quite free from revolutionary sentiments" (25) in order to rationalize the inclusion of his narrative in the authoritative chronicle of events. Lecamus describes his approach to the occupied city as "the crisis of [his] life" and records that "I knew not what I looked for—but something I looked for that should change the world" (131–132). In Dupin's conclusion of his record of events, however, he observes that the occupation's aftermath is surprisingly anticlimactic: "The wonderful manifestation which interrupted our existence has passed absolutely as if it had never been" (254). Everything simply returns to a semblance of normality with remarkable speed.

This turn in Oliphant's narrative accords remarkably well with the experience of those who visited Paris in the months after the fall of the Commune. For example, the socialist poet and proponent of the simple life Edward Carpenter "passed through Paris" during the latter part of the summer of 1871 and records that "the city was quiet. People sat out at the cafés and sipped their *absinthe* as though nothing had happened."[94] As the historian James Joll has written, "Paris, in spite of the defeat of 1870 and the Commune of 1871, soon recovered its reputation as the '*ville lumière*,' the city of fashion, glamour and luxury which other capitals could emulate but never equal."[95] Oliphant herself was perturbed by a sense of the incongruity of quotidian spectacles continuing apace in the wake of traumatic political events. Observing the crowded streets and the "sound of multitudinous feet" in "Three Days in Paris," she asks: "Is this the same city that starved in the siege . . . and that rent herself asunder after in wild revolt and conflict of brother against brother? We are apt to scoff at the return of the old gaiety, the smile and the song that come back too soon, as we chose to think in our wisdom, to lips that had been pinched with misery so terrible."[96] Oliphant explicitly invokes the Commune here, but her manner of doing so is instructive. She construes the civil war in familial terms, as a "conflict of brother against brother," much in the manner that *A Beleaguered City* confronts the living residents of Semur with a disturbing summons from departed members of their own kith and kin. She also self-critically admits to feeling scorn for those who, as in *A Beleaguered City*, treat the occurrence "absolutely as if it had never been." Oliphant observes the Paris Exhibition with the "mingled sympathies" of a "foreign spectator, looking on," but this mingled current of sympathy and incomprehension also clearly informs her allegorical rendering of the revolutionary event of the Commune in *A Beleaguered City*.[97]

As Esther H. Schor comments, when all the different narratives that make up *A Beleaguered City* are read together, the "document of Semur's ordeal bespeaks a far more radical conception of both political and interpretive authority than Dupin's centrist, tolerant, but patriarchal rhetoric can sustain," allowing Oliphant to expose the "conceptual threads that link psychological repression to social oppression" and to explore the ways in which the "enfranchisement of the social body depends on fuller and more complex recognitions of the self."[98] Oliphant's efforts in doing so are all the more remarkable when one considers that her narrative explores these topics with oblique though clearly discernible reference to the Commune. Like her friend Anne Thackeray Ritchie and her literary adversary Mary Elizabeth Braddon, Oliphant navigated the terrain of a dangerous sympathy with the revolutionary militants of the Commune, but as should be clear from the foregoing discussion, she did so in a way that was bolder, more narratively complex and generically audacious. In selecting an epithet with which to introduce a collection of critical essays on Oliphant, D. J. Trela suggests that she was a "gentle subversive."[99] The phrase echoes Robert Lee Wolff's characterization of Braddon as a "crypto-radical" during the early 1880s, as well as Carol Hanbery MacKay's account of Ritchie as a "covert [revolutionary]."[100] Yet in Oliphant's novelistic encounter with the Commune, she came much closer than did Braddon or Ritchie to offering a *genuinely* subversive exploration of the destabilization of bourgeois subjectivity in the face of a revolutionary event, which, although it stops far short of the kind of outright endorsement offered by the Commune's supporters in Britain, nonetheless sketched out the parameters of a form of radical recognition. As the following chapters will show, this pattern of uncomfortable recognition was taken up in different quarters by a diverse array of writers.

CHAPTER 4

"Dreams of the Coming Revolution"

GEORGE GISSING'S *WORKERS IN THE DAWN*

In *Culture and Society* (1958), Raymond Williams characterizes George Gissing's first novel, *Workers in the Dawn* (1880), as an example of Gissing's "negative identification" with the working class—a novel in which he "had been an evident radical."[1] Williams suggests that "it is a characteristic of the negative identification that it breaks up at points of real social crisis and reacts into an indifference to politics, recantation, or sometimes violent assault on the cause that has been abandoned."[2] *Workers in the Dawn* is an important text in this regard, as it provides material with which to examine Gissing's retrospective treatment of a "real social crisis"—the Parisian workers' uprising of 1871—and to chart his repeated acts of narrative displacement and occlusion. For his own part, Gissing claimed that *Workers in the Dawn* was a "*Tendenz-Roman*" and that the novel's engagement with the "terrible social evils" of poverty and social deprivation meant that he had acted as "a mouthpiece of the advanced Radical party," but this assertion of moral purpose had its limits.[3] At a number of important moments in the narrative's development, Gissing invokes the specter of the Commune or, more discreetly, the forms in which its defeat was registered in London, only to deflect and redirect readers' attention. The death of a relatively minor character, John Pether, who openly sympathizes with the Commune, marks the moment in the novel after which all direct, explicit reference to the Commune ceases, at the same time as his death inaugurates a chain of displacements, through which the Commune's continued presence is registered negatively, detectable only at the edges and in the interstices of Gissing's novelistic canvas.

Williams, in his discussion of Gissing, adds that while "nothing is to be gained from simple negative identification, . . . its breakdown can be instructive," suggesting that such a pattern of breakdown is discoverable in Gissing's later novels, including *Demos* (1886) and *The Nether World* (1889), casting Gissing in the role of a disillusioned reformer who eventually came to regard all worldly projects of social transformation with a weary kind of disdain.[4] In 1888, Edith Sichel identified Gissing in similar terms as the leading representative of the "Pessimistic" school of philanthropy, describing him as a novelist whose "pessimism . . . , which allows him to believe in none but the blackest of futures, causes him at the same time and from sheer hopelessness to accept the present with . . . resignation."[5] Sichel even suggested that *Demos* was "written to prove the errors of Socialism and the impracticability of equality."[6] Echoing Sichel's account, Austin Harrison—son of Frederic Harrison, the Positivist and supporter of the Commune who engaged Gissing as a tutor for his son after having read *Workers in the Dawn*—wrote that Gissing's views tended toward "social pessimism." He added: "[Gissing] viewed politics with an almost puerile disdain. He was a voluptuary in pessimism and seemed to delight in social degradation, yet at the same time to loathe it with a fierce intellectual contempt."[7] As this chapter argues, Gissing's gravitation toward this outlook ran through an engagement with the Commune. More fundamentally, it also suggests the extent to which Gissing's naturalistic "Zola-inspired urban fiction" proved incapable of exploiting the novelistic form in a way that could successfully accommodate the revolutionary energies unleashed by the Commune.[8]

John Pether's Dreams

In *Workers in the Dawn*, Gissing's protagonist, Arthur Golding, is torn between the competing ideals of art and social improvement, which forms the basis of a tragic split in his personality, leading him to oscillate between these two poles over the course of the narrative, variously influenced by a series of sometimes sympathetic, sometimes hostile mentors, friends, and lovers, pushing and pulling him in different directions. If Arthur thus appears as something of a straw in the wind, this probably reflects Gissing's own hesitation in pursuing and developing the political trajectory of the novel's earlier sections, which are strangely underwrought. Where one might expect to find explicit political discussion, one finds instead signs of evasion, confirming the novel's status as a curious hybrid of failed *künstlerroman* and frustrated bildungsroman. Gissing sets Arthur's artistic maturation and development against the subdued threat of social upheaval, which various characters conjure up with reference to France's revolutionary history. Gilbert Gresham, Arthur's cynically self-interested guardian and artistic mentor, seeks to dissuade Arthur's childhood friend Helen Norman from her philanthropic endeavors among London's poor with the following warning: "Who can tell what morning you may wake and see these streets of London running with the blood of your friends and relatives. There are knives sharpening now that will before long set right the injustice of centuries, set it right far more quickly than all your gold, if you scattered it all day long about the slums and alleys. Have you studied history? Did you ever read of the French Revolution? Take warning by it, and see your safety while you have time."[9] Given Gresham's fleeting designs on Helen's affections, and his consequent jealousy of Arthur, his reasons for advising Helen about how to use her time, and her inherited wealth, are undoubtedly selfish ones, but his invocation of French political history nevertheless establishes the prominence of the revolutionary example as a counterweight to Helen's reformist, philanthropic aspirations. Gresham's attitude toward this history, which he clearly regards as a salutary warning, rather than a cause for celebration, contrasts sharply with that of the working-class John Pether, whose delirious predictions of revolution are as full-throated and sincere as they are appalling to Arthur's more refined sensibility.

Pether's severe economic difficulties lead Arthur and his friend Mark Challenger to suspect that Pether is "gradually starving to death," but their offer of financial support is met with an indignant rebuke:

> I don't want your money. It isn't friendship to offer it me; it only makes me mad—mad—mad! Look here; I have been reading a newspaper to-day. Do you know how many paupers there are in London? About seventy-thousand! . . . It's coming, I tell you; I know it's coming. I can feel it coming by the trouble in my mind, like I can feel an east wind coming by the pains in my body. . . . These seventy-thousand paupers shall be dressing themselves in the garments of the rich, and warming their frozen limbs in the blood which shall stream like water along the streets! I feel it's coming! (2:306, 310)

Pether's bloodthirsty fantasy of revenge, born of his poverty and deprivation, causes Arthur to "[shrink] back before the man's violence" (2:310). Arthur's response, in turn, serves to marginalize Pether's revolutionary fervor at the same time as it establishes the prominence of Arthur's more temperate variety of Radicalism. Pether and Gresham embody opposing attitudes to the possibility of revolutionary insurgency, with Pether taking the part of an overzealous enthusiast, while Gresham voices an exaggeratedly *haute-bourgeois* cynicism mingled with a trace of genuine apprehension. Arthur sits between these two contrasting positions, yet it is Gresham's manipulative interventions, during his brief time as Arthur's mentor, that lead Arthur to forswear his artistic talents and commit himself, instead, to a life of political involvement. Gissing sets the scene for the elaboration of Arthur's newfound commitment in a Radical Working Men's Club, hosted in the shop of a tin worker named Isaac Spreadbrow on Crown Street. There, Arthur develops his political consciousness through conversations with fellow workers Will Noble, Mark Challenger, and Pether.

Gissing describes Arthur's gravitation toward the Crown Street club as part of a wider trend of politicization among London's working class, as the club itself "was only one of a great number of similar combinations which at this time the glorious spirit of Radicalism was calling into existence throughout the

Metropolis" (2:258). *Workers in the Dawn* was Gissing's novelistic response to a period of increasing political organization that "began to manifest activity towards the end of the year 1870," during which period "the notes of the 'Marseillaise' were occasionally heard in the open streets," while "Republicanism of an advanced type was loudly advocated on numerous platforms and in open-air assemblies" (2:258–259). Gissing's narrator comments that the Franco-Prussian War paradoxically "came to aid" the spread of such sentiments as "hopes of the downfall of tyranny in France and of the establishment once more of a Republic" turned the "thoughts of the poor in England ... in the same direction more strongly than ever" (2:259). The period of excitement after Léon Gambetta's proclamation of the Third Republic on 4 September 1870, "when it was known that Paris, the suffering high-priestess of Liberty, had once again shaken off the degrading yoke of princes and proclaimed the rule of the people" (2:260), provides the backdrop against which Arthur ventures his most politically explicit utterances of the novel.

On the occasion of an "extraordinary meeting" of the Crown Street Club, Arthur delivers an extended speech on the events in France, proclaiming: "The gates of the temple of Liberty have once more been thrown wide open, never, let us hope, to be closed again" (2:260). Arthur accentuates the proximity of England and France, separated only by "some twenty miles of sea" and "a few hours' journey," and adds, "[the French] example will be of inestimable value, of incalculable aid to us in our struggle here in England" (2:260–261). However, Gissing does not develop Arthur's invocation of this geographical proximity, and his passionate assertion of his commitment to the "struggle"—both in England and in France—soon passes from his mind and almost drops out of the narrative altogether, as Arthur's attention becomes embroiled by his marriage to the alcoholic Carrie and, after the marriage disintegrates, the subsequent doomed courtship of his childhood sweetheart, Helen Norman. John Pether, the only member of the club who takes an active interest in the Commune, is eventually consumed by his own revolutionary fervor, after which point the whole tenor of the narrative swerves in a markedly different direction. Gissing passes over in almost total silence the historical actuality that the "gates of the temple of Liberty" were indeed closed in the most brutal fashion several months after Arthur's passionate declaration that the republican example of France "will be unspeakably precious in the sight of us strugglers for right" (2:262). Neither does the novel supply any evidence of Arthur's thoughts about, or his response to, the subsequent drift of events in France during 1871.

One might regard this striking omission as a realistic corollary of the subsequent trajectory of Arthur's deeply troubled life, as the complicated circumstances of his marriage to Carrie make continued involvement with the club particularly difficult and in view of his later oscillation back toward the aesthetic under the influence of Helen Norman. On the other hand, one might equally construe this omission as a sign of hesitance, or unwillingness, on Gissing's part to work through and resolve the political trajectory that his novel had begun to explore. In particular, Gissing's treatment of John Pether's enthusiasm for the Commune is deflationary and linked to Pether's incapacitation during his descent into mental illness. Gissing also represents Pether with recourse to motifs of Gothic horror, linking political radicalization to monstrous somatic degeneration. As Terry Lovell has commented with reference to a slightly earlier tradition of mid-nineteenth-century realism,

> If we accept for the moment the idea that the social class which capitalism itself both produces and fears, the working class, may figure in bourgeois literature of terror as a hideous and fearful monster, then if it is to express that fear in realist fiction, it must be in a form which is recognizable, not disguised as a non-human monster. A condition of the appearance of real fears in recognizable form in realist fiction would seem to be that the fear must be formulated in such a way that it may be overcome in the course of the narrative.[10]

In Gissing's novel, Pether's enthusiasm for the Parisian Communards both confirms and modulates the symbolic identification of working-class radicalism and monstrosity in bourgeois novelistic realism. When Arthur visits Pether for the final time, Gissing's narrator characterizes Pether's expression as "ghastly," and his "jaw-bones seemed almost to pierce through the skin" (3:89), presenting an image of deathly affliction reminiscent of the photographs of the slaughtered Communards with whom Pether identifies.[11] Arthur notices that Pether's "features had altered so since Arthur had last seen him as scarcely to be recognisable" (3:89). Although Arthur momentarily struggles to recognize Pether as a result of his physical deterioration, Pether's unrecognizability also signifies the political distance that has arisen between him and his erstwhile companion. Arthur's interest in French political affairs stops short, after all, of pro-Communard commitment and extends no further than his moderate republican sympathies of late 1870, which are reminiscent of the position taken by Charles Bradlaugh's *National Reformer*.[12] Faced with Pether's support for the Commune, Arthur is caught between human sympathy for his sometime interlocutor at the club and revulsion at the *revolutionary* turn Pether's thought has taken. For Gissing's readers, Pether thus embodies a recognizably human kind of monstrosity, whose bodily and mental collapse goes hand in hand with a challenge to the very boundaries of political and moral respectability that Arthur himself esteems.

Pether's Communard proclivities are mediated through Arthur's gaze. During Arthur's visit to Pether's sickbed, he discovers that Pether had stored up a "great heap of newspapers, . . . those at the top lying open as though they had been lately read," and Mark Challenger informs Arthur that "they are papers with accounts of the Communist rebellion in Paris" (3:89–90). Arthur, in turn, "shuddered involuntarily as he pictured to himself the sick man's thoughts, how they must teem with dreadful images of slaughter," while acknowledging that the reports "doubtless . . . realised to John Pether the dreams of the coming revolution on which he had for years persistently dwelt" (3:90). Pether's manic fixation on newspaper narratives about the Commune and Arthur's anguished and involuntary shudder of repulsion combine to create an impression of the Commune as something in extremis, beyond the pale of both psychological and political normalcy. Shortly before his death, Pether cuts an extraordinarily pathetic figure. During a delirious hallucination of an imagined revolutionary uprising, he calls out to Arthur:

> Wake! Can you sleep whilst the drums are beating and the bells are ringing so loud? Wake, and join yon whilst you have time! We are fifty thousand strong, and already half London is in our hands. Everyone who is ragged or hungry or oppressed, everyone who knows the bitterness of long and hopeless waiting for justice, everyone whom wrong has driven into crime, everyone whom tyranny has made *mad*—all are with us! Hark! Now the drums have ceased, and the firing has begun. They will fight desperately, these rich men, for their bags of gold and their palaces overflowing with luxury. (3:94–95)

Pether's fantasy of revenge, inspired by newspaper narratives of the Commune, culminates with an image of destruction, confirming Arthur's suspicion that Pether's mind "must teem with dreadful images of slaughter." When Pether gives voice to these "dreadful images," however, Gissing makes clear not that Pether's mind dwells on the slaughtered Parisian Communards but that he looks forward instead to the violence of an imagined revolutionary upheaval in London.

The full monstrosity of Pether's vision, which he exclaims, at length, to Arthur, confirms reactionary stereotypes of the Communards and their sympathizers as merciless incendiaries and bloodthirsty killers: "Fire these houses, and kill every living creature that flees from them! It grows dark, but the fires will light us to our work. No pity! No mercy! Aye, the women and children, too! Kill, kill, kill!" (3:95). Pether's hallucination is possibly the most accurate expression in Gissing's oeuvre of Nietzschean *ressentiment*: "the *ressentiment* of those to whom the only authentic way of reaction—that of deeds—is unavailable, and who preserve themselves from harm through the exercise of imaginary vengeance."[13] Pether hardly preserves himself from harm, yet his "exercise of imaginary vengeance" might be said to bear out Fredric Jameson's supposition that the ideologeme of *ressentiment* is crucial to any understanding of Gissing's early novels. Jameson identifies this ideologeme with Gissing's "expression of annoyance at seemingly gratuitous lower-class agitation" and observes that, in the work of the French historian and contemporary of the Commune Hippolyte Taine, the concept will "furnish the inner dynamic for a whole tradition of counter-revolutionary propaganda."[14] Gissing might have found some precedent for Pether's incendiary fantasy in the writings of Communard exiles had he chanced upon a statement "to supporters of the Commune," published by the London-based Revolutionary Commune Group in 1874, in which a group of thirty-three self-professed Blanquist exiles unapologetically claimed their "share of responsibility in the fires that destroyed the instruments of monarchist and bourgeois oppression while protecting [their] fighters."[15] It is more likely, however, that Gissing simply attributed to Pether the kind of motivations that characterized reactionary representations of the Communards in mainstream periodicals, which were full-throated in their condemnation of the Communards' alleged burning of Paris.

John Wilson, writing in the *Quarterly Review*, invoked the "insurgent apparition of the International, with its myriad incendiary hands, and tongues, and pens," an organization that, he went on to suggest, "terribly demonstrates how the speculative delusions palmed on popular ignorance may blaze out in more than metaphorical conflagrations, kindled by popular fanaticisms."[16] Similarly, in the October 1871 issue of the *Dublin Review*, John Baptist Cashel-Hoey glossed the concluding paragraphs of Marx's *The Civil War in France* as an example of an "atheist, murderous, incendiary, predatory" tendency, "aiming at the destruction of the entire existing moral and social order, not in one country only, but throughout the world."[17] He went on to pose the following rhetorical question: "After burning Paris, are we destined to witness London exploded? Why not London as well as Paris?"[18] Paradoxically, however, the scale of the violence to which Pether's imagination turns in the depths of his delirium far more closely resembles the atrocities committed by the Versaillais as they put down the Commune, slaughtering women and children and killing "every living creature" suspected of an association with the Commune.

Other contemporary observers pointed out that the Communards were not necessarily as bloodthirsty as was often claimed, pointing to the kinds of pamphlets and newspapers that Pether is said to hoard. For instance, the Harrow schoolmaster Edward Ernest Bowen, who spent a week of his 1871 Easter vacation in Paris, offered surprisingly favorable eyewitness testimony some years later, in a lecture delivered to the Harrow Liberal Society on 31 October 1887. In this lecture, Bowen commented that "I have before me a pile of newspapers that were sold by the thousands in the streets, the typical journals of the time: the 'Vengeur,' the 'Cri du Peuple,' the 'Mot d'Ordre,' the 'Rappel,'" and he challenged his listeners: "Find, if you can, in one of these, a single word of instigation to disorder, to outrage, or to cruelty."[19] For the purposes of Gissing's narrative, however, the political content of the newspapers that Pether collects is less significant than the vague, ill-defined sense of danger that such propaganda is assumed to pose—of a kind that may "blaze out in more than metaphorical conflagrations," as John Wilson might have put it. In fact, Gissing's attribution of the desire for violence to the novel's only Communard sympathizer, Pether, effectively displaces any attempt to confront the historical actuality of the violence with which the Parisian Communards were themselves suppressed. It is a way of looking at the Commune by not looking at it. As with Bulwer's *The Parisians*, the moment of the Commune's most unequivocal appearance in *Workers in the Dawn* is also a moment of elision and evasion. Where Bulwer's narrative simply breaks off, in Gissing's novel, all explicit reference to the Commune dies with John Pether, whose death inaugurates a chain of topographical and linguistic displacements that combine to prevent any possible deepening of Arthur's political radicalism.

Fire and Snow: Cooling the Incendiary Imagination

Long before Pether's descent into illness, Gissing's narrator characterizes him as a "gloomy fanatic" who "never allowed the sense of his wrongs to sink to rest for a moment" (2:172), not least because he had been "brought up in the workhouse, and suffered cold, and hunger, and cruelty" (2:311) after his mother was executed for murder in the prison where Pether was born. As a consequence of these difficult circumstances, Pether "had at length fanned the fire of wrath within his breast to such an intense glow that it only lacked some special accession of fuel to make it burst forth in all the violence of raging insanity" (2:172). In literal terms, that "fuel" is provided in the form of Pether's collection of inflammable newspapers, while, in figurative terms, one can infer that the reading material contained therein is politically incendiary, at least insofar as it kindles Pether's hallucinatory vision of the Commune in London. Pether's "great heap of newspapers" catches fire, and the ensuing "conflagration spread thence, quick as thought, to the bedclothes" (3:96), consuming him in a blaze that Arthur only narrowly escapes and that leaves Pether's corpse utterly "unrecognisable" (3:97). Pether's politically incendiary aspirations culminate in his death by fire, kindled by the very reading material that motivated his desire to set London's streets ablaze in a frenzied carnival of destruction. Gissing's extension of the metaphor of incendiarism across a number of the chapters in which Pether appears, and its absurd literalization at the moment of his death, could appear as a brutal joke at the expense of Pether's pro-Communard sympathies. Such commitment, Gissing implies, is only conceivable as a consequence of mental derangement, anticipating a later trend for the pathologization of political dissent.[20] At the same time, Pether's incendiary thoughts eventuate in a literal conflagration, putting an end to his fascination with the Commune in the flames of an all-too-real fire. Gissing's comment on the futility of revolutionary enthusiasm also plays out, in microcosm, a tendentious version of the Commune's history in its depiction of Pether's passage from hallucinatory vision to fatal conflagration.

Pether's fixation on the Commune raises the political temperature of the novel, yet Arthur's more muted concern with temperance and working-class respectability goes together with a correspondingly temperate disavowal of Pether's revolutionary mania (an earlier iteration of Cullen's demagogic speeches in *Demos*), dramatized with recourse to the same metaphorical patterning. Gissing figures Arthur's shifting allegiances with related metaphors of fire and heat. After one of Will Noble's speeches at the club, Gissing's narrator describes how "Arthur, in particular, had listened to him with admiration, and had warmed with him into enthusiasm"; Arthur expresses his thanks "in a few words glowing with earnest sincerity," while Noble "returned the young man's warmth with interest" (2:213). Gissing here construes Arthur's early politicization as a form of gentle, but hardly impetuous, warming. By contrast, when Arthur sits with Pether through the watches of the night, shortly before the fire in which Pether dies, Pether's sudden waking and his muttered rendition of passages from his collection of newspapers "sent a chill through Arthur's veins," signaling Pether's state of "mere delirium" and "not healthy consciousness" (3:93). In this regard, at the moment of Pether's death, he appears as only marginally more sympathetic a figure than the drunkard lodger Mr. Briggs in *New Grub Street* (1891), who accidentally sets his lodging house alight in an inebriated stupor, thereby endangering the precious manuscript of Harold Biffen's novel. So reviled is Briggs by his fellow lodgers that he is simply left to burn to death in the blazing building; Biffen himself rushes past Briggs on the landing in his desperate attempt to save his manuscript, and after the fire is extinguished, "Briggs's body [was] brought forth in a horrible condition."[21] Pether's manner of death and his tendency to hoard newspapers also suggests an allusion to the character of Krook in Charles Dickens's *Bleak House* (1852–1853). The gin-soaked Krook unwittingly holds a number of important papers relating to the *Jarndyce v. Jarndyce* legal case on which the novel turns, and he dies as a result of spontaneous combustion. Arnold Kettle once described Krook's death as a "revolutionary image . . . absolutely central to the novel's meaning" because the "whole implication is that processes are involved which can culminate only in explosion and that such explosions are not exceptional and unnatural but the inevitable consequences of the processes themselves."[22] Gissing, meanwhile, praised the rendering of Krook's death as an instance of Dickensian melodrama notable for its "magnificent workmanship," even if it also pressed at "the logical extremes of convention."[23] In *Workers in the Dawn*, Pether's death pastiches Krook's spontaneous combustion in a manner that Eduard Bertz might have regarded as an example of Gissing's Hogarthian realism, but it has the opposite effect from that which Kettle finds to be at work in *Bleak House*.[24] Gissing's allusive tribute to Dickens—part of a more extensive dialogue in which, as Simon James observes, Gissing was always "creatively arguing with the tensions between Dickens's realism and moral purpose"—offered Gissing a means of demarcating the ideological limits of his own novelistic enterprise, conceived, at this point, as a morally purposive vocation.[25] Pether's accidental self-immolation represents a moment of symbolic culmination in the development of the narrative's political trajectory, and on the cusp of the conflagration, Gissing signals a definitive cooling of Arthur's political sympathies, precipitated by Pether's feverish declamations and his unstable lurch toward perceived extremity.

From this point on, Gissing's deployment of the metaphorical language of heat and cold appears only with reference to Arthur's shifting passions for Carrie and Helen—a pattern of imagery that runs concurrently with the political subplot— each of whom, in turn, represents a different pole of attraction in his "double life." His hasty and capricious commitment to the working-class Carrie, whom he rescues from the snow on a dark winter's night, coaxing her back to life with the warmth of a "huge fire" (2:318), arises partly from his philanthropic ideal of social improvement. By contrast, his "purer" love for Helen typifies his growing aesthetic consciousness and his pursuit of an idealized life of art, albeit that Helen also embodies a model of philanthropic good behavior, imbued with the "fire of boundless benevolence" (2:40). On the point of his marriage to Carrie, Arthur recalls his earlier passion for Helen only "as a sort of vaguely remembered joy—a background of dim and fading gold to the rich, warm image of the reigning delight" (2:331). His doomed love for Carrie, meanwhile, rages like a "fire that ceaselessly burned within him" (2:341). The troubles in his relationship with Carrie lead him to dwell, with ever more insistence, on the "heaven-aspiring flame" that he associates with Helen and that "burns upon the altar of the heart" (3:34). As his relationship with Carrie continues to break down, her words are spoken with a "taunting coldness" (3:76), and when Arthur finds a note from Carrie in which she declares that she had "gone for good," Arthur "felt cold in every part of his body" (3:80). These troubles come to a head at the beginning of part 3. The chapter titled "A Climax," in which Carrie declares her intention to leave Arthur, proceeds to relate the death of Pether. Thus, the "fire of . . . consuming jealousy" that "broke out fiercely" (3:86) as a result of Arthur's anxieties about his marriage is partly doused by the more urgent necessity of responding to the calamity of the house fire. After Pether's death, Gissing's deployment of the extended metaphor of heat and cold to observe Arthur's fluctuating passions shifts definitively from politics to romance, signaling the abrupt termination of the novel's political subplot. Ironically, when Arthur eventually does come back into contact with Helen, she is struck down for much of part 3 with a "severe cold" (3:149, 393) as a result of her outdoor philanthropic work among the poor; she spends most of her time recuperating by the fireside, and while her meetings with Arthur bring a "warm glow" (3:156, 194) to her face, the spark of unspoken love that once existed between the two of them is never fully rekindled. This sustained pattern of metaphor, however, indicates a kind of rhetorical displacement whereby the novel's romance plot subtly supersedes and crowds out the novel's political plot, with Pether's violent death by fire functioning as a metonym for the violent suppression of the Commune.

Pether himself, meanwhile, serves largely as a foil for Arthur's development; Pether conveniently disappears from the narrative, along with the political potentiality he represents, at the very moment when Arthur's relationship with Carrie reaches a point of crisis. In fact, Pether's death inaugurates within the novel a chain of not only rhetorical but also topographical displacements in which the Commune's continued presence registers only negatively. One immediate consequence of the fire for Arthur involves his relocation from the lodging room in Huntley Street—which he had initially shared with Mark Challenger and then with Carrie (after their marriage)—to a "garret . . . in a dreary part of Islington" (3:99). He stays for only a short period of time, after which he moves to "a far less agreeable abode in Chapel Street" (3:109), near his temporary place of employment on the Edgware Road. These are just two of a number of relocations and displacements that are forced on Arthur over the course of the novel, but it is notable that the moment of Pether's death coincides with—in fact, precipitates—Arthur's departure from the area in and around Fitzrovia that Thomas Jones and Robert Tombs have described as "the centre of exile social and economic life" for French political refugees in London.[26] These exiles included the generation of *quarante-huitard* refugees who fled France in the wake of the defeated 1848 revolution, as well as the later generation of Communards, who numbered in the thousands.[27] The bulk of the Communards "remained [in Britain] until a partial amnesty was issued in 1879, followed by a complete amnesty in 1880."[28] Gissing himself lived in this area during the two years preceding the publication of *Workers in the Dawn* in March 1880, during which time he inhabited, with his wife, Nell Harrison, two different rooms at 22 Colville Place (close to Charlotte Place), rooms at 31 Gower Place (just south of the Euston Road), as well as at 70 Huntley Street, and rooms in the lodging house owned by the tailor Moses Sageman at 35 Huntley Street. By 30 June 1879, they had moved to 38 Edward Street (now Varndell Street), just north of the Euston Road.[29]

This itinerary closely mirrors the trajectory followed by Arthur Golding, who leaves behind his childhood slum in Whitecross Street and subsequently moves through Little St. Andrew Street, Charlotte Place (1:160, 167), Gower Place (2:190), Huntley Street (2:320), a "garret in Islington" (3:109), Chapel Street (3:109), Hampstead (3:365), Highgate (3:380), and Camden Town (3:383), before his eventual emigration and suicide. Arthur's decision to rent a room on Huntley Street, "affecting a piece of economy very agreeable" to both him and his roommate, Mark Challenger, puts him on a par with those Communards refugees who opted to live in the environs of Fitzrovia, largely as a result of economic necessity (2:320).[30] Arthur passes a large part of his teenage years and early maturity in Charlotte Place, where he is apprenticed to Samuel Tollady, whose shop is located there. Together with Gower Place and Huntley Street, these dwellings constituted part of what Adolphe Smith described as "the political foreign quarter in the Fitzroy Square district, north of Oxford Street," the character of which had been augmented by the "last great rush of political refugees ... after the suppression of the Paris Commune."[31] Tollady's shop on Charlotte Place is but a short distance from Charlotte Street, where the *quarante-huitard* and member of the First International's General Council F. Lassassie ran a well-known barber's shop. Communard exiles are known to have congregated there.[32] Smith confirms the reputation among the exiles of Lassassie's "hairdressing shop and French newspaper agency," indicating a possible source of the incendiary reading materials that cause Pether's untimely death.[33] Charlotte Street was also more widely associated with the circulation of French books and newspapers: Mme. Pirnay ran the Librairie Parisienne, which sold French and foreign newspapers, while the Librairie Cosmopolite contained a reading room with over five thousand French titles. Both institutions were located on Charlotte Street.[34] Arthur, meanwhile, takes particular pride in his job as a printer, remarking: "The newspapers I help to print spread knowledge among thousands every day; it makes me work with energy when I think of it" (2:265), and Gissing's choice of neighborhood lends an aptly political charge to Arthur's enthusiasm for radical print.

Adolphe Smith also records that "in Tottenham Street [which bisects Charlotte Street], the Communist Arbeiter Vereinne [workers' association] had established the headquarters of the German socialist refugees, with whom in spite of the recent [Franco-Prussian] war the French Communists at once and cordially fraternised."[35] At the beginning of 1879, Gissing struck up a friendship with one such German socialist refugee, the twenty-six-year-old Eduard Bertz, and commented that, as a consequence of this friendship, he "occasionally [saw] German socialists who are living in London, [and] also read socialist newspapers."[36] Gissing also published a three-part article, "Notes on Social Democracy," in the *Pall Mall Gazette* in September 1880, in which he focuses primarily on the German exile community and writes critically about Bismarck's antisocialist laws, while briefly referring to the French "exiled Communists."[37] On this evidence, it is tantalizing to speculate that Gissing must only have been at one or two removes from—if he was not in direct contact with—the Communard exiles themselves. Elsewhere in the vicinity of Fitzrovia, the Communard exile Victor Richard ran a greengrocer's shop at 67 Charlotte Street, which, like Lassassie's barber shop, "remained open into the 1880s and 1890s."[38] The wife of Albert Thiesz, the Commune's chief of the postal service, lived at 36 Charlotte Street (under the name of C. Levrey), while Louise Michel took up residence at number 59 and, after her return to Europe from a lengthy period of exile in New Caledonia, organized an International School at number 17 with support from Walter Crane, among others (see figure 4.1).[39]

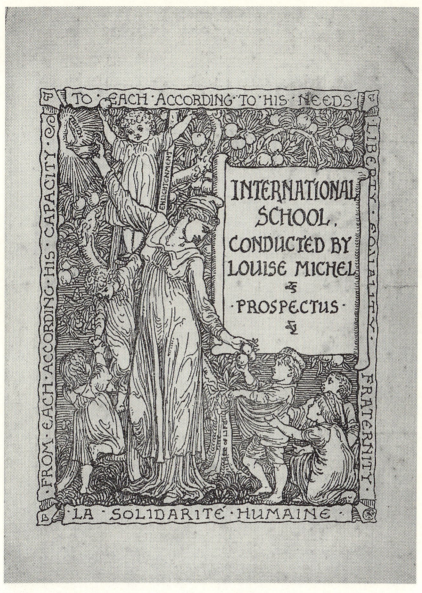

Figure 4.1. Walter Crane, frontispiece, *International School Conducted by Louise Michel: Prospectus* (London: Henry Detloff, 1892). British Library 8305.f.27.4.

Although Michel did not arrive in London until 1890, a decade after Gissing had published *Workers in the Dawn*, it is remarkable to note that her first London residence was located in the very same boarding house at 35 Huntley Street that Gissing and Nell Harrison had vacated during the summer of 1879.[40] Before her arrival in London, Gissing had heard Michel deliver a lecture on "Le Rôle des

Femmes dans l'Humanité" during a visit to Paris in 1888. He commented in a letter to Elizabeth Gaussen, dated 6 October: "It was the first time I had seen this interesting woman; her appearance startled me, she was so terribly like a rather coarse washerwoman. But of course she has fluency enough, & plenty of strong feeling. At one point she aroused loud indignation by describing her 'artistic appreciation' of the scenes of fire during the Commune. It was curious to see the people so stirred by what appeared to an Englishman a simple historical reference."[41] The note of disdain is palpable in Gissing's likening of Michel to a "coarse washerwoman," and yet his making light of the audience's resentment of her allusion to the Commune appears eminently reasonable, despite the disingenuousness of the suggestion that it was no more than "a simple historical reference." Gissing's tone is momentarily disarming when one recalls the forceful rendering of the comparable scene of fire in *Workers in the Dawn*, which transpositions the Parisian conflagration into the British metropolis, but on a much smaller and more containable scale. Indeed, Gissing's amused curiosity in witnessing the response of Michel's French audience must have stemmed, at least in part, from the knowledge that he, too, had found a way of aestheticizing the incendiary threat of the Commune, but in such a way as to make it appear ridiculous, pitiable, and as a result, far less threatening.

This maneuver reveals an important aspect of Gissing's political unconscious. Although *Workers in the Dawn* does not feature in Jameson's pivotal discussion of authentic *ressentiment* in several of Gissing's later novels, Gissing's treatment of John Pether, and Arthur's response to his death, both validates Jameson's reading of Gissing and offers an intriguing moment of local detail. In *The Political Unconscious*, Jameson describes "the situation in which the great realistic novelists . . . are forced, by their own narrative and aesthetic vested interests, into a repudiation of revolutionary change and an ultimate stake in the status quo. Their evocation of the solidity of their object of representation—the social world grasped as an organic, natural, Burkean permanence—is necessarily threatened by any suggestion that the world is not natural, but historical, and subject to radical change."[42] In *Workers in the Dawn*, Pether's death threatens the solidity of Gissing's object of representation in a very precise way, as it is a moment in which a particular feature of the novel's language—namely, the extended metaphor of incendiarism by which Gissing presents the warming and cooling of his characters' fluctuating political commitments—destructively invades and interrupts the diegetic social world of those characters. It is as if the very possibility of Pether's insurgent zeal for revolution presses at the limits of Gissing's novelistic naturalism, threatening to consume not just Pether but the novel itself. The manner of Pether's death also appears as a particularly violent form of the narrative containment strategy, already witnessed in Braddon and Ritchie, which Jameson identifies with the need to "fold everything which is not-being, desire, hope and transformational praxis, back into the status of nature."[43] It is, after all, that most unruly of the elements—fire—that ultimately consumes and dissipates Pether's manic aspirations toward a "transformational praxis."

The Politics of Topography

If the pattern witnessed in *Workers in the Dawn* is thus largely comprehensible within the familiar terms of Jamesonian ideology critique, the spatial politics of the novel suggests a further line of investigation, particularly insofar as Pether's death precipitates an important shift in Arthur's topographical trajectory. The phase of the novel during which Arthur resides in Charlotte Place, Gower Place, and Huntley Street—all streets located firmly within the vicinity of the community of French political exiles—coincides with his most sustained period of political engagement at the club in Crown Street, located "down Tottenham Court Road and across Oxford Street" (2:196), which Mark Challenger proposes that Arthur should join shortly after their move to Gower Place (2:192). After Pether's death, by contrast, Arthur's next moves—first northward to Islington, then westward to Chapel Street, off the Edgware Road, and then on to Hampstead and Highgate—decisively displace him from the neighborhood where the Communard exiles were most densely concentrated. The novel's plotting of Arthur's topographical itinerary thus deprives him of the possibility of developing sustained contact with French revolutionary exiles at the very moment at which the novel's political subplot, concerning Arthur's involvement with the Working Men's Club, could lead toward a deepening of his radical commitments and further exploration of the "perpetual ferment of activity" associated with his work for the club (2:266). Instead, the demands of the narrative's abortive and painful romance plot, centered on Arthur's failing marriage to the alcoholic Carrie, combine with the spatial dislocation necessitated by this plotline in such a way as to preclude Arthur's continued presence in Fitzrovia.

One might consider the utility of this kind of mapping exercise as a form of "distant reading," in which Gissing's London is rendered diagrammatically and what matters is the "matrix of relations [among locations], not a cluster of individual locations."[44] Such an approach risks mistaking geography for geometry, as Claudio Cerreti suggests, flattening out the specificity of a given place by inserting it into a relational diagram. For the purposes of the reading offered here, which foregrounds the importance of Gissing's response to the Commune in the early stages of his novelistic career, it *matters* that Gissing chooses Fitzrovia as the setting for a large part of *Workers in the Dawn*. This is so not only because of the biographical resonances of this choice but also because it sets up a very particular kind of congruence between the imagined space of the novel and the actually existing conditions that obtained in that particular location at the time during which the novel is set and that Gissing evidently relied on to supply verisimilitude and texture. With reference to the Camberwell setting of

Gissing's *In the Year of the Jubilee* (1894), Gail Cunningham notes that Gissing "anatomises a suburb that is destructive of domestic life," adding that Gissing's "locations (most of them actual surviving streets) have a precision that informs meaning."[45] In *Workers in the Dawn*, Gissing is no less precise in his choice of real, surviving locations, and tracing Arthur's trajectory through these places is no less helpful in facilitating the work of interpretation. In this regard, one might say that it is important to think the novel's geography together with its geometry, recognizing, with Cerreti, that "locations as such *are* significant," while also acknowledging that the relations between the different locations of the novel help to elucidate and excavate its political unconscious.[46]

The biographical resonances of Gissing's choice of locations in *Workers in the Dawn* mean that the novel also invites comparison with Gissing's *The Private Papers of Henry Ryecroft* (1903). Gissing presented this book as a fictional autobiography (posthumously edited by "G.G."), which, as Max Saunders has commented, "produces a double effect, of autobiographical material being worked over for aesthetic reasons."[47] Saunders adds: "What Ryecroft exhibits here is really a classic instance of aesthetic sensibility: imagining life as art; his own life as a book."[48] This autobiografictional text registers the "repudiation of revolutionary change" (which Jameson invokes with reference to the genre of novelistic realism) far more concretely and explicitly than is the case in *Workers in the Dawn*. After rambling in the Devonshire countryside near Topsham, the eponymous narrator-protagonist meditates on the "unspeakable blessedness of having a *home*" (in contrast to the series of insecure London digs that preoccupy his memory in the first of the book's four sections) and he records the following observation in his journal: "And to think that at one time I called myself a socialist, communist, anything you like of the revolutionary kind! Not for long, to be sure, and I suspect that there was always something in me that scoffed when my lips uttered such things. Why, no man living has a more profound sense of property than I; no man ever lived, who was, in every fibre, more vehemently an individualist."[49] Ryecroft here registers, in a remarkably candid form, his repudiation and repression of a prior revolutionary commitment and unmistakably declares what Jameson would recognize as Ryecroft's "ultimate stake in the status quo," while simultaneously conflating bourgeois property rights with the necessary preconditions for individual flourishing and self-realization. That this quintessentially ideological reverie occurs immediately after Ryecroft's similarly candid admission that he does not at all "care about the people" of Devon—only "the *places* grow ever more dear to me"—hardly mitigates the general effect.[50] Ryecroft's quasi-revelatory moment of apparent self-knowledge expresses, in microcosm, the basic impulse of Arthur Golding's story: his restless search for a home, as he moves through a succession of digs in Fitzrovia and beyond, is bound up with his conflicted, frequently interrupted, and ultimately frustrated pursuit of artistic self-expression, which Jameson characterizes as "that Utopian fantasy of a life situation in which one would finally have the leisure necessary to write"—or, in Golding's case, to paint.[51] Much as Ryecroft finds it necessary to scoff at his period of youthful revolutionism, Arthur's journey necessarily involves the repudiation of the revolutionary position differently represented by Pether. The further away from Fitzrovia Arthur moves, the less inclined he is toward political activity and discussion, confirming the coincidence of topography and narrative trajectory.

That trajectory sees him seek a life of artistic creativity, which Gissing construes as being opposed to one of political commitment because the two cannot be lived together; in particular, Arthur (like the young Gissing) desires to become a painter, which offers up several parallels with contemporary impressionist responses to the Commune.[52] In a study of post-1871 French impressionism, Albert Boime has traced a process of displacement and marginalization of the Commune roughly analogous to the one that this chapter contends is discoverable in *Workers in the Dawn*. Boime convincingly details how the "Impressionists dealt with specific urban sites and suburban locales so as to recuperate the ground fought over, bloodied, and wasted" during the Commune's suppression, observing that they visited the neighborhoods most closely associated with the Communard insurgency in order to "[free] them from the grim memories of the past and metaphorically [establish] social harmony by immersing them in a flood of dazzling sunlight and color."[53] He meticulously notes the way in which "Impressionism retraces the damaged sites of the Commune, urban intersections, parks, and streets and represents them as bright, flourishing spaces ... promoting the official political ideology with unofficial aesthetic effects."[54] Given the presence of numerous Communard exiles in Fitzrovia during the 1870s and Gissing's familiarity with this neighborhood, one might readily conjecture that Gissing, in *Workers in the Dawn*, was similarly engaged in retracing the "sites of the Commune," provided one accepts Kristin Ross's extension of "the customary temporal and spatial limits of the Commune to include the way it spilled out into ... adjacent scenes."[55]

For Boime, the major impressionist painters, including Claude Monet, Édouard Manet, Auguste Renoir, Edgar Degas, and Gustave Caillebotte, "seized the sites where barricades once stood and restored them to their pristine urban glory, establishing visual parallels and metaphors for the actual rehabilitation of Third Republic France and reassured a still frightened bourgeoisie."[56] Boime reads this repeated gesture of occlusion through deliberate selection—which he identifies in a number of post-1871 impressionist paintings—as evidence of the impressionists' "essentially moderate point of view," which helped establish the conditions for a restorative impulse of "regeneration and renewal," clearing the ground for the utopian impulses of postimpressionist painting.[57] The links between Gissing and impressionism are more auspicious than might at first appear to be the case, given that Gissing is more readily identified with naturalism.[58]

Deborah Parsons has observed that impressionist and naturalist modes are linked by a common aim "to depict a 'reality' that differs from conventional realism," an aim that often involved a "method of adapting to the urban environment" by way of "an intellectualized detachment as opposed to social involvement."[59] Gissing, one might think, dramatizes this very dilemma in the choices faced by Arthur, who ultimately rejects the possibility of "social involvement" in favor of an intellectualized aesthetic ideal. Such parallels are compelling up to a point, but *Workers in the Dawn* can hardly be construed as a straightforward literary expression of the impressionist reclamation of urban space that Boime identifies in the work of Monet, Manet, Degas, and others. Gissing's London is not exactly "bright" or "flourishing," and London had not borne witness to the same scenes of devastation as had Paris. Nevertheless, it is possible to detect a homologous pattern of displacement in *Workers in the Dawn* whereby the Commune is systematically overlooked, ignored, repressed, and forgotten, its presence only detectable in the kind of "small tics and changes of viewpoint" that Paul Wood sees as confirmation that the "Commune and the Prussian war silently haunt Impressionist painting."[60]

After the violent death of Pether, Gissing's novel engages in a comparable process of forgetting and occlusion: the very violence of Pether's death functions as a metonymic substitute for the bloodshed associated with the Commune's suppression, after which point a pattern of topographical displacement sets in. Arthur departs from Fitzrovia and moves westward to Chapel Street, off the Edgware Road, but had he remained in Bloomsbury and instead moved eastward to a different Chapel Street, which runs east from Lamb's Conduit Street toward the junction of Millman Street and Great James Street, he would have encountered the Positivist Church of Humanity at number 19, where Communard refugees gathered during this period for weekly evening classes led by Adolphe Smith.[61] Gissing's connections to the Positivist Society at this time are well-known, but the topographical trajectory of *Workers in the Dawn*, which appears to move in an uncannily opposite direction, confirms Adrian Poole's sense that Gissing's "willed allegiance to the religion of Humanity" was coming under strain and that he was beginning to reject "positivist meliorism in favour of a limited, unambitious ethics of altruism, and above all, mutual pity before the void as the only successful means of tolerating human existence."[62]

In this sense, Gissing's treatment of the Commune in *Workers in the Dawn* anticipates its absent presence in Henry James's *The Ambassadors* (1903), a novel that, according to Scott McCracken, typifies the "paradox of the Commune" insofar as it was frequently "represented through a discourse of its non-representation."[63] McCracken details "James's registration of the event through an absence" in commenting on Lambert Strether's return to Paris during the 1890s, whereupon Strether notices the striking absence of the Palais des Tuileries, which had been destroyed in May 1871 and which kindles in James's protagonist the slow, ruminative workings of his "historic sense."[64] For McCracken, James's discreet evocation of the Commune represents more than just a meditation on Strether's own sense of personal failure and opens out instead into a discussion of how "the consequences of political defeat, the process of dispersal—a dispersal of people, texts, and objects—is absorbed and responded to by modernist aesthetics," such that the "continued existence of disaggregated fragments and vestiges offers the imaginative possibilities of destruction, restoration, or recomposition as collage or montage."[65]

In Gissing's novel, the uncanny nonappearance of the Commune—no exiles appear, for example, despite Arthur's (and Gissing's) proximity to their London haunts—offers an altogether gloomier perspective in which the Commune's suppression is registered through violent metonymy (at the moment of Pether's death), and the subsequent trajectory of the novel's protagonist leads him to despair and eventual suicide. Arthur's story, as Simon James observes, "is full of dead ends," and in this early experimentation with the naturalist novel, the Commune represented for Gissing yet another dead end, both politically and aesthetically.[66] For John Sloan, Gissing's articulation of this "impasse" provides a "series of unique insights into the historical and social conflicts that his fictional world would seek to resolve," and it is certainly true that Gissing's unsentimental exposure of the "inadequacies of liberal humanist values" proves crucial to the production of the novel's "image of deadlock and intellectual exile."[67] From this novel, Sloan suggests, "emerges the subject of Gissing's fiction—the new lower middle-class intellectual who must serve an ideal organic community to which he has no entrance; yet who is unable . . . to theorise his *malaise*."[68] It is less clear, however, why Sloan identifies this malaise with a form of "revolutionary consciousness," and it is hard to see how such a reading could be maintained when fuller consideration is given to Gissing's response to the historical actuality of revolution, as exemplified by the Commune.[69] It is not simply that Gissing's dramatization of Arthur's dilemma of a choice between political involvement and artistic endeavor allegorizes or encapsulates the choice faced by Gissing as a novelist. Rather, in seeking to explore the narrative and aesthetic contours of Arthur's tragic predicament, Gissing finds that the novel (in its naturalistic mode) proves incapable of sustaining any prolonged engagement with the kind of collective and revolutionary political potential called forth by the Commune. Eduard Bertz, meanwhile, recognized the socially critical impulses of his friend's novelistic realism but suggested that Gissing ultimately "sides with the forces that uphold civilisation" and added that "his final word to us is—resignation."[70] In this regard, at least, Gissing is but one of a number of British writers at the fin de siècle who resurrected the Commune in fiction only to discover that he had to kill it off.

CHAPTER 5

Revolution and *Ressentiment*

HENRY JAMES'S *THE PRINCESS CASAMASSIMA*

Scott McCracken's compelling account of the "paradoxical presence of the Commune as absence" in Henry James's *The Ambassadors* concludes by noting that James's negotiation of the Commune, which recalls that of Gissing, abuts a later "modernist conjuncture, [which] as Perry Anderson reminded us . . . , occurred in 'imaginative proximity [with] social revolution.'"[1] McCracken writes that "for James, as for later modernists, his treatment of the past is always also about what is to come," even as James's response to the Commune simultaneously finds itself in tune with a wider current of "active forgetting."[2] As has been considered elsewhere in this book, some of James's contemporaries registered the Commune's presence in more forthright and literal terms, with sometimes interesting consequences. Mary Elizabeth Braddon, for example, associated the presence of Communard exiles in London with an underworld of criminal conspiracy. After *Under the Red Flag*, Braddon returned to the Commune in later novels of 1880s, including the sensational murder mystery *One Life, One Love* (1890), in which she figures Claude Morel, a Communard refugee and bookbinder notable for his disagreeable "physiognomy," as a murderer who "bears the brand of Cain upon his forehead."[3] The journalist and poet George R. Sims's *The Mysteries of Modern London* (1906) plumbs similar depths. "In London," Sims writes, "because it is the capital of the world, are the mysteries of many lands. London is a city of refuge for the outcasts of the Continent."[4] Following the pattern of urban exploration established by pioneering sociologists such as Henry Mayhew and Charles Booth, Sims pursues his observations to the "quiet cafés and restaurants and clubs hidden away in back streets in which men and women meet and eat, drink, dance, and play cards according to their mood, and plot between whiles the deeds that will be ranked with the master crimes of the age."[5]

Communard refugees in London had carved out such spaces "hidden away in back streets." Bernard Porter has argued that the relatively liberal climate of late-Victorian Britain meant that "revolutionaries of all political and national complexions enjoyed more liberty of action... than they had anywhere else in Europe between 1850 and 1880," adding that the "events of 1871—the Paris commune and the exodus of communards to Britain after its suppression—made little difference to this, even though it might have been expected to."[6] While the refugees were thus able, for the most part, to escape the ocular attentions of the state, they were visible enough to attract a different kind of attention in national newspapers. On 2 February 1872, for example, the *Graphic* included an illustration of "The Communist Refugees' Co-operative Kitchen in Newman Passage," signed by the Communard illustrator George Montbard, depicting a communal soup kitchen located in Fitzrovia (see figure 5.1). Like Félix Régamey and numerous others, Montbard had fled to London in the wake of the Commune's defeat. In being deemed newsworthy, these spaces were simultaneously rendered an object of spectacular, public observation. Sims, on the other hand, moves from simple observation to paranoid and fervid speculation, blending the genre of urban anthropological writing, associated with Mayhew's *London Labour and the London Poor* (1851) or Booth's *Life and Labour of the People in London* (1889), with the sensational genre of the urban mystery in a manner that recalls Braddon's traversal of the same terrain.[7] In doing so, Sims figures political exiles as a potential source of social destabilization and crime. In particular, he focuses attention on the French quarter in Soho—a stone's throw from Newman Passage—and suggests: "In the dingy lodging-houses of the side streets of Soho the French murderer and murderess may be leading quiet and simple lives while the Parisian police are searching for them through the length and breadth of France."[8] Sims makes no direct reference to the Commune here, but readers familiar with his poem "In a Cellar in Soho," published in *The Dagonet Ballads* (1879), could hardly fail to make the connection to the delirious exclamations of the "tempest-tost" Communard exile who features in that poem, mourning his dead wife, Marguerite, from the relative security of the titular cellar, while imagining that the visiting priest is an emissary of Versailles.[9]

With regard to Sims's exploration of the mysteries of London's underworld, Mark Seltzer observes that "Sims's works sensationalize the mysteries beneath the humdrum surface and posit lurid secrets to be detected; they incite and cultivate a fascination with the underworld that converts it into a bizarre species of entertainment."[10] Seltzer's account of Sims's dual focus on "policing and entertainment" recalls the dangerous sympathies on display in Braddon's and Ritchie's popular fictions of the Commune, novels that conjure the threat of communist political insurgency for the purpose of popular consumption, only to contain it by way of a careful discursive policing operation.[11] Like Braddon's *One Life, One Love*, Sims also entertains what Seltzer characterizes as a "paranoid vision of London conspiracies," oriented around secret societies and the machinations of political exiles, leading him to project a fantasy of surveillance, which Seltzer

Figure 5.1. George Montbard, "The Communist Refugees' Co-operative Kitchen in Newman Passage," *Graphic*, 3 February 1872, 96. Mary Evans Picture Library.

takes to be intimately connected with the narrative techniques of novelistic realism.[12] As Seltzer superbly demonstrates, Henry James's 1886 novel *The Princess Casamassima* is similarly preoccupied with this atmosphere of uneasy toleration, mingled with the ocular fascinations of surveillance. Building on McCracken's discussion of James's "familiar modernist aesthetic," the rereading of that novel presented here focuses on James's negotiation of the Commune in order to assess his role in consolidating a conservative-aestheticist construction of culture's relationship to revolution.[13]

Subterraneous Politics

Serialized in the *Atlantic Monthly* in fourteen installments between September 1885 and October 1886, James's ninth novel trains its unyielding attention on the cluster of anarchists gathered around the effete bookbinder Hyacinth Robinson and his surlier confrere Paul Muniment. This group looks back at the Commune as a heroic example of revolutionary activism, buoyed up by the reminiscences of the "passionate refugee" Eustache Poupin, who "had come to England after the Commune of 1871, to escape the reprisals of the government of M. Thiers, and had remained there in spite of the amnesties and rehabilitations."[14] Hyacinth's and Poupin's status as artisans, trained in the craft of bookbinding, might lead one to recall that some leading Communards, notably Eugène Varlin, were known to be bookbinders, and Lissagaray records that no fewer than 106 bookbinders were subject to Versaillais reprisals after the suppression of the Commune.[15] Of those who escaped, Dante Gabriel Rossetti sponsored a "book-binding Communist" during the Commune's immediate aftermath.[16] James's novel, meanwhile, memorializes the Commune by allowing it to function as a screen for the projection of lurid hopes on the part of a motley crew of anarchist artisans and revolutionary exiles, while the eponymous Princess embodies a form of bohemian-aristocratic curiosity in the workings of the revolutionary underground that is sometimes mistaken for police surveillance.

The plot of *The Princess Casamassima* largely revolves around the invocation of an unknown and, James implies, largely unknowable anarchist conspiracy, which extends across the continent, even though the bulk of the novel is set in London. Like Gissing, James is concerned to map the political topography of the metropolis's dingy backstreets, hole-and-corner pubs, and artisans' workshops, which make up the "huge, swarming, smoky, human city" of London (1:209). Whereas Gissing never fully resolves the ocular dilemmas precipitated by his novelistic desire to scrutinize working-class political organization, such that the possibility of revolutionary praxis is ultimately occluded and written out of his narratives altogether, James thematizes this very problematic in the person of Princess Casamassima (Christina Light), whose bohemian rejection of her adopted aristocratic class identity goes together with an inquisitive desire "to know something, to learn something, to ascertain what really is going on" (1:203). She is the sort of person for whom Osmond Waymark, the young novelist in Gissing's *The Unclassed* (1884), claims to write when he asserts that his "novel such as no one has yet ventured to write" will be "for men and women who like to look beneath the surface, and who understand that only as artistic material has human life any significance."[17] Like Gissing's 1889 novel *The Nether World*, James's *The Princess Casamassima* explores London's occluded underworld but finds it to be a space of revolutionary political intrigue as much as grinding poverty.

According to Eileen Sypher, James's novel, like Joseph Conrad's *The Secret Agent* (1907), tentatively suggests that "the desire to contain [the threat of revolution] implies not only the desire to distance ... but also the opposing desire to look at the spectacular and forbidden."[18] James explains in the preface to the 1908 New York edition that he plunges Hyacinth, the novel's tragic protagonist, into the "more than 'shady' underworld of militant socialism," such that the topographical undertaking, which proceeds from street to street, is cut across by the need to plumb the depths of London's "subterraneous politics."[19] Insofar as James's preface offers a reliable account of the novel's gestation, *The Princess Casamassima* can be said to have arisen from two related but distinct impulses: James's "attentive exploration of London" (v) and his equally careful, if rather more speculative, excavation of the city's "sinister anarchic underworld," the "suggested nearness" of which "to all our apparently ordered life" can only be evoked by way of "loose appearances, vague motions and sounds and symptoms, just perceptible presences and general looming possibilities" (xxi). With this comment, James exposes the epistemological ground of his endeavor as shaky underfoot and uncertain in the extreme, calling to mind the way in which earlier British responses to the Commune had foregrounded the unstable nature of the boundary between fact and fiction, partly as a consequence of the intense ideological polarization precipitated by the Commune. James takes this epistemological uncertainty and converts it into something resembling an ontological condition of modernity. As he comments in the preface, "the value I wished most to render and the effect I wished most to produce were precisely of our not knowing, of society's not knowing, but only guessing and suspecting and trying to ignore, what 'goes on' irreconcileably, subversively, beneath the vast smug surface" (xxii). Even as the tone of James's preface suggests a supremely confident *knowingness*, he cannot avoid signaling the profound lacuna, or absence of knowledge—even for the purposes of his novelistic venture—that haunts his attempt to get to grips with the pressing question of inequality and the related prospect of social revolution.

Many of James's critics have pointed to the way in which his preface signals a kind of empathic, tabooed sympathy between author and protagonist. Michael Anesko, for instance, notes that "James projects himself in the personality of his protagonist."[20] Discussing James's "crisis over representing Hyacinth," Eileen Sypher suggests that James "imagines Hyacinth as a 'lesser James'—what James would have been like had he been shut out from the world of upper-class culture, a sort of putative son, a Hyacinth to his Apollo."[21] In likening his protagonist to himself in this manner, James steps onto the terrain differently navigated by Braddon and Ritchie, though his negotiation of this dangerous sympathy is far more complexly handled. He inflects this sympathy toward the prospect of revolutionary desire through a narrative voice that projects a relentlessly ironic distantiation from the anarchist artisans' expressions of political commitment. This ironic perspective frames Hyacinth's eventual rejection of the "imbecility" and "palaver" (James, *Princess*, 2:68) that characterizes the conversations at the Sun and Moon pub, at least according to James's narrator, and albeit that Hyacinth's rejection comes tragically too late. For Sypher, the ultimate failure of Hyacinth's quest allows James to "achieve a catharsis of his own desires for change," making James akin to a spectator of the tragic action of his own novel.[22] But the novel might also be said to manifest a tragic worldview at a much deeper level, one that always already militates against the revolutionary politics of its dramatic personae, as this chapter explores.

The motley group of disgruntled working men who gather at the Sun and Moon look to French political history as a source of hope and inspiration, much as Arthur Golding and the other "humble, but not ignoble, advocates of freedom" who congregate at the Crown Street club in *Workers in the Dawn* identify with the republican ideals that underpinned the proclamation of the Third Republic on "the glorious 4th of September" in 1870.[23] While part of Gissing's novel unfolds concurrently with the events of the Franco-Prussian War and the Commune, *The Princess Casamassima* is set over a decade after the Commune's defeat, but it looms much larger in James's novel in the portly, rotund figure of the exile Eustache Poupin (whose name can be translated as "chubby-cheeked"). As Wesley H. Tilley explains, "Since the Commune was the best recent instance of a radical threat to the social order, and might recur, the presence of a Communist in London enabled James to suggest the kind of 'sinister anarchic underworld' on which the effect of the *Princess* depends."[24] Poupin is an older, plumper, and more comfortable version of Ritchie's Max Du Parc or Braddon's Gaston Mortemar. In James's novel, he takes on a role of political mentorship and even plays the part of a "surrogate father" for Hyacinth at the bookbindery where they both work, just as Samuel Tollady encourages Arthur Golding's budding political consciousness while teaching him the related craft of printing.[25] And much like John Pether, who focuses insistently on the sheer number of paupers in London ("About seventy-thousand!"), James's narrator relates that Poupin "squeezed in" to the Sun and Moon on one particular evening "and announced, as if it were a great piece of news, that in the east of London, that night, there were forty thousand men out of work" (2:74).[26] For Poupin and Pether, the thousands of unemployed workers offer specious confirmation of their fantasies of collective agency, which find a focal point in their differently mediated experiences of the Commune. Pether and Poupin both share the assumption that a sufficient quantum of immiseration will precipitate insurgency, but in both cases, the assumption proves unfounded. Yet this is partly beside the point, because neither Gissing nor James is interested in imagining the conditions of possibility for social revolution; they are, instead, more concerned to portray their own self-interested iterations of the warped psychology of revolutionary enthusiasm (or fanaticism).

James's narrator treats Poupin in a particularly disparaging manner, suggesting that his identity as a "political exile" represents little more than a performance that has become routine, if not quite ossified:

> Poupin had performed in this character now for many years, but he had never lost the bloom of the outraged proscript, and the passionate pictures he had often drawn of the bitterness of exile were moving even to those who knew with what success he had set up his household gods in Lisson Grove. He was recognised as suffering everything for his opinions; and his hearers in Bloomsbury... appeared never to have made the subtle reflection... that there was a want of tact in his calling upon them to sympathise with him for being one of themselves. He imposed himself by the eloquence of his assumption that if one were not in the beautiful France, one was nowhere worth speaking of.... Muniment had once said to Hyacinth that he was sure Poupin would be very sorry if he should be enabled to go home again (as he might, from one week to the other, the Republic being so indulgent and the amnesty to the Communards constantly extended), for over there he couldn't be a refugee. (2:74–75)

James portrays Poupin as a refugee who has managed to find some measure of domestic comfort in his exile and who has thereby become secure and confident enough in his semipublic role to forgo the opportunity of returning home, thus rendering the claim to suffering associated with his exile dubious at best, if not entirely void. James calls into question the validity of Poupin's victimhood, subtly arraigning him, in the parenthetical invocation of the amnesty, with a charge of moral inconsistency, even hypocrisy, by delicately contradicting Poupin's claim, interspersed through the play of free indirect discourse, that there is nowhere he would rather be than "the beautiful France." James also makes clear, here and throughout, that his narrator possesses the capacity for "subtle reflection" that his characters apparently lack. More significantly, the conversations that take place in the Sun and Moon allow James to effect an important modulation in the conspiracy narrative, as the fear of collective insurgency typified in *The Parisians* here transforms into a more extended, suggestive, and ultimately obfuscatory focus on individual, terroristic action.

The arrival in London of the mysterious "German revolutionist" (2:82) Diedrich Hoffendahl causes particular excitement at the Sun and Moon. Hoffendahl, around whom the novel's foggy conspiracy plot swirls and hovers, is said to have been the instigator of a "great combined attempt, early in the sixties," about which very little detail is given, beyond the fact that Hoffendahl was the only one of forty participants to have been captured and subsequently "scarred and branded, tortured, almost flayed" (2:79). In another passage of free indirect narration, rather than reported speech, Poupin exclaims that "he himself esteemed Hoffendahl's attempt because it had shaken, more than anything—except, of course, the Commune—had shaken it since the French Revolution, the rotten fabric of the actual social order" (2:80). The narrator's knotty and convoluted syntax wryly suggests the slightly confused tenor of Poupin's thought. The parenthetical reference to the Commune, which could belong either to Poupin or to the ironical voice of the narrator, establishes the talismanic force of this historical event for the club's attendees, even as it implicitly frames the political context in which the event should be seen. Small and incidental as the reference might appear in relation to the novel's wider machinery of conspiratorial intrigue, this moment is significant not least because of the way in which James seamlessly blends the historical experience of the Commune with the fictional machinations of Hoffendahl in order to suggest a wider panorama of unknowable conspiracy. Indeed, so far-reaching were the effects of Hoffendahl's coordinated uprising that "there had been editors and journalists transported even for hinting at it" (2:79). One might account for James's exploitation of the Commune as mere "background" with reference to verisimilitude and technique—the Commune features as part of an expected and fittingly naturalistic range of reference for the would-be revolutionaries who congregate at the Sun and Moon—were it not for the subtle ideological work accomplished by this apparently passing remark. In linking the Commune to Hoffendahl's conspiratorial and secretive revolt, "which took place in four Continental cities at once" (2:79), the narrator discreetly situates the Commune in a generic lineage of conspiratorial putschism, rather than popular insurrection, for which historical antecedents can be found in the abortive Blanquist uprising that took place in Paris during May 1839 or the Dresden uprising of May 1849, in which the anarchist Mikhail Bakunin played a leading role.

As Adrian Wisnicki has commented, Hoffendahl's appearance in the novel ensures that its conspiracy plot is made to seem "like a vast, international and potentially earth-shaking affair," even as its source and precise organization remain shrouded in mystery.[27] This aspect of the novel has long divided critics. Lionel Trilling once observed that the novel is "a brilliantly precise representation of social actuality," whereas John Lucas thought it was characterized by "a baffling vagueness."[28] For Mark Seltzer, meanwhile, Hoffendahl's privileged access to the occult and secret knowledge of revolution, which the Princess desires to access but which the novel never discloses, effectively exculpates James from the problem of realist omniscience: "Hoffendahl's God-like power," as Seltzer puts it, "is also the power of the omniscient narrator, a power of unlimited overseeing."[29] Hoffendahl thus enables James to disavow the necessarily compromised authority of his authorship by distinguishing his "'imaginative' penetration of the city from the manipulative vision and supervision of the conspiratorial plotters."[30] *The Princess Casamassima* is a conspiracy novel in which the inner workings of the conspiracy, if it even exists, are never finally revealed, proffering the outlines of a totality in silhouette without ever disclosing a full view of that totality. Unwilling or unable to contemplate the Jamesonian "final horizon" of cultural revolution and class struggle, James instead inserts the novel's revolutionary partisans into a kind of ersatz providential framework, misidentified with the historical process.[31] At the same time, he repeatedly exposes the half-baked schemes of Poupin and his fellow interlocutors at the Sun and Moon to the full glare of his ironic narrator, making these schemes appear as little more than inconsequential chatter. But Hoffendahl's plots belong to a different order of significance, and it is, as one might imagine, his plans that most intrigue the eponymous Princess.

"Agonies of Sympathy": *Ressentiment* before Revolution

James presents the enigmatic and eye-catching Princess as a figure who is obsessed with learning as much as she can about the nature of the struggles, plots, and plans of the revolutionary underground. Her commitment to the techniques of empirical observation is borne out in her statement to Hyacinth, "I have to believe what I see," before she goes on to explain the roots of her voracious curiosity:

> I don't want to teach, I want to learn; and, above all, I want to know *à quoi m'en tenir*. Are we on the eve of great changes, or are we not? Is everything that is gathering force, underground, in the dark, in the night, in little hidden rooms, out of sight of governments and policemen and idiotic "statesmen"—heaven save them!—is all this going to burst forth some fine morning and set the world on fire? Or is it to sputter out and spend itself in vain conspiracies, be dissipated in sterile heroisms and abortive isolated movements? (1:207–208)

The Princess hopes to glean an insight into the march of events by looking insistently and closely at individual members of the working class, "making studies of the people—the lower orders" (2:37)—in the manner of an urban explorer like Mayhew or Booth, at the same time as her voracious desire to amass knowledge conforms to a more *aesthetic* kind of connoisseurship.

After the fall of the Commune, the polemical literature and caricature produced by the Communards became highly prized and much sought after by collectors. An unnamed correspondent for Charles Dickens's *All the Year Round*, for example, published an article titled "How Paris Mourns" in July 1871 and records searching for "back numbers of the cheap publications" produced during the Commune, commenting that it "was odd to note how thoroughly it was understood that these things were literary curiosities, commanding a fancy price."[32] Caricatures were similarly prized: "When we passed into the region of caricature, and set ourselves to collect specimens of the political cartoons which [had] been published in Paris during the last nine months, our task was environed with difficulty. It was dangerous to ask for, and still more dangerous to display and sell some of these. But we peered below the surface and persevered. We scoured the districts of La Chapelle, Belleville, and Montmartre, and whenever we found a print or newspaper shop, endeavoured to establish confidential relations with its proprietor. We frequently failed."[33] The choice of terms ("peered below the surface," "scoured the districts") anticipates James's evocation of subterranean explorations and pedestrian prowling in his 1908 preface. And much as the Princess approaches the revolutionary underground in search of "really characteristic types" (1:203), initially using Captain Sholto as a go-between, the contributor for *All the Year Round* treats the Communards' revolutionary pamphlets, periodicals, and caricature as similarly collectible, rare "specimens," primarily of interest as a consequence of their pecuniary rather than political value. This value had, of course, appreciated because of the sheer danger of holding such material in one's possession owing to the intensity of the Versaillais reprisals, thus creating an extra frisson of mortal peril for the exacting connoisseur.

An even more peculiar anecdote along these lines appeared in *The Bookworm* in 1891, relating the story of an "indefatigable book-hunter, who was observed by a colleague after the Commune to pass his time in prowling about the by-streets of Paris where the soldiers from Versailles were daily engaged in searching for those implicated in the insurrection, and shooting them down wherever they found them."[34] When the collector's friend seeks to remonstrate with him about the risk to his life, the collector replies, "but what is that compared with the chance of picking up some precious manifesto that will make a figure in my collection out of the pocket of a dead Communard!"[35] The collector is able vicariously to experience the "ecstasy of the barricade" (James, *Princess*, 2:207), as Hyacinth's grandfather had known it, coming into proximity with the prospect of a Versaillais bullet, while simultaneously playing the part of a "prowling" soldier of Versailles, albeit with a very different purpose in mind. The collector's urge to aestheticize the revolutionary politics of the Commune in this way is bound up with a structure of dual identification: the collector prowls the streets hunting down the bodies of Communards as if he were one of the soldiers from Versailles; at the same time, however, the presence of real "soldiers from Versailles" exposes him to the risk of being mistaken for an insurgent and thus being shot as if he were a Communard. The Princess's preoccupation with London's revolutionary underground partakes of a comparable dual identification: she seeks to amass knowledge about the revolutionaries to the point where she becomes a part of their world, but her bohemian-aristocratic curiosity also comes to resemble—and is sometimes mistaken for—the attentions of an undercover police agent (1:219).

The Princess is not simply a collector, however; she also claims to want to know about the trajectory of the revolutionary movement in order that she can "ascertain what really is going on" (1:203). Yet insofar as the novel lifts the veil on the revolutionary talk of the "subversive little circle in Bloomsbury" during the "*séances*" that the Princess desires to access, James's revolutionaries, like Gissing's John Pether, are shown to be preoccupied by a politics of envy (1:202). The appearance of this by-now-familiar ideologeme of *ressentiment* proves decisive in Hyacinth's eventual disavowal of his earlier commitments. Hyacinth faces a more sharply drawn version of the choice between a life of art and a commitment to radical politics that consumes Arthur Golding. Taking note of the novel's densely allusive texture, Marcia Jacobson points out that "the working-class protagonist closest to Hyacinth ... is Gissing's Arthur Golding" because Arthur, like Hyacinth, "is orphaned as a child, raised by a poor printer in London whose close friends are political radicals, and gifted with extraordinary artistic talent."[36] Like Arthur, Hyacinth is also a skilled artisan who finds himself torn between two women: the Princess, like Helen Norman, is identified with the privileges of high culture; while Millicent Henning, like Carrie, is more lustily drawn to somatic pleasures and sensuous gratification. With discriminating exactitude, James notes in the preface that Hyacinth's tragedy consists in "his tergiversation" at the "climax of his adventure" (xviii), and if the sense of turning back conjures the underworld of classical myth, particularly the story of Orpheus and Eurydice, then the mythical resonance of Hyacinth's name—alluding to the beautiful youth, beloved of Apollo, who could not withstand the god's love—similarly marks him, like T. S. Eliot's hyacinth girl in *The Waste Land*, as a figure who is bound to suffer.[37] After Hyacinth swears a vow of loyalty to Hoffendahl, he soon becomes disenamored with the demands that the revolutionary underworld might place on him. Unwilling to break his oath, however, Hyacinth, again like Arthur Golding, ultimately chooses suicide as the only means available of cutting the Gordian knot that binds him. Less immediately obvious is Hyacinth's similarity to John Pether, who, like Hyacinth, was born of "a mother who was tried and found guilty of murder."[38] Again recalling John Pether, and more crucially for the purposes of the argument offered here, Hyacinth's tergiversation also sees him give way to the ideologeme of *ressentiment* at a crucial moment in the narrative's development.

The early signs of this tergiversation are detectable during Hyacinth's Continental visit to Paris and Venice, where he discloses in a revealing letter to the Princess that he is unable to conceive of social revolution as anything other than a nihilistic leveling downward:

> The monuments and treasures of art, the great palaces and properties, the conquests of learning and taste, the general fabric of civilisation as we know it, based, if you will, upon all the despotisms, the cruelties, the exclusions, the

monopolies and rapacities of the past, but thanks to which, all the same, the world is less impracticable and life more tolerable—our friend Hoffendahl seems to me to hold them too cheap and to wish to substitute for them something in which I can't somehow believe as I do in things with which the aspirations and the tears of generations have been mixed. (2:229–230)

Hyacinth disowns the possibility that there might be any positive or beneficent relationship between culture and revolution, of the kind imagined by the Communards and their British supporters, at the same time as he recognizes the contradiction that Walter Benjamin phrased more concisely when he wrote: "There is no document of culture which is not at the same time a document of barbarism."[39] If Hoffendahl's revolutionary aspirations were to be realized, Hyacinth augurs, they could only leave a trail of destruction in their wake, drawing all the "monuments and treasures of art, the great palaces and properties" into a vortex of obliteration. During James's tour of France in the autumn of 1882, he had been similarly struck by the visible legacy of destruction bequeathed to France by the Revolution of the late eighteenth century. While visiting the "very considerable ruins of the abbey of Montmajour," he observed: "Wherever one goes, in France, one meets, looking backward a little, the spectre of the great Revolution; and one meets it always in the shape of the destruction of something beautiful and precious."[40] James was sufficiently attuned to the depredations of the ancien régime to add that the Revolution "must also have destroyed [much] that was more hateful than itself," and he could at least content himself with the knowledge that the patina of historical remoteness rendered the Revolution's legacy relatively harmless, even if it also remained disconcertingly visible.[41]

During an earlier visit to Paris in 1872, the more recent events of the Commune had troubled James in a way that he found harder to accommodate in an even-handed manner, at the same time as he detected in the built environment similarly palpable "gashes and scars of the spring of 1871."[42] In a letter to his brother, James gives way, instead, to a sense of dread, writing: "Beneath all this neatness and coquetry, you seem to smell the Commune suppressed, but seething."[43] The spatial metaphor self-evidently prefigures the subterranean imagery of *The Princess Casamassima*—the "immense underworld, peopled with a thousand forms of revolutionary passion and devotion" (2:138–139), which Hyacinth conjures into being for the Princess after his meeting with Hoffendahl—but James also imagines the Commune here as something unruly in its capacity to overwhelm the senses. He struggles to bring his object properly into view—or, rather, he fails fully to sniff it out—figuring the Commune, by way of synecdoche, as something that stands in for the mass of executed Communard bodies that might actually seethe and smell. As Michelle Coghlan puts it, "in overlooking the ruins and instead 'smelling' the Commune's spectral presence below the surface, James not only senses that the revolution is not dead, but also anticipates that ... the revolution will continue to simmer below the surface of the landscape."[44]

By December 1872, James was looking forward to "the next Communist brûlerie & tuerie, which is pretty sure to come sooner or later," and he commented that, when the day arrives, he was sure that he would "suffer agonies of sympathy," prefiguring the complex articulation of sympathy for his protagonist in *The Princess Casamassima*.[45] Scott McCracken has observed that it is not immediately clear, in James's letter, whether the object of his anticipatory sympathy—anticipatory insofar as James cannot bring himself to look back with any resolution at the historical events of the Commune—is "the massive & glittering capital" of Paris or those putative future Communards who will presumably perish during the "tuerie." In a related comment, McCracken also suggests that the Commune "instigated a problem of representation" for James, such that "references to the Commune in James's fiction appear in a dispersed form, as a kind of literary debris or ruins."[46] This "problem of representation," as it appears in *The Princess Casamassima*, revolves around the associated but distinct problem of *ressentiment* as a mode of response to revolutionary commitment.

Hyacinth's letter to the Princess reveals the *ressentiment* that underpins his shifting outlook: "You know how extraordinary I think our Hoffendahl (to speak only of him); but if there is one thing that is more clear about him than another it is that he wouldn't have the least feeling for this incomparable, abominable old Venice. He would cut up the ceilings of the Veronese into strips, so that every one might have a little piece. I don't want every one to have a little piece of anything, and I have a great horror of that kind of invidious jealousy which is at the bottom of the idea of a redistribution" (2:230). In projecting this philistine position onto Hoffendahl—who occupies one of the novel's many absent centers, at the same time as he functions as the vanishing mediator that precipitates Hyacinth's change of heart—Hyacinth demonstrates that he is unable to conceive social revolution, to represent revolution to himself, or the aspirations that might accompany it, outwith a politics of envy. There is an element of mutual misrecognition, as Hyacinth looks to the Princess as a priestess of high culture, despite her purely adoptive aristocratic background, while she fetishizes him as a "genuine," "authentic" specimen of the social revolution, despite his growing doubts. After he returns from the Continent, he pays a visit to Poupin in Lisson Grove but finds that Poupin's "phrases about humanity" no longer have the same capacity to "thrill him" as was the case before his trip abroad. When Poupin implores Hyacinth to speak to him of his "divine" Paris, he is nonplussed to hear Hyacinth "praise to him the magnificent creations of the arch-fiend of December" (2:241). In learning of Hyacinth's broadly positive response to Napoleon III's embellishment of Paris, under the auspices of Baron Haussman's program of urban renewal, Poupin is caught on the horns of a "terrible dilemma," too pained "to admit that anything in the sacred city was defective" yet unwilling to "concede that it could owe any charm to the perjured monster of the second Empire, or even to the hypocritical, mendacious republicanism of the regime before which the sacred Commune had gone down in blood and fire" (2:241). Poupin resolves his dilemma, rejecting the politics of both the Second Empire and the Third Republic, by anticipating a time "when it's ours," when Paris will have fallen into the hands of a revivified Commune, during which period he fondly imagines that "[the city] will be finer still" (2:241–242).

Poupin, one might think, looks forward, at this point, to the "next Communist brûlerie & tuerie" that James, in 1872, had thought "pretty sure to come sooner or later." Yet Hyacinth recoils at this expression of hopelessly voluntaristic revolutionary sentiment: "Everywhere, everywhere, he saw the ulcer of envy— the passion of a party which hung together for the purpose of despoiling another to its advantage" (2:241). His shift in outlook concludes the second volume of the 1886 first edition. Poupin's fond imagining of a revivified Commune, which briefly recalls the events of 1871, coincides with the tragic modulation of Hyacinth's sympathies, definitively sealing his change of heart, such that he can only comprehend Poupin's revolutionary rhetoric through the interpretative paradigm of *ressentiment*. Poupin's forward-looking vision, already hedged by the well-established ironic distantiation of the ever-vigilant narrator, is further contained by Hyacinth's recourse to "the ultimate negative category of *ressentiment*."[47] Hyacinth becomes a diagnostician of *ressentiment*, and his newfound commitment to the defense of high culture, kindled during his Continental tour, goes together with a Nietzschean conviction that the actions of Communard insurgents, like Poupin, are born solely of a desire for vengeance, rooted in envy, and a desire to punish the rulers, rather than to liberate the oppressed. As Howard Caygill explains, this perspective misses the fact that the Communards' revolt "was directed not against any 'noble morality' of Empire, but against the *ressentiment* of an existing slave*holders* revolt in morals."[48] Thus, in "not seeing what was new and expansive in the Commune, seeing it only as regression," the Nietzschean perspective adopted by Hyacinth fundamentally misunderstands the Commune's "fusion of resistance and affirmation."[49]

In this regard, the horizon of Hyacinth's political vision becomes scarcely distinguishable from John Pether's delirious fantasy of vengeance. Although Hyacinth himself eventually comes to revile such fantasies, after an initial spurt of vainglorious enthusiasm, he proves incapable of imagining any motivation for social revolution that does not originate from the ideologeme of *ressentiment*. Pether embodies *ressentiment*, whereas Hyacinth diagnoses it, or at least he claims to do so; but it is useful to recall Jameson's comment here that "the theory of *ressentiment* . . . will always itself be the expression and the production of *ressentiment*."[50] This formulation is particularly compelling insofar as Hyacinth is concerned, not least because of his status as a "tormented youth" of more than natural sensibility, as James describes him in the preface (viii), condemned by circumstance to live in relative poverty, but who nonetheless aspires to enter the palaces of high culture. In seeking to climb out of this tormenting double bind, Hyacinth projects the motive of "invidious jealousy" onto those who occupy the very space of economic and cultural exclusion that he seeks to leave behind, but this maneuver, as Jameson makes clear, is itself an exemplary manifestation of the very *ressentiment* that Hyacinth diagnoses in others. Elsewhere in the preface, James informs readers that Hyacinth is "jealous of all the ease of life of which he tastes so little" and thus finds himself "bitten, under this exasperation, with an aggressive, vindictive, destructive social faith" (xvii). Hyacinth, then, both embodies and diagnoses revolutionary *ressentiment*, combining in his own person the polarity that Gissing divided between John Pether and Arthur Golding. That Hyacinth eventually relinquishes this "social faith" and emerges instead as a disillusioned interpreter of the imagined resentment that underpins it, might bring him closer to the view that James freely expounds in his own voice in the preface, but it does little to exculpate Hyacinth, or James, from the Jamesonian problematic.

Tragedy, Revolution, and Repetition

James's iteration of this ideologeme is more sophisticated than Gissing's, and *The Princess Casamassima* is ultimately a more successful novel than *Workers in the Dawn*; but in the last analysis, James clearly performs a version of the same containment strategy that has already been observed to be at work in Gissing, Braddon, Ritchie, Bulwer, and others. When James calls attention to Hyacinth's "lively inward revolution" in the preface (xvii), in order to signal (and preempt) Hyacinth's turn from social revolution to cultural solipsism, from politics to aesthetics, his choice of the word "revolution" is hardly accidental. Indeed, given the close proximity of James's confession of his "weakness of sympathy" for the novels of George Eliot, and particularly Eliot's efforts to show her characters' "adventures and their history... as determined by their feelings and the nature of their minds" (xv), attentive readers could hardly fail to notice yet another thread in the dense fabric of textual allusion, which draws James's only political novel into dialogue with Eliot's *Felix Holt, the Radical* (1866). *Felix Holt*, it can be added, stands in the same relation to the Eliot canon as does *The Princess Casamassima* to James's. Eliot's portrayal of Esther Lyon's "inward revolution" in *Felix Holt* is neither worldly nor political; rather, it is an intensely personal and subjective affair, such that Felix's moralized preaching and commitment to betterment through education bears its only real fruit in Esther's moment of choice at the novel's conclusion, where she rejects her claim to the Transome estate.[51] At this crucial moment, as Stefanie Markovits comments, Eliot "shifts the focus from the political revolution implied by the title of the novel to Esther Lyon's 'inward revolution,'" and she does so in a way that forecloses a properly political resolution to the social antagonisms investigated by the novel.[52] It is debatable whether the prospect of political revolution ever really enters the imaginative horizon of Eliot's novel, as Markovitz suggests, but James's deliberate echoing of this basic structure and narrative trajectory should be obvious, even without his direct borrowing of the phrase "inward revolution." Hyacinth's "lively inward revolution" effaces any trace of the historical experience of revolution associated with the Commune insofar as it interiorizes his claim to pursue a politics of direct action in the external world, foregrounding instead his "romantic curiosity," his intensity of perception, and the sensitivity of his nature—an orientation, in short, that bears all the hallmarks of an *aesthetic* attitude to the world. James, in fact, dramatizes the process whereby a revolutionary artisan comes to embrace the very aesthetic attitude that led some high-art connoisseurs to collect Communard manifestos as "literary curiosities," but the tragic conclusion of that process also signals a more problematic statement of Hyacinth's nonbelonging in the realm of high culture and his reduction of social revolution to a politics of envy. In this sense, James's novel shares with Gissing's *Workers in the Dawn* a political unconscious that prioritizes the occlusion of revolutionary commitment through recourse to the ideologeme of *ressentiment*.

Yet James does not simply repeat Gissing (or Eliot or Turgenev). He also thematizes repetition as a problem that bears directly on the dilemmas faced by both political revolutionaries *and* novelists. As Margaret Scanlan perceptively argues, "What haunts Hyacinth the would-be terrorist also haunts James, the fear that every new thing is actually the old in disguise," and she adds that, in James's novel, "the specter of repetition stalks every person, every political or artistic endeavor, every new activity."[53] Hyacinth freely acknowledges to the Princess that "there is nothing original about me at all" (1:204). This preoccupation is also particularly visible in the novel's concern with heredity, not least Hyacinth's desperate attempt to escape the stain of his mother's crime and his "loathing of the idea of a *repetition*" (3:231). He ultimately betrays his vow to Hoffendahl because of his reluctance to conform to, and thereby repeat, the pattern established by his mother in her murder of Hyacinth's father, Lord Frederick Purvis. In thus refusing to play the part of the political revolutionary, Hyacinth is, in fact, rebelling against the maternal overdetermination of his life's course. And behind Hyacinth's mother stands his grandfather. During his visit to his "ancestral city" of Paris, the spirit of Hyacinth's maternal grandfather, who perished on a barricade during the revolution of 1848, accompanies him as he pursues his flâneur's itinerary around the city, learning to regard Paris as a "tremendously artistic and decorative" city (2:209). Hyacinth pointedly neglects to make contact with the "three or four democratic friends, ardent votaries of the social question" (2:209–210), whose contact details Poupin had supplied, and instead takes Paris in something of a holiday humor. Hyacinth is more concerned to direct his strolling toward "theatres, galleries, walks of pleasure" (2:211), and he finds:

"What was supreme in his mind to-day was not the idea of how the society that surrounded him should be destroyed; it was, much more, the sense of the wonderful, precious things it had produced, of the brilliant, impressive fabric it had raised. That destruction was waiting for it there was forcible evidence, known to himself and others, to show; but since this truth had risen before him, in its magnitude he had become conscious of a transfer, partial if not complete, of his sympathies" (2:210). Hyacinth makes clear that he believes there is an intrinsic connection between revolution and destruction, as he begins to arrive at an aestheticist position premised on a rejection of political involvement.

The novel's thematic preoccupation with such patterns of repetition and cyclicality—which brings the vocations of the revolutionary and the novelist into uncomfortable proximity, yoking together the aesthetic and the political in a deathly embrace—uncannily recalls James's apparent certainty that the Commune would recur "sooner or later" in his letter of December 1872. The cyclical pattern of revolutionary recurrence also animates the revisions that James made to the text through its different versions, from manuscript to the *Atlantic Monthly* serialization to the first edition of 1886 and then the New York edition of 1908. John Kimmey records that "in the holograph James has the Poupins leaving Paris in 1851 when Louis Napoleon seized power as a prelude to proclaiming himself Emperor, and Hyacinth going to Paris in June, 1870, one month before the Franco-Prussian War rather than in June, 1883."[54] In the early stages of the novel's gestation, as this makes clear, Poupin was a *quarante-huitard*, which explains why the narrator describes him as a "Republican of the old-fashioned sort, of the note of 1848, humanitary and idealistic, infinitely addicted to fraternity and equality" (1:87–88). Poupin, however, *becomes* a Communard as a consequence of James's revisions. *Quarante-huitardes*, of course, numbered among the Communards, but in choosing definitively to characterize Poupin as a Communard, James introduces the Commune into the novel as a result of the temporal displacement involved in the work of revision: 1848 *becomes* 1871, much as Poupin *becomes* a Communard.

The risk, here, is that James simply reads back the Communard presence in the novel onto the earlier revolutionary upheaval of the midcentury, allowing a Communard exile into the novel, as it were, by the back door, as a Communard-in-name-only whose republican politics "of the old-fashioned sort" belongs to a different era, a different revolution. The effect of such displacement is to negate the originality and novelty of the Commune by inserting it into a prior sequence of revolutionary upheavals. Yet this would matter very little to someone whose conception of revolution is cyclical and who treats the possibility of revolutionary social transformation as if it were a natural phenomenon, as does the Princess when she tells Hyacinth: "I have been here now a year and a half, and, as I tell you, I feel that I have seen. It is the old régime again, the rottenness and extravagance, bristling with every iniquity and every abuse, over which the

French Revolution passed like a whirlwind" (2:114). There is a remarkable congruence between the Princess's severe diagnosis of English society and James's own view of the "English upper class," as expressed in a letter of 6 December 1886 to Charles Eliot Norton: "The condition of that body seems to me to be in many ways very much the same rotten and *collapsible* one as that of the French aristocracy before the revolution—minus cleverness and conversation. Or perhaps it's more like the heavy, congested and depraved Roman world upon which the barbarians came down. In England the Huns and Vandals will have to come *up*— from the black depths of the (in the people) enormous misery.... At all events, much of English life is grossly materialistic and wants blood-letting."[55] One might recall, in reading these remarks, Gerard Manley Hopkins's momentary identification with the Commune in his letter to Robert Bridges ("I am afraid some great revolution is not far off. Horrible to say, in a manner I am a Communist") or John Ruskin's breakthrough realization in *Fors Clavigera* that the "*Real* war in Europe" is not the war between nations but the war between classes.[56] James ever so briefly flirts with such protorevolutionary ideas. More immediately, the letter also suggests the way in which *The Princess Casamassima* offsets James's much-remarked identification with his protagonist by offering a countervailing point of identification. The Princess's antipathy toward the ruling class is unmistakable, but the source of this antipathy is telling. As Marcia Jacobson puts it, "Her interest in revolution dates from a quarrel with her husband and is colored by resentment of him for trying to control her and by resentment of the titled and moneyed class he represents."[57] Jacobson then adds: "The egotism that refers the problem of social change to her need for vengeance prevents the Princess from ultimately gaining the knowledge she seeks."[58] On this reading, then, the Princess herself is the main subject of *ressentiment* in the novel. Although she appears for much of the novel as a collector—much as James, in his preface, identifies his own novelistic enterprise with a voracious tendency to record and horde "many impressions" (v)—her real motivation might, in fact, be much closer to that of Hyacinth than she would ever willingly disclose.

For Deaglán Ó Donghaile, the essential impulse of *The Princess Casamassima* is conservative, as James's exploration of the "aesthetic and cultural threats" posed by his "abstract construction of revolutionary change" allows him "to present the possibility of any radical social transformation as an inherently negative, fundamentally anti-cultural ... phenomenon."[59] Ó Donghaile continues that Hyacinth "speaks for" James when he frames the redistributive impetus of revolution as little more than a politics of envy.[60] One need not see Hyacinth as a simple mouthpiece for James in order to arrive at a similar conclusion. As Fredric Jameson puts it, "ideology is not something which informs or invests symbolic production; rather the aesthetic act is itself ideological, and the production of aesthetic or narrative form is to be seen as an ideological act in its own right, with the function of inventing imaginary or formal 'solutions' to unresolvable social contradictions."[61] The ideological character of James's aesthetic act in *The Princess Casamassima* consists precisely in the way in which the novel gives "social contradictions" the appearance of being "unresolvable." The far-reaching crisis in the formation and reproduction of bourgeois subjectivity instigated by the Commune is played out, in varying degrees, through the pages of almost all of the novels discussed in this book, from the "high," protomodernist realism of James to the popular novels of Braddon and Bulwer Lytton. Each writer offers a different iteration of the same "formal 'solutions,'" which revolve around the individuation of a collective aspiration, reducing the properly political and social claims of the Commune to a form of personal egotism.

In *The Princess Casamassima*, James focuses on a protagonist who enters into an after-the-fact proximity with the Commune—it is a consequence of Hyacinth's friendship with Poupin, rather than direct participation—which triggers and deepens a moment of acute personal crisis. But even as James broaches the political challenge posed by the prospect of social revolution, the very form of his novelistic enterprise proves, on Jameson's terms, ultimately incapable of resolving the contradictions that it exposes between the individual and the collective, the personal and the political; and insofar as James finds recourse to the ideologeme of *ressentiment* in dramatizing Hyacinth's dilemma, *The Princess Casamassima* can be said to occlude these contradictions, in the way outlined earlier. In a particularly pertinent discussion of the novel, Mike Fischer suggests that James's "aestheticization of political praxis not only converts political processes into static reifications, but also provides the dominant hegemony with the illusion that it has truly addressed the concerns of political radicalism through the minor concessions it makes to anarchism's convincing drama of terror."[62] The account just given is a compelling one, but it is also important to recall that James offers a very specific kind of "theatrical" resolution in the novel, which he explicitly identifies with the genre of tragedy. With reference to Hyacinth, James comments in the preface that his protagonist's "aggressive, vindictive, destructive social faith . . . would move to pity and terror only by the aid of some deeper complication," namely, that "he should fall in love with the beauty of the world, actual order and all, at the moment of his most feeling and most hating the famous 'iniquity of its social arrangements'" (xvii). James's deliberate invocation of tragic catharsis sets up the terms of Hyacinth's self-division as a properly irreconcilable antithesis, figuring the split between culture and social revolution as incommensurable, and thereby echoing (deliberately or otherwise) a dominant trope of anti-Communard discourse. For Jameson, James's novels share with those of Joseph Conrad a certain "strategy of aestheticization," which, in James's case, goes together with the "metaphor and the ideal of theatrical representation."[63] In *The Princess Casamassima*, it is ultimately the Princess herself who proves crucial to this strategy, which relies heavily on the novel's widely discussed metaphors of theatricality.[64]

For instance, James implies in the preface that an unspecified audience will be moved to "pity and terror" and that these spectators might thus find some form of aesthetic or moral edification in the tragic tale of the "wretched little bookbinder" (1:85). Hyacinth, too, sometimes appears dimly aware of his own tragic status, reflecting that "he was to go through life in a mask, in a borrowed mantle; he was to be, every day and every hour, an actor" (1:81). At the tragic climax of the novel, which lacks any kind of denouement, James also stages the Princess's discovery of Hyacinth's dead body, after his suicide, in theatrical fashion. In the narrator's framing of the scene, it is Schinkel whose gaze briefly captures the tableau of Hyacinth's dead body, lying "as if he were asleep," alongside "a horrible thing, a mess of blood, on the bed, in his side, in his heart," before the Princess "covered it up" (3:242). Initially, Schinkel and the Princess struggle to gain entry to Hyacinth's locked room, but after Schinkel forces the door, it is ultimately the Princess who "[sees] everything" (3:242). The narrator does not expand on this resonant phrase, but given the extensive visual economy at work in this novel, one might suppose that it carries a special freight of figurative meaning. The Princess's penetration of the revolutionary underground affords her, at the last, a singular kind of access to a unique spectacle of tragic suffering, where she not only enjoys the privilege of a front-row seat but in which she has actually played a leading part. One might ultimately think, then, that James's carefully hedged self-identification with Hyacinth in the 1908 preface is, in fact, something of a ruse, or a careful decoy, given that his real point of identification is with the Princess Casamassima herself.

In Mark Seltzer's Foucauldian reading of the novel, James's experiments with narrative technique reveal an "uneasiness concerning the shame of power"; for Seltzer, James's "turning away from the style of omniscient narration [of his earlier novels] toward the technique of the 'central recording consciousness' . . . displaces the authority of the narrative voice and disavows any direct interpretative authority over the action."[65] Seltzer adds that this "omniscient authority is held up to scrutiny, and indicted, in being transferred to, or displaced upon, the masters of the revolution."[66] Seltzer thereby partially excuses James from the allegedly "authoritarian" tendencies of realist omniscience in suggesting that the novel concentrates such powers in Hoffendahl, whom James figures as the unseen puppet master of the revolution, even as Seltzer acknowledges that James finally remystifies the "realist policing of the real" by identifying realism's policing function, in a recuperative gesture, with "the 'innocent' work of the imagination."[67] Yet James's evident accentuation of the tragic spectacularity of Hyacinth's death also invites a different kind of attention to the novel's concern with looking and seeing. It is, ultimately, the Princess—not Hoffendahl, let alone Hyacinth—who bears witness to the tragic action of the novel's ending; *she* is moved to pity and terror, as is unobtrusively marked in the "strange low cry [that] came from her lips" (3:242). In the last instance, then, it is not so much the masters of the revolution who see everything, thereby acting as a repository for the "bad" side of realist omniscience (as Seltzer suggestively argues), but the Princess, who finally achieves, in some measure, the occulted knowledge about the trajectory of the revolutionary underground that she hoped to attain, even as her own commitment to that cause remains ironically held in suspension, despite her apparent feeling for Hyacinth. It is not so much that James apprehends revolution through the mode of tragedy here; instead, he responds to the tragic character of defeated revolutionary commitments with a (re)privatization of the tragic: Hyacinth's death is a deeply private affair, after all, which does not unfold against a backdrop of world-historical events, even if he inhabits a milieu that is touched by their afterglow.

Deaglán Ó Donghaile suggests that *The Princess Casamassima* discloses an even broader assumption on James's part that "culture is a private affair, at odds with the material and unjust processes of the 'outer world,'" which also partly explains why the Princess understands Hyacinth's "troubled condition as that of being denied access to the kind of culture that she . . . freely enjoys."[68] Yet in encouraging readers to imagine Hyacinth's tragedy as one of social exclusion—figuring him as a kind of radicalized Jude the Obscure, *avant la lettre*—James also writes out of existence another possibility. That is to say, a different version of Hyacinth's commitment to social revolution might differently resolve the problem of the apparent incommensurability between art and revolutionary commitment, in being based on a fundamentally antagonistic assumption that culture, far from being a private affair, is a profoundly collective one, intimately bound up with the very processes of material, political, and social struggle that James uses the novel to traduce. It hardly needs to be stated, by this point, that this countervailing vision of culture was both defended by and embodied in the Commune. To construe the Commune in these terms would be to recognize the stark reality of its defeat as a tragedy different in kind from the version imagined by James, and it is to this possibility that chapter 6 will now turn.

CHAPTER 6

The Uses of Tragedy

ALFRED AUSTIN'S *THE HUMAN TRAGEDY* AND
WILLIAM MORRIS'S *THE PILGRIMS OF HOPE*

The two poets who are discussed in this chapter address the Commune far more directly than did Henry James, and in doing so, they take up more explicit positions than James on the question of the appropriate genre with which to register the Commune's significance. Both William Morris and Alfred Austin, like James, explore the relationship between tragedy and revolution, but they do so from very different standpoints. Morris, in particular, was one of a number of fin-de-siècle socialist poets who grappled with the problem of how to relate to, and retrospectively valorize, the Commune's *failure*. By contrast, the staunch conservative and middling poet Alfred Austin saw in the Commune an occasion considerably to revise and extend *The Human Tragedy*, a long poem that had first appeared in two cantos in 1862. The new edition of 1876 adds two further cantos (renamed as acts) in which Austin's protagonists widen the ambit of their wanderings to encompass both the Italian struggle for national liberation of the late 1860s and the Parisian events of 1871, which Austin frames under the auspices of a homespun theory of tragic suffering. Austin had been foreign affairs correspondent for the *Standard* during the Franco-Prussian War and the Commune, and this firsthand experience apparently motivated his decision to revise his pseudophilosophical verse epic. As he commented in his autobiography: "All I then saw [in 1871] was a fortuitous aid to me, of the most valuable kind, in the writing a few years later of the Fourth Canto of *The Human Tragedy*, and the completion of that poem by the terrible illustration of the too often tragic results of the yearning of many noble minds for the time when a generous, universal and peaceful Cosmopolitanism will, to cite a pertinent phrase of Tennyson's, 'Keep a fretful world in awe.'"[1] Austin's apparent endorsement of "a generous, universal and peaceful Cosmopolitanism" went together with ardent support for British imperialism, and he toed an uncritically pro-Conservative line in his leaders for the *Standard*. When Austin launched the monthly *National Review* in March 1883, a conservative periodical that he edited between 1883 and 1897, an early article by Philip H. Bagenal was titled "The International, and Its Influence on English Politics." Following the sensationalist tone set by Lord Salisbury and other conservative commentators, Bagenal concluded his article with a lurid warning: "The men of 1870 [sic] still live and act.... Marx is dead, but his work goes on."[2] Austin, meanwhile, in an editorial note on "current politics," which appeared in the second issue, quoted a speech by Adolphe Thiers that he saw as an "allusion... to the possible resurrection of the Commune," suggesting that the event still preoccupied him.[3]

Austin is largely unread today, and the controversy that surrounded his transparently political appointment as poet laureate following a four-year hiatus after Tennyson's death, on the say-so of the Conservative prime minister Lord Salisbury, has not aided his posthumous reputation.[4] For Herbert Tucker, Austin's 1876 revised and extended version of *The Human Tragedy* is characterized by "repellent stoicism."[5] It is primarily of interest here insofar as it reveals the distinctive and telling choice of generic terrain with which Austin chose to register the impact of the Commune. By contrast, Morris, another poet who had been briefly considered for the laureateship (to his considerable bemusement), adapts and consciously localizes an epic, or heroic, register in *The Pilgrims of Hope* (1885–1886) in order to celebrate the Communards' struggle from a standpoint of political commitment and solidarity—seeking to find a language with which to sustain, rather than contain and disavow, the possibility of revolutionary activism. Morris had explored the epic tradition at much greater length in his poetry of the 1860s and 1870s, and the heroic character of *Pilgrims* also animates a microculture of socialist verse that appeared across a variety of political periodicals during the 1880s, as is discussed in the last section of this chapter. Reading Morris's and Austin's poetic responses to the Commune together reveals some surprising affinities but also establishes a clear line of demarcation in their starkly contrasting uses of tragedy as both a genre and a sociopolitical orientation.

"I to Neither Camp Belong": Austin's *The Human Tragedy*

Austin prefaced the 1889 edition of *The Human Tragedy* with a lengthy essay titled "On the Position and Prospects of Poetry," in which he sets out a homespun theory of tragedy that he claims to be "universally and enduringly true."[6] The historical scope of the poem's four acts spans from 1857 to 1871, and writing about himself ("the poet") in the third person, Austin comments that "the sight of the smoking ruins of the chief buildings in the French capital fired by the Communists is indelibly impressed on his remembrance," adding that he "cannot but think these mighty events may be celebrated in verse as the accompaniment or chorus of a tragedy of more individual interest" (xl). For Austin, then, the "appalling and memorable event" of the Commune was not in and of itself tragic but instead provides a suitably world-historical backdrop for the interwoven romantic travails of the poem's two bourgeois protagonists, Godfrid and Gilbert (xxxvii). Austin's claim to *celebrate* the "mighty events" of the Commune invokes the negative affirmation of tragic catharsis, which goes together with a streak of deeply conservative pessimism, personified in the poem by Godfrid. Austin articulates the basic terms of this pessimism (which he prefers to think of as an Epicurean stoicism) in his introduction, where he writes: "A tragedy Life is, and a tragedy it must ever remain. But it is a noble tragedy, ennobled by action, struggle, conflict . . . and ever and anon illuminated by joy, exultation, and happy pathos" (xli–xlii). Austin's insertion of the Commune into a framework of tragic "exultation" should not be confused with an attempt to valorize its political aims, not least because his tragic worldview proclaims in advance that the human condition is a matter of transhistorical permanence and is therefore immutable. In this respect, *The Human Tragedy* starkly contrasts with the more political mode of celebration that Morris adopts in his political writings about the Commune and in *The Pilgrims of Hope* (as will be seen), in which Morris finds recourse to an epic register of encomium with which to celebrate the Communards' defeat.

Austin's "philosophic theory," from which *The Human Tragedy* takes its title, is that tragedy constitutes a transhistorical invariant of the human condition and that "Life, looked at largely . . . is tragic . . . because the tragedy is due, not to man's vices, but to his virtues" (xxxviii). Austin enumerates these virtues as "Sexual Love, Religious Sentiment, Patriotism, and Humanity," which form "the four principal agents, or protagonists," of the poem's "solemn drama," such that the poem's human characters simply personify these abstract virtues across the poem's four acts (formerly cantos) that unfold in rather stilted stanzas of ottava rima (xxxviii–xxxix). In act 4, Humanity joins the three other virtues, which have cumulatively entered the stage in each of the previous acts, while Godfrid and Gilbert transfer from a recently liberated Rome to war-torn Paris, along with their respective partners, Miriam and Olympia. Godfrid and Olympia's rather more intimately human tragedy revolves around the fact that their love can never ripen to fruition as a consequence of Olympia's devout religious sensibilities—she is a nun. Gilbert and Miriam, meanwhile, join the Communards, and in doing so, they embody what Austin characterizes in the introduction as "the Worship of Humanity," which is "a creed much in favour in our day" but which "has brought with it a war of classes bitterer even than that of nations, and has already exacted its tribute of anguish, in the merciless struggles of the Paris Commune" (xxxix). In act 3, Godfrid joins Gilbert and Miriam in shared enthusiasm for the patriotic cause of Italian unification, and they fight together under Garibaldi's leadership at the Battle of Mentana in 1867; but in act 4, his "solitary conscience" (270) reaches a plateau of anagnorisis, and he is moved to set out the philosophical basis of his (and, by extension, Austin's) tragic worldview in response to a naïve question from Olympia about the causes of the "dread carnage" in Paris (269).

Godfrid considers how best to "make her understand the woes / Of either camp, and why the twain have fought" (269), and resolves on an explanation that recognizes the tragic incommensurability of competing goods that clash at the level of "conscience against conscience" (272). Godfrid thus exhorts Olympia:

> See then, my child, the Tragedy, and see
> What feeds it. Love, Religion, Country, all
> That deepest, dearest, most enduring be,
> That make us noble, and that hold us thrall. (272)

Godfrid here surveys the exploits of the poem's first three acts, which deal with Love, Religion, and Country in turn, before explaining that "once again this Tragedy ... hath, meseems, / In Paris struck the lurid light of war" (272). His decision to frame the Commune as part of this tragic schema precludes in advance any possibility of partisan commitment on his part, though it jars oddly against his earlier willingness to commit to the cause of Italian independence, which he never explicitly renounces. Nevertheless, he does repudiate the Commune, not in political or ideological terms but owing to a world-weary indifference born of his newfound tragic outlook:

> Another dream, another watchword 'tis,
> This strident Commune shrills upon the wind,
> Which to it Love, Religion, Country, is—
> Level Equality for all Mankind.
> Hence once again the man-made bullets whiz
> 'Gainst man man-made. (272)

It is not hard to recognize in this view, despite its clunky syntax, the seeds of a deeply conservative position that a priori identifies *any* attempt to achieve political or social equality as an illusory "dream" that will inevitably lead to violent disorder. Godfrid's exclamation also suggests a relinquishment on his part of his earlier faith in a liberal progressivist teleology, which he espouses in act 3 against the backdrop of the Italian campaign, where he proclaims: "I still must hope, the lingering dawn despite, / That slow we move, through liberty, to light" (218). Upon the advent of the Commune, however, Godfrid appears to abandon this forlornly Whiggish teleology, without any explicit reckoning, as he comes to see history instead as an arena of waste and suffering that can only be met with an attitude of stoic withdrawal and skeptical spectatorship.

The pseudophilosophical scaffolding that Austin retrospectively constructs around *The Human Tragedy* echoes Nietzsche's view that the historical optimism of the Enlightenment should be equated with the "death of tragedy."[7] Godfrid's abandonment of a Whiggish view of progress might thus be said to facilitate his adoption of the tragic worldview that he takes up most fully in act 4. Enlightenment rationality poses a threat to the tragic aesthetic, for Nietzsche, precisely because of its nonaesthetic commitment to transparent discourse and philosophical understanding. It first enters classical drama in the plays of Euripides, but Nietzsche also identifies a latter-day version of the Socratic optimism that he disclaims in *The Birth of Tragedy* (1871) with the world-making aspirations of revolutionary struggle, which he conceives as a manifestation of slave morality. As Richard J. White explains, Nietzsche identifies "Socratic optimism" with the "optimistic ideals of 'Socratic Christianity'—equal rights for all, the dignity of labour, and so on."[8] Austin allows Godfrid's friend and former rival in love, Gilbert, to act as a rather unconvincing spokesperson for this revolutionary and optimistic orientation. When Gilbert and Miriam travel to France during 1871, as republican followers of Garibaldi, Gilbert describes the Commune, in a letter to Godfrid, as the arrival of a moment "When Freedom, born in panoply of power, / With godlike brain shall renovate the earth, / And Light and Right, and all fair things, shall flower!" (255). He implores Godfrid to "shed the tatters worn traditions wind / Around the barrenness of [his] shivering mind" and "no more live dead," in order that he might see "Future's dawning daylight" and share in Gilbert's "Faith in Mankind" (255–256). Insofar as the poem dramatizes the tragic "jar / Of conscience against conscience" (272), Godfrid's conclusive rejection of Gilbert's partisanship stakes out the terms of the poem's conservatism, with an echo of Nietzsche and Wagner's *Ring Cycle*, as Godfrid questions: "Who shall build new faith / 'Mid ruins such as these! The Gods have died, / The beautiful grand Gods, and but their wraith / Haunts the forsaken spot they sanctified" (257). Such are the strictures of Godfrid's fate—as defined for him by Austin— that he ultimately joins the ranks of the departed, thereby lending his name a rather weightier significance than the poem merits. In a gesture of noble selfsacrifice, he lends his Red Cross armband to Gilbert and Miriam during the bloody street fighting of the Commune's last days in order to assist their escape from the soldiers of Versailles, and as a consequence, he and Olympia are later shot in the cross fire, her nun's habit having failed to provide the protection that he thought it would: "He pierced by ball that fought for faith of old, / She by their shaft who 'gainst all faith rebel" (312). The poem's tragic climax, then, focuses not so much on the defeat of the Commune but on the private tragedy of repressed love and missed opportunity that finds its only consummation in this moment of shared death. Austin, it can be added, disavows the properly tragic character of the Commune's defeat by reasserting a framework of individual, rather than collective, suffering.

By contrast, one of the most memorable critical endeavors to think tragedy and revolution together is to be found in Raymond Williams's *Modern Tragedy* (1966), in which Williams reflects on the way in which revolution "is born in pity and terror: in the perception of a radical disorder," before going on to note that "it is equally tragic in its action, in that it is not against gods or inanimate things that its impulse struggles, but against other men."[9] Tragedy, then, is both an originary cause and the most likely modality of revolution, but this does not lead Williams to a recalcitrant embrace of reaction or a repudiation of revolution *tout court*; on the contrary, he argues that "to see revolution in this tragic perspective is the only way to maintain it."[10] With particular reference to the Commune, Henri Lefebvre offers a related observation; in likening the Commune to a revolutionary fete, he comments that "un grand groupe sociale . . . se reconnait dans et par une fête, dont le côté 'chahut' n'est que l'ombre. La tragédie antique fut une fête. Autour de ces grands jeux ou la Grèce se trouvait et se reconnaissait, il y a avait la tragédie, la résurrection des héros morts."[11] For Lefebvre, the group that recognized itself during the revolutionary fete of the Commune was, quite simply, the people of Paris. If the Commune was a tragedy, it was *their* tragedy. It is clear, then, that Lefebvre is willing to think about the Commune under the sign of the tragic, and he goes on to explain that this is why he used an epigraph from Sophocles's *Women of Trachis* for his book *La Proclamation de la Commune, 26 Mars 1871* (1965). Yet it is equally clear that both Lefebvre, whose study of the Commune adopts an avowedly affirmative and solidaristic register, and Williams, who was, in a different way, intellectually committed to the long revolution for social and economic democracy, rely on a markedly dissimilar conception of tragedy than that which is to be encountered in Austin's *The Human Tragedy*.

In Austin's poem, Godfrid's refusal to take sides is a consequence of the sublime indifference induced by his acceptance of a tragic fatalism. As Godfrid informs a group of Communards: "I to neither camp belong. / For, brothers mine, I fear you miss your way, / Aiming at too much right through too much wrong" (282). Godfrid again stops short of an outright repudiation of the Commune, temporizing instead by identifying it with both "right" and "wrong" simultaneously, while framing the Communards' revolutionary struggle in terms of tragic hamartia. Yet Godfrid's ostensibly open-minded, even pluralistic, attempt to maintain an air of studied neutrality is offset by the narrator's rather more partial assessment of events, since the disembodied narrative voice of the poem, with its pretensions to epic grandeur, likens the Communards to "proletarian hordes" who "had broken through the flimsy line / Of strained Civilisation, and now strode, / Grim apparitions,—with its dainties fine / And gauds abandoned making their abode, / And littering all the spot, like bristly swine" (278). The Communards reappear in a more familiar guise, here, as barbarians at the gates of high culture. Their struggle may be ennobled by the support of honest enthusiasts like Gilbert, who "looked a nobler and completer type / Of those one saw around" and "who, since that he / *Was* nobler, could more keenly feel the stripe / Of contumelious destiny"; but ultimately, however, the narrator declares that the Commune can only deliver the "gloomy glee / Of vain resistance, famine, failure, hate / Fevered to fiery point prescribed by Fate" (291). If Godfrid sometimes assumes the air of a conscience-stricken liberal, then Austin's narrator consistently reassures his readers that they are, in fact, in the presence of a guide whose political predilections are rather more Burkean in dismissing the chaos wrought by the swinish multitude.

Williams's negotiation of the relationship between revolution and tragedy, by contrast, is, as Terry Eagleton suggests, bound up with a two-pronged argument that tragedy is both "a profoundly ordinary affair" and, in riposte to conservative pessimists like Austin, "that it has assumed in our time the shape of an epic struggle which can in principle be resolved."[12] The world-historical coordinates of that "epic struggle" are defined by the depredations of the capitalist mode of production and the resulting conflict between antagonistic social classes, and even as revolutions might be said to occur in response to these properly tragic conditions of modernity, they also proffer the possibility of a resolution that Austin's conservative orientation assumes to be impossible. For Austin, the fact of the Commune's defeat led him retroactively to assume the necessity of its defeat. Eagleton, meanwhile, explains that the tragic dimension of modernity consists in the fact that "we can neither discard the values of justice and democracy, nor brush aside their appalling historical cost in the name of some triumphalist teleology."[13] For conservatives and liberals, this tragic contradiction barely registers because "the former ... may be less than zealous about such questions as social justice" in the first place, while "the latter [appear] to believe that it can be realized without major upheaval."[14] In this respect, Morris's valorization of the Commune in *The Pilgrims of Hope* offers an instructive contrast to Austin's tragic fatalism insofar as Morris seeks to mobilize a comparably epic register but in a way that more successfully recognizes and elucidates the nature of the contradiction identified by Eagleton and Williams.

Heroic Encomium in Morris's *The Pilgrims of Hope*

Like Austin, Morris was prepared to view the Commune through the prism of tragedy. He described it as "the greatest tragedy of modern times" in his 1887 *Commonweal* article "Why We Celebrate the Commune of Paris" and added that "this great tragedy has definitely and irrevocably elevated the cause of Socialism to all those who are prepared to look on the cause seriously, and refuse to admit the possibility of ultimate defeat."[15] He also linked this understanding of the Commune's tragic character to a celebration of the possibility of heroic martyrdom and sacrifice:

> I say solemnly and deliberately that if it happens to those of us now living to take part in such another tragedy it will be rather well for them than ill for them. Truly it is harder to live for a cause than to die for it, and it injures a

man's dignity and self-respect to be always making noisy professions of devotion to a cause before the field is stricken.... But with the chance of bodily sacrifice close a-head there come also times of trial which either raise a man to the due tragic pitch or cast him aside as a useless and empty vapourer.[16]

Morris invokes a revolutionary understanding of virtue ethics in relation to the Commune, celebrating the virtues of courage and fortitude, at the same time as he implicitly offers a model of *collective*, rather than individual, heroism. The Commune, as he put it in his 1885 lecture "The Hopes of Civilization," was a "heroic attempt [that] will give hope and ardour in the cause as long as it is to be won," and he figures the protagonist of the struggle—"the Paris workman"—as a collective entity.[17] Morris also carries over what Herbert Tucker characterizes as a "regimen of transpersonal narrative *Bildung*" into *The Pilgrims of Hope*, a poem in which Morris's proletarian protagonist, Richard, conceives of himself as no more or less than "an atom of the strife."[18] Yet even as Morris constructs the poem's Communard martyrology in heroic terms, he also steers clear of what Williams would regard as utopianism, in the pejorative sense, or revolutionary romanticism, which consists in the "suppression or dilution of [the] quite inevitable fact" of an equation between revolution and tragedy.[19]

Such recognition, however, does not lead Morris to abandon revolutionary politics; on the contrary, the class position of Morris's protagonist, who is a joiner by trade, offers a riposte to Austin's elitist and traditionalist conception of tragedy at the same time as *The Pilgrims of Hope* supplies an implicit answer to Austin's criticism of Morris's poetry of the 1860s and 1870s. In Austin's study *The Poetry of the Period* (1870), a collection of articles reprinted from *Temple Bar*, he argued that Morris's early poetry "surrendered ... wholly to the retrospective tendency of [the] time," adding that "he ignores the present, and his eyelids close with a quiet sadness if you bid him explore the future."[20] The Commune of 1871 would, in the fullness of time, supply Morris with the necessary impetus to reckon with the "true tale" of the past, present, and future, though one might add that Austin's earlier judgment about *The Earthly Paradise*, which reads like a comment on the poem's prefatory "Apology," overlooks the extent to which the "retrospective" tendency of Morris's poetic during this period often involved both radical adaptation of its source material and elements of sociopolitical critique.[21] Indeed, the closing couplet of *The Pilgrims of Hope* takes up a newly politicized version of the flight to the past, together with a hopeful vision of the future, but it anchors itself firmly in the present with Richard's forceful declaration: "I cling to the love of the past and the love of the day to be, / And the present, it is but the building of the man to be strong in me."[22] Having borne witness to the Commune's defeat, Richard devotes himself to a life of continuing political commitment: he remembers the "bygone sorrow" but refuses to give in to it; he does not "hide away from the strife" of coming struggles because of the memory of pain and loss.[23] On the contrary, he embraces it.

In Morris's utopian romance *News from Nowhere* (1890), he organized the representation of an imagined period of revolutionary struggle around a similar recognition of the simultaneously heroic and tragic character of revolution. As Old Hammond informs the nineteenth-century utopian visitor, the "second birth" of the world could hardly take place "without a tragedy."[24] At the same time, however, he explains what the onset of the revolution meant: "The sloth, the hopelessness, and if I may say so, the cowardice of the last century, had given place to the eager, restless heroism of a declared revolutionary period."[25] Without doubt, Morris saw in the Commune a precedent for the "eager, restless heroism" of the revolutionary struggle that brings Nowhere into being, much as he had earlier explored the heroic character of the Commune in *The Pilgrims of Hope*, in which an epic register brushes up against the "plain diction of the realist mode."[26] This aspect of the poem's stylistic duality has long been recognized by its commentators. For example, Morris's erstwhile comrade John Bruce Glasier characterized the poem as a "proletarian epic" that was, at the same time, the "most objective or realistic" of all Morris's poems.[27] Herbert Tucker writes in similar terms, describing the poem as a "hip-pocket epic on the march towards utopia."[28] Florence Boos, meanwhile, comments that the poem offers an "unusual mixture of wry humour and impassioned advocacy, pastoral romance and urban realism."[29] For Anne Janowitz, *The Pilgrims of Hope* manifests an "interventionist poetic" that situates it within a communitarian tradition of romantic poetry that "no longer presents itself as a complaint against industrialism or a nostalgia for the past, but as a strategy for a material, not a transcendent future."[30] By Morris's own estimation, *The Pilgrims of Hope* was "the best short poem" he had written.[31]

The poem recounts the early life and politicization of its two protagonists (Richard and his unnamed wife), Richard's travails at work as a consequence of his socialist activism, and the entrance into their lives of a "new friend" in book 9, the middle-class socialist convert Arthur, with whom Richard's wife falls in love. As this painful fact comes to light, the three comrades uneasily agree to travel together to "unseen Paris, and the streets made ready for war," in order to participate in the Commune's "day of the deeds and the day of deliverance."[32] In book 10, "Ready to Depart," Richard discovers the love that exists between Arthur and his wife in a manner that recalls the first two acts of Austin's *The Human Tragedy*, which revolve around the complex love triangle encompassing Godfrid, Gilbert, and Olive. When Gilbert eventually discovers Godfrid's love for his wife Olive, "He stood transfixed, reading the pictured tale, / And then completing it by his own woe: / Incarnate revelation, come at last, / Explaining each fresh puzzle of the past" (134). This revelation of "love's stern hopelessness"

(135) constitutes the would-be tragic action of the poem's first two acts, and Olive's subsequent death, attributed rather hastily to "weariness of heart" (137), precipitates a brotherly bond between the two male principals, who proceed to join together in the "godlike Cause" of the struggle for Italian independence (138). By the time Godfrid and Gilbert transfer to Paris in 1871, their affections have settled respectively on Olympia (a nun) and Miriam (a militant republican). In *The Pilgrims of Hope*, Morris compresses the emotional tribulations of Austin's first two acts into the final three books of his poem and transposes the love triangle from England to the scene of the Parisian revolution. Richard's acceptance of the transfer of his wife's affections also enables Morris to present a nuanced socialist-feminist argument in *The Pilgrims of Hope*; as Florence and William Boos write, Morris identifies "an emotional test which the new socialist ethic will present to [heterosexual] *men*," thereby lending an emotional complexity to his three protagonists' involvement in the Commune that is almost entirely lacking in *The Human Tragedy*, despite Austin's best efforts.[33]

The realist patina that animates *The Pilgrims of Hope* is detectable in the focus on Richard's work as a socialist agitator, preaching "in street-corners . . . / To knots of men," and his weary routine of alienated labor as a joiner in and around "the purlieus of Soho"; the account of London as a "monstrous tomb" and an "easy-going hell" also dimly recalls James Thomson's *The City of Dreadful Night* (1874).[34] At the same time, however, Morris deploys an epic register that localizes and historically particularizes his prior interest in the chivalric world of Arthurian romance and the heroic landscapes of the Norse sagas. Richard's repeated focus on "deeds to be done," for example, recalls the Völsung king's invocation of "the deed that dies not" in book 1 of Morris's *Sigurd the Volsung* (1876).[35] Even more crucially in this regard, Richard's arrival in Paris during the Commune allows him to experience "the hope of the day that was due—/ . . . now, real, solid and at hand," along with the "promise of spring-tide," which, in turn, leads him to apostrophize his mother in the following terms:

> O mother, mother, I said, hadst thou known as I lay in thy lap,
> And for me thou hopedst and fearedst, on what days my life should hap,
> Hadst thou known of the death that I look for, and the deeds wherein
>   I should deal,
> How calm had been thy gladness! How sweet hadst thou smiled on my weal!
> As some woman of old hadst thou wondered, who hath brought forth a god
>   of the earth,
> And in joy that knoweth no speech she dreams of happy birth.[36]

Morris alludes here to the panoply of classical gods born of mortal women, many of whom had appeared, however briefly, in his earlier poetry. The very nonspecificity of the allusion means that it encompasses a range of possible analogues. One might think of Perseus, the son of Jove and Danaë, who features in the first of the two April tales in *The Earthly Paradise* (1868–1870), titled "The Doom of King Acrisius," and who proclaims his lineage as "the son of Danaë, / ... And those that know, call me the son of Jove"; or one might think of Hercules, the son of Jove and Alcmene, who appears in the first of the two December tales, "The Golden Apples."[37] Similarly, Morris's 1875 translation of Virgil's *Æneid* refers to the story of the birth of Romulus (book 1, ll. 272–277; book 6, ll. 777–780), the son of Ilia (Rhea Silvia) and Mars, while his 1887 translation of Homer's *Odyssey* briefly mentions Alcmene (book 11, ll. 266–268) and Antiope, "Who boasted her that one while in the arms of Zeus [Jove] she had lain, / And Amphion thence and Zethus had borne, his children twain" (book 11, ll. 261–262).[38] One might also recall that some of these figures are mythologically reputable as founders of cities and ancient civilizations. Perseus, for example, is the founder of Mycenae and the Perseid dynasty, while Amphion and Zethus "first built up and settled Thebes of the gates sevenfold" (book 11, l. 263).[39] Romulus, according to legend, was the founder of Rome. Although Richard is clearly not literally the son of a god, Morris's playful allusion in *The Pilgrims of Hope* affirms the epic register of the poem, at the same time as it bears out a modified version of Raymond Williams's observation that "successful revolution ... becomes not tragedy but epic: it is the origin of a people and its valued way of life."[40] As this comment might be taken to suggest, part of the reason that Morris strains toward an epic register in *The Pilgrims of Hope* has to do with his attempt symbolically to convert the historical tragedy of 1871 into something resembling a heroic origin story, or the creation of a new epos, for the late nineteenth-century socialist movement.

Richard, his wife, and Arthur together play a part in "the first fight of the uttermost battle whither all the nations wend"; they were "part of it all, the beginning of the end."[41] After the death of Arthur and his wife, who die as martyrs for the revolutionary cause, Richard returns to England with an aspiration to found a new way of life in a re-visioned London, together with his son, "That two men there might be hereafter to battle against the wrong."[42] As Anne Janowitz writes, the Commune "was an image that belonged entirely to the socialist movement by the 1880s and 1890s," and Morris's poetic reconstruction of it enabled him to "make palpable not only the contemporary political links between the Commune and the struggle for socialism in Britain, but also the connections between the values of the Commune and a set of values already deep in a British communitarian tradition"—a tradition that Janowitz identifies in the poetry of the Chartist movement.[43] Morris's exploration of Richard's experience during the Commune also produces what Florence Boos regards as a form of "revolutionary commitment [that] is deepened by tragic loss," which, in turn, offers a marked contrast to the form of stoic withdrawal and tragic fatalism endorsed by Austin.[44]

Morris's discovery of a heroic epos in the arena of *contemporary* history reimagines the cultural significance of tragic sacrifice in revolutionary terms, in stark contrast to Austin's cultural and political conservatism. With the deaths of Godfrid and Olympia, Austin assumes that the sacrifice that concludes *The Human Tragedy* enjoys tragic status because of the incommensurability between Godfrid's atheism and Olympia's religious commitment, which prevents the fruition of their love during the course of their lives; the tawdry pathos of the poem's ending, such as it is, really concerns a missed opportunity at the level of personal, private life, with the Commune merely serving as an appropriately world-historical backdrop. Their sacrifice facilitates the escape of Gilbert and Miriam, who are thus denied the possibility of dying for their cause. Insofar as the poem solicits a formulaically conceived moment of cathartic release, it does so by containing the Commune's radical challenge to the sanctity of bourgeois individualism within a loosely Hegelian paradigm of "conflict between incompatible goods."[45] *The Pilgrims of Hope*, by contrast, exposes that challenge to full view. While Godfrid sacrifices himself from a position of Olympian indifference to the social revolution of the Commune, Arthur and his unnamed lover do so from a position of partisan commitment, beholden to the possibility of "relinquishing a form of life which is inherently exploitative so that another, more just one may be brought to birth."[46] In this regard, Terry Eagleton's reflections on tragic sacrifice are especially pertinent: "It is not that the end of happiness must be abandoned for that of sacrifice, *eudaimonia* forsaken for ascesis. It is rather that the full achievement of the former tragically entails the latter—that the breaking and remaking of human powers may prove essential to their general flourishing."[47] In this respect, Morris astutely utilizes the ending of *The Pilgrims of Hope* to establish the basis of a form of revolutionary commitment that, in being oriented toward the virtues of courage and fortitude, thereby implicitly critiques the bloodlessly bureaucratic void of bourgeois and reformist politics.

Laying claim to epic grandeur for the Commune was, in part, a means by which Morris could assail the ubiquitous anti-Communard demonology that had been laboriously constructed by mainstream commentators (as discussed elsewhere in this book). Such a claim also elevates the Commune to a higher plane than the shallow vapidity of bourgeois society, against which the Communards and its later socialist defenders like Morris had set themselves. This helps to explain why Austin attributes to his protagonist a nagging sense of the Communards' *worthiness*: "I can but lag behind, / Sceptic, yet see withal the dupes that die / For falsest faith are somewhat more than I!" (272). Even as Godfrid decries what he perceives to be the falsity of the Communards' "faith," he is struck by the sense that they somehow possess a greater dignity than he does and are of a higher moral caliber. This is not simply the *mauvais foi* of the bourgeois subject in the face of insurgent "proletarian hordes"; instead, it signals a more threatening possibility that an unnameable collective protagonist might emerge to usurp the place of the bourgeois hero and whose defeat might register as a more properly tragic occurrence by revealing the cloistered, private sufferings of Godfrid and his ilk as relatively trifling and insignificant by comparison. Godfrid momentarily contemplates this possibility, but Austin does not explore it further. In *The Pilgrims of Hope*, by contrast, Morris seeks to discover a poetic that might enable such a collective protagonist to come to the fore. Even as the poem focuses on the "narrow circle" of the three principal characters, it also accentuates the prospect of an intergenerational inheritance of radical commitment that goes beyond any single family.[48] In book 13, "The Story's Ending," Richard reflects:

> I have heard it told since then,
> And mere lies our deeds have turned to in the mouths of happy men,
> And e'en those will be soon forgotten as the world wends on its way,
> Too busy for truth or kindness. Yet my soul is seeing the day
> When those who are now but children the new generation shall be,
> And e'en in our land of commerce and the workshop over the sea,
> Amid them shall spring up the story; yea the very breath of the air
> To the yearning hearts of the workers true tale of it all shall bear.[49]

Richard's suggestion that the workers of the future will seek a "true tale" of the Commune evokes the plethora of professedly authoritative eyewitness accounts that circulated in Britain in the wake of the Commune, many of which were explicitly hostile to the Communards.[50] In *The Pilgrims of Hope*, by contrast, Morris's poetic mediation of the Commune projects a contrastively heroic story that can be passed on, from generation to generation, among workers "in our land of commerce and the workshop over the sea." Against the "mere lies" of the Commune's opponents, Morris asserts a poetics of heroic commemoration that mobilizes an epic register, singing the "deeds of the helpers of menfolk to every age and clime," but one that is simultaneously and uncomfortably shot through with realist immediacy.[51] Morris does not thereby suppress the Commune's tragic character; rather, he puts tragedy to use in a way that holds out a promise of political fulfillment in the future.

The Poetics of Martyrdom in Fin-de-Siècle Socialist Verse

The French historian Georges Haupt has pointed to the way in which the Commune, after its suppression, lived on as an important symbol for the emergent socialist movement across Europe. Annual celebrations provided occasions in which sectarian animosities between different groupings and organizations could be temporarily put aside. In the year following the inaugural London commemoration of the Commune, Morris delivered a lecture, titled "The Hopes of Civilization" (1885), to the Hammersmith branch of the Socialist League in which he argued that the Communards' "heroic attempt" provides an example to "all Socialists" that "will give hope and ardour in the cause as long as it is to be won";

he added that "we feel as though the Paris workman had striven to bring the day-dawn for us, and had lifted the sun's rim over the horizon, never to set in utter darkness again."[52] For Morris, the suppression of the Commune acted as an impetus to commemorate its defeat and to communicate the responsibility of the living to create a meaning for the otherwise futile sacrifice of "thousands of brave and honest revolutionists at the hands of the respectable classes."[53] As Haupt comments, in an essay titled "The Commune as Symbol and Example," "The transformation in the reception and projection of the images of the 1871 insurrection interwoven with the general evolution of ideology, are in themselves a historical phenomenon which deserves careful study."[54] The kind of documents that fall within the scope of Haupt's study include "pamphlets, newspaper articles, speeches, songs, plays, and poems, as well as a considerable iconography," and he focuses on the French and German context, paying particular attention to the disputes over the Commune's legacy that took place between Marx and Bakunin and later between Lenin and Kautsky.[55]

The reception and projection of images about the Commune also preoccupied the socialist movement in Britain during the 1880s, and this was especially visible in the movement's poetry. *The Pilgrims of Hope*, in particular, played an important localized role in securing the Commune's symbolic status in Britain. During the socialist revival of the 1880s, a number of other poems dedicated to or otherwise concerned with the martyred Communards appeared in fin-de-siècle socialist periodicals, including the monthly journal *To-Day: Monthly Magazine of Scientific Socialism*, edited by Ernest Belfort Bax, and the Socialist League's journal, *Commonweal*, edited by Morris between 1885 and 1890. According to Elizabeth Miller, "the political value of the poetry" that appeared in such fin-de-siècle socialist periodicals can be identified not with "formal innovation" but rather in its "capacity to draw together readers of the radical press into an alternative culture made familiar by appeals to the past and brought to life by oral poetic forms."[56] The Commune provided one of the predominant points of reference for such politicized "appeals to the past."

The regular poetry column is one of the most immediately noticeable features of the *Commonweal*, the official organ of the Socialist League. Jostling against the closely printed propagandistic articles, branch reports, and notes on the news of the day, the numerous poems and marching songs stood out, first and foremost, in visual terms, simply by virtue of being written in verse. Catherine Robson has referred to this visual identity of poetry in the periodical press as being bound up with the "aura of unmarked space that would alert [the Victorian newspaper-reader's] attention to the presence of a poem on a densely printed page."[57] In this respect, *Commonweal* continued a tradition of radical periodical print culture that can be traced back to the Chartist newspapers of the 1830s and 1840s (most notably the *Northern Star*), in which poetry featured as a prominent part of the cultural life of a wider political movement. During the course of Morris's tenure as editor, a wide range of poets appeared within the pages of *Commonweal*, and as Ingrid Hanson points out, many of them looked to "a history of violent revolution on the Continent which is both unifying and, crucially, unfinished."[58] Between 1885 and 1887, over thirty poems by Ferdinand Freiligarth, Heinrich Heine, Ludwig Pfau, Georg Herwegh, and Karl Beck appeared in translations by James Leigh Joynes, the ex-Eton master and member of the Socialist League. Many of these poems reflect on the revolutionary events of 1848. The journal also published Laura Lafargue's English translations of poems by the Communard militants Eugène Pottier and Louise Michel.[59] Other frequent contributors to the poetry column included the journalists Fred Henderson and Reginald A. Beckett, the anarchist David Nicoll, and the trade union organizer Tom Maguire, as well as Morris himself, whose *Pilgrims of Hope* offered a poetic centerpiece in the socialist movement's literary output during the mid-1880s.

The poetics of martyrdom that found expression in poems about the Commune was not exclusively identified with Morris. Beyond the explicitly socialist periodical press, Walter Crane published a short poem, "In Memory of the Commune of Paris: Born March 18, 1871, Died in June the Same Year," in *Black and White* on 4 April 1891, accompanied by a full-page illustration with the same title (see figure 6.1). Crane's title sentimentally personifies the Commune, in the manner of an epitaph that might appear on the gravestone of an infant that died young, but the first line of the poem immediately shifts the reader's attention to the "winged shape with waving torch aflame, / Wild with the winds of March and streaming hair," depicted in the accompanying illustration, which offers a more militant allegorical representation of the Commune as an angel rising above "the storm-clouds" to "declare / Her message."[60] The first stanza poses a rhetorical question, querying the identity of the unknown "winged shape," and the second stanza takes up and answers the question as follows: "A star, through drifting smoke of praise and blame, / The toilers' beacon, still to reappear / With spring-tide hopes, new quickening year by year, / Since bright in Freedom's dawn the COMMUNE came."[61] Several years after the publication of Morris's *Pilgrims of Hope*, Crane asserts a comparable poetic of cyclical regeneration, organized around the renewal of "spring-tide hopes" and the turning of the year that informed the socialist movement's radical calendar of commemoration.[62] Crane's third stanza, meanwhile, turns again to remind readers that the poem's allegorical figure met with a violent end: "Her blood lies still upon the hands that slew," even as she proffers a mnemonic token of "what men dared and suffered, and their fate / Who ruled a city once FOR ALL AND EACH."[63] Crane's winged angel of the Commune, an anti-*pétroleuse* who defiantly holds aloft a flaming torch and wears a red bonnet with an artisan's hammer affixed to her waistband, belongs to a long line of allegorical female figures who "personified the glory of the revolutionary struggle."[64] Yet Walter Benjamin's remarks about Paul Klee's *Angelus Novus* (1920) are also uncannily apt in this context, in that Crane's angel of the

Figure 6.1. Walter Crane, "In Memory of the Commune of Paris: Born 18 March 1871, Died in June the Same Year," *Black and White*, 4 April 1891, 285. Image in Public Domain.

Commune, like Benjamin's angel of history, would also "like to stay, awaken the dead, and make whole what has been smashed."[65]

Crane's poem and illustration celebrating the Commune's memory sit uncomfortably in the pages of the mainstream periodical *Black and White*. Such poems were more commonly to be found in the socialist press. One might, for example, turn to a short poem by Pakenham Thomas Beatty, the Anglo-Irish poet and friend of George Bernard Shaw, which appeared in *To-Day* in May 1886.[66] Beatty's twenty-line poem in blank verse, "The Last Barricade of the Commune," recounts the narrative of a child being shot on an abandoned barricade. Beatty reworks and drastically desentimentalizes the anecdote of the boy with a pocket watch that supplied Victor Hugo with material for one of the poems that appears in the June section of *L'Année Terrible* (1872).[67] The opening lines of Beatty's poem follow a group of Versaillais soldiers in the "plying of their bloody trade." Beatty's Communard speaker follows the soldiers' activities up until the point where they

> swore
> Sullenly that no more blood was to spill.
> Then marched; but when they reached the barricade
> We had abandoned last, a little head
> Lifted its golden curls, and a child said:
> "Vive la Commune"—and then stood still and smiled,
> Folding his little arms across his breast—
> Until one beast, more beast-like than the rest,
> Suddenly raised his gun and shot the child.[68]

In describing the barricade of the title as that which "We had abandoned last," Beatty's speaker identifies with the anonymous collective of murdered Communards, thus framing the short narrative that follows within clearly defined parameters of sympathy for the defeated and repulsion at the cruelty of their suppressors. Indeed, the telltale "we" is the only pronoun in the poem that indicates any sense of the speaker's perspective or position in relation to the events narrated, thereby suggesting that the speaker, singly or with others, occupies an impossible position of witness, even after all the barricades have been abandoned and their other defenders apparently shot. In recounting the child's gesture of innocent defiance and the abrupt brutality of the response it elicits, Beatty fights shy of tear-jerking sentimentality, provoking moral indignation instead, the function of which is to consolidate a solidaristic kind of commemoration among the readership of the socialist journal *To-Day*.

Four months after the appearance of Beatty's poem in *To-Day*, Morris published a poem in *Commonweal* in remembrance of the Commune by the thirty-four-year-old American poet, Charles Edwin Markham. Markham would later become known as the poet laureate of Oregon between 1923 and 1931. He gained popular notoriety with his 1898 ekphrastic poem "The Man with the Hoe," which was inspired by Jean-François Millet's 1862 painting of that name and which called attention to the plight of agricultural laborers. Markham's poem for *Commonweal*, titled "The Song of the Workers (Remembering the Martyrs of the Commune)," deploys a performative language of remembrance that relies on motifs of romance familiar from Morris's socialist chants and his wider oeuvre. Markham's speaker asserts:

> We'll not forget, O comrades, how ye met the ravening hordes—
> How shone out over all the earth the splendour of your swords;
> How they lit up all the Future, all the golden years to be,
> When the burden shall be lifted and the worker shall be free.
>
> We'll remember how ye rallied, faced the ancient Wrong in wrath,
> How your swords that lie in ruins cut the centuries a path.
> We'll not forget your forms that loomed upon the barricades,
> Nor how ye looked from silent eyes when laid asleep with spades.[69]

Markham uses the slightly clunky heptameter couplets that Morris had deployed in his 1875 translation of Virgil's *Æneid*, titled *The Æneids of Virgil Done into English Verse*. Markham's images also call to mind the wider visual, and particularly photographic, culture surrounding the Commune. His reference to "silent eyes . . . laid asleep with spades" evokes the series of "'morgue' photographs," which, as Jeannene Przyblyski suggests, "provide a vision of grim finality to the Commune's embrace of a spurious, photographic aestheticism" in numerous images of barricades.[70] For Markham, although the Communards' figurative swords may "lie in ruins," to be replaced by the spades of their gravediggers, the heroic defeat was not in vain. On the contrary, the speaker asserts that the "splendour of [their] swords / . . . lit up all the Future, all the golden years to be," giving confidence to the *Commonweal* readership that the historical agency of the proletariat was not only assured but actively on the wing. Following Morris's approach in *The Pilgrims of Hope*, Markham articulates the kind of active, future-oriented memorialization characteristic of the nineteenth-century socialist movement, even as the imagined weaponry (swords rather than rifles) suggests a curiously outmoded kind of combat.

On 16 March 1889, Reginald A. Beckett's poem "The Eighteenth of March" appeared in *Commonweal*. Beckett's title alludes to the date on which the people of Montmartre prevented government troops from confiscating National Guard cannons, shooting generals Lecomte and Thomas in the process. The official proclamation of the Commune came later on 28 March, but 18 March passed over into legend as the originary moment of the insurrection. Beckett, whose poems appeared regularly in *Commonweal*, imagines a dialogue between a "rich man" and a "workman," each of whom couches his attitude toward the

Commune—respectively hostile and sympathetic—in terms of a struggle for his children's well-being. The "workman," moreover, appears with "sword in hand, his life at stake," echoing Markham's deployment of a Morrisian rhetoric of heroic valor.[71] Beckett's speaker rallies readers with a call to remembrance in the face of indifference or forgetfulness:

> Brothers, they fought our battle; yet, O shame!
>   We know them not, or spurn their dust with scorn;
> How then shall we make good that glorious claim
>   For which they longed amid their lives forlorn?
> Yet when we share their ardour and their aim
>   The life they died to bear us will be born.[72]

Beckett and Markham both faced the problem of finding a language in which the Communards' "ardour" might be reactivated, but they did so in the absence of a political conjuncture that might allow for such a process to take place. It is unclear in Beckett's poem, for example, whether the projected moment of shared "ardour" will arrive as a result of voluntaristic assertion of will on the part of the reader or whether a more far-reaching and revolutionary shift in the balance of social and class forces would first be necessary. Much like Beatty's position of impossible witness, Beckett's poem cannot, in and of itself, embody or manifest that shared "ardour" and common "aim" without asserting a premature claim to the birth of the "life they died to bear us."

Another *Commonweal* poet, and member of the Socialist League, also reflected on the Commune in verse, though more obliquely than the poets just discussed. Fred Henderson published his first volume of poetry at the tender age of sixteen, and he published a more substantial volume, *Echoes of the Coming Day: Socialist Songs and Rhymes*, in 1887. In his third and final volume, *By the Sea, and Other Poems* (1892), Henderson included the poem "A Song for To-Day," which begins as follows:

> Who will sing us the song of to-day?
>   The lance is broken and knights are dead:
>   Their sun went down over France blood-red,
> And the last of them all was long since clay;
>   Sung and resung, let them rest at last
>   With fame full writ in their own dead past:
> Come—who will sing us the song of to-day?[73]

Henderson does not explicitly identify "blood-red" France with the brutal suppression of the Commune by the Versaillais during the Bloody Week of May 1871, but this opening stanza nevertheless gestures toward a certain kind of discursive exhaustion with the poetics of martyrdom and commemoration familiar from Morris's *Pilgrims of Hope* and the poems discussed earlier. In the final section of Morris's poem, which appeared in *Commonweal* in July 1886, Richard, after telling the tale of the Commune's defeat at the hands of Adolphe Thiers's "brutal war-machine," finds solace in the fact that "Year after year shall men meet with the red flag over head, / And shall call on the help of the vanquished and the kindness of the dead."[74] Richard also initially thinks of his friend Arthur as "a perfect knight of old time as the poets would have them to be."[75] Morris deployed a similar rhetoric of chivalric valor in some of the other poems he contributed to socialist periodicals.[76] Henderson's speaker, by contrast, implies that the singing and resinging of the deeds of those whom Morris elsewhere referred to as the "valiant dead" (in "All for the Cause") might somehow block, or forestall, the emergence of a genuinely contemporary and present-oriented radical poetics.[77] The anxiety to which Henderson gives voice has been articulated more recently, in a different context, by Alain Badiou, who comments in discussion of the Commune on the way in which a certain form of "*commemoration* also happens to proscribe its *reactivation*."[78]

Henderson had written to Morris in 1885, enclosing some of his youthful verse, only to receive a rather indifferent response. Morris wrote to Henderson: "You feel strongly and poetically, you think you have expressed your feelings in your verses, but you have not done so, because you have not compelled others (sympathetic people of course), to feel with you," before adding: "Pray don't be down-cast because you have tried to write poetry and failed."[79] Later during the 1880s, Henderson stayed with Morris at Kelmscott House while he worked as a journalist at the *Star*, suggesting that a measure of fellow feeling developed between the two men.[80] Even so, Henderson's "A Song for To-Day" appears implicitly to critique the assumptions at work in the socialist movement's poetry of commemoration. Henderson's speaker proceeds with an attempt to answer the rhetorical question posed in the first stanza of the poem by offering a series of injunctions to would-be poets concerning the appropriate subject matter for the songs of today projected in the title: "Tell of keen war with the devil's throngs," "Tell of the cause of the poor who sink," "Tell of the women and men grown gray / With lonely labour and scant delight," "Tell of the children that swarm and die / In loathsome dens where Despair is king," and so on.[81] The seemingly naturalistic impulse to focus on the depredations of contemporary capitalism jars against the vocabulary of Morrisian romance, introduced at the outset with the reference to the heroic deeds of dead knights, whose bodies lie moldering in the grave and which Henderson would rather consign to the realm of the "dead past." This tension, as discussed earlier, also animated Morris's own poetic engagement with the Commune in *The Pilgrims of Hope*, in which the poem's realist impulses brush up against an epic register.

Aside from being a potential riposte to Morris, what else might Henderson's implied exhaustion with the socialist movement's poetics of martyrdom express? In 1874, Friedrich Engels responded to Blanquist commemorations of the

Communards with a rebuke: "what a want of criticism to declare the Commune to be sacred and infallible."[82] According to Georges Haupt, Engels's comments can partly be put down to his frustration that "the insistence on the idealised reality ... of the Commune was likely to push the movement back towards the outlooks of the Romantic socialism" of the earlier nineteenth century.[83] The work of commemoration, Haupt suggests, even when it is undertaken in a spirit of militancy and solidarity, can nonetheless forestall a more critical discussion of a movement's limitations and blind spots. In a *Commonweal* review of Eleanor Marx's translation of Lissagaray's *History of the Paris Commune of 1871* (1886), Ernest Belfort Bax commented in a similar vein: "We wish that every true Socialist at heart whose head is led astray by disintegrative tendencies would read, mark, learn and inwardly digest the important lessons of this volume. The cause was wrecked in 1871, in great part at least, ... because of well-meaning conceited, faddy, cantankerous persons, who wasted time in long-winded speeches about personal matters, etc., and who would neither do any work themselves nor let any one else do it."[84] Far from consolidating a poetics of martyrdom, Bax's prosaic candor foregrounds a critique of the Commune's political failure, in order to guide the strategic direction of "Socialist organisations ... in existence to-day."[85] Bax's later text, *A Short History of the Paris Commune* (1895), included a final chapter titled "The Lessons of the Commune," in which he argued that the Commune demonstrated "the supreme necessity of an organisation comprising a solid body of class-conscious proletarians and other Socialists."[86] Bax also reprinted Marx's *The Civil War in France* (1871) as an appendix, indicating his broad agreement with Marx's criticisms of the Commune, which, as Roland Boer notes, produced a "distinct ambivalence, if not tension, in [Marx's] thoughts on the nature of the state after a communist revolution."[87] By seeking to draw "lessons" from the Commune's defeat, Bax looked to the Commune as an imperfect example, in Haupt's terms, rather than a symbol in need of retroactive deliverance.

Writing in a similarly dyspeptic and critical mode, the right-leaning Fabian George Bernard Shaw commented with reference to "an anniversary celebration" of the Commune:

> I was struck by the fact that no speaker could find a eulogy for the Federals which would not have been equally appropriate to the peasants of La Vendée who fought for their tyrants against the French revolutionists. ... Nor could the celebrators find any other adjectives for their favourite leaders of the Commune than those which had recently been liberally applied by all the journals to an African explorer whose achievements were just then held in the liveliest abhorrence by the whole meeting. The statements that the slain members of the Commune were heroes who died for a noble ideal would have left a stranger quite as much in the dark about them as the counter statements, once common enough in our newspapers, that they were incendiaries and assassins.[88]

Shaw's book *The Quintessence of Ibsenism* (1891), in which these remarks appear, had its origin as a contribution to a series of talks hosted by the gradualist Fabian Society, during the spring of 1890, "put under the general heading 'Socialism in Contemporary Literature.'"[89] The context for Shaw's iconoclastic assault on the socialist movement's martyrology, which he condemned as insufficiently specific in its content, was bound up with his attempt to position himself as a pragmatic gradualist, in opposition to the revolutionary politics of the Socialist League and the Social Democratic Federation. Shaw directed his criticism against the perceived inadequacy of the rhetoric of commemoration, yet even Morris, who frequently spoke from the platform at such anniversary celebrations, shared similar reservations. He wrote to his daughter Jenny on the occasion of the 1887 commemoration: "I have to speak, which I don't quite like; because although it is proper & right to celebrate the day, one has by this time said all one has to say on the subject."[90] Morris, like Henderson and Shaw, privately acknowledged the possibility of discursive exhaustion, or rhetorical fatigue, as a danger for this kind of repeated, public performance of celebratory passion mixed with moral indignation.

As Morris's remarks attest, the problem of how to relate to, and retrospectively valorize, the Commune's *failure* created a tension in the socialist periodical press between the motivational need to celebrate heroic defeat, in order to justify sacrifices both past and present, and the evaluative need critically to assess the reasons that underlay the defeat (and it is not altogether surprising that this tension roughly corresponded to the division between poetry and prose). This tension between theory and partisanship is also borne out in Julia Nicholls's identification of the two principal interpretative frameworks with which the socialist movement looked back at the Commune, seeing it as both a "quotidian event" and an episode of "violent trauma," which Nicholls maps onto the division between realist and celebratory readings of its significance.[91] Enzo Traverso, meanwhile, characterizes Marx's response to the suppression of the Commune as a part of a "dialectic of defeat," such that the particular defeat itself constituted a single moment in a larger, multifaceted pattern of expansion and development: "The dimension of such a defeat was overwhelming, but did not shake the faith of Marx in the historical growth of socialism. Three decades later, mass socialist parties existed in all European countries."[92]

In the texts discussed here, the poems of Beatty, Markham, Beckett, and Morris accentuate the Communards' heroism, imbuing the Commune's suppression with an aura of martyrdom that makes critique, if not proscribed, then certainly difficult to negotiate—and all the more so given the appearance of articles by ex-Communards, such as Édouard Vaillant, in the pages of the very same *Commonweal* journal. Bax, Henderson, and Shaw, by contrast, articulate a certain frustration with this discursive construction of the Commune's afterlife. Their engagements are still oriented toward the future (or the future as it bears on the present) but differently so. Vaillant, meanwhile, invoked the Commune as "the first act of the universal drama . . . that will not end until every chain, social and political, has been broken by popular strength."[93] This is not to suggest that Morris was uncritical or that Bax was not sometimes given to celebrating the Communards' heroism; rather, it indicates a point of discursive tension with the fin-de-siècle socialist movement's propagandistic apparatus, whereby analysis could not always be made to dovetail neatly with affirmation and where the impulse of critique frequently brushes up against the impetus to encomium. The Commune, as Haupt puts it, existed as both symbol and example for the early socialist movement, but these two forms of retroactive mobilization did not sit together neatly. As Kristin Ross observes, "weighing the Commune's successes or failures" and seeking to ascertain "in any direct way the lessons it might have provided or might continue to provide for the movements, insurrections, and revolutions that have come in its wake" are largely futile endeavors because "it is not at all clear . . . that the past actually *gives* lessons."[94] This contested historical terrain was similarly traversed by a number of the period's popular novelists, whose work, as earlier chapters of this book have explored, was no less forcefully involved in consolidating the Commune's symbolic status, albeit to markedly different ends. Chapter 7, meanwhile, turns to discuss a writer who was both a popular novelist and a socialist (of sorts) whose engagement with the Commune saw him take up a number of important ideas discussed elsewhere in this book.

CHAPTER 7

"It Had to Come Back"

H. G. WELLS'S *WHEN THE SLEEPER WAKES*

Despite the eventual suppression and defeat of the Commune, it became a crucially important talisman for the emerging socialist movement in Britain at the fin de siècle. As Morris wrote in "Why We Celebrate the Commune of Paris," "The Commune of Paris is but one link in the struggle which has gone on through all history of the oppressed against the oppressors; and without all the defeats of past times we should now have no hope of the final victory."[1] Other socialists' imaginative horizons were much narrower and more temporally circumscribed. Henry Mayers Hyndman, the former Tory radical and leader of the Social Democratic Federation (SDF) relied on a provocative allusion to the Commune in order to elucidate his approbation for the achievements of the Metropolitan Board of Works. In his pamphlet *A Commune for London* (1887), Hyndman celebrates the "enormous changes ... which have been made in well-to-do London in our own time," noting that the "modifications have gone on at an ever-increasing rate of progress," so much so that "a mere recital of what has been done in the last quarter of a century scarcely gives an idea, even to those who have witnessed it, of the transformation which has been wrought."[2] Hyndman's "mere recital" of the achievements of the Metropolitan Board of Works (constituted in 1855), including the completion of New Oxford Street and the Holborn Viaduct, the great Main Drainage Scheme, and the laying out of Battersea, Victoria, and Finsbury Parks, is particularly impressive as an example of nineteenth-century London's "continuous process of demolition and reconstruction," described by Lynda Nead.[3] Hyndman's roll call of achievements indicates that the response of fin-de-siècle socialists to the reality of metropolitan growth was not exclusively constrained within the discursive framework of Morris's romantic anti-urbanism, even as the Commune provided a common point of reference for socialists of various different organizations and ideological persuasions.

A COMMUNE FOR LONDON: ENVISAGING MUNICIPAL SOCIALISM

It is particularly noticeable that Hyndman had recourse to the Commune in sketching out his vision of a better-planned built environment, organized according to human need, rather than profit, not least because his reference cuts against mainstream invocations of the Commune as a synonym for chaotic conflagration. According to Eric Hobsbawm, the Commune provoked an "international outburst of hysteria among the rulers of Europe and among its terrified middle classes."[4] Hyndman elsewhere debunked reactionary misrepresentations of the Commune, writing in *The Historical Basis of Socialism in England* (1883): "Whilst the middle class is content, as a rule, to think of the insurrection as an affair of petroleuses and dynamitards, the Socialist party constantly recalls that . . . Paris was never so peaceful nor were so few crimes ever committed within a like period as during the supremacy of the much abused Commune."[5] In *A Commune for London*, by contrast, a certain indeterminacy and semantic instability hover around the very word "Commune," given that Hyndman makes no direct reference to the Parisian events of 1871. Indeed, Hyndman's use of the indefinite article in his title suggests an older meaning of the word, associated with the smallest administrative division of French territorial organization, which belongs in the series commune, canton, arrondissement, department, region. In France, the word's origins can be traced to the twelfth century, but the existence of the communes as territorial divisions of municipal governance began during the period following the French Revolution, which saw communes replace parishes (*la paroisse*) as the lowest level of newly secularized civic administration. Noting the political fervor that developed in Paris during the Prussian siege of 1870–1871, Gareth Stedman Jones points out that some radical and red republicans "engendered a new language of revolutionary patriotism" that made explicit appeal to the revolutionary Commune of Paris of August 1792: "The potency of the term '*Commune*' derived from the fact that it concentrated within one word the idea of national defence, of local democracy and of revolution."[6] During the early 1880s, after the "socialist revival" in Britain had begun to gather pace, British socialists commemorated the defeated Parisian Commune of 1871, but they did so in the absence of any homegrown revolutionary uprising, such that their focus sometimes shifted, as in Hyndman's case, to issues of local democracy.

As a mode of civic governance, the nearest English equivalent to a commune is the civil parish, although the comparison is partly misleading because some urban communes in France are closer in size to English districts, which tend to comprise several parishes. Morris played on this apparent affinity in *News from Nowhere*, where William Guest learns that the future society's "units of management" operate at the level of "a commune, or a ward, or a parish": "for we have all three names, indicating little real distinction between them now, though time was there was a good deal."[7] Morris's projected conflation of commune and parish, as well as Hyndman's choice of title for his pamphlet, is particularly significant because the word's meaning in English was also heavily overdetermined by the historical events of 1871. The first edition of the *Oxford English Dictionary* offered three separate definitions, the first of which referred to the word's historical derivation from the Latin word *communia*, while the second referred to French territorial divisions governed by a mayor and municipal council. The third definition offered the following: "the government on communalistic principles established in Paris by an insurrection for a short time in the spring of 1871" and "the revolutionary principles and practices embodied in the latter, and advocated by its adherents, the communards."[8] British socialists like Morris and Hyndman, whose ideological commitments involved a desire retroactively to valorize the Communards' struggle, played on this ambiguity, allowing the Commune of 1871 to figure both directly and indirectly in their rhetoric.

In this respect, Hyndman's pamphlet invokes the Commune's memory, without explicitly mentioning the events of 1871, in order to argue for various projects of urban redevelopment under municipal control and thereby implicitly disassociates the Commune from its status as a byword for destruction. Scott McCracken similarly connects the history of the Commune to a longer-term and "gradual process where the particularity of the individual nineteenth-century city was displaced by a more abstract and international sense of the urban: not *a* city, but citi*ness*."[9] He adds: "The threat of insurrection embodied in the memory of the Commune persists as an idea of what the city might become, and, as an idea of the possible rather than the actual, this idea necessarily exceeds the reality of any one city."[10] This abstract and international sense of what a city could be underlies Hyndman's comparison of London with "such turbulent centres as Paris, Berlin, Vienna or Brussels," linking the reform-oriented politics of urban renewal to the revolutionary turmoil of urban insurrection.[11] At the national level, meanwhile, Hyndman also complains that the people of Manchester, Liverpool, Birmingham, Glasgow, Edinburgh, Leeds, and Newcastle "have if anything rather an exaggerated notion of the importance of their respective cities," whereas "London alone is deficient in this characteristic of municipal pride."[12] In *A Commune for London*, Hyndman set out to address this perceived deficiency, while simultaneously preparing the ground for the SDF's electoral agenda on the London County Council (LCC).

Unlike the abstentionist Socialist League, Hyndman's SDF was more willing to engage in the practical politicking of the LCC. The LCC was an experiment in municipal government that was established in 1889, under the aegis of the 1888

Local Government Act. A former SDF member, John Burns, even met with some measure of success in this area. Burns, who had played a leading role in the London Dock Strike, was elected as an LCC councillor for Battersea in 1889 and sided with the Progressive majority on the new LCC. In elaborating the achievements of the LCC, Burns, like Hyndman, rhetorically invoked the Commune. Trumpeting the achievements of the LCC Progressives in an article published in the *Nineteenth Century*, titled "The London County Council I. Towards a Commune," Burns wrote in March 1892: "Much that was considered Utopian and impracticable three years ago is being secured, and much more on the verge of realisation."[13] Burns's pejorative use of the word "Utopian" here functions as a foil against which he extolls the advantages of municipal control of roads and services. Burns conceptualized utopia as a realm of unrealizable potentiality, set against the more pragmatic actuality of municipal socialism. In response to criticism from the future Conservative politician R. E. Prothero, a self-styled "ordinary ratepaying elector," Burns replied with another article in which he more openly acknowledged the allusion to the Commune, writing that "a commune means to me, as it meant to the workers of Paris, a free city in a free country—a community possessing all the powers of a free people for its civic, social, physical, and artistic development, uncontrolled by any power other than that to which it voluntarily consents."[14] He also clearly dissociated this vision from the red-baiting "phantasms of plunder, brigandage, and bacchanalian debauchery" that the "wild tribe of shrieking journalists" had "unjustly associated with the Commune of Paris" twenty-one years ago and that Prothero had revived.[15]

Like Hyndman and Burns, Annie Besant, another SDF member, similarly looked to developments in local government as an instance of "changes practicable among men and women as we know them" and invoked the memory of the Commune in doing so.[16] In an essay titled "Industry under Socialism," published by George Bernard Shaw in his collection *Fabian Essays in Socialism* (1889), Besant suggested that the Conservative politician C. T. Ritchie's 1888 Local Government Act, which laid the legislative basis for the LCC's formation, "has established the Commune"; in dividing England into "districts ruled by County Councils," Ritchie had, according to Besant, "created the machinery without which Socialism was impracticable."[17] She envisaged this administrative apparatus developing County Farms, where "all the small industries necessary in daily life should be carried on in it, and an industrial commune thus built up."[18] Besant characterized the social form of the Commune as the wave of the future, arguing that the "best form of management during the transition period, and possibly for a long time to come, will be through Communal Councils," established on a democratic basis, such that "the power of selection and dismissal within the various sub-divisions should lie with the nominees of the whole Commune."[19] Besant imagines a way of turning Ritchie's Local Government Act against itself and converting it into a vehicle for socializing the means of production, with the commune as the decisive social unit.

Mindful of these debates about municipal socialism, Morris invoked the historical Commune as an example of radically democratic decentralization. The importance of decentralization in Morris's political philosophy is clearly identifiable in his unsympathetic review of Edward Bellamy's state-socialist utopian romance *Looking Backward* (1888), where he commented that, in a socialist society, "it will be necessary for the unit of administration to be small enough for every citizen to feel himself responsible for its details, and be interested in them."[20] Morris's "vision of social transformation" was, as Kristin Ross has shown, "predicated on a large voluntary federation of free associations existing at the local level," which Ross identifies as a "new vision of revolution based on communal autonomy and the loose federation or association of these autonomous units" developed in the wake of the Commune's "freeing itself from the power and authority of the State."[21] Insofar as it is possible to extract any social model from Morris's own utopian vision in *News from Nowhere*, it relies on an imagined federation of such decentralized communes, and as Ross has pointed out, a number of Morris's contemporaries, including Peter Kropotkin and Élisée Reclus, saw "the commune as the revolutionary form of the future."[22] In Morris's lecture "Dawn of a New Epoch" (1886), he celebrates the fact that "the idea of local administration is pushing out that of centralized government," citing the Commune as an example of this tendency: "to take a remarkable case: in the French Revolution of 1793 the most advanced party was centralizing: in the latest French Revolution, that of the Commune of 1871, it was federalist."[23]

Morris's response to the achievements of the LCC was more measured. In a late lecture, "Communism" (1893), he commented that the LCC "has in it a promise of better days, and has already done something to raise the dignity of life in London amongst a certain part of the population."[24] His approval was tempered, however, by his recognition that the gains made—in the form of "parks and other opens spaces, planting of trees, establishment of free libraries and the like"—are "very unequally distributed, that they are gains rather for certain portions of the middle-class than for working people."[25] He was also uncompromising in his assertion that "we must not lose sight of the very obvious fact that these improvements in the life of the larger public can only be carried out at the expense of some portion of the freedom and fortunes of the proprietary classes."[26] Morris, unlike Hyndman, omits any mention of infrastructural projects, limiting his approval to the ameliorated provision of services and amenities. By contrast, Hyndman celebrates a city of improved circulation (by road and rail) and better infrastructure, along with the open spaces, public parks, and amenities. The building of new roads, avenues, bridges, and railway lines and the improvement of the Embankment all constitute evidence of what Patrick Joyce has described as London's "creation as a city of free circulation," which "defined [the city] in governmental terms" during the mid-nineteenth century—the period described by Hyndman, prior to the formation of the LCC.[27] This remaking of the city, as Joyce demonstrates, was tied to a project of liberal political governance concerned not only with the free movement of persons but also with "freeing" the city as a space for the more commodious circulation of capital. Morris's maximalist articulation of the ideal of full communism, written partly in response to the reformist gains of the LCC, remained truer to the Communards' ideal of social revolution through urban insurrection, even as Hyndman, Burns, and Besant attempted to appropriate the symbolic resonance of the Commune for the purpose of their LCC electoral agenda.

The liberal *Daily Chronicle* also recounted the LCC's achievements in a special edition of the newspaper, which first appeared on 18 February 1895. The paper's special commissioners reprinted a booklet, *New London: Her Parliament and Its Works* (1895), containing chapters on the LCC Works Committee, as well as the LCC's contributions to municipal provision of sports facilities, educational opportunities, a fire service, improved dwellings, and numerous amenities. The booklet is accompanied by a series of cartoons and drawings produced by, among others, Edward Burne-Jones, Walter Crane, Joseph Pennell, and Herbert Railton. Crane's striking frontispiece, titled "Unification of London: A Suggestion for the Lord Mayor's Show under the London County Council," depicts a procession of men and women, dressed in loose-fitting, free-flowing garments, carrying banners celebrating "Municipal Progress," "Municipal Lighting," "Municipal Water Supply," "Municipal Markets," "Municipal Education," "No Slums," "Municipal Tramways," "Municipal Docks & Warehouses," "Municipal Work for Unemployed," and "Playgrounds and Open Spaces" (see figure 7.1).[28] The two stewards at the front of the procession are decked out in particolored blouses, suggestive of the pseudomedieval garb worn by the inhabitants of Morris's Nowhere, which, as Morris's utopian protagonist learns, lies "somewhat between that of the ancient classical costume and the simpler forms of the fourteenth-century garments, though it was clearly not an imitation of either."[29] At the same time, Crane's marching workers take forward the very cause of progress that he had depicted in his 1891 *Black and White* allegorical representation "In Memory of the Commune of Paris," as well as in his memorial cartoon—"Vive la Commune!"—distributed as a supplement to the Socialist League's *Commonweal* journal for 24 March 1888 (see figure 7.2). As Morna O'Neill writes, this cartoon became "part of a new international mythology of socialism

Figure 7.1. Walter Crane, frontispiece, "Unification of London: A Suggestion for the Lord Mayor's Show under the London County Council," *New London: Her Parliament and Its Work* (London: Edward Lloyd, 1895). British Library 10350.h.22.

advanced, in part, by the imagery that suffused Crane's other political cartoons."[30] Hyndman celebrated municipal patriotism in *A Commune for London*, and Crane lent it a distinctly medievalist inflection in "Unification of London," deploying a visual rhetoric familiar from his earlier commemorations of the Commune.

Figure 7.2. Walter Crane, "Vive la Commune!," *Commonweal*, 24 March 1888, printed on fine paper and distributed as a supplement. Image in Public Domain.

"Trouble in the Underways":
H. G. Wells's *When the Sleeper Wakes*

G. K. Chesterton responded to this climate of medieval municipalism in his antiutopian satire *The Napoleon of Notting Hill* (1904), in which he imagines the disastrous consequences of a whimsical tilt toward municipal patriotism in a projected future, some eighty years hence, with consequences that call to mind the destructive violence of the Commune's last days. Chesterton was aware of Crane's "decorative curves" and once disclaimed socialists in general on the grounds that "a man of their sort will have a wife in pale green and Walter Crane's 'Triumph of Labour' hanging in the hall."[31] In *Napoleon*, Chesterton also satirizes the modern innovation of County Councils, putting the following words into the mouth of Juan del Fuego, the ex-president of Nicaragua, who contrasts the value of experiential understanding with the empty formalism of rationalizing state institutions: "Do you really mean to say that at the moment when the Esquimaux has learnt to vote for a County Council, you will have learnt to spear a walrus?"[32] Del Fuego speaks from a position of patriotic commitment to the experiential and the particular, his own nation having recently been absorbed by a larger imperial federation, thus making his reference to "a County Council" as an example of such rationalizing, absorptive tendencies particularly pointed in view of the various progressive defenses of the LCC quoted earlier. In Chesterton's novella, the bureaucrat Barker represents the statist position, and he always professes to speak in the name of "the interests of the public" (47) and "the public good" (165) because of his position as a state functionary. Chesterton figures forth his response to Barker's doublespeak through the diptych of Adam Wayne and Auberon Quin, whose revanchist medievalism bears striking similarities to the Morrisian variety on display in Crane's celebration of the LCC.

In Chesterton's short (and first) novella, which reworks the trope of the fool-made-king-for-a-day, Auberon Quin becomes the country's quixotic monarch, after a kind of lottery, and proposes to "devote [his] remaining strength to bringing about a keener sense of local patriotism in the various municipalities of London" (75).[33] Quin announces his "Great Proclamation of the Charter of the Cities" at a meeting of the Society for the Recovery of London Antiquities, whose members greet the king's proposal "in an indescribable state of vagueness" (80). To the consternation of London's mercantile class, whose business affairs are subject to significant disruption, each borough is bestowed with a provost, a heraldic coat of arms, and a uniformed corps of guardsmen—satirically realizing the state of affairs imagined in Crane's cartoon—and the city walls are rebuilt. Quin's antiquarian enthusiasms lead to a revival of the "arrogance of the old medieval cities applied to our glorious suburbs" (73), replete with vestrymen in crowns and wreaths, uniformed halberdiers, banners, and coats of arms. However, when Adam Wayne, the earnest young provost of Notting Hill, decides to execute the king's whimsical inclination to revitalize "the neglected traditions of the London boroughs" with po-faced sincerity, the result is a bloody civil war that includes barricades "nearly as high as houses" (218) and vigorous bouts of street fighting, evoking the very violence of the Commune's last days that Hyndman had sought to downplay. The barricades themselves are composed of the "fragments" of the "vast machinery of modern life" (162)—including omnibuses and chimney pots—recalling the process of *bricolage* that Kristin Ross finds to be at work in the Communards' construction of their Parisian barricades.[34]

The concatenation of urban growth and urban insurrection similarly animated H. G. Wells's *When the Sleeper Wakes*, first serialized in the *Graphic* between 7 January and 6 May 1899 and illustrated predominantly by H. Lanos. In an essay titled "Herbert George Wells and His Work" (1902), which first appeared in the *Cosmopolitan Magazine*, Wells's friend Arnold Bennett characterized *When the Sleeper Wakes*, together with *The First Men in the Moon* and "A Story of the Days to Come," as Wells's foremost examples of "prophecy in fiction."[35] Wells's adventure narrative *When the Sleeper Wakes*, in particular, offers parallels with *The Napoleon of Notting Hill* because it contains lengthy passages recounting a hard-fought urban insurrection, though Wells, unlike Chesterton, explicitly recalls the Commune. Wells's preface to the 1921 edition, which he had retitled *The Sleeper Awakes* in 1910, makes clear the text's investment in issues of metropolitan expansion, informing readers that the "present volume takes up certain ideas already very much discussed in the concluding years of the last century, the idea of the growth of towns and the depopulation of the countryside," adding: "The great city of this story is no more ... than a nightmare of Capitalism triumphant."[36] Wells's narrative thus responded to the "crisis of metropolitan experience," characterized by "chronic overcrowding and slum conditions," that Matthew Beaumont construes as a crucial influence on the "incipient anti-communist imaginary" that emerged during the fin de siècle in response to the "irruption of the Paris insurrection into middle-class consciousness."[37] When the eponymous sleeper, Graham, awakes from his "cataleptic trance" after an interval of two hundred years, he discovers a world—and a metropolis—transformed.[38] It is a world that Graham effectively owns, as Wells's adaptation of Washington Irving's Rip Van Winkle formula sees Graham's investments and savings steadily accrue during his two-hundred-year slumber to such an extent that he wakes to find himself in the position of sole Master and Owner of half the world. A greatly expanded London has become, along with Edinburgh, Portsmouth, Manchester, and Shrewsbury, one of a few great conurbations that constitute the dominant centers of population in Britain, while similar conurbations exist abroad.

London's projected population of thirty-three million inhabitants is "beyond Graham's imagination" but very much in keeping with Wells's predilection speculatively to intensify the perceived contradictions and developing trends of the society he saw around him (*Sleeper*, 148). As he put it in his *Experiment in Autobiography* (1934), *When the Sleeper Wakes* was "essentially an exaggeration of contemporary tendencies: higher buildings, bigger towns, wickeder capitalists and labour more downtrodden than ever."[39] During a flight in an aeropile (or monoplane) between London and Paris, Graham later surveys "the ruin of the houses that had once dotted the country" and notices "the vast treeless expanse of country from which all farms and villages had gone, save for crumbling ruins" (204). Graham's flight intimates the spatialized politics of the novel, as he is briefly informed by the aeronaut as they fly over Paris "about 'trouble in the underways,'" a remark that "Graham did not heed at the time" (206). Much as the underground race of Morlocks feature as a menacing presence in Wells's earlier 1895 novella *The Time Machine*, as do the Vril-ya in Edward Bulwer Lytton's *The Coming Race*, Graham later learns about the suffering slave class employed by the Labour Company only when he "penetrated downward, ever downward, towards the working places" (271).[40] From the magisterial and exhilarating height of his aeropile cockpit, Graham fails to perceive the existence of a subterranean undercurrent of popular discontent, the source of which emanates, appropriately enough, from Paris.

Remarkably, given that the narrative is set sometime around the year 2100, memories of the Commune persist in the future society and offer a focal point of revolutionary optimism against the plutocratic rule of the Council, an organization that came into being in order to manage Graham's affairs during his long slumber. The earliest reference to the Commune appears in the midst of the novel's first insurgency, during which forces aligned with Ostrog, an ostensibly revolutionary opponent of the Council, liberate Graham from the Council's imprisonment, only for Graham subsequently to get lost in the sprawling passageways of the metropolis. At this point in the narrative, the popular forces are seemingly aligned with Ostrog's revolt against the Council, but Graham later discovers the existence of a revolution within the revolution, which Ostrog attempts to suppress and which he identifies with a memory of the Commune: "Ostrog brought flattering reports [to Graham] of the development of affairs abroad. In Paris and Berlin, Graham perceived that he was saying, there has been trouble, not organised resistance indeed, but insubordinate proceedings. 'After all these years,' said Ostrog, when Graham pressed inquiries; 'the Commune has lifted its head again. That is the real nature of the struggle, to be explicit.' But order had been restored in these cities" (232). The Commune emerges as a source of fear for the Bonapartist figure of Ostrog. The revivified Commune also provides a beacon of hope against the swift bureaucratic ossification of Ostrog's rebellion. Graham soon learns that Ostrog cynically attempted to overthrow the Council by means of a carefully manipulated popular uprising, which he set on foot simply in order to secure power for himself.

According to Ostrog, the "social discontent" that gave rise to the Communard uprising stems from the Labour Company's autocratic organization of the forces of production, foregrounding class antagonism as a dominant cause of revolutionary sentiment. The Labour Company figures as a dystopian version of the industrial army imagined in Edward Bellamy's *Looking Backward*—a book that Wells briefly invokes in chapter 2. Having thus identified the "real nature of the struggle," Ostrog becomes remarkably candid about his own will to power in overthrowing the Council: "We had to stir up their discontent, we had to revive the old ideals of universal happiness—all men equal—all men happy—no luxury that everyone may not share—ideas that have slumbered for two hundred years. You know what? We had to revive these ideals, impossible as they are—in order to overthrow the Council" (233). Much like Victor de Mauleon in Bulwer's *The Parisians*, Ostrog's alignment with forces of popular revolt is purely opportunistic and instrumental, and much like Adam Wayne in the comparatively parochial setting of Notting Hill, Ostrog finds himself in the position of a demagogue in danger of being displaced by the very popular forces he has mobilized: "There is trouble. Multitudes will not go back to work. There is a general strike. Half the factories are empty and the people are swarming the Ways. They are talking of a Commune" (233–234). Ostrog also declares the outmoded unfeasibility of collective revolutionary agency, asserting that "the days when the People could make revolutions are past" (235). For Ostrog, this stance is linked to his Nietzschean propensities and aristocratic hauteur. As he puts it to Graham, "The coming of the aristocrat is fatal and assured. The end will be the Over-man—for all the mad protests of humanity" (239). In a recreational dancehall, Graham later sees "marble busts of men whom that age esteemed great moral emancipators" (259), including Grant Allen, Richard Le Gallienne, and Nietzsche.

Wells's elaboration of Ostrog's anti-Communard elitism anticipates the stance taken by the playwright (and Wells's fellow Fabian) George Bernard Shaw, whose four-act play *Man and Superman* (written in 1903 and first performed in 1905) borrowed its title from Nietzsche.[41] Shaw similarly inserted some particularly disparaging remarks about the Commune into the 1907 German edition of *The Perfect Wagnerite* (1898). These remarks were incorporated into the third English edition of the text, published in 1913. In the context of a wider dismissal of the Impossibilist (or revolutionary) socialism of the First International, Shaw comments: "The suppression of the Paris Commune, one of the most tragic examples in history of the pitilessness with which capable practical administrators and soldiers are forced by the pressure of facts to destroy romantic amateurs and theatrical dreamers, made an end of melodramatic Socialism."[42] While many of the popular novelists of the Commune sought to frame the event within the generic confines of melodrama, its more forthright defenders found recourse instead to epic, as did Morris in *The Pilgrims of Hope*. In belatedly seeking to write the Commune's obituary, Shaw attempted to carve out a position of hegemony for Fabian reformism and gradualism, casting a tendentious ideological modification within the socialist movement in terms of a passing generic fashion. Shaw anchored this exercise in apologetics for Adolphe Thiers's mass slaughter of the Communards in pragmatic commitment to "the pressure of facts," yet it is noticeable that Shaw does not accompany this appeal with any specification of the particular "facts" he has in mind, such that his professed empiricism swiftly plunges into resolute abstraction.

Shaw expanded on his dismissal of the Commune in the preface to the 1908 edition of *Fabian Essays in Socialism*, where he wrote: "Anyone who looks at the portraits of the members of the Paris Commune can see at a glance that they compared very favourably in all the external signs of amiability and refinement with any governing body then or now in power in Europe. But they could not manage the business they took upon themselves; and Thiers could."[43] Shaw's focus on the pragmatic management of "business" dovetails with his earlier critique of the revolutionary romanticism of the Communards, whom he dismissed as mere "amateurs" and "theatrical dreamers." In *When the Sleepers Wakes*, Wells repeatedly identifies Graham as the very embodiment of an idealist dreamer, so much so that he is described as a throwback to the outmoded ideals of the nineteenth century. After his mysterious lapse into slumber during the nineteenth century—a period during which he suffered with insomnia and suicidal thoughts—Graham is confusedly described by his solicitor and next of kin as "a fanatical Radical—a Socialist—or typical Liberal, as they used to call themselves, of the advanced school. Energetic—flighty—undisciplined" (19). On Shaw's terms, then, Graham's solidarity with the novel's twenty-second-century Communards could be explained as a natural extenuation of these flighty and undisciplined tendencies. The Positivist Frederic Harrison wrote in similar terms of his encounter with Communard exiles, whom he described as "cultivated and high-minded men who had flung themselves into the struggle on impulse, and with no very clear idea whither it might lead them."[44]

In this regard, Graham also recalls the bohemian "best elements of the bourgeoisie" that, according to Walter Benjamin, sided with the Commune because of its "spontaneous energy and ... enthusiasm."[45] Benjamin had in mind the poet Arthur Rimbaud and the painter Gustave Courbet. In a different sense, Graham, the imagined Master and Owner of the World, embodies an archetypal bourgeois who, by dint of an eccentric commitment to the ideal of universal equality, allies himself with the forces of revolution against tyranny, oppression, and, crucially, his own global expanse of capital. Whereas Benjamin argues that "it was fatal for the workers' rebellions of old that no theory of revolution had directed their course"—even if this absence of theory made possible the "enthusiasm" and "energy" he celebrates—in Wells's narrative, Graham's very *flightiness* ultimately holds out a promise of victory at the revolution's crucial moment, as he takes to his aeropile to repel Ostrog's invading fleet of warplanes.[46] Graham's heroic act of self-sacrifice, which echoes Arthur Golding's suicidal downward plunge into the abyss of Niagara Falls at the end of Gissing's *Workers in the Dawn*, does not guarantee triumph but leaves open the narrative's "horizon of possibility," to borrow a phrase that Phillip E. Wegner uses to characterize the similarly ambiguous ending of Yevgeny Zamyatin's *We* (1924).[47] The availability of this horizon in *When the Sleeper Wakes*, and its subsequent disappearance from Wells's comparable prophetic fictions, marks an important turning point in his development as a novelist, as this chapter elaborates.

"There Will Be No Commune Here": A Commune in London

In "Paris, the Capital of the Nineteenth Century," included as the 1939 "Exposé" of the *Arcades Project*, Benjamin comments:

> Just as the *Communist Manifesto* ends the age of professional conspirators, so the Commune puts an end to the phantasmagoria that dominates the earliest aspirations of the proletariat. It dispels the illusion that the task of the proletarian revolution is to complete the work of '89 in close collaboration with the bourgeoisie. This illusion had marked the period 1831–1871, from the Lyons riots to the Commune. The bourgeoisie never shared in this error. Its battle against the social rights of the proletariat dates back to the great Revolution, and converges with the philanthropic movement that gives it cover and that was in its heyday under Napoleon III.[48]

When the Sleeper Wakes dramatizes these conflicting interests, with Ostrog embodying bourgeois class consciousness in his readiness to suppress the insurgent workers, whom he describes as "swarming yelping fools in blue" (239). The final third of Wells's narrative follows Graham's realignment with and support for the popular forces, whose "blue canvas" uniforms recall the blue blouses of the Parisian working classes during the Commune of 1871. The stakes of Graham's decision to ally himself with the revolt against Ostrog are made clear when his Japanese bodyguard, Asano, disclaims the prospect of "a commune!" by warning Graham: "They would rob you of your property. They would do away with property and give the world over to mob rule" (253). Wells's novel clearly identifies the historical Commune with a potential reemergence of revolutionary and anticapitalist sentiment, which appears as a destabilizing force against the Bonapartist authoritarianism personified in Ostrog's Nietzschean will to power. Insofar as Wells's speculative narrative concretizes contemporary anxieties, Ostrog appears as an embodiment of the bourgeois fear of working-class self-organization. It is thus hardly surprising that the Commune features as the focus of Ostrog's apprehension and as a channel for the expression of his disdain for the "common man," whom he characterizes as a "helpless unit" (236).

The Parisian rising of 2100 is, like the Commune of 1871, "pacified": Graham learns in overhearing the propagandistic argot of the Babble Machines that "all resistance is over" and that the "black police," called in by Ostrog and composed of soldiers from colonial territories in Senegal and the Consolidated African Companies, have taught "a lesson to the disorderly banderlog of this city" (251). Wells's allusive use of the Hindi portmanteau word "Bandar-log," coined by Rudyard Kipling in *The Jungle Book* (1894) to describe the imaginary monkey-people of the Seeonee jungle, suggests that the Babble Machines' propaganda is designed to dehumanize the insurgent workers, much in the manner that the Communards of 1871 were portrayed by hostile caricaturists as simian-featured drunkards.[49] The propaganda of Ostrog's regime thus closely resembles the anti-Communard rhetoric of some contemporary French commentators, including Léon Daudet and Théophile Gautier, who, in Kristin Ross's words, "aimed at establishing a massive racially constituted category that would include in one breath animals, workers (particularly working-class women), barbarians, savages, and thieves."[50] But while the Parisian revolt in *When the Sleeper Wakes* is suppressed, the rebellion spreads to England, contradicting Asano's assertion that "there will be no Commune here," and Ostrog's decision to call the "black police" to London is decisive in shifting Graham's allegiance to the revolutionary forces (253–254).

Wells's brief rendition of the Parisian revolt, however, is notable for its parallels with and departures from the events of 1871. Wells invokes the brutality of the Versaillais in the Babble Machines' reference to the fact that the black police "once or twice . . . got out of hand, and tortured and mutilated wounded and captured insurgents, men and women" (251). Yet Wells's racialization of the Versaillais—displacing the source of the repressive violence onto the colonial "other"—betrays reluctance, on his part, to confront the historical actuality of the Commune as a civil war between opposing classes. At the same time, the Babble Machines proclaim in telegraphic fashion: "The Parisians exasperated by the black police to the pitch of assassination. Dreadful reprisals. Savage times come again. Blood! Blood! Yaha! . . . Law and order must be maintained" (252). In this sense, the rising of 2100 follows a cyclical pattern established by the revolution of 1871, in which the Communards' execution of the archbishop of Paris and several other hostages was widely condemned in the English press for its apparent brutality, even as the surviving Communards explained and justified these actions with reference to the Versaillais's execution of Communard captives.[51] In this regard, it is noteworthy that the mediatization of atrocities, reprisals, and counterreprisals in Wells's narrative clearly identifies the insurgents' violence as a response to the torture and mutilation inflicted on their captured comrades. Wells's narrative thus obliquely confirms, or lends weight to, pro-Communard historiography. Yet by setting this compressed rendition of Parisian events in a speculatively imagined future, Wells's narrative implicitly makes a wider claim about patterns of historical causation and agency, from which readers might draw inferences about the likelihood, or otherwise, that familiar and recurring modes of insurrectionary activity will produce predictably disappointing outcomes.

The novel's first reference to the Commune appears in the chapter "The Old Man Who Knew Everything," in which the old man encountered by Graham comments on the insurgency against the Council as follows: "'Fighting and slaying, and weapons in hand, and fools bawling freedom and the like,' said the old man. 'Not in all my life has there been that. These are like the old days—for sure—when the Paris people broke out—three gross of years ago. That's what I mean hasn't been. But it's the world's way. It had to come back. I know. I know'" (121–122). He appears only briefly and calls to mind the character of Old Hammond, the communist sage of Bloomsbury in Morris's *News from Nowhere*, who similarly acts as a bearer of historical consciousness in the narrative. Unlike Morris's articulate and expansive utopian host, Wells's old man appears lugubrious and distracted by the march of events. He makes reference to the Commune as a phenomenon that has "come back" and suggests that it fits a wider pattern of recognizable activity colloquially described as "the world's way," identifying the revolutionary upheaval of 2100 with Nietzsche's concept of eternal return. Within the horizon of Wells's speculative narrative, the imagined uprising against the Council appears, at least to the old man, as a recurrence of the Commune of 1871. However, as many commentators have pointed out, the Commune of 1871 itself appeared to contemporaries as a recurrence of the revolutionary sentiments that animated Paris's history as a city of revolution. As Priscilla Parkhurst Ferguson comments, the "long shadow cast by the Commune over the Third Republic looked all the darker by virtue of insistent, inescapable parallels with 1793."[52] In *The Psychology of Revolution* (1913), the French crowd psychologist Gustave Le Bon wrote in similar terms, characterizing every successful "popular revolution" as a "temporary return to barbarism" and speculating that "if the Commune of 1871 had lasted, it would have repeated the Terror."[53]

By imagining the repetition of such events projected two hundred years into the future, Wells reinscribes Paris's status as a locus of revolutionary activity at the same time as he envisages a transversal process whereby the defeat of revolution in Paris acts as the spark for a potentially victorious workers' uprising in London. Wells himself had voiced the very same idea in a letter to Elizabeth Healey of 23 March 1888, in which he commented that "the Commune which sank at Paris will rise next in London. That is the star we wait for."[54] A decade before he came to write *When the Sleeper Wakes*, Wells identified the Commune as a symbol of hope in his own political constellation. During this period, Wells attended meetings of the Hammersmith branch of the Socialist League, which took place in the coach house of Morris's Hammersmith residence and which doubtless motivated his sympathetic attitude toward the Commune. As Wells's biographers

Norman and Jeanne MacKenzie point out, the "memory of the Paris Commune was still fresh" at such meetings, not least because there were "old Communards among the audiences at Kelmscott House as well as fugitives from Bismarck's anti-socialist laws" in Germany.[55] In *When the Sleeper Wakes*, by contrast, the old man's insertion of the Communard rebellion into a longer temporal sequence stretching back over "three gross of years" invokes the older, etymological meaning of the word "revolution," suggesting that the events of 2100 represent little more than the next phase in the turning of history's wheel, according to a fatalistic Nietzschean cosmology of eternal return in which no revolutionary upheaval could ever introduce the prospect of genuine rupture and transformation.

The Commune and Eternal Return

The concept of eternal return, or recurrence, featured prominently in the writings of Friedrich Nietzsche, and Karl Löwith regards it as the central organizing concept of Nietzsche's heavily aphoristic philosophical system.[56] Nietzsche's formulation of eternal return in *The Gay Science* (1882), *Thus Spake Zarathustra* (1883–1891), and *Ecce Homo* (1888) was indebted to models of cyclical time derived from the writings of the ancient Pythagoreans, Empedocles, and Heraclitus. Nietzsche, in turn, was an important figure in Wells's cultural milieu, and his ideas fed into the wider current of fin-de-siècle pessimism in which Bernard Bergonzi has situated Wells's early romances.[57] Wells's reliance on Nietzsche was also part of Nietzsche's broader literary apotheosis in Britain and Ireland, which encompassed William Butler Yeats and George Bernard Shaw, among others. Meanwhile, in the French context, Colette E. Wilson has persuasively shown how Nietzsche's idea of active forgetfulness provides a useful "model for understanding the post-Commune universe inhabited by Zola, Maxime Du Camp and their contemporaries."[58] It should already be clear that Nietzsche's influence on Wells, detectable as it is in *When the Sleeper Wakes*, makes him an equally important figure for critical understanding of English mediations of the Commune.

Alexander Tille's English translation of *Thus Spake Zarathustra* appeared in 1896, three years before the serialization of *When the Sleeper Wakes* commenced in the *Graphic*, and provoked several discussions of Nietzsche's thought in mainstream periodicals. In *Thus Spake Zarathustra*, the prophetic Zarathustra's animals instruct him that he is "the teacher of eternal recurrence" and that it is his duty to preach the "doctrine" that "all things recur eternally, ourselves included; and that we have been there infinite times before, and all things with us."[59] Several of Nietzsche's early reviewers concurred with Löwith about the importance of this concept. A. Seth Pringle Pattison proclaimed it to be "the central doctrine of his philosophy" in the *Contemporary Review*, while W. Wallace, in the *Academy*, characterized it as the "ultimate secret on which Nietzsche's system rests."[60] For Löwith, Nietzsche's iterations of eternal recurrence revolve around a crucial paradox, neatly formulated by Löwith's English translator J. Harvey Lomax, who comments that Nietzsche's "ostensibly unified allegory of eternal recurrence splits into two irreconcilable parts, one cosmological and the other anthropological—one portraying the goalless revolution of the universe, the other, a superhuman act of the human will that consummates the self-overcoming of nihilism."[61] On this understanding, recurrence manifests itself as both an "unwilled, physical fact," thereby replacing "ancient cosmology with modern physics," and as "the willing of an ideal [that] replaces Christian faith in the afterlife with the will to self-eternalization and a new way of life."[62] Given that Nietzsche began to formulate the concept in the wake of the Commune, it takes on a particular resonance in its cosmological iteration as a way of containing the threat of political rupture embodied in the Commune, pitting the Communards' iconoclastic assertion of revolutionary agency against an all-engulfing prospect of eternity and the endless reduplication of the same.

Walter Benjamin noted the appearance of a closely related "cosmological speculation" in *L'Eternité par les Astres* (1872), the final book of the revolutionary and ex-Communard Auguste Blanqui, written during his last imprisonment.[63] Ben Carver, meanwhile, points to the similarity between Blanqui's astral vision of infinite worlds and Wells's *A Modern Utopia*, which imagines a "parallel planet beyond Sirius" where "every man, woman and child alive has a Utopian parallel."[64] For Benjamin, however, Blanqui's acquiescence in this Nietzschean vision represents the very moment at which he "yields to bourgeois society."[65] Benjamin argues that Blanqui's elaboration of the cosmology of eternal return, from which he quotes extensively, offers up an "infernal vision" and represents Blanqui's "unconditional surrender" to "a society that projects this image of the cosmos—understood as an image of itself—across the heavens."[66] Benjamin suggests that the concept's emergence in Blanqui's thought after the Commune's defeat encapsulates his intellectual submission to bourgeois society and a retreat from his earlier revolutionary convictions.

Nietzsche's own hostility to the Commune bears out such an interpretation. In *The Birth of Tragedy*, published one year after the defeat of the Commune and first translated into English in 1909, Nietzsche obliquely responded to the Commune with the comment, ostensibly concerning Alexandrian culture, that "there is nothing more terrible than a barbaric slave class, who have learned to regard their existence as an injustice, and now prepare to take vengeance, not only for themselves, but for all generations."[67] Against this background, Nietzsche's concept of eternal recurrence appears as a cosmological complement to his more explicitly counterrevolutionary theory of *ressentiment*, which posits that a so-called slave class preserve themselves from harm through the pursuit of "imaginary vengeance" directed against their masters.[68] Fredric Jameson argues that the theory of *ressentiment* plays a crucial role in Nietzsche's "historical master narrative," which revolves around the contention that the entire Judeo-Christian ethical tradition, as well as later developments such as socialism or any form of democratic egalitarianism, constitutes the slaves' revenge, which simultaneously infects the masters with the same "slave mentality—an ethos of charity—in order to rob them of their natural vitality and aggressive, properly aristocratic insolence."[69] One of Jameson's commentators, William C. Dowling, aptly comments that the ideologeme of "ressentiment is invoked by a nineteenth-century bourgeoisie and its intelligentsia as the mindless and destructive envy that the have-nots of society always and universally feel towards the haves, thus utterly denying the origins in economic exploitation of all discontent from below, of Peterloo and Chartism and the Paris commune."[70] It is particularly noteworthy that Morris, one of the Commune's foremost British defenders, showed himself to be carefully attuned to the reactionary character of this theory when he wrote, defending the idea of revolution in "How We Live and How We Might Live" (1884), that "it is not revenge we want for poor people, but happiness."[71] By contrast, Ostrog, the Bonapartist Nietzschean overman, appears in Wells's novel as an exemplary diagnostician and opponent of proletarian *ressentiment*, recalling Arthur Golding's attitude to John Pether in Gissing's *Workers in the Dawn* and Hyacinth Robinson's tragic tergiversation in James's *The Princess Casamassima*. Yet Wells clearly presents Ostrog as the story's villain, suggesting the confusion of Wells's ultimate stance in relation to the reality of class antagonism. Indeed, it is only when one reads *When the Sleeper Wakes* with reference both to the theory of *ressentiment* and the concept of eternal recurrence that it becomes possible to disclose Wells's true position in relation to the events he narrates.

In framing the projected Communard resurgence as a manifestation of eternal return ("It's the world way. It had to come back."), Wells flattens out the tremors and reverberations of that particular insurgency, along with the insurgents' claims to novelty, by extending the temporal horizon to such an extent that the insurgents' actions appear as little more than the latest incarnation of a timeless, fixed pattern. In doing so, he thereby forecloses in advance the prospect of social transformation with or without the intervention of the Bonapartist figure of Ostrog, whose actions Wells clearly does not celebrate. Such a view ran counter to Marx's assertion of the Commune's novelty, as he argued that "this was the first revolution in which the working class was openly acknowledged as the only class capable of social initiative, even by the great bulk of the Paris middle class—shopkeepers, tradesmen, merchants—the wealthy capitalists alone excepted."[72] Yet Marx also observed: "It is generally the fate of completely new historical creations to be mistaken for the counterparts of older, and even defunct, forms of social life, to which they may bear a certain likeness," hence the attempts of the Commune's opponents to depict it as a return of the medieval communes or to construe the Commune's "antagonism...

against the state power" as an "exaggerated form of the ancient struggle against over-centralization."[73]

Benjamin followed Marx in asserting that the Commune represented a break in the long nineteenth century's historical sequence of revolutions, dispelling "the illusion that the task of the proletarian revolution is to complete the work of '89 in close collaboration with the bourgeoisie." In "Paris, Capital of the Nineteenth Century," Benjamin argued that "the collapse of the Second Empire and the Commune of Paris" served as timely reminders that "the pomp and splendour with which commodity-producing society surrounds itself, as well as the illusory sense of security, are not immune to dangers."[74] For Benjamin, such disturbances fundamentally threatened the bourgeois "phantasmagorias" of the marketplace and civilization, identified with differing economic and technological determinations, including the Parisian arcades, the haphazard urban experiences of the flâneur, and Haussmann's transformations of Paris. Benjamin's dissection of these phantasmagorias leads him to draw the Commune into a constellation with the Nietzschean vision of eternal recurrence, though, for Benjamin, Nietzsche's concept shares an affinity with the inner logic of equivalence that Marx had discovered in the commodity.[75] According to Benjamin, "In the idea of eternal recurrence, the historicism of the nineteenth century capsizes," such that "every tradition, even the most recent, becomes the legacy of something that has already run its course in the immemorial night of the ages."[76] Socialist attempts to memorialize the Commune's heroic defeat as the founding moment in an unprecedented tradition of proletarian revolution would thereby be negated at birth, according to the cosmological logic of the concept.

Benjamin certainly reflected on the concept of eternal return, but this did not imply endorsement on his part, as he also offered a critical account of the reasons underlying its emergence in Nietzsche's post-1871 writings. In Convolute D of the *Arcades Project*, "Boredom, Eternal Return," Benjamin includes several extracts from Nietzsche's posthumously collected *The Will to Power* (1901) and comments that "the notion of eternal return appeared at a time when the bourgeoisie no longer dared count on the impending development of the system of production they had set going," not least because of the shock that had been delivered to bourgeois society by the sudden emergence of the Commune.[77] In Convolute J on Baudelaire, Benjamin more explicitly draws out his view of the concept's status as an ideological reflex of economic forces:

> The idea of eternal recurrence transforms the historical event itself into a mass produced article. But this conception also displays, in another aspect—on its obverse side, one could say—a trace of the economic circumstances to which it owes its sudden topicality. This was manifest at the moment the security of the conditions of life was considerably diminished through an accelerated

succession of crises. The idea of *eternal* recurrence derived its luster from the fact that it was no longer possible, in all circumstances, to expect a recurrence of conditions across any interval of time shorter than that provided by eternity.[78]

The Commune was a particularly acute manifestation of crisis that threatened to undermine capitalist circuits of production and exchange, interrupting an economic dispensation that facilitates the accumulation of private property. In this context, Benjamin suggests, the idea of eternal recurrence offered antisocialists like Nietzsche a convenient metaphysical stabilization of this contingent set of social relations by reducing the possibility of historical transformation to yet another "mass produced article" for consumption, much as Wells's novel fulfilled a similar function in the literary marketplace. Benjamin captures the way in which the concept of eternal return commoditizes "the historical event," even as it denies any validity to the notion of historical "progress," at the same time as he identifies the conjunctural cause of its emergence in Nietzsche's thought as a response to a period of instability and capitalist crisis. Benjamin, by contrast, defended the idea that "progress has its seat not in the continuity of elapsing time but in its interferences," arguing that "for the materialist historian, every epoch with which he occupies himself is only prehistory for the epoch he himself must live in. And so, for him, there can be no appearance of repetition in history, since precisely those moments in the course of history that matter most to him, by virtue of their index as 'fore-history,' become moments of the present day and change their specific character according to the catastrophic or triumphant nature of the day."[79] Benjamin's militant presentism, which he elsewhere sets against positivist historicism, in turn motivates his own view of the Commune as an event that "[dispelled] the illusion that the task of the proletarian revolution is to complete the work of 1789 hand in hand with the bourgeoisie."[80] For Benjamin, the historical experience of the Commune inaugurated a new phase in the class struggle organized according to the logic of confrontation rather than accommodation, antagonism rather than compromise.

"No Certainty of Either Victory or Defeat"

Benjamin's reading of Nietzsche's concept of eternal recurrence aptly reveals it, in Esther Leslie's words, as the necessary "complement of a crisis-ridden capitalism, in which what is true is truly the unconscious acknowledgement that there is nothing new to come, because no future can be imagined in the context of the current economic order."[81] While Wells may not have read Nietzsche at first hand, Nietzsche's ideas certainly influenced a number of his novels—as John Batchelor and others have recognized—and discussion of eternal recurrence featured prominently in early reviews of Nietzsche's work when it first began to appear in English translation.[82] As such, the resurfacing of the concept of eternal recurrence in *When the Sleeper Wakes*, where it is invoked with explicit reference to the Commune, helps clarify the ideological stakes of Wells's mobilization of "prophecy in fiction" (to borrow Arnold Bennett's words). Wells's equivocation over Graham's role in the revolt demonstrates that he is ultimately unable to imagine a future beyond a moderately reformed version of the "current economic order," but his disavowal of the possibility of revolutionary rupture, as encapsulated in the Commune, entailed the relinquishment of his youthful enthusiasm for such politics. As he had put it in his 1888 letter to Elizabeth Healey, in which he praised the Commune, "I sympathise most, of all parties in the world, with Wm. Morris and the Revolutionary circle in London."[83] As Wells moved closer to the gradualist Fabian Society, which he eventually joined for a period of five years between 1903 and 1908, he necessarily left behind his earlier commitments, but the essential gesture of disavowal is already present in *When the Sleeper Wakes* and is equally detectable in his subsequent comments on the book. Wells explicitly repudiated the novel's original ending in his preface to the revised edition of 1910, where he wrote that, "with a few strokes of the pen," he had "eliminated certain dishonest and regrettable suggestions that the People beat Ostrog": "My Graham dies, as all his kind must die, with no certainty of either victory or defeat."[84] Wells registered the Commune's posthumous impact, almost thirty years after the event, but ultimately disavowed the Communards' revolutionary and socialist internationalism in the name of a more technocratic transnationalism on display in his later advocacy of a World State.

The narrative of class struggle and popular insurgency on display in *When the Sleeper Wakes* does not reach an affirmative conclusion but meets only with ambivalence and irresolution, which partly suggests why Wells remained troubled by a nagging sense of the novel's artistic failure, which he associated with the "marks of haste not only in the writing of the latter part, but in the very construction of the story."[85] In particular, he rejected the "ill-conceived latter part," which "was pushed to its end," and pointed out that he "had in hand another book, *Love and Mr. Lewisham*, which had taken a very much stronger hold upon [his] affections than this present story."[86] In his 1910 preface, Wells's evident dissatisfaction with the narrative quality of this early romance potentially conceals a different, more political discomfort that he had made more explicit elsewhere. In September 1906, in a letter to the editor of the *Daily Express* refuting attacks on his novel *In the Days of the Comet* (1906), Wells identified himself as being "in no way a representative of any Socialist organization" but "merely a private, unorthodox, and rebellious member of the Fabian Society."[87] The following year, in a letter to the editor of the *Magazine of Commerce*, dated 5 August 1907, he explicitly repudiated revolution in his assertion that "the methods of transition from the limited individualism of our present to the scientifically organised State, which is the Socialist ideal, must be gradual, tentative and various," and he reassured his readers that "the advent of a strongly Socialistic Government to power would mean no immediate revolutionary changes at all."[88]

Wells's mobilization of the concept of eternal return in *When the Sleeper Wakes* offers an early signal of his gravitation in this reformist direction and discloses the full extent of the paradox that Löwith identified in Nietzsche's idea. Much as the concept refuses to settle on either side of its cosmological and anthropological iterations, so does the indeterminacy of the conclusion of *When the Sleeper Wakes* ultimately reveal the narrative's equivocation over the resurgence of the Commune, leaving readers unsure whether Wells depicts a tragic defeat—recapitulating the historical example of the 1871 rising—or a heroic gesture of self-sacrifice in which Graham's skill in the aeropile secures victory for the revolutionary forces. Even if the latter option were seen to be true, one might still entertain the possibility that the victorious revolution would ossify. In this sense, the conclusion of *When the Sleeper Wakes* dramatizes the paradox central to Nietzsche's concept. Graham's willful attempt to alter the course of events abides by Zarathustra's injunction to "save the past . . . and to change every 'It was' into a 'thus I would have it,'" while acting out Wells's own youthful desire to see the Commune's "star" rise again in London.[89] In this regard, Graham enacts the anthropological iteration of Nietzsche's concept, in which recurrence appears as an ethical task to be accomplished. The individualized scope of Graham's narrative is set against the much grander scale of revolutionary upheaval, encompassing the actions of multiple, unseen revolutionary committees organizing to repel Ostrog's invading air force, gesturing toward the possibility of collective revolutionary agency. Yet, at the conclusion of the narrative, Graham's heroic act of self-sacrifice in defense of the revolution leaves the novel open-ended and unresolved, suggesting a refusal, on Wells's part, to take any definitive stance on the wider question of revolutionary agency, even as Graham's sympathies are unambiguously delineated.

Graham's passionate and heroic devotion to the cause certainly manifests a recurrence of the Communards' revolutionary commitment. Yet Graham also faces the tangible prospect of defeat, and it is here that the second, cosmological iteration of Nietzsche's concept—as "physical metaphysics"—becomes relevant. Bernd Magnus identifies this second sense with a suggestion that "a finite number of states of the world is destined to unfold in time—which is infinite, not finite. Hence, given the finite number of possible states of the world and the infinity of time, any single state of the world must recur. More than that, it must recur eternally: the eternal recurrence of the same."[90] According to this logic, the nonexistence in world history of a successful revolutionary prototype, and the historical fact of the Paris Commune's defeat in 1871, necessarily condemns

Graham's revolt to the same fate as the defeated historical Communards, because the possibility of their final victory does not belong among "the finite number of possible states of the world"; otherwise it would already have been witnessed. The logic appears curiously circular (and so the wheel turns), but there is enough evidence in *When the Sleeper Wakes* to suggest that Wells mobilized precisely this paradoxical circularity in order to contain and disavow the Commune's revolutionary potential. If, as the old man comments, the Commune "had to come back," then the "world's way" immediately foredooms it to renewed defeat.

Wells's achievement in *When the Sleeper Wakes* was to imagine a scenario in which the entire world's stock of private property has been concentrated into the hands of a single individual, who, upon his inheritance of this worldwide monopoly, decides to disown it in the name of a resurgent Communard praxis. Yet the novel obscures its stance in relation to that praxis, illuminating the distance between Wells and the older generation of socialist revivalists, such as Morris and Crane, whose commemorations of the Commune were grounded in an unabashedly affirmative belief in the possibility—and the possibly imminent prospect—not only of the Commune's repetition but of its successful vindication in victorious class struggle. Wells toyed with hopes of such a victory during his youthful visits to meetings of Morris's Socialist League, but he found himself unable to translate such hopes into his later experiments in fiction without considerable qualification. If, as the French historian George Haupt has commented, the Commune was both a symbol and an example for the emergent fin-de-siècle socialist movement, then for Wells and his fellow Fabian Bernard Shaw, it was a symbol that they had to disavow in order to establish their claim to mastery of the rhetorical terrain that had heretofore been occupied by an older generation of avowedly revolutionary socialists.[91] In an inversion of the more typical phenomenon whereby youthful rebels outflank their political predecessors to the left, Wells and Shaw instead gravitated steadily rightward.

When the Sleeper Wakes occupies an important waypoint in Wells's development as a novelist and as a political thinker, insofar as none of his later scientific romances even entertain the possibility of class struggle and revolutionary insurrection as an agent of social change. *In the Days of the Comet* imagines a global "Awakening" precipitated by the "new gas" contained in a comet that enters the Earth's atmosphere, thereby inaugurating an era of "peace on earth and good will to all men"—but the narrative function of the gas is to displace any prospect that human agency might precipitate such a transformation.[92] *When the Sleeper Wakes*, then, offers important insights about the particular trajectory of Wells's intellectual and political development, but it also presents an interesting modulation of the fin-de-siècle subgenre of prophetic fiction known as cacotopianism, which, as Matthew Beaumont has convincingly shown, was, unlike dystopian fiction, "concerned less with repudiating the literary expression of utopianism than with combating its practical embodiment in the proletariat."[93] As Beaumont points out, the array of cacotopian narratives—including Samuel Bracebridge Hemyng's *The Commune in London* (1871), E. H. Berens and I. Singer's *The Story of My Dictatorship* (1894), and Charles Gleig's *When All Men Starve* (1898)—explicitly respond to the anxieties engendered by the Commune, which "shaped the social imaginary of an entire generation" in Britain as well as France.[94] Such texts, Beaumont argues, wage "a fictional offensive by forging the rhetorical tools of an anti-revolutionism that, by filling their readers' imaginations with the spectral symbols of a fictional socialist menace, sought expressly to influence bourgeois class consciousness."[95] The cacotopia also "incorporates a 'utopian function'" because the prophetic, anticipatory narrative structure, which depicts revolution as "an infernal state of social flux," simultaneously "conscripts reactionary political instincts in support of a utopian model of capitalism supposedly implicit in the present."[96] Wells's response to the Commune in *When the Sleeper Wakes* modulates these features of the cacotopian genre, at the same time as his engagement with the primal scene of bourgeois anxiety—namely, the revolutionary possibility of proletarian self-organization and democratic self-governance—speaks to concerns about labor and class antagonism that were far more widely distributed in the fiction of the period.[97]

Given Wells's broadly reformist orientation, occupying the softer flank of the fin-de-siècle socialist movement, he was hardly in a position to offer a full-throated endorsement of the capitalist mode of production, and *When the Sleeper Wakes* in no way offers a "utopian" or recuperative resolution to the class conflicts depicted in the novel, in the manner that Beaumont identifies with the cacotopian genre. Rather, pessimism is the keynote of Wells's text, a characteristic that it shares with many of Wells's early romances, notably *The Time Machine* (1895) and *The Island of Doctor Moreau* (1896), as well as Gissing's response to the Commune in *Workers in the Dawn*. For Beaumont, the "ideological force" of cacotopian texts "depends on their belief that capitalism can abolish class conflict, and that the working class can be rendered quiescent."[98] One finds no such ideological self-assurance in Wells, yet neither can he bring himself to have any confidence in the proletariat as an agent of its own emancipation. Graham's death neatly symbolizes this dilemma: while his death represents the potential termination of the novel's revolutionary uprising, that uprising was, in part, a revolt prosecuted against Graham's very status as the Master and Owner of half the world. Graham's death is thus as much a crisis for the prevailing system of property relations that obtains within the novel as it is for the revolution that he leads, but Wells does not elaborate on the consequences of this contradiction. On the contrary, he abandons his narrative at the very moment that the projected revolution is about to enter its decisive phase: the precise point at which the novel's bourgeois protagonist vacates the stage, leaving it empty for the anonymous revolutionary masses to see through the revolt they have initiated to ultimate victory or final defeat.

Wells's disavowal—or, one might say, avoidance—of collective revolutionary agency in fact ushers in the more properly utopian phase in his literary production, from which all traces of working-class self-organization mysteriously vanish. Publication of *When the Sleeper Wakes* in 1899 was followed with Wells's most self-evidently programmatic utopias: *Anticipations* (1901), *Mankind in the Making* (1903), and *A Modern Utopia* (1905). One might also recall that *A Modern Utopia*, *The World Set Free* (1915), and *The Shape of Things to Come* (1933) all resort to some form of enlightened aristocracy or benevolent dictatorship, drawing on Wells's proposals for a World State, which he first outlined in *Anticipations*. As Duncan Bell has pointed out, Wells's later "cosmopolitan socialism" was "vanguardist insofar as the primary agents of change—and the ideal rulers of the future society—were a transnational technocratic elite."[99] In this respect, the qualified affinity of *When the Sleeper Wakes* with the cacotopian propensity for counterrevolutionary propaganda opens the way for Wells to enter all the more securely into a new period of literary and political activity, in which his Fabian reformism dovetails neatly with a commitment to the version of "compensatory" and "prophylactic" utopianism that Beaumont identifies with the state socialism of Edward Bellamy and the Fabians of the 1880s.[100] Wells's narrative reenactment of Communard struggle thus paradoxically serves to occlude the possibility that such a revolutionary orientation might gather momentum as a practical, political current during the early twentieth century.

CHAPTER 8

Conclusion

LOOKING WITHOUT SEEING

In bringing such a heterogeneous gathering of writers into dialogue, this book has not set out to delineate a positivistic, comprehensive mapping of the British response to the Commune; rather, it has aimed to elucidate the dominant patterns and striations of that response by investigating some of its major textual iterations. In this respect, the book has sought to demonstrate some of the ways in which the prospect of social revolution was perceived as a threat—sometimes amorphous and unknowable, sometimes detailed and precise—to the ruling social and cultural order during the closing decades of the nineteenth century. The scale and extent of this reaction was, paradoxically, an index of the Commune's success, at least according to the logic set out by Michelle Coghlan, which is to say that "movements provoke reaction precisely insofar as they unsettle the terms of the lived and the possible."[1] Like all defeated revolutions, the Commune retains some of its original capacity to unsettle, and this necessarily means that any traversal of its history or its representation will, whether knowingly or unknowingly, work either to renovate and repair that capacity or to contain it.

Leon Trotsky commented in the introduction to his 1925 book *Literature and Revolution*, written during the early years of the Bolshevik revolution: "Our policy in art, during a transitional period, can and must be to help the various groups and schools of art which have come over to the Revolution to grasp correctly the historic meaning of the Revolution, and to allow them complete freedom of self-determination in the field of art, after putting before them the categorical standard of being for or against the Revolution."[2] It would be churlish to claim that there were not certain writers in Britain who took up positions either "for or against" the revolution proclaimed on 18 March 1871, but it has not been the aim of this book to judge the writers discussed in it according to a version of the binary "categorical standard" that Trotsky outlines. As Peter Starr has written (with reference to the work of Henri Lefebvre), the Commune just as readily precipitated a state of confusion as it did clear-cut condemnation or endorsement.[3] The Commune, in any case, did not survive long enough for many writers to "come over" to it in any other way than belatedly, retrospectively, and commemoratively (with all the complications that this latter term involves). Many of those who did write about it, even in the realm of fiction, were more concerned to think about their relation to the historical event in spatial terms, presenting themselves (or their characters) as being either *above* or *below* the scene of revolution, either viewing it from an Olympian height or emerging into it from subterranean depths. With this in mind, it is useful to recall Theodor Adorno's aforementioned comment that "the historical moment is constitutive of artworks; authentic works are those that surrender themselves to the historical substance of their age without reservation and without the presumption of being superior to it."[4] Put simply, in the field of popular fiction, almost all of the Commune's detractors in Britain uncritically assumed a position of superiority, which assured their artistic failure in dealing with it.

Examples are plentiful. In act 4 of Alfred Austin's *The Human Tragedy*, the poem's chief protagonist, Godfrid, surveys the Communards "From the lone perch of sorrow's fearless height."[5] One of the poem's more uncharitable reviewers quipped that *The Human Tragedy* is really "a glorified three-volume novel in verse," and there is some truth in this assertion, at least insofar as Godfrid's assumed position of elevated solitude closely mirrors the spatial disposition of many of the most overtly anti-Communard novels discussed in the earlier chapters of this book.[6] Many of the protagonists seek a position of elevation from which to "enjoy the spectacle" of the Commune's defeat, as a correspondent for the *Graphic* put it when the likelihood of the Versaillais victory became clear (see figure 8.1).[7]

In the climactic chapter of Alexandra Orr's *The Twins of Saint Marcel*, titled "Paris on Fire," the protagonists assemble on the roof of their townhouse on the morning when the Versailles troops enter Paris. Their house just so happens to be "higher than those opposite": "from our attic windows we could see many of the rising grounds of the city."[8] Surveying the scene with the aid of "M. Brunel's opera glasses" leads Aurée, the first-person narrator, to exclaim: "What a spectacle! What beauty! far beyond the river we looked over a sea of fresh green foliage, ... which hiding the palaces and houses of all kinds carried the eye on to the Arc de Triomphe rising above them."[9] From this vantage point, the assembled group witnesses the impending destruction of the city at a safe distance, Aurée's vision of natural beauty acting as a momentary relief from her subsequent narration of the burning of the Ministère de Finance and the Tuileries, which causes her to weep uncontrollably. Aurée's neighbor Clémence even professes to be able to detect "fragments of burnt paintings" and "smouldering velvets," blown along the breeze, which causes Aurée to worry that "these fragments come from some of our dear pictures" in the Louvre.[10]

Figure 8.1. James Dromgole Linton, "Waiting for the End—A Sketch on the Terrace of St. Germain," *Graphic*, 3 June 1871, 512–513. Mary Evans Picture Library.

James F. Cobb frames the Bloody Week from a similar vantage point, allowing his protagonists to ascend "to the roof of the house," where "a sad but magnificent spectacle was displayed before them."[11] Cobb's narrator lists the "Tuilieries, the ex-Prefecture of Police, the Palais de Justice, and the Hôtel de Ville" among the threatened buildings and observes: "This unexampled letting loose of human fury seemed, indeed, like an outbreak from hell itself; the whistling of the shells, the roar of the cannons, the harsh grating of the *mitrailleuses*, the sharp crack of the fusillade, formed the fantastic orchestra to this most tragic, but most splendid spectacle—to this magnificent panorama of fire, of which no description can give any but the faintest idea."[12] By construing the fighting as a "most tragic, but most splendid spectacle"—splendid because of the bourgeois victory, tragic because of the threat posed to cultural and architectural monuments—Cobb asserts the primacy of a deracinated mode of aesthetic apprehension. Like spectators at the opera or visitors to an exhibition, Cobb's bourgeois protagonists can be assured that the soon-to-be-defeated revolution will not seriously upset their position as consumers of the spectacle, even if the destruction momentarily reframes their vision of the urban picturesque as a "magnificent panorama of fire."

Charles Glyn strikes a related note in John Oxenham's *Under the Iron Flail*. When the Versailles troops enter the city, he, along with three others, "spent pretty nearly all that day on the roof," where he finds himself "gazing with wonder and regret on the spectacle": "It was the strangest combination of opposites imaginable. Here on the roof we four stood as peacefully as though we had come up simply to take tea; while down below surged, and swarmed, and yelled, and screamed a nation gone mad."[13] Once again, the Commune interrupts the serene rituals of bourgeois existence, but the interruption is only momentary and made to seem less threatening in being figured as an unreasonable outburst of "maddened beasts" that "[run] amok to satisfy their own wild passions," rather than a considered, rational challenge to the dominant social order.[14] Henry Guiron, the repentant Communard in William Barry's *The Dayspring*, takes up a similar position "in a covered verandah on the roof from which nearly all Paris seemed visible" during the last days of the fighting.[15] Barry's novel offers a slight modulation of the familiar motif in that Guiron, given his former sympathies for the Commune, experiences the "spectacle" as "his own Day of Judgement," allowing Barry to present the scene as one of atonement and expiation on Guiron's part for his past "incendiary deeds."[16] Conveniently enough, the injured Guiron is attended by both a doctor and a priest, who unite to minister to the simultaneously physical and spiritual "pathology" of Guiron's communism.

Orr's *The Twins of Saint Marcel* was published in 1872, while Barry's *The Dayspring* first appeared in 1903. During the interim, several other novelists of the Commune shared their apparent desire to gain representational mastery over the defeated revolution by rising above it. Discursively speaking, this marked desire for symbolic elevation recalls the architectural strategy adopted by the French bourgeoisie in the wake of the Commune's defeat, as they attempted to reassert ideological and symbolic control over the capital. The Communards themselves had well understood the intrinsically political quality of public space; in Stewart Edwards's assessment, the Commune "was not just a ritualistic acting out of repressed desires but the active conquest of urban time and space, a restructuring of the city."[17] One of the currents in the confluence of factors that underlay the revolutionary events of 1871 was the working-class resentment that had welled up in response to Baron Haussmann's embellishment of Paris. This extensive project, a brainchild of the Emperor, involved the construction of spacious boulevards, widened streets, public parks, gardens, and numerous monuments in order to create an image of civic affluence. This remaking of the city, implemented between 1852 and 1870, was a form of social cleansing insofar as it forced working-class Parisians out of the center of the city and into the suburbs, partly with the intention of obliterating the material and architectural conditions that underlay Paris's long history of urban revolt and street insurrection.

The emergence of the Commune briefly reversed this process. As Kristin Ross writes, "The workers who occupied the Hôtel de Ville [and] who tore down the Vendôme Column were not 'at home' in the centre of Paris; they were occupying enemy territory, the circumscribed proper place of the dominant social order. Such an occupation, however brief, provides an example of . . . *détournement*— using the elements or terrain of the dominant social order to one's own ends, for a transformed purpose; integrating actual or past productions into a superior construction of milieu."[18] David Harvey has similarly remarked on the way that "buildings and monuments were deeply political symbols to Parisians" during the nineteenth century.[19] In his discussion of the prolonged construction of the Basilica of Sacré-Coeur on the heights of Montmartre in the wake of the Commune, Harvey offers a perceptive account of the Commune's repercussions for the built environment. The Basilica project, which was sponsored by the Thiers government at the behest of the new archbishop of Paris, exemplifies the symbolic usage and ideological consecration of civic space in the interest of promoting patriotic and conformist consciousness. Harvey argues that the project was undertaken with the intention of resecuring the bourgeoisie's "symbolic domination of Paris," while simultaneously effacing the lived memory of the Commune by physically renovating one of its key strongholds.[20]

The various British novelists who conclude their fictions of the Commune from a position of panoramic elevation sought to reassert bourgeois dominance in similarly spatial terms. In doing so, they recognized that the restoration of ruling-class political supremacy went together with a restoration of the antediluvian symbolic order, toward which their humble efforts made a minor contribution. As Braddon's narrator blithely puts it in *Under the Red Flag*, after the fall of the Commune, "Paris was Paris again."[21] As *novelists*, however, their widespread preoccupation with the symbolism of elevation recycled a hackneyed and almost exhausted trope. Priscilla Parkhurst Ferguson observes that "one of the most frequent strategies of [nineteenth-century] writers and tourists alike is to view the city from afar, most strikingly from a height," and this "view of the city from afar becomes a staple among topoi in the nineteenth century, an urban variant of the more general romantic taste for panoramas."[22] "The panorama," Ferguson continues, "offers one means of creating unity" and thus belongs to "a long line of utopics that allow us to identify with the city, to know it, or to feel that we do."[23] While Ferguson identifies various earlier manifestations of this utopian impulse toward unity as a "revolutionary" motif, it is clear that the novelists of the Commune discussed here fantasize a rather more exclusive, counterrevolutionary form of "unity" that relies on the prior suppression of proletarian insurrection and the attendant threat posed by such insurrectionary forces to the structural unity of the capitalist social order.[24] By converting the unrest associated with the Commune's last days into spectacular panoramas of destruction, these authors rewrite an episode of class struggle as a form of deracinated mass entertainment.

The pattern of neurotic repetition that can be detected when these novels are read together, which betrays a collective desire to master the trauma of a revolutionary challenge to the status quo, was also bound up with an orientation toward the mass market in popular fiction. As Michelle Coghlan has written with reference to the Commune's "spectacular afterlife as spectre and spectacle" in nineteenth-century America, the Commune's *"virality* as a sensation" heralded the advent of proletarian revolution as a commodified article of consumption.[25] In Walter Benjamin's terms, the popular fictions of the Commune unwittingly engage in the transformation of "the historical event itself into a mass produced article," which, in turn, renders the historical process unthinkable in a properly revolutionary sense.[26] Yet this way of novelizing the historical event of the Commune ultimately offers little more than a way of looking (from an assumed position of symbolic dominance) without really *seeing*. John Oxenham's protagonist reveals the basic contours of this quintessentially bourgeois myopia when he observes: "Terrible, horrible things were being done almost under our eyes. Their details were fortunately hidden, but what we did see fascinated us, and we did not go down even to eat."[27] One might diagnose this morbid fascination, and associated loss of appetite, as the manifestation of a uniquely bourgeois neurosis that surfaces when the essential structure of class domination that underpins bourgeois society becomes a little too visible for comfort. Yet the harder Oxenham's protagonists look ("we watched with horror, it was impossible not to watch"), the less they really see of the Versaillais's brutal implementation of class vengeance (and the *bourgeois ressentiment* that goes with it).[28] This particular way of not seeing what the Commune really meant was widely distributed throughout the popular fiction of the period, much as it might provide one possible explanation for Edward Bulwer Lytton's failure to complete *The Parisians*.

But what did the Commune really mean? Commentators of right and left—Salisbury, Ruskin, Arnold, Marx—agreed that it precipitated what Raymond Williams would think of as an "emergent" (as opposed to dominant or residual) structure of feeling, inaugurating a new and unprecedented phase in the struggle against bourgeois society organized around a forthright recognition of class antagonism.[29] For Marx, the Commune was the "initiation of the social revolution of the nineteenth century."[30] In a letter to Ludwig Kugelman, dated 17 April 1871, Marx elaborated that "whatever the immediate outcome may be, a new point of departure, of importance in world history, has been gained."[31] Given the nature of the Commune, it was difficult for those opposed to it to launch a "process of attempted incorporation" in the traditional sense, so they instead developed uncoordinated strategies of containment, with varying degrees of sophistication, and these have been the chief object of discussion in this book.[32] Among themselves, however, the surviving Communards were less certain about whether the Commune represented the inauguration of an emergent historical period or the reanimation of a past one. Gustave Paul Cluseret, the Commune's first delegate of war, argued in 1873 that the Communards' chief aim was to "finish what had been left incomplete in 1793."[33] Writing in the Socialist League's *Commonweal* journal in April 1885, Édouard Vaillant agreed: "The Commune of Paris . . . was not a separatist effort of egotistical isolation. It was on the contrary, as in 1793, the effort of revolutionary Paris to rally all the forces of the

Revolution within the nation, to take the direction of the country by all its people."[34] By contrast, the Communard artist Gustave Courbet (according to John Milner) "rejected . . . comparisons [with 1789] as inappropriate to the unique historical circumstances of his own time."[35] Likewise, the Hungarian Communard Léo Frankel argued in 1877 that "[the Commune] was a new kind of revolution with a new objective," identifying its novelty with the fact that "it was a workers' revolution."[36]

Similarly, Jacques Vingtras, the supremely irascible protagonist of Jules Vallès's *L'Insurgé*, professes, "m'est venu aussi le dédain de la défroque jacobine. / Tout ce fatras de la légende de 93 me fait l'effet du tas de guenilles effrangées et déteintes que l'on vient offrir au père Gros, le chiffonnier, dans son échoppe de la rue Mouffetard, ouverte à tous les vents" (I have grown contemptuous of Jacobin hand-me-downs. / All that shit about the legend of '93 affects me just like the faded, filthy tatters offered to old Gros, the ragman, in his shop on rue Mouffetard which the wind whistles through all day).[37] He expands on this reasoning elsewhere: "Souvent même, je plante là 89 et 93 pour me trouver simplement en face de moi, et pour suivre ma pensée" (Often I even slough off '89 and '93 to be face-to-face with myself so I can follow my thought).[38] In being open to all the winds ("ouverte à tous les vents") and following his thought wherever it leads, Vingtras diffidently asserts the novelty of the Commune, in a manner that recalls Benjamin's observation that the Commune "[dispelled] the illusion that the task of the proletarian revolution is to complete the work of 1789 hand in hand with the bourgeoisie."[39] Vallès, in Jerrold Seigel's estimation, "consistently rejected models derived from the past," especially "in his politics."[40]

By contrast, where Cluseret and Vaillant celebrate the Commune as the continuation of an earlier revolutionary tradition, their rhetorical strategy brings them into proximity with those who sought to circumscribe and contain the insurgent potential of the Commune's legacy by making it knowable as an instance of repetition, a reiteration of something that had come before. Several of the more hostile novelists of the Commune were keen to assert such historical parallels, and one relatively recent historian joins them in seeing the Commune as the French Revolution's "farewell to history."[41] One of the earliest mobilizations of this tactic is to be found in *All the Year Round*, where an unnamed correspondent concludes an 1871 article, "How Paris Mourns," by quoting a snatch from book 3 of Carlyle's *The French Revolution* on the Bals à Victime and proceeds to observe, in an allusion to Ecclesiastes, that "the thing which has been is the thing which shall be, and Paris and the Parisians have not altered a jot since then."[42]

The fact that many of the popular novelists of the Commune simultaneously found recourse to providential plots, reading providence into the workings of history, also bears on the anxiety about revolution and repetition. Faith in providence is, after all, one of the oldest manifestations of the desire for omniscience and elevation. One of the functions of the providential plot, as Peter Brooks has observed with reference to a later current of modernist writing, is to subsume individual experience "to that of mankind, to show the individual as a significant repetition of a story already endowed with meaning."[43] Such obsession with repetition is precisely what consumes Hyacinth Robinson in James's *The Princess Casamassima*, much as Wells's exploration of Graham Vane's involvement with the revolutionary movement in *When the Sleeper Wakes* turns on the Nietzschean concept of eternal return. In these texts, the desire for symbolic mastery in the wake of the Commune, absent any sense of providential security, produces instead a kind of narrative vertigo, as the protagonists cannot quite convince themselves that their experience constitutes a properly "significant repetition of a story already endowed with meaning."

Many of the popular novels discussed in this book, notably those of Braddon, Ritchie, and Barry, present young men who fall in with the revolutionary fraternity of the Commune only for their authors subsequently to extricate them, while carefully circumscribing the extent of any possible imaginative sympathy for the Commune in the manner discussed elsewhere in this book. With Hyacinth Robinson and Arthur Golding, James and Gissing, respectively, find recourse to a different kind of extrication from the prospect of sustained revolutionary commitment: namely, suicide. As was argued in chapter 5, Hyacinth's suicide marks the tragic conclusion of James's thematization of repetition in *The Princess Casamassima* as a problem that confronts both revolutionaries and novelists. Gissing, meanwhile, appears partly to have shared Marx's sense of an emergent, and therefore novel, historical conjuncture, at least insofar as he described *Workers in the Dawn*, in a letter to his brother, as a novel about "earnest young people striving for improvement in, as it were, the dawn of a new phase of civilisation."[44] For Gissing, however, it was a false dawn, and at the novel's conclusion, Arthur Golding throws himself into the Niagara Falls, making his manner of death roughly comparable to Graham Vane's more heroic demise in *When the Sleeper Wakes*. In Gissing's and Wells's narratives, the protagonists' dying moments involve a vertiginous fall from a great height. Insofar as James accentuates the tragic aspect of Hyacinth's narrative, his death might also be said to involve a fall, albeit complicated by the fact that his tragedy takes place in the figurative space of the revolutionary underground. For Hyacinth and Arthur, in particular, their contact with or proximity to revolutionary militants opens up a tragic gulf that illuminates the incommensurability of the competing claims of culture and political commitment. In these novels, the two cannot be thought together, let alone lived together.

Faced with what Kristin Ross characterizes as the Commune's democratic "transvaluation of the very idea of art and of abundance," many of the writers considered in this book responded by seeking, in a variety of ways, to cauterize the psychic wound inflicted on bourgeois subjectivity.[45] They sought to contain the challenge posed to bourgeois conceptions of culture by reasserting the sanctity of the cultural as a space of privilege and by identifying the Communards, or revolutionary commitment in general, with a nihilistic urge for destruction. In *The Dayspring*, for example, William Barry attributes the following sentiment to the Communard and Blanquist Émile Eudes: "Paris shall belong to the proletarians, or Paris shall be no more."[46] That this zero-sum logic more accurately captures the nature of the bourgeois reaction to the Commune did not seriously trouble any of those writers who projected such motivations onto the Communard revolutionaries. Barry's narrator adds: "The proletarians had been conquered; they would have their revenge," aligning Eudes's fictional remarks with the by then well-established ideologeme of *ressentiment*.[47] Eudes is just one of a number of historical Communards who make cameo appearances in Barry's novel, lending it an air of rough-and-ready historical verisimilitude. In fact, no fewer than twenty-four historical Communards either appear, sometimes very briefly, or are fleetingly mentioned in *The Dayspring*.[48] Other writers worked from a more limited palette. Kathleen's assiduous pursuit of Sérizier provides the melodramatic climax of Braddon's *Under the Red Flag*, while Max Du Parc and his mentor Caron share the company of General Dombrowski in Ritchie's *Mrs Dymond*. Ernest Durand, the fictional Communard protagonist of Francis Henry Gribble's *The Red Spell*, finds himself perturbed to discover that Charles Delescluze, the Commune's delegate for war, is more concerned to draft "inspiriting proclamations and decrees" than to organize the resistance during the Commune's last days.[49] And in Maria M. Grant's *Lescar, the Universalist*, the novel's heroine-turned-*pétroleuse*, Faustine, is last seen "riding by Raoul Regnau [sic], on the day of the proclamation of the Assembly, through the streets of Paris on a white charger," before her death during the fighting.[50]

According to Richard Maxwell, the "impression made by ... 'world-historical figures'" in much nineteenth-century historical fiction "stems largely from the limits on his, or her, appearances."[51] In the preceding examples, the popular novelists of the Commune follow these strictures, which stem from Walter Scott's advice in an 1813 letter to Richard Sainthill Jones. According to Scott, "where historical characters are introduced [into fiction] it ought only to be incidentally," and he added that they should be introduced "in such a manner as not to interfere with established truth."[52] Needless to say, in the popular historical fictions of the Commune (as is doubtless the case with all historical fiction), the authors were not abiding by an "established truth." Rather, they were contributing to the construction of a partial and ideologically motivated version of the "truth." Much of the historical romance fiction relied, in more or less explicit terms, on claims to veracity set out in contemporaneous historical writing, and the sources of particular fictionalized episodes of the Commune can be fairly easily traced to one or another of these contemporary historical accounts. As discussed in chapter 3, Ritchie explicitly invokes the authority of Maxime Du Camp, while Braddon similarly relies on Du Camp's *Les Convulsions de Paris* for an extended episode in *Under the Red Flag*. In *The Dayspring*, which was first published in 1903, Barry would have been able to make use of Thomas March's *The History of the Paris Commune of 1871* (1896), and Barry fairly clearly transposes many of the historical Communards who appear in his novel directly from the pages of March's history. March, in turn, frequently relies on citations from Du Camp, F. de la Brugère's *Histoire de la Commune de Paris en 1871* (1871), Ernest Daudet's *L'Agonie de la Commune* (1871), and Marshal Patrice de MacMahon's *L'Armée de Versailles, depuis Sa Formation jusqu'à la Complète Pacification de Paris* (1871).

To take one short example of the process of cross-fertilization between history and fiction, Victor Bénot and the relatively unknown Colonel Boursier appear very briefly in Barry's novel in a passage that closely follows March's narration of their alleged burning of the Palais Royale and the Imperial Library, situated in buildings adjoining the Louvre, and March directs readers to citations from De la Brugère and Du Camp.[53] Various other episodes in the novel offer up similar parallels, and such comparisons could easily be multiplied to encompass other novels. The crossover between fiction and history is also observable in the number of war correspondents (G. A. Henty, William Westall, Henry Kingsley) who turned their firsthand experience of the Franco-Prussian War and the Commune into fiction. Barry, who happened to be a Catholic priest, presumably imagined he was making recourse to what Scott might have regarded as the "established truth" about the Commune, drawn from historical sources, but as the historian March occasionally discovered in his own assiduous comparison of such sources, the truth could be rather slippery. In one particularly revealing footnote, March notices that Marshal MacMahon's account of the reoccupation of Père Lachaise differs substantially from that given by Du Camp and he remarks rather limply: "It is impossible to reconcile the two accounts, and unfortunately there are no other authorities to appeal to," since "not one of the authorities, Communist or other, was present at the Père Lachaise at the time, and therefore all accounts are equally dependent upon second-hand testimony."[54] March appears not to have been overly perturbed by the methodological problems posed by this crux, as he is elsewhere willing to treat both MacMahon *and* Du Camp as wholly reliable authorities whose anti-Communard word ought to be taken at face value. Yet as various narrative vignettes about particular Communards made their way from the "authoritative" accounts into the historical romance narratives of popular novelists, these authors allowed the patina of historical verisimilitude to continue the work of reinscribing an ideological construction of the event itself.

This mutual implication of history in fiction and fiction in history links these two modes of historical narration as a site of political contestation. March is no less forthright than Barry concerning his anxiety about repetition and the prospects of recurrence. Barry's narrator explains: "It is necessary that we should know [Emile Vaillant's] thought, for it lives on."[55] March, meanwhile, explains in his introduction: "To the Governments of every civilized country [the] Commune is an object-lesson which cannot, or at least should not, be lost sight of, for the human passions and aspirations which found expression then are still in existence, and may again, under different guises, make manifest their depth and power."[56] In framing his narrative in this way, March lays bare the ideological stakes of his decision to retell the Commune's story, over two decades after its defeat. Much like the authors of historical romance, he promises a narrative replete with "incidents . . . of thrilling interest."[57] Yet his mode of narration, which relies on the studious marshaling of "facts" culled from elsewhere, precludes any real attempt on his part to investigate "the human passions and aspirations" that he proclaims to be at the root of the matter. By the end of the book, March simply reduces the Communards to "ill-natured children" and "animals."[58] While many of the popular fictions of the Commune frequently echo such rhetoric, they also partially complexify it by offering up individuated narratives of entirely fictional (and ultimately repentant) Communard partisans. In doing so, these writers delineate the terms of a dangerous sympathy with the revolutionary motivations of the Commune, thereby enabling them to adopt a relatively more nuanced view of the "human passions and aspirations" that underpinned it. The very fictionality of these Communards allowed for an extension of imaginative sympathy that was more difficult to accomplish in unambiguously historical writing, where different pressures had to be negotiated. Even as they extend a reactionary repudiation of the Commune, some of these novels simultaneously explore the parameters of a more liberal sensibility that seeks to understand, rather than castigate, while nonetheless remaining several steps short of endorsement.

The limits of that liberal sensibility are not hard to identify. It is useful to recall, at this point, Fredric Jameson's highly illuminating discussion of the historical novel, a genre born in the crucible of revolution. Jameson observes, "the moment of revolution—the absolute Event, so to speak—is always a matter of absolute dichotomization: whatever happens later on, the 'lyric illusion' is always the moment in which everyone has to take sides, for or against, and . . . this stark simplification then poses unique dilemmas for narrative representation."[59] The pressure of this "absolute dichotomization," Jameson continues, often "leads . . . to a kind of allegorical treatment unsuitable to the novel as a form and [presents] impossible obstacles for any genuinely novelistic narration," hence the frequent recourse of so many popular novelists of the Commune to the representational calculus of melodrama, with its (bourgeois) heroes and (Communard) villains.[60] In the case of William Barry, a novelist who tries harder than most to extend the fullest possible imaginative sympathy to his Communard protagonist, the pressure to "take sides" (in Jameson's sense) nonetheless reappears in drastic fashion at the novel's conclusion, which offers up a profoundly ideological exculpation of Adolphe Thiers by allowing him to grant a strictly one-off pardon to Henry Guiron, at the behest of Guiron's priest (Barry was a priest, one might recall): "You, at least, can say that Adolphe Thiers was no blood-drinker," as the fictionalized Thiers puts it (in the third person) with a rather unconvincing air of jocular bonhomie.[61]

Henry James, meanwhile, explained his avoidance of the genre of the historical novel by setting out a frank account of its perceived aesthetic limitations. As he argued in a letter to the American novelist Sarah Orne Jewett, dated 5 October 1905,

> The "historical novel" is, for me, condemned... to a fatal *cheapness*, for the simple reason that the difficulty of the job is inordinate.... You may multiply the little facts that can be got from pictures and documents, relics and prints, as much as you like—*the* real thing is almost impossible to do, and in its essence the whole effect is as nought: I mean the invention, the representation of the old CONSCIOUSNESS, the soul, the sense, the horizon, the vision of individuals in whose minds half the things that make ours, that make the modern world were non-existent.[62]

Even though there was no great gulf of time between the advent of the Commune and the subsequent appearance of numerous popular novels that worked the Commune into fiction, James's remarks about "fatal *cheapness*" could be applied, without too much trouble, to most of the historical romances discussed in this book. Jameson makes it possible to historicize James's intuitive sense of the failure of the late nineteenth-century historical novel in offering a timely reminder that it was "historically a narrative form generated by the passage from the old [feudal] order to a bourgeois society, as well as the representation of that historical passage."[63] He goes on to question "whether the historical novel... can function as a useful generic category for novels which issue from and represent wholly different kinds of historical convulsions."[64] In this respect, the failure of the historical novel, as such, to meet the challenge of the Commune, especially given its own history as a genre intimately bound up with the process of late eighteenth- to mid-nineteenth-century bourgeois revolution, constitutes a broader kind of looking without seeing: very many fin-de-siècle novelists addressed themselves to the Commune, but very few can be said to have understood it. To proffer such an analysis in the first place, however, must surely depend on whether one regards the Commune as a fundamentally unprecedented *kind* of historical convulsion or whether one instead sees it as a repetition of a familiar pattern.

Careful readers of this book will already have noticed that there is, ultimately, no "great" historical novel of the Commune among the texts discussed here.

Leaving aside Zola's *La Débâcle* (1892) as a possible exception, it is not the purpose of this book to argue that there is such a novel. Reading James's intuitive supposition alongside Jameson's theoretical reflections offers one possible explanation for this situation, which, after all, relates only to a relatively minor episode in literary history. But the fact that it is only a minor episode in *literary* history discloses something potentially more significant about the nature of the relationship between literature and social revolution, at least insofar as the institution of literature (in its current iteration) derives so much of its status, such as it is or once was, from the very social and economic dispensation that the revolutionary process would seek to transform. James's own exploration of the prospects for social revolution, as inaugurated by the Commune, shuns the gaudy multiplication of "little facts" in favor of a considerably more complex attempt to discover the "real thing." Yet even as James self-consciously avoids the popular genre of historical fiction in his novelistic engagement with the Commune, he, like Gissing, runs up against the limits of form, for the novel, as Franco Moretti explains, "exists not as a critique, but as a *culture of everyday life*," and it is "an *a priori* condition of this 'symbolic form'" that "the significance of history does not lie in the 'future of the species,' but must be revealed within the more narrow confines of a circumscribed and relatively common individual life."[65] This is part of the reason, Moretti goes on to suggest, why the classical bildungsroman reveals a fundamental "incompatibility between the novelistic world and revolutionary crisis, as the latter indicates the moment when the great superindividual forces, in addition to being 'inevitable,' become irresistible: heedlessly tearing to shreds all the plots, all the networks that had been so carefully woven."[66] Even as James consciously exploits this incompatibility in Hyacinth's narrative of failed *bildung*, he remains, ultimately, too resistant to the idea that revolutionary energies might be allowed to tear up his own carefully woven plots to be able to discover the "real thing" of revolution.

In contrast to Moretti's account of the bildungsroman, Jameson's discussion of the historical novel strikes a slightly different note: "The historical novel as a genre cannot exist without [the] dimension of collectivity, which marks the drama of the incorporation of individual characters into a greater totality, and can alone certify the presence of History as such. Without this collective dimension, history, one is tempted to say, is again reduced to mere conspiracy, the form it takes in novels which have aimed for historical content without historical consciousness and which remain therefore merely political in some more specialized sense."[67] At the risk of overextending Jameson's argument, one might observe that James's evident fascination with "mere conspiracy" in *The Princess Casamassima*—which both echoes and aesthetically elevates the discourse of conspiracy on display in any number of popular novels of the Commune (from Bulwer to Braddon and beyond)—went together with an obvious rejection of the "dimension of collectivity." Hyacinth Robinson's tragedy is, as was argued in chapter 5, a fundamentally private affair, which loosely identifies the novel as an abortive bildungsroman. In this regard, one might say that *The Princess Casamassima* does not fail *as a novel* (in the way that James thought the historical novel condemned to failure); rather, it fails to represent the "real thing" of social revolution precisely insofar as it reduces history to "mere conspiracy" and figures forth its "historical content without historical consciousness." This is not to make James culpable for such a failure (if that is what it should be called): on the contrary, in brushing up against the limits of novelistic form, he in fact makes it possible to discern the lineaments of a properly structural problem, thereby snatching a different kind of victory from the jaws of defeat. Contemporary ecocritics recognize a similar problem when they point to the realist novel's intrinsic incapacity to reckon with the scale of the civilizational danger posed by climate change. Wells, on the other hand, moved in a different generic direction in his early experiments with scientific romance; as discussed in chapter 7, in *When the Sleeper Wakes*, Wells adumbrates the emergence of a certain undecidability vis-à-vis the role of human agency in history that will later come to be associated with modernist poetics and practices of reading, frequently organized around the repression of politics and an open-ended multiplicity in the choice of interpretations, as set against the pressure to "take sides" (which is not to say that there were not also modernists who took sides).

In different ways, all of the writers considered in this book beg a still more challenging question about the capacity of literature, both as an institution and as a mode of apprehension frequently bound up with an aesthetic disposition, to achieve an accurately textured and fully "realistic" representation of revolutionary motivation and practice. This, in turn, will have far-reaching consequences for how readers (and critics) who lack the concrete experience of a revolutionary conjuncture might interpret and apprehend such motivations and practices, but I do not propose to open that question here. It is, of course, somewhat unfashionable to write about "revolutionary practice" today, at least insofar as such reflections continue, however implicitly, to pose the prospect of social revolution as a live problem.[68] Those who would cavil about such matters need only ask themselves some simple questions: Can one really be confident that one's preferred mode of social organization (which usually amounts to a more or less modified version of the status quo of capitalist realism) will persist in its basic contours for the next twenty-five to thirty years? If not, what will take its place? These rhetorical questions—which invite moderates of all stripes to scrutinize the confidence of their convictions at a time of intensifying ideological polarization, passionate intensities, and widespread civil unrest—will doubtless appear as naïve hostages to fortune, but they are not intended as a predictive statement. They are, rather, an attempt drastically to simplify, and thereby to approximate and reanimate, the questions that the Commune posed to those contemporary observers in Britain who identified, in one way or another, with the dominant liberal structure of feeling, often from a position of quite fragile superiority. The very fact of the Commune's working existence, albeit short-lived, forced such observers to confront the real possibility of social revolution, which, in however minimal a fashion, disturbed a whole set of psychic, cultural, and intellectual investments in the status quo. This book has sought to tell the story of that disturbance as it affected the literary culture of late-Victorian Britain.

Acknowledgments

In the course of writing this book, I have received support of various kinds from many different people, too numerous to mention here. I would, however, like to set out some brief acknowledgments. During the early stages of my research, Scott McCracken, Jo McDonagh, Drew Milne, Sara Thornton, Catherine Maxwell, and Sophie Gilmartin all offered helpful suggestions and advice. I am also particularly grateful to Matthew Beaumont and Florence S. Boos, both of whom kindly read sections of the manuscript in draft and offered characteristically insightful and incisive comments that improved the final version of the book, as did the comments of the anonymous readers at Rutgers University Press, as well as those of the series editor, Kristin Ross. As is customary, but no less true for being customary, I should remind readers that I remain solely responsible for any errors.

Along the way, various conversations with Matthew Ingleby, Ed Birch, Luke Roberts, David Grundy, Michelle Coghlan, and Joe Davidson proved to be sources of stimulation and encouragement, and I am doubly thankful to Matthew for inviting me to present an earlier version of chapter 2 at the London Nineteenth-Century Studies seminar. Similarly, I am obliged to Frankie Hines and David Cunningham for an invitation to present a working draft of chapter 4 at Westminster's departmental research seminar in English literature and cultural studies. Both occasions helped me to consolidate a sense of the book's overall trajectory and to refine some of its arguments. A travel grant from Jesus College, Oxford, allowed me to undertake research trips to visit the Eugene W. Schulkind Paris Commune Collection at the University of Sussex and the Siege and Commune Special Collection at Northwestern University, and I am particularly grateful to Jason Nargis at Northwestern for his assistance and warm reception. I would also like to thank David Southern, at Duke University Press, for his assistance in making available an otherwise elusive volume of Thomas Carlyle's correspondence during the coronavirus lockdown.

An earlier version of chapter 7 was published as "'It Had to Come Back': The Paris Commune and H. G. Wells's *When the Sleeper Wakes*," in *ELH* 86, no. 2 (2019): 525–554, and I am thankful to the journal's anonymous readers who offered some timely and helpful comments.

At Rutgers University Press, it has been a pleasure to work with Micah Kleit and Elisabeth Maselli. I am also particularly grateful to Kristin Ross, both for her invitation to publish the book under the auspices of this series and for her support and encouragement during the writing process. Her various books on the Commune have long been a source of tremendous intellectual stimulation, and I struggle to imagine how this book would have taken shape without the benefit of these works.

Lastly, my deepest gratitude is reserved for my *sýntrofos*, Eva Nanopoulos, for her boundless patience and intellectual companionship throughout the period in which I wrote this book.

Notes

PREFACE

1. Raymond Williams, *The Long Revolution*, 3rd ed. (Harmondsworth, UK: Pelican, 1971), 10.
2. Eugene Schulkind, *The Paris Commune of 1871* (London: Historical Association, 1971), 10.
3. Walter Crane, "In Memory of the Commune of Paris: Born March 18, 1871, Died in June the Same Year," *Black and White* 1, no. 9 (4 April 1891): 274.
4. Thomas March, *The History of the Paris Commune of 1871* (London: Swan Sonnenschein, 1896), 1.
5. Robert H. Sherard, *Oscar Wilde: The Story of an Unhappy Friendship* (London: Greening, 1905), 35. Deaglán Ó Donghaile aptly comments that "the ruin symbolised for Wilde the recent history of urban insurgency, its ruin etching the story of political insurrection and its 'symbolic form' into the very materiality of the city." Ó Donghaile, *Oscar Wilde and the Radical Politics of the Fin de Siècle* (Edinburgh: Edinburgh University Press, 2020), 174.
6. See Perry Anderson, "Origins of the Present Crisis," in *English Questions* (London: Verso, 1992), 15–47. Anderson developed these ideas in collaboration with Tom Nairn in a series of articles for the *New Left Review*. For a concise account of the Nairn-Anderson thesis, see Ellen Meiksins Wood, *The Pristine Culture of Capitalism: A Historical Essay on Old Regimes and Modern States*, 2nd ed. (London: Verso, 2015), 11–17.
7. Perry Anderson, "Components of the National Culture," in *English Questions*, 97.
8. See Chris Baldick, *The Social Mission of English Criticism, 1848–1932* (Oxford, UK: Clarendon, 1983).
9. Adolphe Smith, "Political Refugees," in *London in the Nineteenth Century*, by Walter Besant (London: Adam and Charles Black, 1909), 399.
10. See Matthew Beaumont, *Utopia Ltd.: Ideologies of Social Dreaming in England, 1870–1900*, 2nd ed. (Chicago: Haymarket, 2009), 134–140.
11. Algernon Charles Swinburne to William Michael Rossetti, 1 June 1871, in *The Swinburne Letters*, ed. Cecil Y. Lang, 6 vols. (New Haven, CT: Yale University Press, 1959–1962),

2:146. See Jacques Rancière, *Hatred of Democracy*, trans. Steve Corcoran, 3rd ed. (London: Verso, 2014).

12. See Schulkind, *Paris Commune of 1871*; Stewart Edwards, *The Paris Commune, 1871* (London: Eyre and Spottiswoode, 1971); Jacques Rougerie, *Paris Libre, 1871* (Paris: Éditions du Seuil, 1971); Jacques Rougerie, *La Commune, 1871* (Paris: Presses Universitaires de France, 1988); Jacques Rougerie, *Paris Insurgé: La Commune de 1871* (Paris: Gallimard, 1995); Alain Dalotel, Alaine Faure, and Jean-Claude Freiermuth, *Aux Origines de la Commune: Le Mouvement des Réunions Publiques à Paris, 1868–1871* (Paris: Maspero, 1980); Robert Tombs, *The War against Paris, 1871* (Cambridge: Cambridge University Press, 1981); Robert Tombs, *The Paris Commune, 1871*, 2nd ed. (London: Routledge, 1999); Gay L. Gullickson, *Unruly Women of Paris: Images of the Commune* (Ithaca, NY: Cornell University Press, 1996); Martin Phillip Johnson, *The Paradise of Association: Political Culture and Popular Organization in the Paris Commune of 1871* (Ann Arbor: University of Michigan Press, 1996); Carolyn J. Eichner, *Surmounting the Barricades: Women in the Paris Commune* (Bloomington: Indiana University Press, 2004); John M. Merriman, *Massacre: The Life and Death of the Paris Commune of 1871* (New Haven, CT: Yale University Press, 2014).

13. Kristin Ross, *The Emergence of Social Space: Rimbaud and the Paris Commune*, 2nd ed. (London: Verso, 2008); Peter Starr, *Commemorating Trauma: The Paris Commune and Its Cultural Aftermath* (New York: Fordham University Press, 2006); Colette E. Wilson, *Paris and the Commune, 1871–78: The Politics of Forgetting* (Manchester, UK: Manchester University Press, 2007); Philip M. Katz, *From Appomattox to Montmartre: Americans and the Paris Commune* (Harvard: Harvard University Press, 1998); J. Michelle Coghlan, *Sensational Internationalism: The Paris Commune and the Remapping of American Memory in the Long Nineteenth Century* (Edinburgh: Edinburgh University Press, 2016). See also Karine Varley, *Under the Shadow of Defeat: The War of 1870–71 in French Memory* (Basingstoke, UK: Palgrave, 2008).

14. Beaumont, *Utopia Ltd.*, 129–168.

15. Matthew Beaumont, "A Communion of Just Men Made Perfect: Walter Pater, Romantic Anti-Capitalism and the Paris Commune," in *Renew Marxist Art History*, ed. Warren Carter, Barnaby Haran, and Frederic J. Schwartz (London: Art Books, 2013), 103; Scott McCracken, "The Author as Arsonist: Henry James and the Paris Commune," *Modernism/Modernity* 21, no. 1 (January 2014): 73.

16. Albert Boime, *Art and the French Commune: Imagining Paris after War and Revolution* (Princeton, NJ: Princeton University Press, 1995); Gonzalo J. Sánchez, *Organizing Independence: The Artists Federation of the Paris Commune and Its Legacy, 1871–1889* (Lincoln: University of Nebraska Press, 1997); John Milner, *Art, War and Revolution in France, 1870–1871: Myth, Reportage and Reality* (New Haven, CT: Yale University Press, 2000); Bertrand Tillier, *La Commune de Paris, Révolution sans Images? Politique et Représentations dans la France Républicaine (1871–1914)* (Seyssel, France: Champ Vallon, 2004); Adrian Rifkin, *Communards and Other Cultural Histories: Essays by Adrian Rifkin*, ed. Steve Edwards (Leiden, Netherlands: Brill, 2016); Julia Nicholls, *Revolutionary Thought after the Paris Commune, 1871–1885* (Cambridge: Cambridge University Press, 2019).

CHAPTER 1 — INTRODUCTION

1. Edmund Gosse, "Tennyson," *New Review* 7, no. 42 (November 1892): 520–521.

2. For a classic study of this period in literary history, see John Carey, *The Intellectuals and the Masses: Pride and Prejudice among the Literary Intelligentsia, 1880–1939* (London:

Faber and Faber, 1992). For discussion of the explicitly anticommunist politics of some modernists, see also David Ayers, *Modernism, Internationalism and the Russian Revolution* (Edinburgh: Edinburgh University Press, 2018), 201–203.

3. Gosse, "Tennyson," 517.

4. Gosse, 518.

5. Gosse, 520.

6. Edmund Gosse, "The Influence of Democracy on Literature," *Contemporary Review* 59 (April 1891): 523–524. Gosse reprinted both essays in his 1893 volume of essays *Questions at Issue* (London: William Heinemann, 1893), in which his Tennyson obituary appears under the title "Tennyson—and After."

7. Gosse, "Influence," 524.

8. John Leighton, *Paris under the Commune; or, The Seventy-Three Days of the Second Siege*, 3rd ed. (London: Bradbury, Evans, 1871), 372.

9. Karl Marx, "First Draft of 'The Civil War in France,'" in *Political Writings*, vol. 3, *The First International and After*, ed. David Fernbach (Harmondsworth, UK: Penguin, 1992), 249.

10. Jürgen Osterhammel, *The Transformation of the World: A Global History of the Nineteenth Century*, trans. Patrick Camiller (Princeton, NJ: Princeton University Press, 2014), 135. For a fuller discussion, see Alice Bullard, *Exile to Paradise: Savagery and Civilization in Paris and the South Pacific, 1790–1900* (Stanford, CA: Stanford University Press, 2000).

11. Thomas C. Jones and Robert Tombs, "The French Left in Exile: *Quarante-huitards* and Communards in London, 1848–80," in *A History of the French in London: Liberty, Equality, Opportunity*, ed. Debra Kelly and Martyn Cornick (London: Institute of Historical Research, 2013), 169.

12. Eric Hobsbawm, *The Age of Empire, 1875–1914*, new ed. (London: Abacus, 2010), 84.

13. Priscilla Parkhurst Ferguson, *Paris as Revolution: Writing the Nineteenth-Century City* (Berkeley: University of California Press, 1994), 188.

14. George Moore, *Confessions of a Young Man* (London: Swan Sonnenschein, Lowrey, 1888), 158.

15. Friedrich Nietzsche, *The Works of Friedrich Nietzsche*, vol. 10, *A Genealogy of Morals*, ed. Alexander Tille, trans. William A. Haussmann (London: Macmillan, 1897), 26. For Gosse's interest in Nietzsche, see Rachel Potter, *Modernism and Democracy: Literary Culture, 1900–1930* (Oxford: Oxford University Press, 2006), 28; and M. E. Humble, "Early British Interest in Nietzsche," *German Life and Letters* 24, no. 4 (July 1971): 329.

16. Robert C. Holub, *Nietzsche in the Nineteenth Century: Social Questions and Philosophical Interventions* (Philadelphia: University of Pennsylvania Press, 2018), 140. Holub suggests that the Commune represented for Nietzsche "an indication of the decline in European man, the destruction of what is valuable and worth preserving in past human experience" (142). For discussion of Nietzsche's aristocratic dread of the Commune, as expressed in *The Birth of Tragedy*, and his general hostility to the idea of working-class self-emancipation, see Marc Sautet, *Nietzsche et la Commune* (Paris: Le Sycomore, 1981); and Dominic Losurdo, *Nietzsche, the Aristocratic Rebel: Intellectual Biography and Critical Balance-Sheet*, trans. Gregor Benton (Leiden, Netherlands: Brill, 2019), 26–30. See also Nancy S. Love, *Marx, Nietzsche, and Modernity* (New York: Columbia University Press, 1986), 141, 164–166.

17. Jacques Rancière, *Hatred of Democracy*, trans. Steve Corcoran, 3rd ed. (London: Verso, 2014), 68.

18. Eleanor Marx, "March 18: The Paris Commune—A Letter of Eleanor Marx" (17 March 1893), *Labour Monthly* 22, no. 3 (March 1940): 158.

19. See Kristin Ross, *Communal Luxury: The Political Imaginary of the Paris Commune* (London: Verso, 2015), 58.

20. Ross, 58.

21. Ross, 6.

22. Ross, 6.

23. Gosse, "Influence," 527.

24. K. Marx, "The Civil War in France: Address of the General Council," in *Political Writings*, vol. 3, *The First International and After*, ed. David Fernbach (Harmondsworth, UK: Penguin, 1992), 214.

25. Gosse, "Influence," 529.

26. Gosse, 529.

27. Karl Marx, "The Class Struggles in France: 1848 to 1850," in *Surveys from Exile: Political Writings*, vol. 2, ed. David Fernbach (Harmondsworth, UK: Penguin, 1992), 131.

28. Algernon Charles Swinburne, *The Letters of Algernon Charles Swinburne*, ed. Edmund Gosse and Thomas James Wise, 2 vols. (London: William Heinemann, 1918), 1:xiii.

29. Algernon Charles Swinburne to William Michael Rossetti, 1 June 1871, in *Letters of Algernon Charles Swinburne*, 1:94. For the standard critical edition of Swinburne's letters, see *The Swinburne Letters*, ed. Cecil Y. Lang, 6 vols. (New Haven, CT: Yale University Press, 1959–1962), 2:146.

30. Swinburne to Rossetti, in *Swinburne Letters*, 2:146–147.

31. For discussion of "the fundamental problem of choice of evidence" in relation to the Commune, see Eugene Schulkind, *The Paris Commune of 1871* (London: Historical Association, 1971), 7–8. For a brief overview of the Commune's heavily contested historiography, see David A. Shafer, *The Paris Commune: French Politics, Culture, and Society at the Crossroads of the Revolutionary Tradition and Revolutionary Socialism* (New York: Palgrave Macmillan, 2005), 111–118.

32. Gay L. Gullickson, *Unruly Women of Paris: Images of the Commune* (Ithaca, NY: Cornell University Press, 1996), 2.

33. Pascale Casanova, *The World Republic of Letters*, trans. M. B. DeBevoise (Cambridge, MA: Harvard University Press, 2004), 24.

34. For Giorgio Agamben's elucidation of the concept of "bare life" as the "original—if concealed—nucleus of sovereign power," see Agamben, *Homo Sacer: Sovereign Power and Bare Life*, trans. Daniel Heller-Roazen (Stanford, CA: Stanford University Press, 1998), 6.

35. Théophile Gautier, *The Works of Théophile Gautier*, ed. and trans. F. C. de Sumichrast, 12 vols. (New York: International Publishing, 1900–1903), 10:352–353. Edmond de Goncourt was similarly worried about the Venus de Milo, commenting in his journal on 18 April 1871, "it is thought that [the Communard artist Gustave] Courbet is on her track, and the silly employees [of the Louvre] fear the worst if the fanatical modernist lays his hands on the classical masterpiece." Edmond de Goncourt and Jules de Goncourt, *Pages from the Goncourt Journal*, ed. and trans. Robert Baldick (Oxford: Oxford University Press, 1988), 186. John M. Merriman, a historian of the Commune, writes that the Commune's Federation of Artists was, in fact, deeply "concerned with protecting the artistic treasures of the Louvre from being damaged by Versaillais shells." Merriman,

Massacre: The Life and Death of the Paris Commune of 1871 (New Haven, CT: Yale University Press, 2014), 69.

36. Casanova, *World Republic of Letters*, 29.

37. Marx, "Civil War in France: Address of the General Council," 228.

38. Goncourt and Goncourt, *Pages from the Goncourt Journal*, 194.

39. Casanova, *World Republic of Letters*, 24.

40. Casanova, 24.

41. Casanova, 24.

42. Raymond Williams, "The Bloomsbury Fraction," in *Problems in Materialism and Culture: Selected Essays* (London: Verso, 1980), 158. For a fuller discussion of the Pre-Raphaelite Brotherhood's status as an artistic vanguard in Victorian Britain, see Wendy Graham, *Critics, Coteries, and Pre-Raphaelite Celebrity* (New York: Columbia University Press, 2017), chap. 1.

43. Dante Gabriel Rossetti to William Bell Scott, 2 October 1871, in *The Correspondence of Dante Gabriel Rossetti*, ed. William E. Fredeman, Roger C. Lewis, and Jane Cowan, 10 vols. (Cambridge, UK: D. S. Brewer, 2002–2015), 5:165. An account of the "Red Benevolent Society," written by "an English Officer under the Commune," was published in the pages of the *Pall Mall Gazette* on 18 September 1871. See "The Communists in London," *Pall Mall Gazette* 14, no. 2058 (18 September 1871): 3.

44. Dante Gabriel Rossetti to John Lucas Tupper, 16 December 1871, in *Correspondence*, 5:205. The editors speculate that the Leverdays in question "may have been ... a relative of Emile Leverdays (1835–1890) who published a number of political pamphlets in 1870 and was part of the Commune movement in 1871" (5:205). It appears more likely that it was, in fact, Émile Leverdays himself, whose role in the Commune was minimal but who followed many of his comrades into exile.

45. "Nécrologie," *Le Radical*, 12 September 1890, n.p. [2].

46. W. M. Rossetti, *The Diary of W. M. Rossetti*, ed. Odette Bornand (Oxford: Oxford University Press, 1977), 256–257. In a letter to Walt Whitman, thanking Whitman for sending his "fine verses on the Parisian catastrophes," Rossetti elaborated on his support for the Commune, writing: "My own sympathy (unlike that of most Englishmen) was very strongly with the Commune—i.e. with extreme, democratic, and progressive republicanism." W. M. Rossetti to Walt Whitman, 9 July 1871, in *Selected Letters of William Michael Rossetti*, ed. Roger W. Peattie (University Park and London: Pennsylvania State University Press, 1990), 274.

47. Dante Gabriel Rossetti to Ford Madox Brown, 30 January 1873, in *Correspondence*, 6:51.

48. See Angela Thirlwell, *Into the Frame: The Four Loves of Ford Madox Brown* (London: Chatto and Windus, 2010), 100.

49. Justin McCarthy, *Reminiscences*, 2 vols (London: Chatto and Windus, 1899), 1:315.

50. William Holman Hunt, *Pre-Raphaelitism and the Pre-Raphaelite Brotherhood*, 2 vols. (London: Macmillan, 1905), 2:314.

51. See Jules Andrieu, "The Paris Commune: A Chapter towards Its Theory and History," *Fortnightly Review* 10, no. 59 (November 1871): 571–598. For the English Positivists' defense of the Commune, see Royden Harrison, ed., *The English Defence of the Commune 1871* (London: Merlin, 1971).

52. Andrieu, "Paris Commune," 573. For a study of Andrieu's libertarian political thought and orientation, see Maximilien Rubel's introduction in *Notes pour Servir à*

l'Histoire de la Commune de Paris en 1871, by Jules Andrieu, ed. Maximilien Rubel, 7–40 (Paris: Payot, 1971).

53. Walter Crane, *An Artist's Reminiscences* (London: Methuen, [1907]), 106.

54. General Cluseret, "The Paris Commune of 1871: Its Origin, Legitimacy, Tendency, and Aim," *Fraser's Magazine* 7, no. 39 (March 1873): 360.

55. Paschal Grousset, "How the Paris Commune Made the Republic," *Time: A Monthly Miscellany of Interesting and Amusing Literature* 1 (April 1879): 106.

56. Jules Vallès, "Quatrevingt-Treize," *Examiner* 3449 (7 March 1874): 237.

57. Régamey's work as an illustrator is discussed at more length in chapter 2; Louise Michel, "The Strike: A Drama," *Commonweal: A Revolutionary Journal of Anarchist Communism* 7, no. 281 (19 September 1891): 113; 7, no. 282 (26 September 1891): 117–118; 7, no. 283 (3 October 1891): 121–122; 7, no. 284 (10 October 1891): 125; 7, no. 287 (31 October 1891): 137–139; 7, no. 292 (5 December 1891): 157–158; 7, no. 293 (12 December 1891): 161.

58. For discussion of Vermersch's journal, see Scott McCracken, "The Commune in Exile: Urban Insurrection and the Production of International Space," in *Nineteenth-Century Radical Traditions*, ed. Joseph Bristow and Josephine McDonagh (Basingstoke, UK: Palgrave, 2016), 126.

59. Édouard Vaillant, "Vive la Commune!," *Commonweal* 1, no. 3 (April 1885): 17.

60. Vaillant, 17.

61. William Morris, *Journalism: Contributions to "Commonweal," 1885–1890*, ed. Nicholas Salmon (Bristol, UK: Thoemmes, 1996), 549.

62. Julia Nicholls, *Revolutionary Thought after the Paris Commune, 1871–1885* (Cambridge: Cambridge University Press, 2019), 2.

63. Ross, *Communal Luxury*, 102.

64. Matthew Arnold to Mary Penrose Arnold, 20 March 1871, in *The Letters of Matthew Arnold*, ed. Cecil Y. Lang, 6 vols. (Charlottesville: University of Virginia Press, 1996–2002), 4:25.

65. Matthew Arnold to Mary Penrose Arnold, 31 May 1871, in *Letters*, 4:37.

66. Thomas Carlyle to John Carlyle, 29 May 1871, in *The Collected Letters of Thomas and Jane Welsh Carlyle*, ed. Ian Campbell, Aileen Christianson, and David Sorensen, 48 vols. (Durham, NC: Duke University Press, 1970–2020), 47:208–209.

67. John Ruskin, "Letter 7: Charitas," 1 July 1871, *Fors Clavigera*, in *The Works of John Ruskin*, ed. E. T. Cook and Alexander Wedderburn, 39 vols. (London: George Allen, 1903–1912), 27:127.

68. George Eliot to Alexander Main, 14 November 1872, in *The George Eliot Letters*, ed. Gordon S. Haight, 9 vols. (London: Oxford University Press, 1954–1978), 5:326.

69. [Lord Salisbury], "The Commune and the Internationale," *Quarterly Review* 131, no. 262 (October 1871): 550.

70. Peter Keating, *The Haunted Study: A Social History of the English Novel, 1875–1914*, 2nd ed. (London: Fontana, 1991), 352.

71. For a compelling account of how "Victorian writers of both fiction and history were intensely pre-occupied with the question of how—and whether—the recent past could be written into the national historical narrative" and related anxieties about "multiplicity" in the writing of history, see Helen Kingstone, *Victorian Narratives of the Recent Past: Memory, History, Fiction* (Basingstoke, UK: Palgrave, 2018), 14.

72. See Jonathan Nield, *A Guide to the Best Historical Novels and Tales* (London: Elkin Matthews, 1902), 88–89; Ernest Albert Baker, *A Guide to Historical Fiction* (London:

NOTES TO PAGES 14–19

George Routledge, 1914), 292–297. Baker's main focus falls on English and French novels of the Franco-Prussian War, and he excludes most of the female authors included in the list, probably on the (shaky) grounds that he regarded their efforts as a form of "sensation" fiction, rather than historical novels proper.

73. Keating, *Haunted Study*, 353.

74. Keating, 355–356.

75. John Oxenham, *Under the Iron Flail* (London: Cassell, 1905), 287. The chapter titles belong to James F. Cobb, Alexandra Orr, and Oxenham, respectively. John Oxenham was a pseudonym used by the journalist William Arthur Dunkerley.

76. In this sense, these novels offer minor variations on a major theme of Victorian fiction that is intimately bound up with the disavowal of any revolutionary challenge to private property. For a thoroughgoing discussion of the centrality of property to Victorian fiction, see Jeff Nunokawa, *The Afterlife of Property: Domestic Security and the Victorian Novel* (Princeton, NJ: Princeton University Press, 1994).

77. Peter Brooks, *Reading for the Plot: Design and Intention in Narrative*, new ed. (Cambridge, MA: Harvard University Press, 1992), 6–7. For a fuller account of the uses of providence in Victorian fiction, see Thomas Vargish, *The Providential Aesthetic in Victorian Fiction* (Charlottesville: University of Virginia Press, 1985).

78. Edward Bulwer Lytton, *The Parisians*, 2 vols (London: Routledge, 1878), 2:354.

79. James F. Cobb, *Workman and Soldier: A Tale of Paris Life during the Siege and the Rule of the Commune* (London: Griffith and Farran, 1880), 300–301; Oxenham, *Under the Iron Flail*, 355.

80. Fredric Jameson, *The Political Unconscious: Narrative as a Socially Symbolic Act*, new ed. (London: Routledge, 2002), 4.

81. Jameson, 4.

82. William Barry, *The Dayspring* (New York: Dodd, Mead, 1904), 322. The British edition was published by T. Fisher Unwin in 1903.

83. Mary Elizabeth Braddon, *Under the Red Flag* (Leipzig: Bernard Tauchnitz, 1883), 118.

84. Ross, *Communal Luxury*, 63.

85. William Morris, *News from Nowhere* (1890), in *The Collected Works of William Morris*, ed. May Morris, 24 vols. (London: Longmans, Green, 1910–1915), 16:133.

86. Braddon, *Under the Red Flag*, 127.

87. Gosse, "Influence," 528.

88. Georg Lukács, *The Meaning of Contemporary Realism*, trans. John Mander and Necke Mander (London: Merlin, 1979), 34.

89. Theodor Adorno, *Aesthetic Theory*, trans. Robert Hullot-Kentor (London: Continuum, 2004), 240.

CHAPTER 2 — REFUGEES, RENEGADES, AND MISREPRESENTATION

1. Thomas Carlyle, *The French Revolution: A History*, 3 vols. (London: Chapman and Hall, 1871), 1:222.

2. Carlyle, 1:222.

3. Carlyle, 1:222.

4. See, for example, Ronald Paulson, *Representations of Revolution, 1789–1820* (New Haven, CT: Yale University Press, 1983); Ian R. Christie, *Stress and Stability in Late Eighteenth-Century Britain: Reflections on the British Avoidance of Revolution* (Oxford,

UK: Clarendon, 1984); Ceri Crossley and Ian Small, eds., *The French Revolution and British Culture* (Oxford: Oxford University Press, 1989); Keith Hanley and Raman Selden, eds., *Revolution and English Romanticism: Politics and Rhetoric* (New York: St. Martin's, 1990); Kelvin Everest, ed., *Revolution in Writing: British Literary Responses to the French Revolution* (Milton Keynes, UK: Open University Press, 1991); Mark Philp, ed., *The French Revolution and British Popular Politics* (Cambridge: Cambridge University Press, 1991); Alison Yarrington and Kelvin Everest, eds., *Reflections of Revolution: Images of Romanticism* (London and New York: Routledge, 1993); M. O. Grenby, *The Anti-Jacobin Novel: British Conservatism and the French Revolution* (Cambridge: Cambridge University Press, 2001); Andrew M. Stauffer, *Anger, Revolution, and Romanticism* (Cambridge: Cambridge University Press, 2005); Kevin Gilmartin, *Writing against Revolution: Literary Conservatism in Britain, 1790–1832* (Cambridge: Cambridge University Press, 2007); Colin Jones, Josephine McDonagh, and Jon Mee, eds., *Charles Dickens, "A Tale of Two Cities," and the French Revolution* (Basingstoke, UK: Palgrave 2009).

5. George Levine, *The Boundaries of Fiction: Carlyle, Macaulay, Newman* (Princeton, NJ: Princeton University Press, 1968), 136–137.

6. Levine, 138.

7. Chris R. Vanden Bossche, *Carlyle and the Search for Authority* (Columbus: Ohio State University Press, 1991), 63, 89.

8. Thomas Carlyle to John Carlyle, 29 May 1871, in *The Collected Letters of Thomas and Jane Welsh Carlyle*, ed. Ian Campbell, Aileen Christianson, and David Sorensen, 48 vols. (Durham, NC: Duke University Press, 1970–2020), 47:182, 208.

9. E. S. Beesly, "The Paris Revolution," in *The English Defence of the Commune (1871)*, ed. Royden Harrison (London: Merlin, 1971), 64.

10. [William Stigand], "The Commune of Paris," *Edinburgh Review* 134, no. 274 (October 1871): 563.

11. Stigand, 563.

12. Frederic Harrison, "The Fall of the Commune," *Fortnightly Review* 10, no. 56 (August 1871): 131.

13. Harrison, 131.

14. Walter Crane, *An Artist's Reminiscences* (London: Methuen, [1907]), 102.

15. Kristin Ross, *Communal Luxury: The Political Imaginary of the Paris Commune* (London: Verso, 2015), 14. For a fuller discussion of the popular reunions, see Alain Dalotel, Alaine Faure, and Jean-Claude Freiermuth, *Aux Origines de la Commune: Le Mouvement des Réunions Publiques à Paris 1868–1871* (Paris: Maspero, 1980).

16. Leslie Mitchell, *Bulwer Lytton: The Rise and Fall of a Victorian Man of Letters* (London: Hambledon and London, 2003), 157.

17. Mitchell, 221.

18. Juliette Atkinson, *French Novels and the Victorians* (Oxford: Oxford University Press, published for the British Academy, 2017), 346.

19. Owen Meredith, "Prefatory Note (by the Author's Son)," in *The Parisians*, by Edward Bulwer Lytton, 2 vols. (London: Routledge, 1878), 2:v. Subsequent citations to *The Parisians* refer to this edition and appear parenthetically in the text.

20. Walter Benjamin, *The Arcades Project*, trans. Howard Eiland and Kevin McLaughlin (Cambridge, MA: Harvard University, 1999), 85–86.

21. Benjamin, 99.

22. Benjamin, 790.

23. David L. Pike, *Subterranean Cities: The World beneath Paris and London, 1800–1945* (Ithaca, NY: Cornell University Press, 2005), 110–111.

24. Pike, 75.

25. See, for example, Rosalind Williams, *Notes on the Underground: An Essay on Technology, Society, and the Imagination*, new ed. (Cambridge, MA: MIT Press, 2008), 192–194; for discussion of Carlyle's treatment of the French Revolution in this light, see Albert J. LaValley, *Carlyle and the Idea of the Modern: Studies in Carlyle's Prophetic Literature and Its Relations to Blake, Nietzsche, Marx, and Others* (New Haven, CT: Yale University Press, 1968), 122, 127–128.

26. Ross, *Communal Luxury*, 14.

27. Karl Marx and Frederick Engels, *The Communist Manifesto*, ed. David McLellan (Oxford: Oxford University Press, 1998), 27.

28. For a discussion of the anxieties about the "red republican" conspiracies in the context of the Italian Risorgimento with reference to Collins and Disraeli, see Albert D. Pionke, *Plots of Opportunity: Representing Conspiracy in Victorian England* (Columbus: Ohio State University Press, 2004), 101–132. See also Adrian S. Wisnicki, *Conspiracy, Revolution and Terrorism from Victorian Fiction to the Modern Novel* (London and New York: Routledge, 2008), 89–110.

29. Stigand, "Commune of Paris," 526.

30. Stigand, 526.

31. Edmond de Goncourt and Jules de Goncourt, *Pages from the Goncourt Journal*, ed. and trans. Robert Baldick (Oxford: Oxford University Press, 1988), 185.

32. Mary Elizabeth Braddon, *Under the Red Flag* (Leipzig: Bernhard Tauchnitz, 1883), 219.

33. [Henry Du Pré Labouchère], *Diary of the Besieged Resident in Paris: Reprinted from "The Daily News," with Several New Letters and Preface* (London: Hurst and Blackett, 1871), 379.

34. [Lord Salisbury], "The Commune and the Internationale," *Quarterly Review* 131, no. 262 (October 1871): 553, 550.

35. Salisbury, 554–555.

36. Matthew Beaumont, *Utopia Ltd.: Ideologies of Social Dreaming in England, 1870–1900*, 2nd ed. (Chicago: Haymarket, 2009), 135.

37. Beaumont, 145.

38. Edward Bulwer Lytton, *The Coming Race* (Edinburgh: William Blackwood, 1871), 292.

39. Beaumont, *Utopia Ltd.*, 48.

40. Pike, *Subterranean Cities*, 113.

41. Pike, 107.

42. Braddon, *Under the Red Flag*, 142. As the Versaillais invade Paris, the narrator is similarly convinced that "thirty-thousand men are said to be . . . communicating with each other by underground passages" (207–208).

43. Mary Elizabeth Braddon, *One Life, One Love: A Novel* (London: Simpkin, Marshall, Hamilton, Kent, 1891), 335.

44. Karl Marx, "The Civil War in France: Address of the General Council," in *Political Writings*, vol. 3, *The First International and After*, ed. David Fernbach (Harmondsworth, UK: Penguin, 1992), 212.

45. For a brief discussion of critical realism as it pertains to Georg Lukács's reading of Balzac, see Dominick LaCapra, *History, Literature, Critical Theory* (Ithaca, NY: Cornell University Press, 2013), 14–15.

46. Mitchell, *Bulwer Lytton*, 221, xix.

47. Edward Bulwer Lytton, *Pamphlets and Sketches* (London: George Routledge, 1875), 170.

48. Allan Conrad Christensen, *Edward Bulwer-Lytton: The Fiction of New Regions* (Athens: University of Georgia Press, 1976), 174.

49. Stigand, "Commune of Paris," 563.

50. John M. Merriman, *Massacre: The Life and Death of the Paris Commune of 1871* (New Haven, CT: Yale University Press, 2014), 256. The precise number of Communards killed during the Bloody Week remains a source of controversy among historians. Robert Tombs argues a revisionist case that the death toll has been exaggerated, while Karin Varley questions Tombs's downward revision (from around twenty-five thousand to between fifty-seven hundred and seventy-four hundred), suggesting that "there remain distinct possibilities that the figures which were obtained by Tombs may be incomplete." See Robert Tombs, "How Bloody Was *La Semaine Sanglante* of 1871? A Revision," *Historical Journal* 55, no. 3 (September 2012): 679–704; Karine Varley, "Reassessing the Paris Commune of 1871: A Response to Robert Tombs, 'How Bloody Was *La Semaine Sanglante*? A Revision,'" *H-France Salon* 3, no. 1 (2011): 22.

51. Tombs, "How Bloody Was *La Semaine Sanglante* of 1871?," 699. Some brief questions about Tombs's hypothesis may be raised here. For example, he assumes that the court-martial proceedings afforded prisoners the dignity of an individual hearing ("Let us assume for the sake of argument that it took ten minutes on average to bring in a prisoner, elicit details, present some basic evidence"; Tombs, 699), whereas contemporary reports of court-martial proceedings suggest that "prisoners [were] judged and condemned in batches of fifty," which, if true, would rather upend Tombs's estimates. See "Justice Satisfied," *Graphic* 3, no. 83 (24 June 1871): 585. Tombs relies on assiduous archival research into cemetery records in Paris, dismissing the possibility that the Versaillais may have disposed of bodies, either through burial or cremation, at a distance from Paris in order deliberately to conceal the full scale of what Tombs freely recognizes was a "terrible atrocity." One contemporary report suggests that the bodies of Communards summarily executed in La Roquette were taken away in "seven railway-vans." To where, one might wonder, and why make use of railway vans? Were it to be established that bodies of dead Communards were transported outside of Paris by rail (perhaps no further than Satory), Tombs would need to widen the ambit of his necrological rummaging quite considerably. See "The Civil War in Paris," *Illustrated London News* 58, no. 1655 (17 June 1871): 596.

52. "Foreign News," *Graphic* 3, no. 79 (3 June 1871): 518.

53. Thomas Vargish, *The Providential Aesthetic in Victorian Fiction* (Charlottesville: University of Virginia Press, 1985), 24.

54. Matthew Arnold, "The Future of Liberalism," in *Irish Essays and Others* (London: Smith, Elder, 1882), 143.

55. Matthew Arnold to Mary Penrose Arnold, 20 March 1871, in *The Letters of Matthew Arnold*, ed. Cecil Y. Lang, 6 vols. (Charlottesville: University of Virginia Press, 1996–2002), 4:25.

56. Chris Baldick, *The Social Mission of English Criticism, 1848–1932* (Oxford, UK: Clarendon, 1983), 49–50.

57. James F. Cobb, *Workman and Soldier: A Tale of Paris Life during the Siege and the Rule of the Commune* (London: Griffith and Farran, 1880), 100–101.

58. John Oxenham, *Under the Iron Flail* (London: Cassell, 1905), 363.
59. William Morris, *Political Writings: Contributions to "Justice" and "Commonweal," 1883–1890*, ed. Nicholas Salmon (Bristol, UK: Thoemmes, 1994), 234–235.
60. Matthew Arnold, *Essays in Criticism*, 3rd ed. (London: Macmillan, 1875), 29.
61. Matthew Arnold to Mary Penrose Arnold, 28 March 1871, in *Letters*, 4:27.
62. Matthew Arnold to Mary Penrose Arnold, 11 June 1871, in *Letters*, 4:40.
63. Raymond Williams, "Utopia and Science Fiction," in *Problems in Materialism and Culture: Selected Essays* (London: Verso, 1980), 201.
64. Williams, 201.
65. Williams, 201.
66. Ross, *Communal Luxury*, 93.
67. Matthew Arnold, *Culture and Anarchy* (London: Smith, Elder, 1869), 101.
68. John Ruskin, *Fors Clavigera*, in *The Works of John Ruskin*, ed. E. T. Cook and Alexander Wedderburn, 39 vols. (London: George Allen, 1903–1912), 27:116.
69. Ruskin, 27:116.
70. Ruskin, 27:122.
71. Ruskin, 27:167.
72. Ruskin, 27:127.
73. Judith Stoddart, *Ruskin's Culture Wars: "Fors Clavigera" and the Crisis of Victorian Liberalism* (Charlottesville: University of Virginia Press, 1998), 88–89.
74. Ruskin, *Fors Clavigera*, 27:117.
75. Stoddart, *Ruskin's Culture Wars*, 115.
76. [Eliza Lynn Linton], *The True History of Joshua Davidson* (London: Strahan, 1872), 267. Subsequent citations refer to this edition and appear parenthetically in the text.
77. W. J. Linton, *The Paris Commune* (Boston: Reprinted from *The Radical* for September, 1871), 18.
78. W. Linton, 25.
79. W. Linton, 25. For discussion of W. J. Linton's political trajectory, see Gregory Claeys, *Citizens and Saints: Politics and Anti-Politics in Early British Socialism* (Cambridge: Cambridge University Press, 1989), 306–309.
80. Eliza Lynn Linton, *The True History of Joshua Davidson, Christian and Communist*, 6th ed. (London: Chatto and Windus, 1874), v–vi.
81. E. Linton, vi.
82. E. Linton, vii.
83. Jan-Melissa Schramm, *Censorship and the Representation of the Sacred in Nineteenth-Century England* (Oxford: Oxford University Press, 2019), 121.
84. Linton, *True History* (6th ed.), viii.
85. Adolphe Smith, "Political Refugees," in *London in the Nineteenth Century*, by Walter Besant (London: Adam and Charles Black, 1909), 399.
86. See Rosemary Ashton, *Victorian Bloomsbury* (New Haven, CT: Yale University Press, 2012), 208.
87. Smith, "Political Refugees," 399–400.
88. Smith, 401.
89. Anne Thackeray Ritchie, *Mrs Dymond* (London: Smith, Elder, 1885), 514.
90. Ritchie, 514–515.
91. Ritchie, 515.
92. Ritchie, 515.

93. Anne Ritchie, *Records of Tennyson, Ruskin and Browning* (London: Macmillan, 1892), 126.

94. See Caroline Corbeau-Parsons, "Crossing the Channel," in *Impressionists in London: French Artists in Exile 1870–1904*, ed. Caroline Corbeau-Parsons (London: Tate, 2017), 15.

95. See Edward Morris, *French Art in Nineteenth-Century Britain* (New Haven, CT: Yale University Press, 2005), 85.

96. Morris, 158–159.

97. "The French Siege of Paris," *Illustrated London News* 58, no. 1651 (20 May 1871):492.

98. See Anna Gruetzner Robins, "Alphonse Legros: Migrant and Cultural Ambassador," in Corbeau-Parsons, *Impressionists in London*, 117.

99. Thomas Carlyle, *Chartism* (London: James Fraser, 1840), 57, 8.

100. See, for example, Deirdre David, *Fictions of Resolution in Three Victorian Novels: "North and South," "Our Mutual Friend," "Daniel Deronda"* (Basingstoke, UK: Macmillan, 1981), 3–49. David Lodge points out that the mid-century "Condition of England" novels were also heavily influenced by "memories and myths of the French Revolution," and particularly Carlyle's narration of that history in *The French Revolution*. See David Lodge, "The French Revolution and the Condition of England: Crowds and Power in the Early Victorian Novel," in Crossley and Small, eds., *The French Revolution and British Culture*, 127.

101. Carolyn Lesjak, *Working Fictions: A Genealogy of the Victorian Novel* (Durham, NC: Duke University Press, 2006), 26.

CHAPTER 3 — DANGEROUS SYMPATHIES

1. Prosper-Olivier Lissagaray, *History of the Commune of 1871*, trans. Eleanor Marx (London: Reeves and Turner, 1886), 79. The first edition appeared in French in 1876: *Histoire de la Commune de 1871* (Brussels: Librairie Contemporaine de Henri Kistemaeckers, 1876).

2. Louise Michel, *La Commune* (Paris: P. V. Stock, 1898), 140.

3. Carolyn J. Eichner, *Surmounting the Barricades: Women in the Paris Commune* (Bloomington: Indiana University Press, 2004), 18.

4. Eichner, 3.

5. Gay L. Gullickson, *Unruly Women of Paris: Images of the Commune* (Ithaca, NY: Cornell University Press, 1996), 3. See also Eugene Schulkind, "Socialist Women during the 1871 Paris Commune," *Past & Present* 106 (February 1985), 124–163; and Edith Thomas, *The Women Incendiaries*, new ed. (Chicago: Haymarket, 2007).

6. "Civil War in Paris," *Times*, March 20, 1871, 9.

7. "Civil War in Paris," 9.

8. See Margaret Oliphant, *Memoir of the Life of Laurence Oliphant and of Alice Oliphant, His Wife*, new ed. (London: William Blackwood, 1892), 232–233; for Austin's claim that he vacated Paris on 8 February, immediately after the "Election in the Capital of Representatives in the National Assembly," and did not return until "Thiers had possession of the City," see Alfred Austin, *The Autobiography of Alfred Austin, Poet Laureate, 1835–1910*, 2 vols. (London: Macmillan, 1911), 2:86–87; Henry Vizetelly, *Paris in Peril*, 2 vols. (London: Tinsley Brothers, 1882), 2:262. See also F. B. Smith, "Some British Reactions to the Commune," in *Paradigm for Revolution? The Paris Commune, 1871–1971*, ed. Eugene Kamenka (Canberra: Australian National University Press, 1972), 76. For a fuller discussion of

British special correspondents working in Europe during the Franco-Prussian War, see Catherine Waters, *Special Correspondence and the Newspaper Press in Victorian Print Culture, 1850–1886* (London: Palgrave Macmillan, 2019), 97–130.

9. "The New Revolution in Paris," *Standard*, March 21, 1871, 5.

10. "Our Paris Letter," *Englishwoman's Domestic Magazine* 79 (1 July 1871): 54.

11. Elisabeth Jay, *British Writers and Paris, 1830–1875* (Oxford: Oxford University Press, 2016), 185.

12. "Our Paris Letter," 54.

13. Mary Elizabeth Braddon, *Under the Red Flag* (Leipzig: Bernhard Tauchnitz, 1883), 163. Subsequent citations refer to this edition and appear parenthetically in the text.

14. "Women in Revolt," *Englishwoman's Domestic Magazine* 79 (1 July 1871): 59.

15. Gullickson, *Unruly Women of Paris*, 178. For a wide-ranging discussion of press representations of Communard women and the emergence of the figure of the *pétroleuse*, see Gullickson, 159–190.

16. Priscilla Parkhurst Ferguson, *Paris as Revolution: Writing the Nineteenth-Century City* (Berkeley: University of California Press, 1994), 154.

17. Anne Thackeray Ritchie, *Mrs Dymond* (London: Smith, Elder, 1885), 454. Subsequent citations refer to this edition and appear parenthetically in the text.

18. George Eliot, *Impressions of Theophrastus Such* (Edinburgh: William Blackwood, 1879), 185–186.

19. Across the Atlantic, the same image was published in *Harper's Weekly* on 8 July 1871. This image is discussed in Michelle Coghlan's *Sensational Internationalism: The Paris Commune and the Remapping of American Memory in the Long Nineteenth Century* (Edinburgh: Edinburgh University Press, 2016), 31–33. Chapter 1 of Coghlan's book deftly surveys the "visual culture of gender panic" in postbellum US responses to the Commune and offers suggestive parallels with the material considered here.

20. Bertall, *The Communists of Paris 1871: Types–Physiognomies–Characters; with Explanatory Text Descriptive of Each Design Written Expressly for This Edition by an Englishman* (London: Buckingham, 1873), image no. 39, n.p. "Bertall" was the pseudonym of the anti-Communard caricaturist Charles Albert d'Arnoux.

21. Peter Keating, *The Haunted Study: A Social History of the English Novel 1875–1914*, 2nd ed. (London: Fontana, 1991), 356.

22. Alexandra Orr, *The Twins of Saint-Marcel: A Tale of Paris Incendié* (Edinburgh: William P. Nimmo, 1872), 231.

23. Robert Lee Wolff, *Sensational Victorian: The Life and Fiction of Mary Elizabeth Braddon* (New York: Garland, 1979), 269.

24. See Wolff, 277–299.

25. Wolff, 304.

26. Mrs. John Waters, *A Young Girl's Adventures in Paris during the Commune* (London: Remington, 1881), 241. Waters's narrative first appeared as *Nellie Montel; or, Three Months under the Commune* in serial form across five installments in volume 24 of the *Churchman's Shilling Magazine and Family Treasury* between October 1878 and February 1879.

27. Orr, *Twins of Saint-Marcel*, 338.

28. Orr, 298.

29. Orr, 332.

30. G. A. Henty, *A Woman of the Commune* (London: F. V. White, 1896), 20–21. For a useful comparative discussion of Henty's novel and Edward King's *The Red Terror*

(1895), focusing on the way in which they "[revive] to reinter the Commune," see Coghlan, *Sensational Internationalism*, 56–70 (quote on 63). King's novel was published in America by Henry T. Coates with the title *Under the Red Flag; or, The Adventures of Two American Boys in the Days of the Commune*. It was presumably retitled for the British market in order to avoid confusion with Braddon's novel. For some further examples of the providential worldview in fictions of the Commune, see chapter 1, 14–15.

31. Edward King, *The Red Terror; or, The Adventures of Two American Boys under the Red Flag of the Commune* (London: Cassell, 1895), 463.

32. Thomas Vargish, *The Providential Aesthetic in Victorian Fiction* (Charlottesville: University of Virginia Press, 1985), 2, 4.

33. Vargish, 4.

34. Maxime Du Camp, *Les Convulsions de Paris*, 5th ed., 4 vols. (Paris: Librairie Hachette, 1881), 1:207–224. For Robert Tombs's description of Du Camp, see *The Paris Commune, 1871* (London: Routledge, 1999), 142.

35. See Maxime Vuillaume, *Mes Cahiers Rouge au Temps de la Commune*, 5th ed. (Paris: Société d'Éditions Littéraires et Artistiques, 1900), 100–101.

36. Colette E. Wilson, *Paris and the Commune 1871–78: The Politics of Forgetting* (Manchester, UK: Manchester University Press, 2007), 93. Wilson elaborates that Du Camp was one of the leading figures among the "anti-Communard bourgeoisie" and notes that "it was this group's 'memory' of Paris and the Commune which was to crystallize into the accepted 'history' of this event as exemplified by Du Camp's *Les Convulsions de Paris*" (15).

37. Hayden White, *The Content of the Form: Narrative Discourse and Historical Representation*, 2nd ed. (Baltimore: Johns Hopkins University Press, 1990), 37.

38. White, 37.

39. Lissagaray, *History of the Commune of 1871*, 436.

40. Orr, *Twins of Saint-Marcel*, iii.

41. Orr, iii. For Orr's source, see Francisque Sarcey, *Le Siège de Paris: Impressions et Souvenirs* (Paris: E. Lachaud, 1871). In Arnold Bennett's preface to *The Old Wives' Tale* (1908), a novel that features an episode set in Paris during the siege and the Commune, he notes that he researched the novel by reading aloud to his wife "Sarcey's diary of the siege." Bennett, *The Old Wives' Tale* (London: Hodder and Stoughton, 1911), ix.

42. See, for example, Orr, *Twins of Saint-Marcel*, 297–299, 301, 306.

43. For discussion of the sympathetic response of British workers to the Commune, see Royden Harrison, "Marx, Engels and the British Response to the Commune," in *Revolution and Reaction: The Paris Commune, 1871*, ed. John Hicks and Robert Tucker (Amherst: University of Massachusetts Press, 1973), 96–110.

44. Wolff, *Sensational Victorian*, 303.

45. See, for example, "Notes and News," *Academy* 536 (12 August 1882): 119; G. Monod, "Contemporary Life and Thought in France," *Contemporary Review* 43, no. 2 (February 1883): 174–175.

46. Ferguson, *Paris as Revolution*, 178.

47. Ferguson, 189.

48. Pascale Casanova, *The World Republic of Letters*, trans. M. B. DeBevoise (Cambridge, MA: Harvard University Press, 2004), 127.

49. See Elisabeth Jay, "'In Her Father's Steps She Trod': Anne Thackeray Ritchie Imagining Paris," *Yearbook of English Studies* 36, no. 2 (2006): 197–211. Jay focuses on Ritchie's earlier Parisian narrative *The Story of Elizabeth* (1863).

50. Winifred Gérin, *Anne Thackeray Ritchie: A Biography* (Oxford: Oxford University Press, 1981), 203.

51. Anne Thackeray Ritchie, *The Correspondence and Journals of the Thackeray Family*, ed. John Aplin, 5 vols. (London: Pickering and Chatto, 2011), 2:82. For another account of Ritchie's visit to Paris in 1871, see Ritchie, *Thackeray's Daughter: Some Recollections of Anne Thackeray Ritchie*, comp. Hester Thackeray Fuller and Violet Hammersley, 2nd ed. (Dublin: Euphorian, 1952), 122–123.

52. Ritchie, *Correspondence and Journals*, 2:83.

53. Ritchie, 2:82.

54. Ritchie, 3:204.

55. Ritchie, 2:82.

56. For further discussion of this spectatorial politics of elevation, see chapter 8.

57. The phrase "mob horror" belongs to Brian Hamnett. For a discussion of its mobilization in Dickens's two historical novels, *Barnaby Rudge* (1841) and *A Tale of Two Cities*, see Hamnett's *The Historical Novel in Nineteenth-Century Europe: Representations of Reality in History and Fiction* (Oxford: Oxford University Press, 2011), 117–124.

58. Waters, *Young Girl's Adventures in Paris*, 191; Braddon, *Under the Red Flag*, 88; Orr, *Twins of Saint-Marcel*, 298.

59. Carol Hanbery MacKay, *Creative Negativity: Four Victorian Exemplars of the Female Quest* (Stanford, CA: Stanford University Press, 2001), xi.

60. Eichner, *Surmounting the Barricades*, 11.

61. Eichner, 8.

62. See Sally Ledger, *The New Woman: Fiction and Feminism at the Fin de Siècle* (Manchester, UK: Manchester University Press, 1997), 21–23; Ann Heilmann, *New Woman Strategies: Sarah Grand, Olive Schreiner, and Mona Caird* (Manchester, UK: Manchester University Press, 2004), 165–168.

63. Gérin, *Anne Thackeray Ritchie*, 220.

64. Anne Thackeray Ritchie, *Records of Tennyson, Ruskin and Browning* (London: Macmillan, 1892), 75. The chapter on Ruskin was written in 1887 for *Macmillan's* and was first published as an essay in *Harper's Magazine* in March 1890.

65. Ritchie, 82. See chapter 2.

66. For King's chapter, see "Dombrowski at Dinner," in *Red Terror*, 252–263.

67. Hamnett, *Historical Novel in Nineteenth-Century Europe*, 123.

68. The concluding paragraphs of Ritchie's penultimate chapter closely follow and, in some places, directly translate an episode drawn from volume 3 of Du Camp's *Les Convulsions de Paris*, in which he narrates the Communard M. Gablin's apparent prevention of the burning of the Ministère de la Marine by locking a group of incendiaries in a room. See Du Camp, 3:95; Ritchie, *Mrs Dymond*, 509–510.

69. Esther Schwartz-McKinzie, introduction to *Mrs Dymond*, by Anne Thackeray Ritchie (Stroud, UK: Sutton, 1997), xii. For a related discussion of the novel in these terms, see Carol Hanbery MacKay, "Tradition, Convergence, and Innovation: The Literary Legacy of Anne Thackeray Ritchie," *Victorian Review* 36, no. 1 (Spring 2010): 174–175.

70. Schwartz-McKinzie, xii.

71. Gérin, *Anne Thackeray Ritchie*, 196. While Oliphant became a firm friend of Ritchie, her distinct lack of admiration for Braddon's writing is a matter of record. Oliphant published a sharply critical anonymous attack on Braddon, titled "Novels," which appeared in *Blackwood's Magazine* in 1867.

72. Merryn Williams, *Margaret Oliphant: A Critical Biography* (Basingstoke, UK: Macmillan, 1986), 98. See also Oliphant, *Memoir of the Life of Laurence Oliphant*, 233.

73. Margaret Oliphant, *The Autobiography of Margaret Oliphant: The Complete Text*, ed. Elisabeth Jay (Oxford: Oxford University Press, 1990), 137.

74. See John Oxenham, *Under the Iron Flail* (London: Cassell, 1902), 240, 255.

75. [Margaret Oliphant], "Three Days in Paris," *Blackwood's Magazine* 124, no. 756 (October 1878): 455. Merryn Williams lists this article among Oliphant's numerous contributions to *Blackwood's* in his biography of Oliphant. See Williams, *Margaret Oliphant*, 209.

76. Oliphant, "Three Days in Paris," 456.

77. Oliphant, 473.

78. Oliphant, 473.

79. Oliphant, *Memoir of the Life of Laurence Oliphant*, 233.

80. Margaret Oliphant, *A Beleaguered City, Being the Narrative of Certain Recent Events in the City of Semur, in the Department of the Haute Bourgogne; A Tale of the Seen and the Unseen* (London: Macmillan, 1880), 204, 54. Subsequent citations refer to this edition and appear parenthetically in the text.

81. Kristin Ross, *The Emergence of Social Space: Rimbaud and the Paris Commune*, 2nd ed. (London: Verso, 2008), 42.

82. Esther H. Schor, "The Haunted Interpreter in Oliphant's Supernatural Fiction," in *Margaret Oliphant: Critical Essays on a Gentle Subversive*, ed. D. J. Trela (Selinsgrove, PA: Susquehanna University Press, 1995), 91.

83. Karl Marx, "The Civil War in France: Address of the General Council," in *Political Writings*, vol. 3, *The First International and After*, ed. David Fernbach (Harmondsworth, UK: Penguin, 1992), 203.

84. Marx, 203.

85. Marx, 268. See also 219.

86. Henri Lefebvre, "La Commune: Dernière Fête Populaire," in *Images of the Commune / Images de la Commune*, ed. James A. Leith (Montreal: McGill-Queen's University Press, 1978), 43. For another suggestive reading of the Commune's "festive" character, see Ann Rigney, "Remembering Hope: Transnational Activism beyond the Traumatic," *Memory Studies* 11, no. 3 (2018): 375.

87. Lissagaray, *History of the Commune of 1871*, 301–302, 306. As Adrian Rifkin notes, the problem of political censorship under the Second Empire meant that many artists and performers experienced the Commune as a creative liberation. See Rifkin, "Cultural Movement and the Paris Commune," in *Communards and Other Cultural Histories: Essays by Adrian Rifkin*, ed. Steve Edwards (Leiden, Netherlands: Brill, 2016), 193.

88. Charles Quentin, *Through the Storm*, 3 vols. (London: Hurst and Blackett, 1880), 3:213. Quin published under the pseudonym "Charles Quentin."

89. Georg Lukács, *The Historical Novel*, trans. Hannah and Stanley Mitchell (London: Merlin, 1989), 285. The book was first published in Moscow in 1937. As Ian Duncan has observed, Lukács's "main claim or premise" is that "an authentic realism is one that reveals the dialectical form of history." Duncan, "History and the Novel after Lukács," *Novel: A Forum on Fiction* 50, no. 3 (2017): 388.

90. Lukács, *The Historical Novel*, 285.

91. Fredric Jameson, *The Antinomies of Realism* (London: Verso, 2013), 267.

92. Francis Henry Gribble, *The Red Spell* (London: Frederick A. Stokes, 1895), 98.

93. Gribble, 191.

94. Edward Carpenter, "Saved by a Nose: A Bit of an Autobiography," in *Sketches from Life in Town and Country, and some Verses* (London: George Allen, 1908), 212.

95. James Joll, *Europe since 1870: An International History*, 2nd ed. (Harmondsworth, UK: Penguin, 1976), 32.

96. Oliphant, "Three Days in Paris," 474.

97. Oliphant, 462.

98. Schor, "Haunted Interpreter," 106.

99. D. J. Trela, "Introduction: Discovering the Gentle Subversive," in Trela, *Margaret Oliphant*, 12.

100. Wolff, *Sensational Victorian*, 277; MacKay, *Creative Negativity*, xi.

CHAPTER 4 — "DREAMS OF THE COMING REVOLUTION"

1. Raymond Williams, *Culture and Society, 1780–1950*, new ed. (Harmondsworth, UK: Penguin, 1982), 178.

2. Williams, 264.

3. George Gissing to Frederic Harrison, 9 July 1880, and George Gissing to Algernon Gissing, 8 June 1880, in *The Collected Letters of George Gissing*, vol. 1, *1863–1880*, ed. Paul F. Mattheisen, Arthur C. Young, and Pierre Coustillas (Athens: Ohio University Press, 1990), 1:289, 282.

4. Williams, *Culture and Society*, 180.

5. Edith Sichel, "Two Philanthropic Novelists: Mr. Walter Besant and Mr. George Gissing," *Murray's Magazine* 3, no. 16 (April 1888): 507, 515.

6. Sichel, 511.

7. Austin Harrison, *Frederic Harrison: Thoughts and Memories* (London: William Heinemann, 1926), 81–82.

8. Matthew Ingleby, *Nineteenth-Century Fiction and the Production of Bloomsbury: Novel Grounds* (London: Palgrave, 2018), 94.

9. George Gissing, *Workers in the Dawn: A Novel*, 3 vols. (London: Remington, 1880), 2:179–180. Subsequent citations refer to this edition and appear parenthetically in the text.

10. Terry Lovell, *Consuming Fiction* (London: Verso, 1987), 93.

11. See Jeannene M. Przyblyski, "Revolution at a Standstill: Photography and the Paris Commune of 1871," *Yale French Studies* 101 (2001): 54–78; Donald E. English, "Political Photography and the Paris Commune of 1871: The Photographs of Eugène Appert," *History of Photography* 7, no. 1 (1983): 31–42.

12. Adolphe S. Headingley (also known as Adolphe Smith) comments in his biography of Bradlaugh that "Bradlaugh maintained a very reserved attitude during the whole of the agitation consequent on the Communard rising in Paris. He never advocated the cause of the Commune; the most he did was to urge that the Parisians should be allowed fair play." Headingley, *The Biography of Charles Bradlaugh* (London: Remington, 1880), 259.

13. Friedrich Nietzsche, *A Genealogy of Morals*, vol. 10 of *The Works of Friedrich Nietzsche*, ed. Alexander Tille (London: Macmillan, 1897), 35.

14. Fredric Jameson, *The Political Unconscious: Narrative as a Socially Symbolic Act*, new ed. (London: Routledge, 2002), 189. As Peter Starr comments, Taine's seven-volume history of France, *Les Origines de la France Contemporaine* (1875–1894), traces a process of "decomposition originating in the French Revolution" that "culminated in the events of the année terrible, most notably, the Franco-Prussian War and Paris Commune."

Starr, *Commemorating Trauma: The Paris Commune and Its Cultural Aftermath* (New York: Fordham University Press, 2006), 38.

15. Revolutionary Commune Group, "To Supporters of the Commune," in *The Paris Commune of 1871: The View from the Left*, ed. Eugene Schulkind (London: Jonathan Cape, 1972), 238.

16. [John Wilson], "Economic Fallacies and Labour Utopias," *Quarterly Review* 131, no. 261 (July 1871): 261.

17. [John Baptist Cashel-Hoey], "The International Society," *Dublin Review* 17, no. 34 (October 1871): 463.

18. Cashel-Hoey, 464.

19. W. E. Bowen, *Edward Bowen: A Memoir* (London: Longmans, Green, 1902), 350. Bowen's lecture, "The Commune of Paris, 1871," is included as an appendix (336–356). W. E. Bowen was Edward Bowen's nephew.

20. For discussion of this phenomenon, see, for example, the chapter "Resistance: Pathologising Dissent," in Bruce M. Z. Cohen, *Psychiatric Hegemony: A Marxist Theory of Mental Illness* (London: Palgrave Macmillan, 2016), 169–204.

21. George Gissing, *New Grub Street: A Novel*, 3 vols. (London: Smith, Elder, 1891), 3:185.

22. Arnold Kettle, "Dickens and the Popular Tradition," in *Marxists on Literature: An Anthology*, ed. David Craig (Harmondsworth, UK: Penguin, 1975), 237. For a pertinent discussion of the assumed relationship between alcohol and spontaneous combustion, given that Krook appears to subsist on gin, see also Gaston Bachelard, *The Psychoanalysis of Fire*, trans. Alan C. M. Ross (Boston: Beacon, 1964), 93–98.

23. George Gissing, *Charles Dickens: A Critical Study* (London: Blackie, 1898), 57–58. As Simon J. James notes, "Gissing's anxiety about his inheritance from his literary parent involves avoidance of the aesthetic mistakes and even betrayals of the father, but also the repayment of gratitude." James, *Unsettled Accounts: Money and Narrative in the Novels of George Gissing* (London: Anthem, 2003), 37.

24. Eduard Bertz, "George Gissing: Ein Real-Idealist," in *George Gissing: The Critical Heritage*, ed. Pierre Coustillas and Colin Partridge (Abingdon, UK: Routledge, 1995), 149–156.

25. James, *Unsettled Accounts*, 52.

26. Thomas C. Jones and Robert Tombs, "The French Left in Exile: *Quarante-huitards* and Communards in London, 1848–80," in *A History of the French in London: Liberty, Equality, Opportunity*, ed. Debra Kelly and Martyn Cornick (London: Institute of Historical Research, 2013), 172.

27. Jones and Tombs, 169.

28. Jones and Tombs, 169.

29. See Robin Woolven, "George Gissing's London Residences, 1877–1891," *Gissing Journal* 39, no. 4 (2003): 5–15; Richard Dennis, "The Place of Bloomsbury in the Novels of George Gissing," *Opticon 1826* 7 (2009): 1–10.

30. Jones and Tombs, "French Left in Exile," 172.

31. Adolphe Smith, "Political Refugees," in *London in the Nineteenth Century*, by Walter Besant (London: Adam and Charles Black, 1909), 399–400.

32. See P. K. Martinez, "Paris Communard Refugees in London, 1871–1880" (PhD diss., University of Sussex, 1981), 77.

33. Smith, "Political Refugees," 401.

34. Michel Rapoport, "The London French from the Belle Epoque to the End of the Inter-war Period (1880–1939)," in Kelly and Cornick, *History of the French in London*, 256.

35. Smith, "Political Refugees," 400.

36. George Gissing to Algernon Gissing, 21 December 1879, in *Collected Letters*, 1:226.

37. [George Gissing], "Notes on Social Democracy—II," *Pall Mall Gazette* 32, no. 4853 (11 September 1880): 10. In a manner that roughly corresponds to the division between Arthur Golding and John Pether, Gissing expressed a generally sympathetic view of the moderate, reformist demands of the German socialist movement but also warned of the "dangerous fanaticism" of its revolutionary fringes. Gissing, "Notes on Social Democracy—I," *Pall Mall Gazette*, 32, no. 4851 (9 September 1880): 10.

38. Jones and Tombs, "French Left in Exile," 190.

39. Stanley Hutchins, "The Communard Exiles in Britain," *Marxism Today* 15, no. 3 (March 1971): 90–92; 15, no. 4 (April 1971): 117–120; 15, no. 6 (June 1971): 180–186.

40. Hutchins, 91. Other Communards who are known to have lived in and around Bloomsbury include Prosper-Olivier Lissagaray, Charles Malato, Jean-Baptiste Clément, Napoléon la Cécilia, Charles Longuet, Francis Jourde, and Georges Pilotell. See Hutchins, 117–120.

41. George Gissing to Elizabeth Gaussen, 6 October 1888, in *Collected Letters*, 3:256.

42. Jameson, *Political Unconscious*, 180–181.

43. Jameson, 181.

44. Franco Moretti, *Graphs, Maps, Trees: Abstract Models for a Literary Theory* (London: Verso, 2005), 54.

45. Gail Cunningham, "The Riddle of Suburbia: Suburban Fictions at the Victorian Fin de Siècle," in *Expanding Suburbia: Reviewing Suburban Narratives*, ed. Roger Webster (Oxford, UK: Berghahn, 2000), 63–64. For an extended discussion of *Workers in the Dawn* in these terms, including a map of Arthur's residential mobility, see Richard Dennis, "Mapping Gissing's *Workers in the Dawn*," *The Gissing Journal* 46, no. 4 (October 2010), 1–20.

46. Claudio Cerreti, quoted in Moretti, *Graphs, Maps, Trees*, 54.

47. Max Saunders, *Self Impression: Life-Writing, Autobiografiction, and the Forms of Modern Literature* (Oxford: Oxford University Press, 2010), 130.

48. Saunders, 130.

49. George Gissing, *The Private Papers of Henry Ryecroft* (Westminster, UK: Archibald Constable, 1903), 112–113.

50. Gissing, 113.

51. Jameson, *Political Unconscious*, 192.

52. For Gissing's desire to be a painter, recorded in an 1898 letter to Gabrielle Fleury, see Pierre Coustillas, *The Heroic Life of George Gissing, Part I: 1857–1888*, 2nd ed. (Abingdon, UK: Routledge, 2016), 37.

53. Albert Boime, *Art and the French Commune: Imagining Paris after War and Revolution* (Princeton, NJ: Princeton University Press, 1995), 96.

54. Boime, 45.

55. Kristin Ross, *Communal Luxury: The Political Imaginary of the Paris Commune* (London: Verso, 2015), 6.

56. Boime, *Art and the French Commune*, 45.

57. Boime, 19, 31. Boime construes his critique as a necessary corrective to "the occultation of the Commune in the abundant literature on Impressionism" (19).

58. See, for example, Xavier Baron, "Impressionist London in the Novels of George Gissing," in *Lineages of the Novel: Essays in Honour of Raimund Borgmeier*, ed. Bernhard Reitz and Eckart Voigts-Virchow (Trier, Germany: WVT Wissenschaftlicher Verlag Trier, 2000), 107–117; David Baguley, *Naturalist Fiction: The Entropic Vision* (Cambridge: Cambridge University Press, 1990), 30–31.

59. Deborah Parsons, *Streetwalking the Metropolis: Women, the City and Modernity* (Oxford: Oxford University Press, 2000), 32. Parsons adds elsewhere that "the impressionist impulse . . . to record the subjective experience of modernity" extends "naturalism's aim at the accurate social observation of everyday life." Parsons, "Whirlpools of Modernity: European Naturalism and the Urban Phantasmagoria," in *George Gissing: Voices of the Unclassed*, ed. Martin Ryle and Jenny Bourne Taylor, 2nd ed. (Abingdon, UK: Routledge, 2016), 109.

60. Paul Wood, "The Avant-Garde and the Paris Commune," in *The Challenge of the Avant-Garde*, ed. Paul Wood (New Haven, CT: Yale University Press in association with the Open University, 1999), 122.

61. See Smith, "Political Refugees," 401; Frederic Harrison, *Autobiographic Memoirs*, 2 vols. (London: Macmillan, 1911), 2:32; Mrs. Frederic Harrison, "French Refugees to England in 1871–72," *Cornhill Magazine*, n.s., 18 (May 1905): 607–613. For the Positivists' and the International's activities in support of the refugees, see also Martha S. Vogeler, *Frederic Harrison: The Vocations of a Positivist* (Oxford, UK: Clarendon, 1984), 103–104; Yvonne Kapp, *Eleanor Marx: Family Life, 1855–1883* (London: Virago, 1979), 136–137.

62. Adrian Poole, *Gissing in Context* (London: Macmillan, 1975), 63, 67. See also Martha Vogeler, "Gissing and the Positivists," *Gissing Newsletter* 21, no. 1 (1985): 1–13.

63. Scott McCracken, "The Author as Arsonist: Henry James and the Paris Commune," *Modernism/Modernity* 21, no. 1 (January 2014): 73.

64. McCracken, 73; Henry James, *The Ambassadors* (London: Methuen, 1903), 59.

65. McCracken, "Author as Arsonist," 83.

66. James, *Unsettled Accounts*, 65.

67. John Sloan, *George Gissing: The Cultural Challenge* (London: Palgrave Macmillan, 1989), 30, 15.

68. Sloan, 30.

69. Sloan, 30.

70. Bertz, "George Gissing," 155, 153.

CHAPTER 5 — REVOLUTION AND *RESSENTIMENT*

1. Scott McCracken, "The Author as Arsonist: Henry James and the Paris Commune," *Modernism/Modernity* 21, no. 1 (January 2014): 72, 85. McCracken quotes Perry Anderson, "Modernity and Revolution," *New Left Review* 144 (April 1984): 104.

2. McCracken, "Author as Arsonist," 84, 72.

3. Mary Elizabeth Braddon, *One Life, One Love: A Novel* (London: Simpkin, Marshall, Hamilton, Kent, 1891), 13–14.

4. George R. Sims, *The Mysteries of Modern London* (London: C. Arthur Pearson, 1906), 13.

5. Sims, 13.

6. Bernard Porter, *The Origins of the Vigilant State: The London Metropolitan Police Special Branch before the First World War*, 2nd ed. (Woodbridge, UK: Boydell, 1991), 9.

For a lengthier account of British police surveillance of the exiled Communards, see P. K. Martinez, "Paris Communard Refugees in London, 1871–1880" (PhD diss., University of Sussex, 1981), 421–428.

7. For a study of this subgenre of the realist novel, see Richard Maxwell, *The Mysteries of Paris and London* (Charlottesville: University of Virginia Press, 1992).

8. Sims, *Mysteries of Modern London*, 13.

9. George R. Sims, *The Dagonet Ballads (Chiefly from the Referee)* (London: E. J. Francis, 1879), 24–29. Stanley Hutchins records that Sims was a near neighbor of Henri Rochefort, a journalist who had escaped from New Caledonia after being transported there and who published *La Lanterne* in London. See Hutchins, "The Communard Exiles in Britain," *Marxism Today* 15, no. 6 (June 1971): 185.

10. Mark Seltzer, *Henry James and the Art of Power* (Ithaca, NY: Cornell University Press, 1984), 30.

11. Seltzer, 30.

12. Seltzer, 41.

13. McCracken, "Author as Arsonist," 81–82.

14. Henry James, *The Princess Casamassima: A Novel*, 3 vols. (London: Macmillan, 1886), 1:87. Subsequent citations refer to this edition and appear parenthetically in the text.

15. Prosper-Olivier Lissagaray, *History of the Commune of 1871*, trans. Eleanor Marx Aveling (London: Reeves and Turner, 1886), 500, appendix 37.

16. Dante Gabriel Rossetti to Ford Madox Brown, 30 January 1873, *The Correspondence of Dante Gabriel Rossetti*, ed. William E. Fredeman, Roger C. Lewis and Jane Cowan, 10 vols. (Cambridge: D. S. Brewer, 2002–2015), 6:51.

17. George Gissing, *The Unclassed* (London: Chapman and Hall, 1884), 33.

18. Eileen Sypher, *Wisps of Violence: Producing Public and Private Politics in the Turn-of-the-Century British Novel* (London: Verso, 1993), 28. In this respect, particularly given *The Princess Casamassima*'s intense concern with observation and surveillance, it is telling that, initially at least, James could not bring himself to *look* at the Commune. In April 1871, he wrote to Grace Norton, "I confess that the history of the French people for the past many weeks is something from which I as one *qui les a beaucoup aimés* am fain to avert my face." Henry James to Grace Norton, 13 April 1871, in *The Complete Letters of Henry James, 1855–1872*, ed. Pierre A. Walker and Greg W. Zacharias, 2 vols. (Lincoln: University of Nebraska Press, 2006), 2:401.

19. Henry James, preface to *The Princess Casamassima*, vol. 1 (New York: Charles Scribner's Sons, 1908), xviii, xxii. Subsequent citations refer to this edition and appear parenthetically in the text.

20. Michael Anesko, *"Friction with the Market": Henry James and the Profession of Authorship* (Oxford: Oxford University Press, 1986), 109.

21. Sypher, *Wisps of Violence*, 31.

22. Sypher, 31.

23. George Gissing, *Workers in the Dawn: A Novel*, 3 vols. (London: Remington, 1880), 2:260.

24. Wesley H. Tilley, *The Background of "The Princess Casamassima"* (Gainesville: University of Florida Press, 1960), 7.

25. See Elizabeth Carolyn Miller, "The Inward Revolution: Sexual Terrorism in *The Princess Casamassima*," *Henry James Review* 24, no. 2 (Spring 2003): 159.

26. The pub's Bloomsbury location is not incidental. Stanley Hutchins records that Communard exiles tended to gather at the Blue Posts in Newman Street and the Lord Monson's Arms at 56 Tottenham Street, all located within the vicinity of Bloomsbury. Hutchins, "Communard Exiles in Britain," 184.

27. Adrian S. Wisnicki, *Conspiracy, Revolution, and Terrorism from Victorian Fiction to the Modern Novel* (New York and London: Routledge, 2008), 155.

28. Lionel Trilling, "The Princess Casamassima," in *The Liberal Imagination: Essays on Literature and Society* (Harmondsworth, UK: Peregrine, 1970), 84; John Lucas, "Conservatism and Revolution in the 1880s," in *Literature and Politics in the Nineteenth Century: Essays*, ed. John Lucas (London: Methuen, 1971), 208.

29. Seltzer, *Henry James*, 54.

30. Seltzer, 55.

31. Fredric Jameson, *The Political Unconscious: Narrative as a Socially Symbolic Act*, new ed. (London: Routledge, 2002), 81.

32. "How Paris Mourns," *All the Year Round* 6, no. 137 (15 July 1871): 154. For a related anecdote, see Charles Hervey, "Collectors and Their 'Hobbies,'" *London Society* 46, no. 272 (August 1884): 239.

33. "How Paris Mourns," 153.

34. "Book-collecting," in *The Bookworm: An Illustrated Treasury of Old-Time Literature* (London: Elliot Stock, 1891), 243.

35. "Book-collecting," 243.

36. Marcia Jacobson, *Henry James and the Mass Market* (Tuscaloosa: University of Alabama Press, 1983), 55.

37. For a more extensive discussion of the "sexual ambivalence" signified in Hyacinth's name, see Wendy Graham, "Henry James's Subterranean Blues: A Rereading of *The Princess Casamassima*," *Modern Fiction Studies* 40, no. 1 (Spring 1994): 63.

38. Gissing, *Workers in the Dawn*, 2:311.

39. Walter Benjamin, "On the Concept of History," in *Selected Writings*, vol. 4, *1938–1940*, ed. Howard Eiland and Michael W. Jennings, trans. Edmund Jephcott et al. (Cambridge, MA: Harvard University, 2003), 392.

40. Henry James, *A Little Tour in France* (Leipzig: Bernhard Tauchnitz, 1885), 223–224.

41. James, 224.

42. Henry James to William James, in *The Complete Letters of Henry James, 1872–1876*, ed. Pierre A. Walker and Greg W. Zacharias, 3 vols. (Lincoln: University of Nebraska Press, 2008), 1:114.

43. Henry James to William James, 1:114.

44. J. Michelle Coghlan, *Sensational Internationalism: The Paris Commune and the Remapping of American Memory in the Long Nineteenth Century* (Edinburgh: Edinburgh University Press, 2016), 118.

45. Henry James to Alice James, 16 December 1872, in *Complete Letters of Henry James, 1872–1876*, 1:157.

46. McCracken, "Author as Arsonist," 76.

47. Jameson, *Political Unconscious*, 45.

48. Howard Caygill, *On Resistance: A Philosophy of Defiance* (London: Bloomsbury, 2013), 39.

49. Caygill, 39.

50. Jameson, *Political Unconscious*, 190.

51. George Eliot, *Felix Holt, the Radical*, 3 vols. (Edinburgh: William Blackwood, 1866), 3:259.

52. Stefanie Markovits, *The Crisis of Action in Nineteenth-Century English Literature* (Columbus: Ohio State University Press, 2006), 89. Carolyn Lesjak reads Esther's narrative in similar terms as a "cautionary political allegory" that "mirrors the transformation desired by the text for the working class." Lesjak, *Working Fictions: A Genealogy of the Victorian Novel* (Durham, NC: Duke University Press, 2006), 76.

53. Margaret Scanlan, "Terrorism and the Realistic Novel: Henry James and *The Princess Casamassima*," *Texas Studies in Literature and Language* 34, no. 3 (1992): 382.

54. John Kimmey, *Henry James and London: The City in His Fiction* (New York: Peter Lang, 1991), 188n39.

55. Henry James to Charles Eliot Norton, 6 December 1886, in *Henry James: Letters*, ed. Leon Edel, 4 vols. (Cambridge, MA: Harvard University, 1974–1985), 3:146.

56. Gerard Manley Hopkins to Robert Bridges, 2 August 1871, in *The Collected Works of Gerard Manley Hopkins*, ed. R.K.R. Thornton, Catherine Phillips, et al., 7 vols. (Oxford: Oxford University Press, 2013), 1:209–210; John Ruskin, *Fors Clavigera*, in *The Works of John Ruskin*, ed. E. T. Cook and Alexander Wedderburn, 39 vols. (London: George Allen, 1903–1912), 27:127.

57. Jacobson, *Henry James*, 53.

58. Jacobson, 53.

59. Deaglán Ó Donghaile, *Blasted Literature: Victorian Political Fiction and the Shock of Modernism* (Edinburgh: Edinburgh University Press, 2011), 44.

60. Ó Donghaile, 53.

61. Jameson, *Political Unconscious*, 64.

62. Mike Fischer, "The Jamesian Revolution: A Lesson in Bookbinding," *Henry James Review* 9, no. 2 (Spring 1988): 95.

63. Jameson, *Political Unconscious*, 220. Discussing *The Princess Casamassima*, John Carlos Rowe observes that the novel makes "dominant use of the dramatic arts as metaphors for the theatricality of [the] classed society" depicted in the novel. Rowe, *The Theoretical Dimensions of Henry James* (Madison: University of Wisconsin Press, 1985), 173. See also Fischer, "Jamesian Revolution," 94–95; Seltzer, *Henry James*, 39–42.

64. This point extends Eileen Sypher's contention that it is the Princess, not Hyacinth, who acts as the main "channel through which the projected conservative vision of the novel is articulated"; Sypher adds that the Princess functions as a "decoy figure" and "an alter ego for [James's] narrator." Sypher, *Wisps of Violence*, 37, 45.

65. Seltzer, *Henry James*, 56, 55.

66. Seltzer, 55.

67. Seltzer, 56. For a related account of the identification between James and Hoffendahl, see Collin Meissner, "*The Princess Casamassima*: 'A Dirty Intellectual Fog,'" *Henry James Review* 19, no. 1 (1998): 61–62.

68. Ó Donghaile, *Blasted Literature*, 55. In Seltzer's terms, it might be added that James here reinforces "the nineteenth-century production of the category of 'the literary'" in such a way as to "guarantee an absolute antinomy between the literary and . . . 'the political' domain." Seltzer, *Henry James*, 173.

CHAPTER 6 — THE USES OF TRAGEDY

1. Alfred Austin, *The Autobiography of Alfred Austin, Poet Laureate, 1835–1910*, 2 vols. (London: Macmillan, 1911), 2:89.

2. Philip H. Bagenal, "The International, and Its Influence on English Politics," *National Review* 2, no. 9 (November 1883): 436.

3. Alfred Austin and W. J. Courthope, "Current Politics," *National Review* 1, no. 2 (April 1883): 319.

4. For discussion of this controversy, see Linda H. Peterson, "On the Appointment of the 'Poet Laureate to Her Majesty,' 1892–1896," *BRANCH: Britain, Representation and Nineteenth-Century History*, ed. Dino Franco Felluga, June 2012 extension of *Romanticism and Victorianism on the Net*, last accessed 24 May 2020.

5. Herbert F. Tucker, *Epic: Britain's Heroic Muse, 1790–1910* (Oxford: Oxford University Press, 2008), 508.

6. Alfred Austin, *The Human Tragedy*, new and rev. ed. (London: Macmillan, 1889), xxxix. Subsequent citations to the poem and Austin's introduction refer to this edition and appear parenthetically in the text.

7. Friedrich Nietzsche, *The Birth of Tragedy; or, Hellenism and Pessimism*, vol. 3 of *The Complete Works of Frederick Nietzsche*, ed. Oscar Levy, trans. William A. Haussmann (Edinburgh: T. N. Foulis, 1909), 110.

8. Richard J. White, *Nietzsche and the Problem of Sovereignty* (Chicago: University of Chicago Press, 1997), 63.

9. Raymond Williams, *Modern Tragedy* (London: Chatto and Windus, 1966), 77. For George Lukács's articulation of a remarkably similar notion of tragic "sacrifice" in a revolutionary conjuncture, see "Tactics and Ethics," in *Tactics and Ethics, 1919–1929: The Questions of Parliamentarianism and Other Essays*, trans. Michael McColgan (London: Verso, 2014), 10.

10. Williams, *Modern Tragedy*, 84.

11. Henri Lefebvre, "La Commune: Dernière Fête Populaire," in *Images of the Commune / Images de la Commune*, ed. James A. Leith (Montreal: McGill-Queen's University Press, 1978), 40.

12. Terry Eagleton, *Sweet Violence: The Idea of the Tragic* (Oxford, UK: Blackwell, 2003), 96.

13. Eagleton, 59.

14. Eagleton, 59.

15. William Morris, *Political Writings: Contributions to "Justice" and "Commonweal," 1883–1890*, ed. Nicholas Salmon (Bristol, UK: Thoemmes, 1994), 232–233.

16. Morris, 233.

17. William Morris, "The Hopes of Civilization," *Signs of Change*, in *The Collected Works of William Morris*, ed. May Morris, 24 vols. (London: Longmans, Green, 1910–1915), 23:74.

18. Tucker, *Epic*, 512; William Morris, *The Pilgrims of Hope*, in *Collected Works*, 24:404. Richard's proletarian class position is announced in book 6, "The New Proletarian."

19. Williams, *Modern Tragedy*, 77.

20. Alfred Austin, *The Poetry of the Period* (London: Richard Bentley, 1870), 144.

21. Morris, *Pilgrims of Hope*, 24:406. For a study of *The Earthly Paradise* that runs against the grain of Austin's comments, see Florence S. Boos, *The Design of William Morris' "The Earthly Paradise"* (Lewiston, NY: Edwin Mellen, 1991).

22. Morris, *Pilgrims of Hope*, 24:408.

23. Morris, 24:408.

24. William Morris, *News from Nowhere*, in *Collected Works*, 16:132.

25. Morris, 16:128.

26. Kristin Ross, *Communal Luxury: The Political Imaginary of the Paris Commune* (London: Verso, 2015), 76.

27. John Bruce Glasier, "A Proletarian Epic," *Socialist Review: A Monthly Review of Modern Thought* 17 (1920): 322.

28. Tucker, *Epic*, 510.

29. Florence S. Boos, "Narrative Design in *The Pilgrims of Hope*," in *Socialism and the Literary Artistry of William Morris*, ed. Florence S. Boos and Carole G. Silver (Columbia: University of Missouri Press, 1990), 147.

30. Anne Janowitz, "*The Pilgrims of Hope*: William Morris and the Dialectic of Romanticism," in *Cultural Politics at the Fin de Siècle*, ed. Sally Ledger and Scott McCracken (Cambridge: Cambridge University Press, 1995), 165–166.

31. William Morris to James Mavor, in *The Collected Letters of William Morris*, ed. Norman Kelvin, 4 vols. in 5 (Princeton, NJ: Princeton University Press, 1984–1996), 2:391.

32. Morris, *Pilgrims of Hope*, 24:400.

33. Florence S. Boos and William Boos, "*News from Nowhere* and Victorian Socialist-Feminism," *Nineteenth-Century Contexts* 14, no. 1 (1990): 19.

34. Morris, *Pilgrims of Hope*, 24:386–387, 382, 383.

35. Morris, 24:384, 397; William Morris, *Sigurd the Volsung*, in *Collected Works*, 12:14.

36. Morris, *Pilgrims of Hope*, 24:402, 403. This passage also provides scope for a rereading of book 4, "Mother and Son"—later reprinted in *Poems by the Way* (1891)—as an address in the voice of Richard's mother to a much younger version of the poem's protagonist and narrator. Most of the poem's critics assume, not without reason, that the speaker of book 4 is Richard's wife addressing their recently born child. See, for example, Michael Holzman, "Propaganda, Passion, and Literary Art in William Morris's *The Pilgrims of Hope*," *Texas Studies in Literature and Language* 24, no. 4 (Winter 1982): 382. At the opening of book 5, however, Richard recalls lying in his mother's lap "twenty-five years ago," only to find himself "born again" into the "world of struggle and pain" in the socialist movement, which provides grounds to speculate that the speaker of book 4 could be his mother, rather than his wife. Morris, *Pilgrims of Hope*, 24:380.

37. William Morris, *The Earthly Paradise*, in *Collected Works*, 3:223, 6:3–20.

38. William Morris, *The Æneids of Virgil Done into English Verse*, in *Collected Works*, 11:8–9, 134; William Morris, *The Odyssey of Homer Done into English Verse*, in *Collected Works*, 13:159.

39. Morris, *Odyssey*, 13:159.

40. Williams, *Modern Tragedy*, 64.

41. Morris, *Pilgrims of Hope*, 24:405.

42. Morris, 24:408.

43. Janowitz, "*Pilgrims of Hope*," 177, 175.

44. Boos, "Narrative Design," 165.

45. Tucker, *Epic*, 508. Hegel was convinced that "ragamuffins and vagabonds"—a type among whom he would doubtless have numbered the Communards—are not a fit object of tragic sympathy. See G.W.F. Hegel, "Tragedy as a Dramatic Art," in *Hegel on Tragedy*, ed. Anne Paolucci and Henry Paolucci (New York: Anchor, 1962), 50. For discussion of

Hegel's conception of tragedy as a "conflict of ethical substance," see Williams, *Modern Tragedy*, 33.

46. Eagleton, *Sweet Violence*, 80.

47. Eagleton, 80.

48. Morris, *Pilgrims of Hope*, 24:406. In choosing to describe their relationship as a circle, Richard deliberately avoids describing it as a triangle.

49. Morris, 24:406.

50. See, for example, John Leighton, *Paris under the Commune; or, The Seventy-Three Days of the Second Siege* (London: Bradbury, Evans, 1871); [Frederic Marshall], "A History of the Commune of Paris, by a Resident," *Blackwood's Magazine* 110, no. 669 (July 1871): 118–136; William Gibson, *Paris during the Commune, 1871: Being Letters from Paris and Its Neighbourhood, Written Chiefly during the Time of the Second Siege* (London: Whittaker, 1872); Albert D. Vandam, *An Englishman in Paris: Notes and Recollections*, 2 vols. (London: Chapman and Hall, 1892), 2:329–252; Denis Arthur Bingham, *Recollections of Paris*, 2 vols. (London: Chapman and Hall, 1896); Algernon Bertram Redesdale, *Further Memories*, introduction by Edmund Gosse (London: Hutchinson, 1917), 78–95.

51. Morris, *Pilgrims of Hope*, 24:406.

52. William Morris, "The Hopes of Civilization," in *Collected Works*, 23:74.

53. Morris, 23:74. On the number of Communard dead, see 194n50.

54. Georges Haupt, "The Commune as Symbol and Example," in *Aspects of International Socialism, 1871–1941: Essays by Georges Haupt*, trans. Peter Fawcett, preface by Eric Hobsbawm, 2nd ed. (Cambridge: Cambridge University Press, 2010), 25.

55. Haupt, 29. For a recent account of the ways in which English, Irish, and Scottish socialists commemorated the Commune, see Laura C. Forster, "The Paris Commune in the British Socialist Imagination, 1871–1914," *History of European Ideas* 46, no. 5 (2020): 614–632.

56. Elizabeth Carolyn Miller, *Slow Print: Literary Radicalism and Late Victorian Print Culture* (Stanford, CA: Stanford University Press, 2013), 168.

57. Catherine Robson, "The Presence of Poetry: Response," *Victorian Studies* 50, no. 2 (2008): 260.

58. Ingrid Hanson, "Socialist Identity and the Poetry of European Revolution in *Commonweal*, 1885–1890," in *Poetry, Politics, and Pictures: Culture and Identity in Europe, 1840–1914*, ed. Ingrid Hanson, Wilfred Jack Rhoden, and E. E. Snyder (Oxford, UK: Peter Lang, 2013), 225. Hanson focuses on German and French poems in translation and argues that "the French and German poems of revolution . . . translated in *Commonweal*" furthered "a pan-European myth of martyrdom for the cause which is central to the narrative construction of the movement" (225–226).

59. Laura Lafargue's *Commonweal* translations are Eugene Pottier, "Buried Alive," *Commonweal* 5, no. 170 (13 April 1889): 115; Louise Michel, "To Battle!," *Commonweal* 5, no. 179 (15 June 1889): 189; Pottier, "Plenty," *Commonweal* 5, no. 185 (27 July 1889): 237; Pottier, "Blanqui," *Commonweal* 5, no. 193 (21 September 1889): 301; Pottier, "Marguerite: To My Daughter, M.P.," *Commonweal* 5, no. 196 (12 October 1889): 325; Pottier, "The Anthropophagite," *Commonweal* 5, no. 207 (28 December 1889): 411; Pottier, "Don Quixote," *Commonweal* 6, no. 222 (12 April 1890): 115.

60. Walter Crane, "In Memory of the Commune of Paris: Born March 18, 1871, Died in June the Same Year," *Black and White* 1, no. 9 (4 April 1891): 274.

61. Crane, 274.

62. For discussion of the US socialist movement's radical calendar of Commune commemoration, see J. Michelle Coghlan, *Sensational Internationalism: The Paris Commune and the Remapping of American Memory in the Long Nineteenth Century* (Edinburgh: Edinburgh University Press, 2016), 79–104.

63. Crane, "In Memory of the Commune of Paris," 274.

64. See Gay L. Gullickson, *Unruly Women of Paris: Images of the Commune* (Ithaca, NY: Cornell University Press, 1996), 219.

65. Walter Benjamin, "On the Concept of History," in *Selected Writings*, vol. 4, *1938–1940*, ed. Howard Eiland and Michael W. Jennings, trans. Edmund Jephcott et al. (Cambridge, MA: Harvard University, 2003), 392.

66. See Michael Holroyd, *Bernard Shaw*, vol. 1, *1856–1898: The Search for Love* (London: Chatto and Windus, 1988), 102–104.

67. See Victor Hugo, *L'Année Terrible* (Paris: Michel Lévy Frères, 1872), 319–321. In Hugo's poem, the soldiers are too ashamed to shoot the boy and allow him to go free. Michelle Coghlan discusses several American poems of this period that rework the same anecdote. See Coghlan, *Sensational Internationalism*, 169n62.

68. Pakenham Beatty, "The Last Barricade of the Commune," *To-Day: Monthly Magazine of Scientific Socialism* 5, no. 29 (May 1886): 125. Beatty republished the poem in *Spretae Carmina Musae: Songs of Love and Death* (1893).

69. Charles Edwin Markham, "The Song of the Workers (Remembering the Martyrs of the Commune)," *Commonweal* 2, no. 35 (11 September 1886): 187.

70. Jeannene M. Przyblyski, "Revolution at a Standstill: Photography and the Paris Commune of 1871," *Yale French Studies* 101 (2001): 71–72.

71. Reginald A. Beckett, "The Eighteenth of March," *Commonweal* 5, no. 166 (16 March 1889): 83.

72. Beckett, 83.

73. Fred Henderson, *By the Sea, and Other Poems* (London: T. Fisher Unwin, 1892), 23.

74. Morris, *Pilgrims of Hope*, 24:406.

75. Morris, 24:397.

76. See, for example, William Morris, "The Three Seekers," *To-Day: Monthly Magazine of Scientific Socialism* 1, no. 1 (January 1884): 25–29.

77. William Morris, "All for the Cause," in *Collected Works*, 9:185.

78. Alain Badiou, *The Communist Hypothesis*, trans. David Macey and Steve Corcoran, 2nd ed. (London: Verso, 2015), 138.

79. William Morris to Fred Henderson, 19 October 1885, in *Collected Letters*, 2:471–472.

80. William Morris, *William Morris's Socialist Diary*, ed. Florence S. Boos, 2nd ed. (Nottingham, UK: Five Leaves, 2018), 137–138.

81. Henderson, *By the Sea*, 24.

82. Friedrich Engels, "The Programme of the Blanquist Commune Refugees" (1874), in *The Paris Commune of 1871: The View from the Left*, ed. Eugene Schulkind (London: Jonathan Cape, 1972), 240.

83. Haupt, "Commune as Symbol and Example," 38.

84. Ernest Belfort Bax, "Lissagaray's 'History of the Commune,'" *Commonweal* 2, no. 47 (4 December 1886): 283.

85. Bax, 283.

86. Ernest Belfort Bax, *A Short History of the Paris Commune* (London: Twentieth Century, 1895), 82.

87. Roland Boer, "Marx's Ambivalence: State, Proletarian Dictatorship and Commune," *International Critical Thought* 9, no. 1 (2019): 116. There is not scope here to offer a full account of Marx's reflections on the Commune, though Boer's article offers a useful overview.

88. George Bernard Shaw, *The Quintessence of Ibsenism* (London: Walter Scott, 1891), 126.

89. Shaw, v.

90. William Morris to Jenny Morris, 17 March 1887, in *Collected Letters*, 2:627–628.

91. Julia Nicholls, *Revolutionary Thought after the Paris Commune, 1871–1885* (Cambridge: Cambridge University Press, 2019), 21–77.

92. Enzo Traverso, *Left-Wing Melancholia: Marxism, History, and Memory* (New York: Columbia University Press, 2016), 33–34.

93. See Édouard Vaillant, "Vive la Commune!," *Commonweal* 1, no. 3 (April 1885): 17.

94. Ross, *Communal Luxury*, 2.

CHAPTER 7 — "IT HAD TO COME BACK"

1. William Morris, *Political Writings: Contributions to "Justice" and "Commonweal," 1883–1890*, ed. Nicholas Salmon (Bristol, UK: Thoemmes, 1994), 232–233.

2. H. M. Hyndman, *A Commune for London* (London: Justice Printery, 1887), 3. For a comprehensive account of representations of the changing built environment of nineteenth-century London, see Lynda Nead, *Victorian Babylon: People, Streets, and Images in Nineteenth-Century London*, 2nd ed. (New Haven, CT: Yale University Press, 2011).

3. Hyndman, *Commune for London*, 3–4; Nead, *Victorian Babylon*, 29.

4. Eric Hobsbawm, *The Age of Empire, 1875–1914*, new ed. (London: Abacus, 2010), 84.

5. H. M. Hyndman, *The Historical Basis of Socialism in England* (London: Kegan Paul, Trench, 1883), 421.

6. Gareth Stedman Jones, *Karl Marx: Greatness and Illusion* (Cambridge, MA: Harvard University Press, 2016), 492.

7. William Morris, *News from Nowhere*, in *The Collected Works of William Morris*, ed. May Morris, 24 vols. (London: Longmans Green, 1910–1915), 16:88.

8. James A. H. Murray, ed., *A New English Dictionary on a Historical Basis*, 10 vols. (Oxford, UK: Clarendon, 1888–1928), 2:698. Volume 2, which covered the letter C, was published in 1893.

9. Scott McCracken, "The Commune in Exile: Urban Insurrection and the Production of International Space," in *Nineteenth-Century Radical Traditions*, ed. Joseph Bristow and Josephine McDonagh (Basingstoke, UK: Palgrave, 2016), 114.

10. McCracken, 127.

11. Hyndman, *Commune for London*, 7.

12. Hyndman, 1.

13. John Burns, "The London County Council I. Towards a Commune," *Nineteenth Century* 31, no. 181 (March 1892): 501–502.

14. John Burns, "Let London Live!," *Nineteenth Century* 31, no. 182 (April 1892): 674. For R. E. Prothero's response, see "The London County Council II. Towards Common Sense," *Nineteenth Century* 31, no. 181 (March 1892): 515.

15. Burns, "Let London Live!," 674.

16. Annie Besant, "Industry under Socialism," in *Fabian Essays in Socialism*, ed. George Bernard Shaw (London: Fabian Society, 1889), 151.

17. Besant, 152–153.

18. Besant, 154.

19. Besant, 158.

20. Morris, *Political Writings*, 424–425.

21. Kristin Ross, *Communal Luxury: The Political Imaginary of the Paris Commune* (London: Verso, 2015), 111.

22. Ross, 117.

23. William Morris, "Dawn of a New Epoch," *Signs of Change* in *Collected Works*, 23:138.

24. William Morris, "Communism," *Lectures on Socialism* in *Collected Works*, 23:264.

25. Morris, 23:265.

26. Morris, 23:265.

27. Patrick Joyce, *The Rule of Freedom: Liberalism and the Modern City* (London: Verso, 2003), 106. See also Nead, *Victorian Babylon*, 51–56.

28. Special Commissioners of *The Daily Chronicle*, *New London: Her Parliament and Its Work, Reprinted from "The Daily Chronicle"* (London: Edward Lloyd, 1895).

29. Morris, *News from Nowhere*, 16:14.

30. Morna O'Neill, "'Vive la Commune!': The Imaginary of the Paris Commune and the Arts and Crafts Movement," in *Teaching William Morris*, eds. Jason D. Martinek and Elizabeth Carolyn Miller (Madison, NJ: Farleigh Dickinson University Press, 2019), 109.

31. G. K. Chesterton, *The Common Man* (London: Sheed and Ward, 1950), 231; Chesterton, *A Miscellany of Men* (London: Methuen, 1912), 117. Manuscript evidence shows that Chesterton was working on *Napoleon* between 1897 and 1902, and there are also suggestions that he had been working on it from his schooldays. See William Oddie, *Chesterton and the Romance of Orthodoxy: The Making of GKC, 1874–1908* (Oxford: Oxford University Press, 2008), 267.

32. G. K. Chesterton, *The Napoleon of Notting Hill* (London: John Lane, 1904), 41. Subsequent citations refer to this edition and appear parenthetically in the text.

33. For a roughly contemporaneous (and sincere rather than parodic) example of such antiquarian enthusiasm, see John Horace Round, "The Commune of London," in *The Commune of London and Other Studies* (Westminster, UK: Archibald Constable, 1899), 219–260.

34. Kristin Ross, *The Emergence of Social Space: Rimbaud and the Paris Commune*, 2nd ed. (London: Verso, 2008), 36.

35. Arnold Bennett, "Herbert George Wells and his Work," in *Arnold Bennett and H. G. Wells: A Record of a Personal and a Literary Friendship*, ed. Harris Wilson (Urbana: University of Illinois Press, 1960), 275.

36. H. G. Wells, *The Sleeper Awakes* (London: Collins' Clear-Type Press, 1921), 5–6.

37. Matthew Beaumont, *Utopia Ltd.: Ideologies of Social Dreaming in England 1870–1900*, 2nd ed. (Chicago: Haymarket, 2009), 154. Beaumont cites Raymond Williams's elaboration of the "crisis of metropolitan experience" in *The Country and the City* (London: Chatto and Windus, 1973), 272. See also Raymond Williams, "Metropolitan Perceptions and the Emergence of Modernism," in *Politics of Modernism: Against the New Conformists*, ed. Tony Pinkney, 2nd ed. (London: Verso, 2007), 37–48.

38. H. G. Wells, *When the Sleeper Wakes* (London: George Bell, 1899), 28. Subsequent citations refer to this edition and appear parenthetically in the text.

39. H. G. Wells, *Experiment in Autobiography: Discoveries and Conclusions of a Very Ordinary Brain (since 1866)*, 2 vols. (London: Victor Gollancz and the Cresset Press, 1934), 2:645.

40. For extended discussion of this topic as it bears on Wells's early fiction, see Catherine Redford, "'Great Safe Places Deep Down': Subterranean Spaces in the Early Novels of H. G. Wells," in *Utopias and Dystopias in the Fiction of H. G. Wells and William Morris: Landscape and Space*, ed. Emelyne Godfrey (Basingstoke, UK: Palgrave, 2016), 123–138.

41. In Shaw's article "Nietzsche in English," published in the *Saturday Review* in 1896, he described Nietzsche as a "champion of privilege, of power and of inequality." George Bernard Shaw, "Nietzsche in English," *Saturday Review of Politics, Literature, Science and Art* 81, no. 2111 (11 April 1896): 373–374.

42. George Bernard Shaw, *The Perfect Wagnerite: A Commentary on the Niblung's Ring*, 3rd ed. (London: Constable, 1913), 100. The additional chapter where these remarks appear, "Why He Changed His Mind," was also included in the 1909 Brentano edition published in New York.

43. George Bernard Shaw, "Preface to the 1908 Edition," in *Fabian Essays in Socialism*, ed. George Bernard Shaw (Boston: Ball, 1909), xii.

44. Frederic Harrison, *Autobiographic Memoirs*, 2 vols. (London: Macmillan, 1911), 2:31.

45. Walter Benjamin, *The Arcades Project*, trans. Howard Eiland and Kevin McLaughlin (Cambridge, MA: Harvard University, 1999), 25.

46. Benjamin, 25.

47. Phillip E. Wegner, *Imaginary Communities: Utopia, the Nation, and the Spatial Histories of Modernity* (Berkeley: University of California Press, 2002), 179.

48. Benjamin, *Arcades Project*, 24.

49. See James A. Leith, "The War of Images Surrounding the Commune," in *Images of the Commune / Images de la Commune*, ed. James A. Leith (Montreal: McGill-Queen's University Press, 1978), 138–139.

50. Ross, *Emergence of Social Space*, 149.

51. See, for example, Pierre Vésinier, *History of the Commune of Paris*, trans. J. V. Weber (London: Chapman and Hall, 1872), 241–242; Prosper-Olivier Lissagaray, *History of the Commune of 1871*, trans. Eleanor Marx Aveling (London: Reeves and Turner, 1886), 349–350.

52. Priscilla Parkhurst Ferguson, *Paris as Revolution: Writing the Nineteenth-Century City* (Berkeley: University of California Press, 1994), 153.

53. Gustave Le Bon, *The Psychology of Revolution*, trans. Bernard Miall (London: T. Fisher Unwin, 1913), 329.

54. H. G. Wells to Elizabeth Healey, 23 March 1888, in *The Correspondence of H. G. Wells*, ed. David Clayton Smith, 4 vols. (London: Pickering and Chatto, 1998), 1:95–96.

55. Norman MacKenzie and Jeanne MacKenzie, *The Life of H. G. Wells: The Time Traveller*, rev. ed. (London: Hogarth, 1987), 62.

56. See Karl Löwith, *Nietzsche's Philosophy of the Eternal Recurrence of the Same*, trans. J. Harvey Lomax, with a foreword by Bernd Magnus (Berkeley: University of California Press, 1997). For Löwith, Nietzsche's elaboration of the concept illustrates an "essential connection between nihilism and recurrence" because "on the one hand the idea of the eternal recurrence teaches a new purpose of human existence beyond human

existence, a will to self-eternalization; but it also teaches the exact opposite: a revolving of the natural world in itself, a revolving that is just as selfless as it is goalless, and that includes human life." Löwith, 60.

57. See Bernard Bergonzi, *The Early H. G. Wells: A Study of the Scientific Romances* (Toronto: University of Toronto Press, 1961), 9–11, 22.

58. Colette E. Wilson, *Paris and the Commune 1871–78: The Politics of Forgetting* (Manchester, UK: Manchester University Press, 2007), 11.

59. Friedrich Nietzsche, *Thus Spake Zarathustra: A Book for All and None*, vol. 8 of *The Works of Friedrich Nietzsche*, trans. Alexander Tille (London: Macmillan, 1896), 320. As the publication of Nietzsche's *Complete Works* in English took shape under the editorship of Oscar Levy, this edition was retrospectively renumbered as volume 2.

60. A. Seth Pringle Pattison, "The Opinions of Friedrich Nietzsche," *Contemporary Review* 73 (May 1898): 735; W. Wallace, "'The Works of Friedrich Nietzsche,'" *Academy* 50, no. 1265 (1 August 1896): 77.

61. Löwith, *Nietzsche's Philosophy*, xxiv.

62. Löwith, xxv.

63. Benjamin, *Arcades Project*, 112.

64. H. G. Wells, *A Modern Utopia* (London: Chapman and Hall, 1905), 24; Ben Carver, "'All Good Earthly Things Are in Utopia Also': Familiarity and Irony in the Better Worlds of Morris and Wells," in Godfrey, *Utopias and Dystopias*, 86–87.

65. Benjamin, *Arcades Project*, 111.

66. Benjamin, 112.

67. Friedrich Nietzsche, *The Birth of Tragedy; or, Hellenism and Pessimism*, vol. 3 of *The Complete Works of Frederick Nietzsche*, ed. Oscar Levy, trans. William A. Haussmann (Edinburgh: T. N. Foulis, 1909), 138.

68. Friedrich Nietzsche, *A Genealogy of Morals*, vol. 10 of *The Works of Friedrich Nietzsche*, ed. Alexander Tille, trans. William A. Haussmann (London: Macmillan, 1897), 35. Haussmann translates *ressentiment* as "resentment."

69. Fredric Jameson, *The Political Unconscious: Narrative as a Socially Symbolic Act*, new ed. (London: Routledge, 2006), 188–189.

70. William C. Dowling, *Jameson, Althusser, Marx: An Introduction to the Political Unconscious* (London: Methuen, 1984), 134.

71. William Morris, "How We Live and How We Might Live," in *Collected Works*, 23:3.

72. Karl Marx, "The Civil War in France: Address of the General Council," in *Political Writings*, vol. 3, *The First International and After*, ed. David Fernbach (Harmondsworth, UK: Penguin, 1992), 214.

73. Marx, 211.

74. Benjamin, *Arcades Project*, 15.

75. See Esther Leslie, *Walter Benjamin: Overpowering Conformism* (London: Pluto, 2000), 180–181.

76. Benjamin, *Arcades Project*, 116.

77. Benjamin, 117.

78. Benjamin, 340.

79. Benjamin, 474.

80. Benjamin, 12–13.

81. Leslie, *Walter Benjamin*, 181.

82. John Batchelor, *H. G. Wells* (Cambridge: Cambridge University Press, 1985), 5.

83. Wells to Healey, 23 March 1888, 1:95.
84. H. G. Wells, *The Sleeper Awakes: A Revised Edition of "When the Sleeper Wakes"* ([London]: Thomas Nelson and Sons, 1910), ii.
85. Wells, i.
86. Wells, i.
87. H. G. Wells to the editor of the *Daily Express*, 16 September 1906, in *Correspondence*, 2:106.
88. H. G. Wells to the editor of the *Magazine of Commerce*, 5 August 1907, in *Correspondence*, 2:155.
89. Nietzsche, *Thus Spake Zarathustra*, 198.
90. Löwith, *Nietzsche's Philosophy*, xv. As Löwith puts it, "In the cosmological interpretation . . . recurrence appear[s] not as a 'plan for a new way to live' and a 'will to rebirth' but as destruction and rebirth that happens by nature and that is completely indifferent to all plans made by man." Löwith, 157.
91. See Georges Haupt, "The Commune as Symbol and Example," in *Aspects of International Socialism 1871–1941: Essays by Georges Haupt*, trans. Peter Fawcett, preface by Eric Hobsbawm, 2nd ed. (Cambridge: Cambridge University Press, 2010), 23–47.
92. H. G. Wells, *In the Days of the Comet* (London: Macmillan, 1906), 202, 17.
93. Beaumont, *Utopia Ltd.*, 132.
94. Beaumont, 131.
95. Beaumont, 147.
96. Beaumont, 163.
97. See, for example, David Trotter, *The English Novel in History, 1895–1920* (London: Routledge, 2001), 27–48.
98. Beaumont, *Utopia Ltd.*, 165.
99. Duncan Bell, "Pragmatism and Prophecy: H. G. Wells and the Metaphysics of Socialism," *American Political Science Review* 112, no. 2 (2018): 409.
100. Beaumont, *Utopia Ltd.*, 43, 64.

CHAPTER 8 — CONCLUSION

1. J. Michelle Coghlan, *Sensational Internationalism: The Paris Commune and the Remapping of American Memory in the Long Nineteenth Century* (Edinburgh: Edinburgh University Press, 2016), 158.
2. Leon Trotsky, *Literature and Revolution*, ed. William Keach, trans. Rose Strunsky (Chicago: Haymarket, 2005), 33.
3. Peter Starr, *Commemorating Trauma: The Paris Commune and its Cultural Aftermath* (New York: Fordham University Press, 2006), 2–5, 18–19, 30–32.
4. Theodor Adorno, *Aesthetic Theory*, trans. Robert Hullot-Kentor (London: Continuum, 2004), 240.
5. Alfred Austin, *The Human Tragedy*, new and rev. ed. (London: Macmillan, 1889), 280.
6. "The Human Tragedy," *Saturday Review* 68, no. 1779 (30 November 1889): 629.
7. "Parisian Refugees at St. Germains," *Graphic* 3, no. 79 (3 June 1871): 514.
8. Alexandra Orr, *The Twins of Saint Marcel: A Tale of Paris Incendié* (Edinburgh: William P. Nimmo, 1872), 313.
9. Orr, 313.
10. Orr, 316.

11. James F. Cobb, *Workman and Soldier: A Tale of Paris Life during the Siege and the Rule of the Commune* (London: Griffith and Farran, 1880), 304–305.

12. Cobb, 304–305.

13. John Oxenham, *Under the Iron Flail* (London: Cassell, 1902), 359, 362.

14. Oxenham, 379.

15. William Barry, *The Dayspring* (New York: Dodd, Mead, 1904), 320.

16. Barry, 317.

17. Stewart Edwards, *The Paris Commune, 1871* (London: Eyre and Spottiswoode, 1971), 365.

18. Kristin Ross, *The Emergence of Social Space: Rimbaud and the Paris Commune*, 2nd ed. (London: Verso, 2008), 42.

19. David Harvey, *Paris, Capital of Modernity* (London: Routledge, 2003), 328.

20. Harvey, 332.

21. Mary Elizabeth Braddon, *Under the Red Flag* (Leipzig: Bernard Tauchnitz, 1883), 236.

22. Priscilla Parkhurst Ferguson, *Paris as Revolution: Writing the Nineteenth-Century City* (Berkeley: University of California Press, 1994), 67.

23. Ferguson, 69

24. Ferguson, 69.

25. Coghlan, *Sensational Internationalism*, 3, 8.

26. Walter Benjamin, *The Arcades Project*, trans. Howard Eiland and Kevin McLaughlin (Cambridge, MA: Harvard University, 1999), 340.

27. Oxenham, *Under the Iron Flail*, 363.

28. Oxenham, 363.

29. Raymond Williams, *Marxism and Literature* (Oxford: Oxford University Press, 1977), 121–127.

30. Karl Marx, "The Civil War in France: Address of the General Council," in *Political Writings*, vol. 3, *The First International and After*, ed. David Fernbach (Harmondsworth, UK: Penguin, 1992), 249.

31. Karl Marx to Ludwig Kugelman, 17 April 1871, in *The Paris Commune of 1871: The View from the Left*, ed. Eugene Schulkind (London: Jonathan Cape, 1971), 199.

32. Williams, *Marxism and Literature*, 124.

33. Gustave Paul Cluseret, "The Paris Commune of 1871: Its Origin, Legitimacy, Tendency, and Aim," *Fraser's Magazine* 7, no. 39 (March 1873): 360–361.

34. Édouard Vaillant, "Vive la Commune!," *Commonweal* 1, no. 3 (April 1885): 17.

35. John Milner, *Art, War and Revolution in France, 1870–1871: Myth, Reportage and Reality* (New Haven, CT: Yale University Press, 2000), 147. See also David A. Shafer, *The Paris Commune: French Politics, Culture and Society at the Crossroads of the Revolutionary Tradition and Revolutionary Socialism* (Basingstoke: Palgrave Macmillan, 2005), 140–141.

36. Léo Frankel, "Article on the Commune," in Schulkind, *Paris Commune*, 241.

37. Jules Vallès, *Jacques Vingtras: L'Insurgé, 1871* (Paris: G. Charpentier, 1886), 100. For the translation, see Jules Vallès, *The Insurrectionist*, trans. Sandy Petrey (Englewood Cliffs, NJ: Prentice-Hall, 1971), 61.

38. Vallès, *Jacques Vingtras*, 92; Vallès, *Insurrectionist*, 54–55.

39. Benjamin, *Arcades Project*, 12–13.

40. Jerrold Seigel, *Bohemian Paris: Culture, Politics, and the Boundaries of Bourgeois Life, 1830–1930* (Harmondsworth, UK: Penguin, 1986), 202.

41. See, for example, Cobb, *Workman and Soldier*, 118, 212, 220; Maria M. Grant, *Lescar, the Universalist*, 3 vols. (London: Chapman and Hall, 1874), 3:245. François Furet, *Revolutionary France, 1770–1880* (Oxford: Oxford University Press, 1992), 506.

42. "How Paris Mourns," *All the Year Round* 6, no. 137 (15 July 1871): 155.

43. Peter Brooks, *Reading for the Plot: Design and Intention in Narrative*, new ed. (Cambridge, MA: Harvard University Press, 1992), 280.

44. George Gissing to Algernon Gissing, 2 January 1880, in *The Collected Letters of George Gissing*, vol. 1, *1863–1880*, ed. Paul F. Mattheisen, Arthur C. Young, and Pierre Coustillas (Athens: Ohio University Press, 1990), 1:229.

45. Kristin Ross, *Communal Luxury: The Political Imaginary on the Paris Commune* (London: Verso, 2015), 64.

46. Barry, *Dayspring*, 310.

47. Barry, 310.

48. In addition to Eudes, these are (in order of appearance) Raoul Rigault, Gabriel Ranvier, Edmond Mégy, Théophile Ferré, Jaroslav Dombrowski, Gustave Flourens, Auguste Vermorel, Charles Delescluze, Louis Rossell, Pascale Grousset, Jules Bergeret, Charles Amouroux, Charles Mabille, Gustave Paul Cluseret, L. Boursier, Victor Bénot, Gustave Genton, Louis Benoni Decamps, Théodore Benoist, Adolphe Berthillon, Auguste Blanqui, Antoine Brunel, and Henri Rochefort. Other contemporaneous figures also appear, including Victor Noir, Français-Vincent Raspail, Léon Gambetta, and Adolphe Thiers.

49. Francis Henry Gribble, *The Red Spell* (New York: Frederick A. Stokes, 1895), 69.

50. Grant, *Lescar*, 3:236–237.

51. Richard Maxwell, *The Historical Novel in Europe, 1650–1950* (Cambridge: Cambridge University Press, 2009), 50. Maxwell borrows the Hegelian phrase ("world-historical figures") from Lukács, adding: "The reader may catch a few intimate glimpses of the reigning celebrity—and thus approach the secret-history logic of gauging public catastrophe by reference to private psychology—but such moments are never long sustained" (50–51). In a more recent discussion of the Commune's "insurgent universality," Massimiliano Tomba writes that "One of the characteristics of insurgent universality is the lack of what Hegel called world-historical heroes who play pivotal roles in the progress of world history. When the people are really the protagonists and they act politically, not through representatives and leaders but in their own assemblies, clubs, and councils, then the people don't need big personalities." The proliferation of many different historical Communards in the popular fictions about the Commune is, in part, an effect of the phenomenon Tomba describes, since there were no self-evidently "great personalities" who could "emerge and take up the scene with their own name." See Tomba, *Insurgent Universality: An Alternative Legacy of Modernity* (Oxford: Oxford University Press, 2019), 79.

52. Walter Scott to Richard Sainthill Jones, 12 March 1833, in *The Letters of Sir Walter Scott*, ed. H.J.C. Grierson, 12 vols. (London: Constable, 1932–1937), 3:234.

53. Barry, *Dayspring*, 319; Thomas March, *The History of the Paris Commune of 1871* (London: Swan Sonnenschein, 1896), 291.

54. March, *History*, 336.

55. Barry, *Dayspring*, 322.

56. March, *History*, 1.

57. March, 1.

58. March, 1, 317, 332.

59. Fredric Jameson, *The Antinomies of Realism* (London: Verso, 2013), 270–271.
60. Jameson, 271.
61. Barry, *Dayspring*, 327.
62. Henry James to Sarah Orne Jewett, 5 October 1905, in *Henry James: Letters*, ed. Leon Edel, 4 vols. (Cambridge, MA: Harvard University, 1974–1984), 4:208.
63. Jameson, *Antinomies*, 271.
64. Jameson, 271.
65. Franco Moretti, *The Way of the World: The Bildungsroman in European Culture*, trans. Albert Sbragia, new ed. (London: Verso, 2000), 35.
66. Moretti, 54.
67. Jameson, *Antinomies*, 267.
68. For an illuminating consideration this topic, see Neil Davidson, "Is Social Revolution Still Possible in the Twenty-First Century?," *Journal of Contemporary Central and Eastern Europe* 23, nos. 2–3 (2015): 105–150.

Bibliography

PRIMARY SOURCES

Andrieu, Jules. *Notes pour Servir à l'Histoire de la Commune de Paris en 1871*. Edited by Maximilien Rubel and Louis Janover. Paris: Payot, 1971.

———. "The Paris Commune: A Chapter towards Its Theory and History." *Fortnightly Review* 10, no. 59 (November 1871): 571–598.

Arnold, Matthew. *Culture and Anarchy*. London: Smith, Elder, 1869.

———. *Essays in Criticism*. 3rd ed. London: Macmillan, 1875.

———. *Irish Essays and Others*. London: Smith, Elder, 1882.

———. *The Letters of Matthew Arnold*. Edited by Cecil Y. Lang. 6 vols. Charlottesville: University of Virginia Press, 1996–2002.

Austin, Alfred. *The Autobiography of Alfred Austin, Poet Laureate, 1835–1910*. 2 vols. London: Macmillan, 1911.

———. *The Human Tragedy*. New and rev. ed. London: Macmillan, 1889.

———. *The Poetry of the Period*. London: Richard Bentley, 1870.

Austin, Alfred, and W. J. Courthope. "Current Politics." *National Review* 1, no. 2 (April 1883): 314–320.

Bagenal, Philip H. "The International, and Its Influence on English Politics." *National Review* 2, no. 9 (November 1883): 422–436.

Baker, Ernest Albert. *A Guide to Historical Fiction*. London: George Routledge, 1914.

Barry, William. *The Dayspring*. New York: Dodd, Mead, 1904.

Bax, Ernest Belfort. "Lissagaray's 'History of the Commune.'" *Commonweal* 2, no. 47 (4 December 1886): 283.

———. *A Short History of the Paris Commune*. London: Twentieth Century, 1895.

Beatty, Pakenham. "The Last Barricade of the Commune." *To-Day: Monthly Magazine of Scientific Socialism* 5, no. 29 (May 1886): 125.

Beckett, Reginald A. "The Eighteenth of March." *Commonweal* 5, no. 166 (16 March 1889): 83.

Beesly, E. S. "The Paris Revolution." In *The English Defence of the Commune (1871)*, edited by Royden Harrison, 64–67. London: Merlin, 1971.

Bennett, Arnold. "Herbert George Wells and his Work." In *Arnold Bennett and H. G. Wells: A Record of a Personal and a Literary Friendship*. Edited by Harris Wilson, 260–276. Urbana: University of Illinois Press, 1960.

———. *The Old Wives' Tale*. London: Hodder and Stoughton, 1911.

Bertall [Charles Albert d'Arnoux]. *The Communists of Paris 1871: Types–Physiognomies–Characters; Explanatory Text Descriptive of Each Design Written Expressly for This Edition by an Englishman*. London: Buckingham, 1873.

Bertz, Eduard. "George Gissing: Ein Real-Idealist." In *George Gissing: The Critical Heritage*, edited by Pierre Coustillas and Colin Partridge, 149–156. Abingdon, UK: Routledge, 1995.

Besant, Annie. "Industry under Socialism." In *Fabian Essays in Socialism*, edited by George Bernard Shaw, 150–169. London: Fabian Society, 1889.

Betham-Edwards, Matilda. *Brother Gabriel*. 3 vols. London: Hurst and Blackett, 1878.

Bingham, Denis Arthur. *Recollections of Paris*. 2 vols. London: Chapman and Hall, 1896.

"Book-collecting." In *The Bookworm: An Illustrated Treasury of Old-Time Literature*, 241–244. London: Elliot Stock, 1891.

Bowen, W. E. *Edward Bowen: A Memoir*. London: Longmans, Green, 1902.

Braddon, Mary Elizabeth. *One Life, One Love: A Novel*. London: Simpkin, Marshall, Hamilton, Kent, 1891.

———. *Under the Red Flag*. Leipzig: Bernard Tauchnitz, 1883.

Bulwer Lytton, Edward. *The Coming Race*. Edinburgh: William Blackwood, 1871.

———. *Pamphlets and Sketches*. London: George Routledge, 1875.

———. *The Parisians*. 2 vols. London: Routledge, 1878.

Burns, John. "Let London Live!" *Nineteenth Century* 31, no. 182 (April 1892): 673–685.

———. "The London County Council I. Towards a Commune." *Nineteenth Century* 31, no. 181 (March 1892): 496–514.

Carlyle, Thomas. *Chartism*. London: James Fraser, 1840.

———. *The Collected Letters of Thomas and Jane Welsh Carlyle*. Edited by Ian Campbell, Aileen Christianson, and David Sorensen. 48 vols. Durham, NC: Duke University Press, 1970–2020.

———. *The French Revolution: A History*. 3 vols. London: Chapman and Hall, 1871.

Carpenter, Edward. "Saved by a Nose: A Bit of an Autobiography." In *Sketches from Life in Town and Country, and some Verses*, 212–219. London: George Allen, 1908.

[Cashel-Hoey, John Baptist]. "The International Society." *Dublin Review* 17, no. 34 (October 1871): 447–464.

Chambers, Robert W. *The Red Republic: A Romance of the Commune*. London: G. P. Putnam's Sons, 1895.

Chesterton, G. K. *The Common Man*. London: Sheed and Ward, 1950.

———. *A Miscellany of Men*. London: Methuen, 1912.

———. *The Napoleon of Notting Hill*. London: John Lane, 1904.

"Civil War in Paris." *Times*, March 20, 1871, 9.

"Civil War in Paris, The." *Illustrated London News* 58, no. 1655 (17 June 1871): 596.

Cluseret, Gustave Paul. "The Paris Commune of 1871: Its Origin, Legitimacy, Tendency, and Aim." *Fraser's Magazine* 7, no. 39 (March 1873): 360–384.

Cobb, James F. *Workman and Soldier: A Tale of Paris Life during the Siege and the Rule of the Commune*. London: Griffith and Farran, 1880.

"Communists in London, The." *Pall Mall Gazette* 14, no. 2058 (18 September 1871): 3.

Crane, Walter. *An Artist's Reminiscences*. London: Methuen, [1907].

———. "In Memory of the Commune of Paris: Born March 18, 1871, Died in June the Same Year." *Black and White* 1, no. 9 (4 April 1891): 274.

Derwent, Leith. *King Lazarus: A Novel*. 3 vols. London: Bentley, 1881.

Dickinson, G. Lowes. *Revolution and Reaction in Modern France*. London: George Allen, 1892.

Du Camp, Maxime. *Les Convulsions de Paris*. 5th ed. 4 vols. Paris: Librairie Hachette, 1881.

Eliot, George. *Felix Holt, the Radical*. 3 vols. Edinburgh: William Blackwood, 1866.

———. *The George Eliot Letters*. Edited by Gordon S. Haight. 9 vols. London: Oxford University Press, 1954-1978.

———. *Impressions of Theophrastus Such*. Edinburgh: William Blackwood, 1879.

Engels, Friedrich. "The Programme of the Blanquist Commune Refugees." 1874. In *The Paris Commune of 1871: The View from the Left*, edited by Eugene Schulkind, 239-240. London: Jonathan Cape, 1972.

"Foreign News." *Graphic* 3, no. 79 (3 June 1871): 518.

Frankel, Léo. "Article on the Commune." In *The Paris Commune of 1871: The View from the Left*, edited by Eugene Schulkind, 241. London: Jonathan Cape, 1972.

"French Siege of Paris, The." *Illustrated London News* 58, no. 1651 (20 May 1871): 492.

Gautier, Théophile. *The Works of Théophile Gautier*. Edited and translated by F. C. de Sumichrast. 12 vols. New York: International Publishing, 1900-1903.

Gibson, William. *Paris during the Commune, 1871: Being Letters from Paris and Its Neighbourhood, Written Chiefly during the Time of the Second Siege*. London: Whittaker, 1872.

Gissing, George. *Charles Dickens: A Critical Study*. London: Blackie, 1898.

———. *The Collected Letters of George Gissing*. Vol. 1, *1863-1880*. Edited by Paul F. Mattheisen, Arthur C. Young, and Pierre Coustillas. Athens: Ohio University Press, 1990.

———. *The Nether World: A Novel*. 3 vols. London: Smith, Elder and Co., 1889.

———. *New Grub Street: A Novel*. 3 vols. London: Smith, Elder, 1891.

———. "Notes on Social Democracy—I." *Pall Mall Gazette* 32, no. 4851 (9 September 1880): 10.

———. "Notes on Social Democracy—II." *Pall Mall Gazette* 32, no. 4853 (11 September 1880): 10.

———. "Notes on Social Democracy—III." *Pall Mall Gazette* 32, no. 4855 (14 September 1880): 11.

———. *The Private Papers of Henry Ryecroft*. Westminster, UK: Archibald Constable, 1903.

———. *The Unclassed: A Novel*. 3 vols. London: Chapman and Hall, 1884.

———. *Workers in the Dawn: A Novel*. 3 vols. London: Remington, 1880.

Glasier, John Bruce. "A Proletarian Epic." *Socialist Review: A Monthly Review of Modern Thought* 17 (1920): 322-325.

Goncourt, Edmond de, and Jules de Goncourt. *Pages from the Goncourt Journal*. Edited and translated by Robert Baldick. Oxford: Oxford University Press, 1988.

Gosse, Edmund. "The Influence of Democracy on Literature." *Contemporary Review* 59 (April 1891): 523-536.

———. *Questions at Issue*. London: William Heinemann, 1893.

——. "Tennyson." *New Review* 7, no. 42 (November 1892): 513–523.
Grant, Maria M. *Lescar, the Universalist*. 3 vols. London: Chapman and Hall, 1874.
Gribble, Francis Henry. *The Red Spell*. New York: Frederick A. Stokes, 1895.
Grousset, Paschal. "How the Paris Commune Made the Republic." *Time: A Monthly Miscellany of Interesting and Amusing Literature* 1 (April–September 1879): 106–114, 247–255, 371–378, 492–500, 568–576, 750–760.
Harrison, Austin. *Frederic Harrison: Thoughts and Memories*. London: William Heinemann, 1926.
Harrison, Frederic. *Autobiographic Memoirs*. 2 vols. London: Macmillan, 1911.
——. "The Fall of the Commune." *Fortnightly Review* 10, no. 56 (August 1871): 129–155.
——. "The Revolution of the Commune." *Fortnightly Review* 9, no. 53 (May 1871): 556–579.
Harrison, Mrs. Frederic. "French Refugees to England in 1871–72." *Cornhill Magazine*, n.s., 18 (May 1905): 607–613.
Harrison, Royden, ed. *The English Defence of the Commune 1871*. London: Merlin, 1971.
Hayens, Herbert. *Paris at Bay*. London: Blackie and Son, 1897.
Headingley, Adolphe S. *The Biography of Charles Bradlaugh*. London: Remington, 1880.
Hegel, G.W.F. *Hegel on Tragedy*. Edited by Anne Paolucci and Henry Paolucci. New York: Anchor, 1962.
Henderson, Fred. *By the Sea, and Other Poems*. London: T. Fisher Unwin, 1892.
Henty, G. A. *A Woman of the Commune*. London: F. V. White, 1896.
Hervey, Charles. "Collectors and Their 'Hobbies.'" *London Society* 46, no. 272 (August 1884): 236–240.
Hopkins, Gerard Manley. *The Collected Works of Gerard Manley Hopkins*. Edited by R.K.R. Thornton, Catherine Phillips, et al. Vol. 1. Oxford: Oxford University Press, 2013.
"How Paris Mourns." *All the Year Round* 6, no. 137 (15 July 1871): 150–155.
Hugo, Victor. *L'Année Terrible*. Paris: Michel Lévy Frères, 1872.
"Human Tragedy, The." *Saturday Review* 68, no. 1779 (30 November 1889): 628–629.
Hunt, William Holman. *Pre-Raphaelitism and the Pre-Raphaelite Brotherhood*. 2 vols. London: Macmillan, 1905.
Hyndman, H. M. *A Commune for London*. London: Justice Printery, 1887.
——. *The Historical Basis of Socialism in England*. London: Kegan Paul, Trench, 1883.
James, Henry. *The Ambassadors*. London: Methuen, 1903.
——. *The Complete Letters of Henry James, 1855–1872*. Edited by Pierre A. Walker and Greg W. Zacharias, 2 vols. Lincoln: University of Nebraska Press, 2006.
——. *The Complete Letters of Henry James, 1872–1876*. Edited by Pierre A. Walker and Greg W. Zacharias, 3 vols. Lincoln: University of Nebraska Press, 2008.
——. *Henry James: Letters*. Edited by Leon Edel. 4 vols. Cambridge, MA: Harvard University, 1974–1985.
——. *A Little Tour in France*. Leipzig: Bernhard Tauchnitz, 1885.
——. *The Princess Casamassima*. 3 vols. London: Macmillan, 1886.
——. *The Princess Casamassima*. 2 vols. New York: Charles Scribner's Sons, 1908.
"Justice Satisfied." *Graphic* 3, no. 83 (24 June 1871): 585.
Keenan, Henry F. *Trajan: The History of a Sentimental Young Man, with Some Episodes in the Comedy of Many Lives' Errors*. New York: Cassell, 1885.
King, Edward. *The Red Terror; or, The Adventures of Two American Boys under the Red Flag of the Commune*. London: Cassell, 1895.

[Labouchère, Henry Du Pré]. *Diary of the Besieged Resident in Paris: Reprinted from "The Daily News," with Several New Letters and Preface.* London: Hurst and Blackett, 1871.

Le Bon, Gustave. *The Psychology of Revolution.* Translated by Bernard Miall. London: T. Fisher Unwin, 1913.

Leighton, John. *Paris under the Commune; or, The Seventy-Three Days of the Second Siege.* 3rd ed. London: Bradbury, Evans, 1871.

[Linton, Eliza Lynn]. *The True History of Joshua Davidson.* London: Strahan, 1872.

———. *The True History of Joshua Davidson, Christian and Communist.* 6th ed. London: Chatto and Windus, 1874.

Linton, W. J. *The Paris Commune.* Boston. Reprinted from *The Radical* for September 1871.

Lissagaray, Prosper-Olivier. *Histoire de la Commune de 1871.* Brussels: Librairie Contemporaine de Henri Kistemaeckers, 1876.

———. *History of the Commune of 1871.* Translated by Eleanor Marx. London: Reeves and Turner, 1886.

March, Thomas. *The History of the Paris Commune of 1871.* London: Swan Sonnenschein, 1896.

Markham, Charles Edwin. "The Song of the Workers (Remembering the Martyrs of the Commune)." *Commonweal* 2, no. 35 (11 September 1886): 187.

[Marshall, Frederic]. "A History of the Commune of Paris, by a Resident." *Blackwood's Magazine* 110, no. 669 (July 1871): 118–136.

Marx, Eleanor. "March 18: The Paris Commune—A Letter of Eleanor Marx." 17 March 1893. *Labour Monthly* 22, no. 3 (March 1940): 158–161.

Marx, Karl. "The Civil War in France: Address of the General Council." In *Political Writings*, vol. 3, *The First International and After*, edited by David Fernbach, 187–236. Harmondsworth, UK: Penguin, 1992.

———. "The Class Struggles in France: 1848 to 1850." In *Surveys from Exile: Political Writings*, vol. 2, edited by David Fernbach, 35–142. Harmondsworth, UK: Penguin, 1992.

———. "First Draft of 'The Civil War in France.'" In *Political Writings*, vol. 3, *The First International and After*, edited by David Fernbach, 236–268. Harmondsworth, UK: Penguin, 1992.

Marx, Karl, and Frederick Engels. *The Communist Manifesto.* Edited by David McLellan. Oxford: Oxford University Press, 1998.

McCarthy, Justin. *Reminiscences.* 2 vols. London: Chatto and Windus, 1899.

Meredith, Owen. "Prefatory Note (by the Author's Son)." In *The Parisians*, by Edward Bulwer Lytton, vol. 2, v–vii. London: Routledge, 1878.

Michel, Louise. *La Commune.* Paris: P. V. Stock, 1898.

———. "The Strike: A Drama." *Commonweal: A Revolutionary Journal of Anarchist Communism* 7, no. 281 (19 September 1891): 113; 7, no. 282 (26 September 1891): 117–118; 7, no. 283 (3 October 1891): 121–122; 7, no. 284 (10 October 1891): 125; 7, no. 287 (31 October 1891): 137–139; 7, no. 292 (5 December 1891): 157–158; 7, no. 293 (12 December 1891): 161.

———. "To Battle!" *Commonweal* 5, no. 179 (15 June 1889): 189.

Monod, G. "Contemporary Life and Thought in France." *Contemporary Review* 43, no. 2 (February 1883): 174–175.

Montbard, George. *The Case of John Bull in Egypt, The Transvaal, Venezuela and Elsewhere.* London: Hutchinson, [1896].

Moore, George. *Confessions of a Young Man.* London: Swan Sonnenschein, Lowrey, 1888.

Morris, William. *The Collected Works of William Morris*. Edited by May Morris. 24 vols. London: Longmans, Green, 1910–1915.

———. *The Collected Letters of William Morris*. Edited by Norman Kelvin. 4 vols. in 5. Princeton, NJ: Princeton University Press, 1984–1996.

———. *Journalism: Contributions to "Commonweal," 1885–1890*. Edited by Nicholas Salmon. Bristol, UK: Thoemmes, 1996.

———. *Political Writings: Contributions to "Justice" and "Commonweal," 1883–1890*. Edited by Nicholas Salmon. Bristol, UK: Thoemmes, 1994.

———. *Socialist Diary*. Edited by Florence S. Boos. 2nd ed. Nottingham, UK: Five Leaves, 2018.

———. "The Three Seekers." *To-Day: Monthly Magazine of Scientific Socialism* 1, no. 1 (January 1884): 25–29.

Murray, James A. H., ed. *A New English Dictionary on a Historical Basis*. 10 vols. Oxford, UK: Clarendon, 1888–1928.

"Nécrologie." *Le Radical*, 12 September 1890, n.p. [2].

"New Revolution in Paris, The." *Standard*, March 21, 1871, 5.

Nield, Jonathan. *A Guide to the Best Historical Novels and Tales*. London: Elkin Matthews, 1902.

Nietzsche, Friedrich. *The Birth of Tragedy; or, Hellenism and Pessimism*. Vol. 3 of *The Complete Works of Frederick Nietzsche*. Translated by William A. Haussmann. Edinburgh: T. N. Foulis, 1909.

———. *A Genealogy of Morals*. Vol. 10 of *The Works of Friedrich Nietzsche*. Edited by Alexander Tille. Translated by William A. Haussmann. London: Macmillan, 1897.

———. *Thus Spake Zarathustra: A Book for All and None*. Vol. 8 of *The Works of Friedrich Nietzsche*. Translated by Alexander Tille. London: Macmillan, 1896.

"Notes and News." *Academy* 536 (12 August 1882): 119.

Oliphant, Margaret. *The Autobiography of Margaret Oliphant: The Complete Text*. Edited by Elisabeth Jay. Oxford: Oxford University Press, 1990.

———. *A Beleaguered City, Being the Narrative of Certain Recent Events in the City of Semur, in the Department of the Haute Bourgogne; A Tale of the Seen and the Unseen*. London: Macmillan, 1880.

———. *Memoir of the Life of Laurence Oliphant and of Alice Oliphant, His Wife*. New ed. London: William Blackwood, 1892.

———. "Novels." *Blackwood's Magazine* 102, no. 623 (September 1867): 257–280.

———. "Three Days in Paris." *Blackwood's Magazine* 124, no. 756 (October 1878): 455–474.

Orr, Alexandra. *The Twins of Saint-Marcel: A Tale of Paris Incendié*. Edinburgh: William P. Nimmo, 1872.

"Our Paris Letter." *Englishwoman's Domestic Magazine* 79 (1 July 1871): 54.

Oxenham, John. *Under the Iron Flail*. London: Cassell, 1905.

"Parisian Refugees at St. Germains." *Graphic* 3, no. 79 (3 June 1871): 514.

Pattison, A. Seth Pringle. "The Opinions of Friedrich Nietzsche." *Contemporary Review* 73 (May 1898): 727–750.

Pottier, Eugene. "The Anthropophagite." *Commonweal* 5, no. 207 (28 December 1889): 411.

———. "Blanqui." *Commonweal* 5, no. 193 (21 September 1889): 301.

———. "Buried Alive." *Commonweal* 5, no. 170 (13 April 1889): 115.

———. "Don Quixote." *Commonweal* 6, no. 222 (12 April 1890): 115.

———. "Marguerite: To My Daughter, M.P." *Commonweal* 5, no. 196 (12 October 1889): 325.

———. "Plenty." *Commonweal* 5, no. 185 (27 July 1889): 237.
Prothero, R. E. "The London County Council II. Towards Common Sense." *Nineteenth Century* 31, no. 181 (March 1892): 515-524.
Quentin, Charles. *Through the Storm*. 3 vols. London: Hurst and Blackett, 1880.
Redesdale, Algernon Bertram. *Further Memories*. Introduction by Edmund Gosse. London: Hutchinson, 1917.
Revolutionary Commune Group. "To Supporters of the Commune." In *The Paris Commune of 1871: The View from the Left*, edited by Eugene Schulkind, 235-238. London: Jonathan Cape, 1972.
Ritchie, Anne Thackeray. *The Correspondence and Journals of the Thackeray Family*. Edited by John Aplin. 5 vols. London: Pickering and Chatto, 2011.
———. *Mrs Dymond*. London: Smith, Elder, 1885.
———. *Records of Tennyson, Ruskin and Browning*. London: Macmillan, 1892.
———. *Thackeray's Daughter: Some Recollections of Anne Thackeray Ritchie*. Compiled by Hester Thackeray Fuller and Violet Hammersley. 2nd ed. Dublin: Euphorian, 1952.
Rossetti, Dante Gabriel. *The Correspondence of Dante Gabriel Rossetti*. Edited by William E. Fredeman, Roger C. Lewis, and Jane Cowan. 10 vols. Cambridge, UK: D. S. Brewer, 2002-2015.
Rossetti, W. M. *The Diary of W. M. Rossetti*. Edited by Odette Bornand. Oxford: Oxford University Press, 1977.
———. *Selected Letters of William Michael Rossetti*. Edited by Roger W. Peattie. University Park and London: Pennsylvania State University Press, 1990.
Round, John Horace. *The Commune of London and Other Studies*. Westminster, UK: Archibald Constable, 1899.
Ruskin, John. *The Works of John Ruskin*. Edited by E. T. Cook and Alexander Wedderburn. 39 vols. London: George Allen, 1903-1912.
[Salisbury, Lord]. "The Commune and the Internationale." *Quarterly Review* 131, no. 262 (October 1871): 549-580.
Sarcey, Francisque. *Le Siège de Paris: Impressions et Souvenirs*. Paris: E. Lachaud, 1871.
Savidge, Eugene C. *The American in Paris: A Biographical Novel of the Franco-Prussian War, the Siege and Commune of Paris from an American Standpoint*. Philadelphia: J. B. Lippincott, 1896.
Schulkind, Eugene, ed. *The Paris Commune of 1871: The View from the Left*. London: Jonathan Cape, 1972.
Scott, Walter. *The Letters of Sir Walter Scott*. Edited by H.J.C. Grierson. 12 vols. London: Constable, 1932-1937.
Shaw, George Bernard, ed. *Fabian Essays in Socialism*. London: Fabian Society, 1889.
———. "Nietzsche in English." *Saturday Review of Politics, Literature, Science and Art* 81, no. 2111 (11 April 1896): 373-374.
———. *The Perfect Wagnerite: A Commentary on the Niblung's Ring*. 3rd ed. London: Constable, 1913.
———. "Preface to the 1908 Edition." In *Fabian Essays in Socialism*, edited by George Bernard Shaw, ix-xxii. Boston: Ball, 1909.
———. *The Quintessence of Ibsenism*. London: Walter Scott, 1891.
Sherard, Robert H. *Oscar Wilde: The Story of an Unhappy Friendship*. London: Greening, 1905.

Sichel, Edith. "Two Philanthropic Novelists: Mr. Walter Besant and Mr. George Gissing." *Murray's Magazine* 3, no. 16 (April 1888): 506–518.
Sims, George R. *The Dagonet Ballads (Chiefly from the Referee)*. London: E. J. Francis, 1879.
———. *The Mysteries of Modern London*. London: C. Arthur Pearson, 1906.
Smith, Adolphe. "Political Refugees." In *London in the Nineteenth Century*, by Walter Besant, 399–406. London: Adam and Charles Black, 1909.
Special Commissioners of *The Daily Chronicle*. *New London: Her Parliament and Its Work, Reprinted from "The Daily Chronicle."* London: Edward Lloyd, 1895.
[Stigand, William]. "The Commune of Paris." *Edinburgh Review* 134, no. 274 (October 1871): 511–563.
Swinburne, Algernon Charles. *The Letters of Algernon Charles Swinburne*. Edited by Edmund Gosse and Thomas James Wise. 2 vols. London: William Heinemann, 1918.
———. *The Swinburne Letters*. Edited by Cecil Y. Lang. 6 vols. New Haven, CT: Yale University Press, 1959–1962.
Vaillant, Édouard. "Vive la Commune!" *Commonweal* 1, no. 3 (April 1885): 17.
Vallès, Jules. *The Insurrectionist*. Translated by Sandy Petrey. Englewood Cliffs, NJ: Prentice-Hall, 1971.
———. *Jacques Vingtras: L'Insurgé, 1871*. Paris: G. Charpentier, 1886.
———. "Quatrevingt-Treize." *Examiner* 3449 (7 March 1874): 236–237.
Vandam, Albert D. *An Englishman in Paris: Notes and Recollections*. 2 vols. London: Chapman and Hall, 1892.
Vésinier, Pierre. *History of the Commune of Paris*. Translated by J. V. Weber. London: Chapman and Hall, 1872.
Vizetelly, Henry. *Paris in Peril*. 2 vols. London: Tinsley Brothers, 1882.
Vuillaume, Maxime. *Mes Cahiers Rouge au Temps de la Commune*. 5th ed. Paris: Société d'Éditions Littéraires et Artistiques, 1900.
Wallace, W. "The Works of Friedrich Nietzsche." *Academy* 50, no. 1265 (1 August 1896): 75–77.
Waters, Mrs. John. *A Young Girl's Adventures in Paris during the Commune*. London: Remington, 1881.
Wells, H. G. *The Correspondence of H. G. Wells*. Edited by David Clayton Smith. 4 vols. London: Pickering and Chatto, 1998.
———. *Experiment in Autobiography: Discoveries and Conclusions of a Very Ordinary Brain (since 1866)*. 2 vols. London: Victor Gollancz and the Cresset Press, 1934.
———. *In the Days of the Comet*. London: Macmillan, 1906.
———. *A Modern Utopia*. London: Chapman and Hall, 1905.
———. *The Sleeper Awakes*. London: Collins' Clear-Type Press, 1921.
———. *The Sleeper Awakes: A Revised Edition of "When the Sleeper Wakes."* [London]: Thomas Nelson and Sons, 1910.
———. *When the Sleeper Wakes*. London: George Bell, 1899.
Westall, William. *Her Two Millions*. 3 vols. London: Ward and Downey, 1887.
[Wilson, John]. "Economic Fallacies and Labour Utopias." *Quarterly Review* 131, no. 261 (July 1871): 229–263.
"Women in Revolt." *Englishwoman's Domestic Magazine* 79 (1 July 1871): 59–60.
Wright, Thomas. *Our New Masters*. London: Strahan, 1873.

SECONDARY SOURCES

Adorno, Theodor. *Aesthetic Theory*. Translated by Robert Hullot-Kentor. London: Continuum, 2004.

Agamben, Giorgio. *Homo Sacer: Sovereign Power and Bare Life*. Translated by Daniel Heller-Roazen. Stanford, CA: Stanford University Press, 1998.

Anderson, Perry. *English Questions*. London: Verso, 1992.

———. "Modernity and Revolution." *New Left Review* 144 (March–April 1984): 96–113.

Anesko, Michael. *"Friction with the Market": Henry James and the Profession of Authorship*. Oxford: Oxford University Press, 1986.

Ashton, Rosemary. *Victorian Bloomsbury*. New Haven, CT: Yale University Press, 2012.

Atkinson, Juliette. *French Novels and the Victorians*. Oxford: Oxford University Press, published for the British Academy, 2017.

Ayers, David. *Modernism, Internationalism and the Russian Revolution*. Edinburgh: Edinburgh University Press, 2018.

Bachelard, Gaston. *The Psychoanalysis of Fire*. Translated by Alan C. M. Ross. Boston: Beacon, 1964.

Badiou, Alain. *The Communist Hypothesis*. Translated by David Macey and Steve Corcoran. 2nd ed. London: Verso, 2015.

Baguley, David. *Naturalist Fiction: The Entropic Vision*. Cambridge: Cambridge University Press, 1990.

Baldick, Chris. *The Social Mission of English Criticism, 1848–1932*. Oxford, UK: Clarendon, 1983.

Baron, Xavier. "Impressionist London in the Novels of George Gissing." In *Lineages of the Novel: Essays in Honour of Raimund Borgmeier*, edited by Bernhard Reitz and Eckart Voigts-Virchow, 107–117. Trier, Germany: WVT Wissenschaftlicher Verlag Trier, 2000.

Batchelor, John. *H. G. Wells*. Cambridge: Cambridge University Press, 1985.

Beaumont, Matthew. "A Communion of Just Men Made Perfect: Walter Pater, Romantic Anti-Capitalism and the Paris Commune." In *Renew Marxist Art History*, edited by Warren Carter, Barnaby Haran, and Frederic J. Schwartz, 94–106. London: Art Books, 2013.

———. *Utopia Ltd.: Ideologies of Social Dreaming in England, 1870–1900*. 2nd ed. Chicago: Haymarket, 2009.

Bell, Duncan. "Pragmatism and Prophecy: H. G. Wells and the Metaphysics of Socialism." *American Political Science Review* 112, no. 2 (2018): 409–422.

Benjamin, Walter. *The Arcades Project*. Translated by Howard Eiland and Kevin McLaughlin. Cambridge, MA: Harvard University Press, 1999.

———. *Selected Writings*. Vol. 4, *1938–1940*. Edited by Howard Eiland and Michael W. Jennings. Translated by Edmund Jephcott et al. Cambridge, MA: Harvard University, 2003.

Bergonzi, Bernard. *The Early H. G. Wells: A Study of the Scientific Romances*. Toronto: University of Toronto Press, 1961.

Boer, Roland. "Marx's Ambivalence: State, Proletarian Dictatorship and Commune." *International Critical Thought* 9, no. 1 (2019): 109–127.

Boime, Albert. *Art and the French Commune: Imagining Paris after War and Revolution*. Princeton, NJ: Princeton University Press, 1995.

Boos, Florence S. *The Design of William Morris' "The Earthly Paradise."* Lewiston, NY: Edwin Mellen, 1991.

———. "Narrative Design in *The Pilgrims of Hope*." In *Socialism and the Literary Artistry of William Morris*, edited by Florence S. Boos and Carole G. Silver, 147–166. Columbia: University of Missouri Press, 1990.

Boos, Florence S., and William Boos. "*News from Nowhere* and Victorian Socialist-Feminism." *Nineteenth-Century Contexts* 14, no. 1 (1990): 3–32.

Bragg, Tom. *Space and Narrative in the Nineteenth-Century British Historical Novel.* Abingdon, UK: Routledge, 2016.

Bristow, Joseph, and Josephine McDonagh, eds. *Nineteenth-Century Radical Traditions.* Basingstoke, UK: Palgrave, 2016.

Brooks, Peter. *Reading for the Plot: Design and Intention in Narrative.* New ed. Cambridge, MA: Harvard University Press, 1992.

Bullard, Alice. *Exile to Paradise: Savagery and Civilization in Paris and the South Pacific, 1790–1900.* Stanford, CA: Stanford University Press, 2000.

Carey, John. *The Intellectuals and the Masses: Pride and Prejudice among the Literary Intelligentsia, 1880–1939.* London: Faber and Faber, 1992.

Carver, Ben. "'All Good Earthly Things are in Utopia Also': Familiarity and Irony in the Better Worlds of Morris and Wells." In *Utopias and Dystopias in the Fiction of H. G. Wells and William Morris: Landscape and Space*, edited by Emelyne Godfrey, 75–87. Basingstoke, UK: Palgrave, 2016.

Casanova, Pascale. *The World Republic of Letters.* Translated by M. B. DeBevoise. Cambridge, MA: Harvard University Press, 2004.

Caygill, Howard. *On Resistance: A Philosophy of Defiance.* London: Bloomsbury, 2013.

Christensen, Allan Conrad. *Edward Bulwer-Lytton: The Fiction of New Regions.* Athens: University of Georgia Press, 1976.

———, ed. *The Subverting Vision of Bulwer Lytton: Bicentenary Reflections.* Newark: University of Delaware Press, 2004.

Christie, Ian R. *Stress and Stability in Late Eighteenth-Century Britain: Reflections on the British Avoidance of Revolution.* Oxford, UK: Clarendon, 1984.

Claeys, Gregory. *Citizens and Saints: Politics and Anti-Politics in Early British Socialism.* Cambridge: Cambridge University Press, 1989.

Coghlan, J. Michelle. *Sensational Internationalism: The Paris Commune and the Remapping of American Memory in the Long Nineteenth Century.* Edinburgh: Edinburgh University Press, 2016.

Cohen, Bruce M. Z. *Psychiatric Hegemony: A Marxist Theory of Mental Illness.* London: Palgrave Macmillan, 2016.

Corbeau-Parsons, Caroline. "Crossing the Channel." In *Impressionists in London: French Artists in Exile 1870–1904*, edited by Caroline Corbeau-Parsons, 13–19. London: Tate, 2017.

Coustillas, Pierre. *The Heroic Life of George Gissing, Part I: 1857–1888.* 2nd ed. Abingdon, UK: Routledge, 2016.

Crossley, Ceri, and Ian Small, eds. *The French Revolution and British Culture.* Oxford: Oxford University Press, 1989.

Cunningham, Gail. "The Riddle of Suburbia: Suburban Fictions at the Victorian Fin de Siècle." In *Expanding Suburbia: Reviewing Suburban Narratives*, edited by Roger Webster, 51–70. Oxford, UK: Berghahn, 2000.

Dalotel, Alain, Alaine Faure, and Jean-Claude Freiermuth. *Aux Origines de la Commune: Le Mouvement des Réunions Publiques à Paris, 1868–1871*. Paris: Maspero, 1980.

David, Deirdre. *Fictions of Resolution in Three Victorian Novels: "North and South," "Our Mutual Friend," "Daniel Deronda."* Basingstoke, UK: Macmillan, 1981.

Davidson, Neil. "Is Social Revolution Still Possible in the Twenty-First Century?" *Journal of Contemporary Central and Eastern Europe* 23, nos. 2–3 (2015): 105–150.

Dennis, Richard. "Mapping Gissing's *Workers in the Dawn*." *The Gissing Journal* 46, no. 4 (October 2010): 1–20.

———. "The Place of Bloomsbury in the Novels of George Gissing." *Opticon 1826* 7 (2009): 1–10.

Dowling, William C. *Jameson, Althusser, Marx: An Introduction to the Political Unconscious*. London: Methuen, 1984.

Duncan, Ian. "History and the Novel after Lukács." *Novel: A Forum on Fiction* 50, no. 3 (2017): 388–396.

Eagleton, Terry. *Sweet Violence: The Idea of the Tragic*. Oxford, UK: Blackwell, 2003.

Edwards, Stewart. *The Paris Commune, 1871*. London: Eyre and Spottiswoode, 1971.

Eichner, Carolyn J. *Surmounting the Barricades: Women in the Paris Commune*. Bloomington: Indiana University Press, 2004.

English, Donald E. "Political Photography and the Paris Commune of 1871: The Photographs of Eugène Appert." *History of Photography* 7, no. 1 (1983): 31–42.

Everest, Kelvin, ed. *Revolution in Writing: British Literary Responses to the French Revolution*. Milton Keynes, UK: Open University Press, 1991.

Ferguson, Priscilla Parkhurst. *Paris as Revolution: Writing the Nineteenth-Century City*. Berkeley: University of California Press, 1994.

Fischer, Mike. "The Jamesian Revolution in *The Princess Casamassima*: A Lesson in Bookbinding." *Henry James Review* 9, no. 2 (Spring 1988): 87–104.

Forster, Laura C. "The Paris Commune in London and the Spatial History of Ideas, 1871–1900." *Historical Journal* 62, no. 4 (2019): 1021–1044.

———. "The Paris Commune in the British Socialist Imagination, 1871–1914." *History of European Ideas* 46, no. 5 (2020): 614–632.

Furet, François. *Revolutionary France, 1770–1880*. Oxford: Oxford University Press, 1992.

Gérin, Winifred. *Anne Thackeray Ritchie: A Biography*. Oxford: Oxford University Press, 1981.

Gilmartin, Kevin. *Writing against Revolution: Literary Conservatism in Britain, 1790–1832*. Cambridge: Cambridge University Press, 2007.

Godfrey, Emelyne, ed. *Utopias and Dystopias in the Fiction of H. G. Wells and William Morris: Landscape and Space*. Basingstoke, UK: Palgrave, 2016.

Graham, Wendy. *Critics, Coteries, and Pre-Raphaelite Celebrity*. New York: Columbia University Press, 2017.

———. "Henry James's Subterranean Blues: A Rereading of *The Princess Casamassima*." *Modern Fiction Studies* 40, no. 1 (Spring 1994): 51–84.

Grenby, M. O. *The Anti-Jacobin Novel: British Conservatism and the French Revolution*. Cambridge: Cambridge University Press, 2001.

Gullickson, Gay L. *Unruly Women of Paris: Images of the Commune*. Ithaca, NY: Cornell University Press, 1996.

Hamnett, Brian R. *The Historical Novel in Nineteenth-Century Europe: Representations of Reality in History and Fiction*. Oxford: Oxford University Press, 2011.

Hanley, Keith, and Raman Selden, eds. *Revolution and English Romanticism: Politics and Rhetoric*. New York: St. Martin's, 1990.

Hanson, Ingrid. "Socialist Identity and the Poetry of European Revolution in *Commonweal*, 1885–1890." In *Poetry, Politics, and Pictures: Culture and Identity in Europe, 1840–1914*, edited by Ingrid Hanson, Wilfred Jack Rhoden, and E. E. Snyder, 225–246. Oxford, UK: Peter Lang, 2013.

Hanson, Ingrid, Wilfred Jack Rhoden, and E. E. Snyder, eds. *Poetry, Politics, and Pictures: Culture and Identity in Europe, 1840–1914*. Oxford, UK: Peter Lang, 2013.

Harrison, Royden. "Marx, Engels and the British Response to the Commune." In *Revolution and Reaction: The Paris Commune of 1871*, edited by John Hicks and Robert Tucker, 96–110. Amherst: University of Massachusetts Press, 1973.

Harvey, David. *Paris, Capital of Modernity*. London: Routledge, 2003.

Haupt, Georges. *Aspects of International Socialism, 1871–1914: Essays*. Translated by Peter Fawcett. Preface by Eric Hobsbawm. 2nd ed. Cambridge and Paris: Cambridge University Press; Editions de la Maison des Sciences de l'Homme, 1986.

Heilmann, Ann. *New Woman Strategies: Sarah Grand, Olive Schreiner, and Mona Caird*. Manchester, UK: Manchester University Press, 2004.

Hicks, John, and Robert Tucker, eds. *Revolution and Reaction: The Paris Commune, 1871*. Amherst: University of Massachusetts Press, 1973.

Hobsbawm, Eric. *The Age of Empire, 1875–1914*. New ed. London: Abacus, 2010.

Holroyd, Michael. *Bernard Shaw*. Vol. 1, *1856–1898: The Search for Love*. London: Chatto and Windus, 1988.

Holub, Robert C. *Nietzsche in the Nineteenth Century: Social Questions and Philosophical Interventions*. Philadelphia: University of Pennsylvania Press, 2018.

Holzman, Michael. "Propaganda, Passion, and Literary Art in William Morris's *The Pilgrims of Hope*." *Texas Studies in Literature and Language* 24, no. 4 (Winter 1982): 372–393.

Humble, M. E. "Early British Interest in Nietzsche." *German Life and Letters* 24, no. 4 (July 1971): 327–335.

Hutchins, Stanley. "The Communard Exiles in Britain." *Marxism Today* 15, no. 3 (March 1971): 90–92; 15, no. 4 (April 1971): 117–120; 15, no. 6 (June 1971): 180–186.

Ingleby, Matthew. *Nineteenth-Century Fiction and the Production of Bloomsbury: Novel Grounds*. London: Palgrave, 2018.

Jacobson, Marcia. *Henry James and the Mass Market*. Tuscaloosa: University of Alabama Press, 1983.

James, Simon J. *Unsettled Accounts: Money and Narrative in the Novels of George Gissing*. London: Anthem, 2003.

Jameson, Fredric. *The Antinomies of Realism*. London: Verso, 2013.

———. *The Political Unconscious: Narrative as a Socially Symbolic Act*. New ed. London: Routledge, 2002.

Janowitz, Anne. "*The Pilgrims of Hope*: William Morris and the Dialectic of Romanticism." In *Cultural Politics at the Fin de Siècle*, edited by Sally Ledger and Scott McCracken, 160–183. Cambridge: Cambridge University Press, 1995.

Jay, Elisabeth. *British Writers and Paris, 1830–1875*. Oxford: Oxford University Press, 2016.

———. "'In Her Father's Steps She Trod': Anne Thackeray Ritchie Imagining Paris." *Yearbook of English Studies* 36, no. 2 (2006): 197–211.

Jellinek, Frank. *The Paris Commune of 1871*. London: Gollancz, 1971.
Joll, James. *Europe since 1870: An International History*. 2nd ed. Harmondsworth, UK: Penguin, 1976.
Johnson, Martin Phillip. *The Paradise of Association: Political Culture and Popular Organization in the Paris Commune of 1871*. Ann Arbor: University of Michigan Press, 1996.
Jones, Colin, Josephine McDonagh, and Jon Mee, eds. *Charles Dickens, "A Tale of Two Cities," and the French Revolution*. Basingstoke, UK: Palgrave, 2009.
Jones, Gareth Stedman. *Karl Marx: Greatness and Illusion*. Cambridge, MA: Harvard University Press, 2016.
Jones, Thomas C., and Robert Tombs. "The French Left in Exile: *Quarante-huitards* and Communards in London, 1848–80." In *A History of the French in London: Liberty, Equality, Opportunity*, edited by Debra Kelly and Martyn Cornick, 165–191. London: Institute of Historical Research, 2013.
Joyce, Patrick. *The Rule of Freedom: Liberalism and the Modern City*. London: Verso, 2003.
Kamenka, Eugene, ed. *Paradigm for Revolution? The Paris Commune, 1871–1971*. Canberra: Australian National University Press, 1972.
Kapp, Yvonne. *Eleanor Marx: Family Life, 1855–1883*. London: Virago, 1979.
Katz, Philip Mark. *From Appomattox to Montmartre: Americans and the Paris Commune*. Cambridge, MA: Harvard University Press, 1998.
Keating, Peter. *The Haunted Study: A Social History of the English Novel, 1875–1914*. 2nd ed. London: Fontana, 1991.
Kelly, Debra, and Martyn Cornick, eds. *A History of the French in London: Liberty, Equality, Opportunity*. London: Institute of Historical Research, 2013.
Kettle, Arnold. "Dickens and the Popular Tradition." In *Marxists on Literature: An Anthology*, edited by David Craig, 214–244. Harmondsworth, UK: Penguin, 1975.
Kimmey, John. *Henry James and London: The City in His Fiction*. New York: Peter Lang, 1991.
Kingstone, Helen. *Victorian Narratives of the Recent Past: Memory, History, Fiction*. Basingstoke, UK: Palgrave, 2018.
LaCapra, Dominick. *History, Literature, Critical Theory*. Ithaca, NY: Cornell University Press, 2013.
LaValley, Albert J. *Carlyle and the Idea of the Modern: Studies in Carlyle's Prophetic Literature and Its Relations to Blake, Nietzsche, Marx, and Others*. New Haven, CT: Yale University Press, 1968.
Ledger, Sally. *The New Woman: Fiction and Feminism at the Fin de Siècle*. Manchester, UK: Manchester University Press, 1997.
Lefebvre, Henri. "La Commune: Dernière Fête Populaire." In *Images of the Commune / Images de la Commune*, edited by James A. Leith, 33–45. Montreal: McGill-Queen's University Press, 1978.
———. *La Proclamation de la Commune, 26 Mars 1871*. 2nd ed. Paris: La Fabrique, 2018.
Leith, James A., ed. *Images of the Commune / Images de la Commune*. Montreal: McGill-Queen's University Press, 1978.
———. "The War of Images Surrounding the Commune." In *Images of the Commune / Images de la Commune*, edited by James A. Leith, 101–150. Montreal: McGill-Queen's University Press, 1978.

Lesjak, Carolyn. *Working Fictions: A Genealogy of the Victorian Novel*. Durham, NC: Duke University Press, 2006.

Leslie, Esther. *Walter Benjamin: Overpowering Conformism*. London: Pluto, 2000.

Levine, George. *The Boundaries of Fiction: Carlyle, Macaulay, Newman*. Princeton, NJ: Princeton University Press, 1968.

———. "Taking Oliphant Seriously: *A Country Gentleman and His Family*." *ELH* 83, no. 1 (Spring 2016): 233–258.

Lodge, David. "The French Revolution and the Condition of England: Crowds and Power in the Early Victorian Novel." In *The French Revolution and British Culture*, edited by Ceri Crossley and Ian Small, 123–140. Oxford: Oxford University Press, 1989.

Losurdo, Domenic. *Nietzsche, the Aristocratic Rebel: Intellectual Biography and Critical Balance-Sheet*. Translated by Gregor Benton. Leiden, Netherlands: Brill, 2019.

Love, Nancy S. *Marx, Nietzsche, and Modernity*. New York: Columbia University Press, 1986.

Lovell, Terry. *Consuming Fiction*. London: Verso, 1987.

Löwith, Karl. *Nietzsche's Philosophy of the Eternal Recurrence of the Same*. Translated by J. Harvey Lomax, with a foreword by Bernd Magnus. Berkeley: University of California Press, 1997.

Lucas, John. "Conservatism and Revolution in the 1880s." In *Literature and Politics in the Nineteenth Century: Essays*, edited by John Lucas, 173–219. London: Methuen, 1971.

Lukács, Georg. *The Historical Novel*. Translated by Hannah and Stanley Mitchell. London: Merlin, 1989.

———. *The Meaning of Contemporary Realism*. Translated by John Mander and Necke Mander. London: Merlin, 1979.

———. *Tactics and Ethics, 1919–1929: The Questions of Parliamentarianism and Other Essays*. Translated by Michael McColgan. London: Verso, 2014.

MacKay, Carol Hanbery. *Creative Negativity: Four Victorian Exemplars of the Female Quest*. Stanford, CA: Stanford University Press, 2001.

———. "Tradition, Convergence, and Innovation: The Literary Legacy of Anne Thackeray Ritchie." *Victorian Review* 36, no. 1 (Spring 2010): 164–184.

MacKenzie, Norman, and Jeanne MacKenzie. *The Life of H. G. Wells: The Time Traveller*. Rev. ed. London: Hogarth, 1987.

Markovits, Stefanie. *The Crisis of Action in Nineteenth-Century English Literature*. Columbus: Ohio State University Press, 2006.

Martinez, P. K. "Paris Communard Refugees in London, 1871–1880." PhD diss., University of Sussex, 1981.

Maxwell, Richard. *The Historical Novel in Europe, 1650–1950*. Cambridge: Cambridge University Press, 2009.

———. *The Mysteries of Paris and London*. Charlottesville: University of Virginia Press, 1992.

McCracken, Scott. "The Author as Arsonist: Henry James and the Paris Commune." *Modernism/Modernity* 21, no. 1 (January 2014): 71–87.

———. "The Commune in Exile: Urban Insurrection and the Production of International Space." In *Nineteenth-Century Radical Traditions*, edited by Joseph Bristow and Josephine McDonagh, 113–136. Basingstoke, UK: Palgrave, 2016.

Meissner, Collin. "*The Princess Casamassima*: 'A Dirty Intellectual Fog,'" *Henry James Review* 19, no. 1 (1998): 53–71.

Merriman, John M. *Massacre: The Life and Death of the Paris Commune of 1871*. New Haven, CT: Yale University Press, 2014.

Miller, Elizabeth Carolyn. "The Inward Revolution: Sexual Terrorism in *The Princess Casamassima*." *Henry James Review* 24, no. 2 (Spring 2003): 146–167.

———. *Slow Print: Literary Radicalism and Late Victorian Print Culture*. Stanford, CA: Stanford University Press, 2013.

Milner, John. *Art, War and Revolution in France, 1870–1871: Myth, Reportage and Reality*. New Haven, CT: Yale University Press, 2000.

Mitchell, Leslie. *Bulwer Lytton: The Rise and Fall of a Victorian Man of Letters*. London: Hambledon and London, 2003.

Moretti, Franco. *Atlas of the European Novel, 1800–1900*. London: Verso, 1998.

———. *Graphs, Maps, Trees: Abstract Models for a Literary Theory*. London: Verso, 2005.

———. *The Way of the World: The Bildungsroman in European Culture*. New ed. Translated by Albert Sbragia. London: Verso, 2000.

Morris, Edward. *French Art in Nineteenth-Century Britain*. New Haven, CT: Yale University Press, 2005.

Nead, Lynda. *Victorian Babylon: People, Streets, and Images in Nineteenth-Century London*. 2nd ed. New Haven, CT: Yale University Press, 2011.

Nicholls, Julia. *Revolutionary Thought after the Paris Commune, 1871–1885*. Cambridge: Cambridge University Press, 2019.

Nunokawa, Jeff. *The Afterlife of Property: Domestic Security and the Victorian Novel*. Princeton, NJ: Princeton University Press, 1994.

Oddie, William. *Chesterton and the Romance of Orthodoxy: The Making of GKC, 1874–1908*. Oxford: Oxford University Press, 2008.

Ó Donghaile, Deaglán. *Blasted Literature: Victorian Political Fiction and the Shock of Modernism*. Edinburgh: Edinburgh University Press, 2011.

———. *Oscar Wilde and the Radical Politics of the Fin de Siècle*. Edinburgh: Edinburgh University Press, 2020.

O'Neill, Morna. "'Vive la Commune!': The Imaginary of the Paris Commune and the Arts and Crafts Movement." In *Teaching William Morris*, edited by Jason D. Martinek and Elizabeth Carolyn Miller, 99–114. Madison, NJ: Farleigh Dickinson University Press, 2019.

Osterhammel, Jürgen. *The Transformation of the World: A Global History of the Nineteenth Century*. Translated by Patrick Camiller. Princeton, NJ: Princeton University Press, 2014.

Parsons, Deborah. *Streetwalking the Metropolis: Women, the City and Modernity*. Oxford: Oxford University Press, 2000.

———. "Whirlpools of Modernity: European Naturalism and the Urban Phantasmagoria." In *George Gissing: Voices of the Unclassed*, edited by Martin Ryle and Jenny Bourne Taylor, 2nd ed., 107–118. Abingdon, UK: Routledge, 2016.

Paulson, Ronald. *Representations of Revolution, 1789–1820*. New Haven, CT: Yale University Press, 1983.

Pennybacker, Susan D. *A Vision for London, 1889–1914: Labour, Everyday Life and the LCC Experiment*. London: Routledge, 1995.

Peterson, Linda H. "On the Appointment of the 'Poet Laureate to Her Majesty,' 1892–1896." *BRANCH: Britain, Representation and Nineteenth-Century History*, edited by Dino Franco Felluga, June 2012. Extension of *Romanticism and Victorianism on the Net*. Last accessed 24 May 2020.

Philp, Mark, ed. *The French Revolution and British Popular Politics*. Cambridge: Cambridge University Press, 1991.

Pike, David L. *Subterranean Cities: The World beneath Paris and London, 1800–1945*. Ithaca, NY: Cornell University Press, 2005.

Pionke, Albert D. *Plots of Opportunity: Representing Conspiracy in Victorian England*. Columbus: Ohio State University Press, 2004.

Poole, Adrian. *Gissing in Context*. London: Macmillan, 1975.

Porter, Bernard. *The Origins of the Vigilant State: The London Metropolitan Police Special Branch before the First World War*. 2nd ed. Woodbridge, UK: Boydell, 1991.

Potter, Rachel. *Modernism and Democracy: Literary Culture, 1900–1930*. Oxford: Oxford University Press, 2006.

Przyblyski, Jeannene M. "Revolution at a Standstill: Photography and the Paris Commune of 1871." *Yale French Studies* 101 (2001): 54–78.

Radford, Andrew, and Victoria Reid, eds. *Franco-British Cultural Exchanges, 1880–1940: Channel Packets*. Basingstoke, UK: Palgrave Macmillan, 2012.

Rancière, Jacques. *Hatred of Democracy*. Translated by Steve Corcoran. 3rd ed. London: Verso, 2014.

Rapoport, Michel. "The London French from the Belle Epoque to the End of the Interwar Period (1880–1939)." In *A History of the French in London: Liberty, Equality, Opportunity*, edited by Debra Kelly and Martyn Cornick, 241–279. London: Institute of Historical Research, 2013.

Redford, Catherine. "'Great Safe Places Deep Down': Subterranean Spaces in the Early Novels of H. G. Wells." In *Utopias and Dystopias in the Fiction of H. G. Wells and William Morris: Landscape and Space*, edited by Emelyne Godfrey, 123–138. Basingstoke, UK: Palgrave, 2016.

Rifkin, Adrian. *Communards and Other Cultural Histories: Essays by Adrian Rifkin*. Edited by Steve Edwards. Leiden, Netherlands: Brill, 2016.

Rigney, Ann. "Remembering Hope: Transnational Activism beyond the Traumatic." *Memory Studies* 11, no. 3 (2018): 368–380.

Robins, Anna Gruetzner. "Alphonse Legros: Migrant and Cultural Ambassador." In *Impressionists in London: French Artists in Exile 1870–1904*, edited by Caroline Corbeau-Parsons, 115–119. London: Tate, 2017.

Robson, Catherine. "The Presence of Poetry: Response." *Victorian Studies* 50, no. 2 (2008): 254–262.

Ross, Kristin. *Communal Luxury: The Political Imaginary of the Paris Commune*. London: Verso, 2015.

———. *The Emergence of Social Space: Rimbaud and the Paris Commune*. 2nd ed. London: Verso, 2008.

Rougerie, Jacques. *La Commune, 1871*. Paris: Presses Universitaires de France, 1988.

———. *Paris Insurgé: La Commune de 1871*. Paris: Gallimard, 1995.

———. *Paris Libre, 1871*. Paris: Éditions du Seuil, 1971.

Rowe, John Carlos. *The Theoretical Dimensions of Henry James*. Madison: University of Wisconsin Press, 1985.

Royle, Edward. *Revolutionary Britannia? Reflections on the Threat of Revolution in Britain, 1789–1848*. Manchester, UK: Manchester University Press, 2000.
Rubel, Maximilien. "Préface." In *Notes pour Servir à l'Histoire de la Commune de Paris en 1871*, by Jules Andrieu, ed. Maximilien Rubel, 7–40 (Paris: Payot, 1971).
Sánchez, Gonzalo J. *Organizing Independence: The Artists Federation of the Paris Commune and Its Legacy, 1871–1889*. Lincoln: University of Nebraska Press, 1997.
Saunders, Max. *Self Impression: Life-Writing, Autobiografiction, and the Forms of Modern Literature*. Oxford: Oxford University Press, 2010.
Sautet, Marc. *Nietzsche et la Commune*. Paris: Le Sycomore, 1981.
Scanlan, Margaret. "Terrorism and the Realistic Novel: Henry James and *The Princess Casamassima*." *Texas Studies in Literature and Language* 34, no. 3 (1992): 380–402.
Schor, Esther H. "The Haunted Interpreter in Oliphant's Supernatural Fiction." In *Margaret Oliphant: Critical Essays on a Gentle Subversive*, edited by D. J. Trela, 90–110. Selinsgrove, PA: Susquehanna University Press, 1995.
Schramm, Jan-Melissa. *Censorship and the Representation of the Sacred in Nineteenth-Century England*. Oxford: Oxford University Press, 2019.
Schulkind, Eugene. *The Paris Commune of 1871*. London: Historical Association, 1971.
———. "Socialist Women during the 1871 Paris Commune." *Past & Present* 106 (February 1985): 124–163.
Schwartz-McKinzie, Esther. Introduction to *Mrs Dymond*, by Anne Thackeray Ritchie, ix–xiii. Stroud, UK: Sutton, 1997.
Seigel, Jerrold. *Bohemian Paris: Culture, Politics, and the Boundaries of Bourgeois Life, 1830–1930*. Harmondsworth, UK: Penguin, 1986.
Seltzer, Mark. *Henry James and the Art of Power*. Ithaca, NY: Cornell University Press, 1984.
Shafer, David A. *The Paris Commune: French Politics, Culture, and Society at the Crossroads of the Revolutionary Tradition and Revolutionary Socialism*. New York: Palgrave Macmillan, 2005.
Simmons, Clare A. *Eyes across the Channel: French Revolutions, Party History and British Writing, 1830–1882*. Amsterdam: Harwood, 2000.
Simon, Walter Michael. *European Positivism in the Nineteenth Century: An Essay in Intellectual History*. Ithaca, NY: Cornell University Press, 1963.
Sloan, John. *George Gissing: The Cultural Challenge*. London: Palgrave Macmillan, 1989.
Smith, F. B. "Some British Reactions to the Commune." In *Paradigm for Revolution? The Paris Commune, 1871–1971*, edited by Eugene Kamenka, 64–90. Canberra: Australian National University Press, 1972.
Starr, Peter. *Commemorating Trauma: The Paris Commune and Its Cultural Aftermath*. New York: Fordham University Press, 2006.
Stauffer, Andrew M. *Anger, Revolution, and Romanticism*. Cambridge: Cambridge University Press, 2005.
Stoddart, Judith. *Ruskin's Culture Wars: "Fors Clavigera" and the Crisis of Victorian Liberalism*. Charlottesville: University of Virginia Press, 1998.
Sypher, Eileen. *Wisps of Violence: Producing Public and Private Politics in the Turn-of-the-Century British Novel*. London: Verso, 1993.
Thirlwell, Angela. *Into the Frame: The Four Loves of Ford Madox Brown*. London: Chatto and Windus, 2010.
Thomas, Edith. *The Women Incendiaries*. New ed. Chicago: Haymarket, 2007.

Thwaite, Ann. *Edmund Gosse: A Literary Landscape*. Oxford: Oxford University Press, 1985.

Tilley, Wesley H. *The Background of "The Princess Casamassima."* Gainesville: University of Florida Press, 1960.

Tillier, Bertrand. *La Commune de Paris, Révolution sans Images? Politique et Représentations dans la France Républicaine (1871-1914)*. Seyssel, France: Champ Vallon, 2004.

Tomba, Massimiliano. *Insurgent Universality: An Alternative Legacy of Modernity*. Oxford: Oxford University Press, 2019.

Tombs, Robert. "How Bloody Was *La Semaine Sanglante* of 1871? A Revision." *Historical Journal* 55, no. 3 (September 2012): 679-704.

———. *The Paris Commune, 1871*. 2nd ed. London: Routledge, 1999.

———. *The War against Paris, 1871*. Cambridge: Cambridge University Press, 1981.

Traverso, Enzo. *Left-Wing Melancholia: Marxism, History, and Memory*. New York: Columbia University Press, 2016.

Trela, D. J. "Introduction: Discovering the Gentle Subversive." In *Margaret Oliphant: Critical Essays on a Gentle Subversive*, edited by D. J. Trela, 11-27. Selinsgrove, PA: Susquehanna University Press, 1995.

———, ed. *Margaret Oliphant: Critical Essays on a Gentle Subversive*. Selinsgrove, PA: Susquehanna University Press, 1995.

Trilling, Lionel. *The Liberal Imagination: Essays on Literature and Society*. Harmondsworth, UK: Peregrine, 1970.

Trotsky, Leon. *Literature and Revolution*. Edited by William Keach. Translated by Rose Strunsky. Chicago: Haymarket, 2005.

Trotter, David. *The English Novel in History, 1895-1920*. London: Routledge, 2001.

Tucker, Herbert F. *Epic: Britain's Heroic Muse, 1790-1910*. Oxford: Oxford University Press, 2008.

Vanden Bossche, Chris R. *Carlyle and the Search for Authority*. Columbus: Ohio State University Press, 1991.

Vargish, Thomas. *The Providential Aesthetic in Victorian Fiction*. Charlottesville: University of Virginia Press, 1985.

Varley, Karine. "Reassessing the Paris Commune of 1871: A Response to Robert Tombs, 'How Bloody Was *La Semaine Sanglante*? A Revision.'" *H-France Salon* 3, no. 1 (2011): 20-25.

———. *Under the Shadow of Defeat: The War of 1870-71 in French Memory*. Basingstoke, UK: Palgrave, 2008.

Vogeler, Martha S. *Frederic Harrison: The Vocations of a Positivist*. Oxford, UK: Clarendon, 1984.

———. "Gissing and the Positivists." *Gissing Newsletter* 21, no. 1 (1985): 1-13.

Waters, Catherine. *Special Correspondence and the Newspaper Press in Victorian Print Culture, 1850-1886*. London: Palgrave Macmillan, 2019.

Wegner, Phillip E. *Imaginary Communities: Utopia, the Nation, and the Spatial Histories of Modernity*. Berkeley: University of California Press, 2002.

White, Hayden. *The Content of the Form: Narrative Discourse and Historical Representation*. 2nd ed. Baltimore: Johns Hopkins University Press, 1990.

White, Richard J. *Nietzsche and the Problem of Sovereignty*. Chicago: University of Chicago Press, 1997.

Williams, Merryn. *Margaret Oliphant: A Critical Biography*. Basingstoke, UK: Macmillan, 1986.

Williams, Raymond. *The Country and the City*. London: Chatto and Windus, 1973.

———. *Culture and Society, 1780–1950*. New ed. Harmondsworth, UK: Penguin, 1982.

———. *Marxism and Literature*. Oxford: Oxford University Press, 1977.

———. *Modern Tragedy*. London: Chatto and Windus, 1966.

———. *Politics of Modernism: Against the New Conformists*. Edited by Tony Pinkney. 2nd ed. London: Verso, 2007.

———. *Problems in Materialism and Culture: Selected Essays*. London: Verso, 1980.

———. *The Long Revolution*. 3rd ed. Harmondsworth, UK: Pelican, 1971.

Williams, Rosalind. *Notes on the Underground: An Essay on Technology, Society, and the Imagination*. New ed. Cambridge, MA: MIT Press, 2008.

Wilson, Colette E. *Paris and the Commune, 1871–78: The Politics of Forgetting*. Manchester, UK: Manchester University Press, 2007.

Wisnicki, Adrian S. *Conspiracy, Revolution and Terrorism from Victorian Fiction to the Modern Novel*. London and New York: Routledge, 2008.

Wolff, Robert Lee. *Sensational Victorian: The Life and Fiction of Mary Elizabeth Braddon*. New York: Garland, 1979.

Wood, Ellen Meiksins. *The Pristine Culture of Capitalism: A Historical Essay on Old Regimes and Modern States*. 2nd ed. London: Verso, 2015.

Wood, Paul. "The Avant-Garde and the Paris Commune." In *The Challenge of the Avant-Garde*, edited by Paul Wood, 113–136. New Haven, CT: Yale University Press, in association with the Open University, 1999.

Woolven, Robin. "George Gissing's London Residences, 1877–1891." *Gissing Journal* 39, no. 4 (2003): 5–15.

Yarrington, Alison, and Kelvin Everest, eds. *Reflections of Revolution: Images of Romanticism*. London and New York: Routledge, 1993.

Index

Note: Page numbers in *italics* denote images and associated captions.

Academy, 158–159
Adorno, Theodor, 18, 169
Æneid (Virgil), 129, 136
Æneids of Virgil Done into English Verse, The (Morris), 136
affiches, 71
Agonie de la Commune, L' (Daudet), 177
Alcmene, 129
allegorical female figures, 133–135
All the Year Round (Dickens), 106–107, 174
Alton Locke, Tailor and Poet (Kingsley), 37, 45–46
Ambassadors, The (James), 96, 98
American in Paris, The (Savidge), 13
Amphion, 129
ancien régime, 30, 36, 109
Anderson, Perry, viii–ix, 98
Andrieu, Jules, 9–10
Anesko, Michael, 102
Angelus Novus, 133–135
Année Terrible, L' (Hugo), 135
Anticipations, 167
anticlericalism, 58
anticommunism, 1, 12, 32–33, 40
antidemocratic sentiment, x, 2, 25, 36
Antiope, 129
apocalyptic ideology, 28
apprenticeships, 89–90
Arcades Project, The (Benjamin), 22, 155, 161
Armée de Versailles, depuis Sa Formation jusqu'à la Complète Pacification de Paris, L' (MacMahon), 177

Arnold, Mary Penrose, 33, 173
Arnold, Matthew, x, 12, 33–36
artistic creativity, 95
Artist's Reminiscences, An (Crane), 10
Atkinson, Juliette, 21
Atlantic Monthly, 101, 114
Austin, Alfred, 48, 119–120, 120–125, 125–131, 169
Avenir, L', 11

Babble Machines, 156
Bagenal, Philip H., 120
Baker, Ernest, 13
Bakunin, Mikhail, 105, 132
Baldick, Chris, 33
Barry, William Francis, 13, 16, 17, 171, 175–179
Basilica of Sacre-Coeur, 172
Bastille, storming of, 19
Batchelor, John, 162–163
Battle of Mentana, 121
Bax, Ernest Belfort, 37, 132, 140
Beatty, Pakenham Thomas, 135
Beaumont, Matthew, xi, 28, 165–166
Beck, Karl, 133
Beckett, Reginald A., 133, 136–137, 140
Bee-hive, 20
Beesly, Edward Spencer, ix, 10, 20, 38, 40
Beeton, Isabella, 49
Beeton, Samuel Orchart, 48–49
Beleaguered City, A (Oliphant), 69–78, 75
Bellamy, Edward, 146, 153, 167

Benjamin, Walter, 22, 109, 133–135, 154–155, 159, 161–162, 173–174
Bennett, Arnold, 59, 151, 198n41
Bénot, Victor, 177
Berens, E. H., 166
Bertall (Charles Albert d'Arnoux), 50, 52
Bertz, Eduard, 87, 90, 97
Besant, Annie, 64, 145, 147
Besant, Walter, 40
Betham-Edwards, Matilda, 13, 53
Bible and biblical narratives, 37, 72–73
bildungsroman novels, 65, 80, 180–181
Birth of Tragedy, The (Nietzsche), 123, 159
Bismarck, Otto von, 90, 157
Black and White, 133, *134*, 135, 147
Blackwood's Magazine, 21, 70
Blanquists, 54–55, 85, 105, 138–139, 159, 176
Bleak House (Dickens), 87–88
Bloody Week *(semaine sanglante)*, viii, 6, 17, 32, 39, 74, 137, 170, 194nn50–51
Boer, Roland, 139
Boime, Albert, xi, 95–96
bookbinders, 101, 103
Book of Sibyls, A (MacKay), 64
Bookworm, The (unknown), 107
Boos, Florence, 128
Boos, William, 128
Booth, Charles, 98–99
Bourbon Restoration, 34
Bowen, Edward Ernest, 85
Braddon, Mary Elizabeth: and conspiracy narratives, 27, 29, 98; and context of study, x; and emergence of *pétroleuse* characters, 53; extrication of protagonists from revolutionary commitment, 175; and ideological polarization during Commune era, 21; and Oliphant, 78, 199n71; and overview of study, 13, 16–17; and *pétroleuse* characters, 49; and *ressentiment*, 7; Ritchie compared with, 61, 63–64, 66–67; and subterranean settings in *The Princess Casamassima*, 103; and vengeance, 54–61
Bradlaugh, Charles, 83, 201n12
Bridges, Robert, 115
Brontë, Charlotte, 57
Brooke, Dorothea, 65
Brooks, Peter, 14–15, 175
Brother Gabriel (Betham-Edwards), 13, 53
Brown, Ford Madox, 9, 40, 41
Brugère, F. de la, 177

Burne-Jones, Edward, 147
Burns, John, 145, 147
By the Sea, and Other Poems (Henderson), 137

cacotopianism, xi, 28, 165–167
Caillebotte, Gustave, 95
Caird, Mona, 64–65
Cameron, Julia Margaret, 64
capitalism, 36, 83, 125, 138, 152, 155, 162, 166, 172, 181
caricatures, 106–107, 156
Carlyle, Thomas, 12, 19–20, 29, 45, 174, 196n100
Carpenter, Edward, 77
Carver, Ben, 159
Casanova, Pascale, 6, 7, 8, 60
Case of John Bull in Egypt, The Transvaal, Venezuela and Elsewhere, The (Montbard), 11
Cashel-Hoey, John Baptist, 85
Catholic Church, 16, 66, 177
Caygill, Howard, 111
Central Committee of the National Guard, vii–viii
Cerreti, Claudio, 93–94
Chambers, Robert W., 13
"Charitas" (Ruskin), 36–37
Charles X, 34
Chartism, 38–39, 129
Chartism (Carlyle), 45
Chasse à l'homme dans les catacombs (Manhunt in the Catacombs), 22–23
Chesterton, G. K., 26, 150, 213n31
Christian ethics and morality, 39, 45–46
Church of Humanity, 96
City of Dreadful Night, The (Thomson), 128
civil parishes, 143
Civil War in France, The (Marx), 2, 7, 30, 74, 85, 139
class divisions and conflict, 81; and anti-communism of Commune's opponents, 12–13; in *A Beleaguered City*, 70; in *Joshua Davidson*, 45–46; in *The Parisians*, 23–25; and repetition/cyclicality, 114–115; and Ruskin's ideology, 36–37; and subterranean settings in *The Princess Casamassima*, 106; in *Under the Red Flag*, 55; and Wells's fiction, 152–153, 155–158, 163–167
classical gods, 128–129
Class Struggles in France: 1848 to 1850, The (Marx), 5

INDEX

Clément, Jean-Baptiste, 11
Clement-Thomas, Jacques Leon, vii, 136
Cluseret, Gustave Paul, 10, 173–174
Cobb, James F., 13–14, 33, 170
Coghlan, J. Michelle, xi, 168, 172–173
collectivism, 54–55, 76, 126, 180
Collins, Wilkie, 26
Colvin, Sidney, 9
Coming Race, The (Bulwer-Lytton), 23, 28–31, 35, 152
commemorations of the Commune, 138–139
Commonweal, x, 11, 125, 132–133, 135–140, 147, *149*, 173
Communal Councils, 145–146
Communal Luxury (Ross), xi
"Commune and the Internationale, The" (Salisbury), 28
Commune for London, A (Hyndman), 142, 143–149
Commune in London, The (Hemyng), 166
"Commune of Paris, The" (Beesley), 20
"Commune or Death—The Women of Montmartre, The" (Houghton), 50, *51*
communes (French administrative division), 143
Communeux 1871, Types-Caractères-Costumes, Les (Bertall), 50
Communism, 5, 54–55, 59–60
Communist Arbeiter Vereinne, 90
"Communist Club-Room Near Leicester Square, A" (Régamey), *43*
Communist International, The, 26–28, 54, 85, 90
Communist Manifesto (Marx and Engels), 155
"Communist Refugees' Co-operative Kitchen in Newman Passage, The" (Montbard), 99, *100*
Communists of Paris 1871, The (Bertall), 52
Comte, Auguste, ix, 40
"Concert for the Wounded at the Tuileries," 75
"Condition of England" novels, 45–46, 196n100
Confessions of a Young Man (Moore), 3
Conrad, Joseph, 26, 102, 116
conservatism, 1, 115–116, 119–120, 122, 125
conspiracy plots and narratives, 26–30, 104–105
Contemporary Review, 2, 158
Convulsions de Paris, Les (Du Camp), 58, 177, 199n68
Correspondence and Journals of the Thackeray Family, The, 62

Cosmopolitan Magazine, 151
Coghlan, Michelle, 109–110
County Councils, 150
Courbet, Gustave, 20, 154, 174
Crane, Walter, viii, 10, 21, 90, *91*, 133–135, *134*, 147, *148*
Criminal Law Amendment, 27
crowd psychology, 157
Crown Street Club, 82
cultural universalism, 6
Culture and Anarchy (Arnold), 33, 35
Culture and Society (Williams), 79
Cunningham, Gail, 94
cyclicality, 114, 133, 156–158, 158–162, 162–164, 175. *See also* eternal return

Dagonet Ballads, The (Sims), 99
Daily Chronicle, 147
Daily Express, 163
Daily News, 27
Dalotel, Alain, xi
Dalou, Jules, 41
Daudet, Ernest, 177
Daudet, Léon, 156
"Dawn of a New Epoch" (Morris), 145
Dayspring, The (Barry), 13, 16, 171, 176–177
Débâcle, La (Zola), 180
Degas, Edgar, 95, 96
democratization, 36, 146
Demos (Gissing), 79–80
Derwent, Leith, 13
Dickens, Charles, 45, 57, 63, 68, 87–88, 106
Dilettante Aristocracy, 29
Disraeli, Benjamin, 26, 45
distant reading, 93
divine order, 14–15, 56
Dmitrieff, Elisabeth, 64
Dombrowski, Jaroslav, 66
Dominicans, 58–59
"Dominicans d'Arcueil, Les," 58
"Doom of King Acrisius,The" (Morris), 129
Dowling, William C., 160
Downfall, The (Zola), 13
Dresden uprising (1849), 105
Dublin Review, 85
Du Camp, Maxime, 58, 68, 74, 158, 177, 198n36, 199n68
Dunkerley, William Arthur (Oxenham pen name), 33–34
Durand, Philip, 60
dystopian fiction, x, 29, 153, 165. *See also* cacotopianism

Eagleton, Terry, 125, 130
Earthly Paradise, The (Morris), 126, 129
Ecce Homo (Nietzsche), 158
Echoes of the Coming Day: Socialist Songs and Rhymes (Henderson), 137
Edinburgh Review, 20, 27, 28, 32
Edwards, Stewart, xi, 171
Eichner, Carolyn J., xi, 47, 64
"Eighteenth of March, The" (Beckett), 136
Eliot, George, 13, 38, 45, 50–53, 57, 65, 67–68, 112–113
Eliot, T. S., 1, 108
Empedocles, 158
Engels, Friedrich, 138–139
English naturalism, 16
English Positivism, 10
Englishwoman's Domestic Magazine, 48, 49
Enlightenment, 122–123
"Envoi" character, 30–32
epistemology, 102
eternal return, 157–158, 158–162, 162–164, 175
Eternité par les Astres, L' (Benjamin), 159
eudaimonia, 130
Eudes, Émile, 55, 176, 218n48
Euripides, 123
Eurydice, 108
Examiner, 10
execution of Communards, 22, 32, 38, 59, 72. *See also* Bloody Week *(semaine sanglante)*
exiles, 8–9, 29
Experiment in Autobiography (Wells), 152
eyewitness accounts of the Commune, 131

Fabian Essays in Socialism (Shaw), 145, 154
Fabian Society, 140, 154, 163, 165, 167
facticity, 58–59
Falkland (Bulwer-Lytton), 31
"Fall of the Commune, The" (Frederic), 20
Federation of Artists, 74, 188n35
Felix Holt, the Radical (Eliot), 37, 45, 68, 112–113
Félix Régamey, 10–11
feminism, 47, 57, 64, 69, 128
Ferguson, Priscilla Parkhurst, 3, 60, 157, 172
Ferré, Théophile, 55
First Men in the Moon, The (Wells), 151
Fischer, Mike, 116
Fitzrovia, 95
Fitzroy Square, 9–10
Flaubert, Gustave, 68
Flourens, Gustave, 54

Fors Clavigera (Ruskin), 36–37, 66, 115
Forster, E. M., 23
Fortnightly Review, 10, 20
Fourth Canto, 119
Franco-Prussian War: in *The Dayspring*, 177; and European imperial anxieties, ix–x; and political mobilization in Paris, vii; in *The Princess Casamassima*, 28, 114; and seizure of Parisian National Guard cannons, 47; and siege of Paris, 7, 21, 27, 31, 59–60, 76–77, 96, 143; and *The Twins of Saint Marcel*, 57; in *Workers in the Dawn*, 82, 103
Frankel, Léo, 174
Fraser's Magazine, 10
Freiligarth, Ferdinand, 133
French Assembly, 36
"French Communists in London" (Régamey), 44
French Revolution: British responses to, 19; Commune equated with, 105, 115, 139, 174; and "Condition of England" novels, 196n100; depicted in *The Parisians*, 23; and imagery of Paris, 8, 109; impact in Britain, 14, 45, 81; and origins of municipal socialism, 143–144, 146; and spatial politics of *Workers in the Dawn*, 93; and *A Tale of Two Cities*, 63
French Revolution: A History, The (Carlyle), 19–20, 174
Froude, James Anthony, 10
"Function of Criticism, The" (Arnold), 34

Gambetta, Léon, 82
Garibaldi, Giuseppe, 121, 123
Gaskell, Elizabeth, 45
Gaussen, Elizabeth, 92
Gautier, Théophile, 6–7, 7–8, 156
Gay Science, The (Nietzsche), 158
gender norms, 49, 56–57
Gérin, Winifred, 61, 69
German refugees, 90
Gissing, George: context of *Workers in the Dawn*, 79–80; and eternal return, 160; motivations of characters, 80–86; and overview of study, 15, 16; and pathologization of political dissent, 86–93; pessimism in writings, 166; and politics of *ressentiment*, ix–x, 7, 108; and politics of topography, 93–97; and self-sacrifice, 155
Glasier, John Bruce, 127
Gleig, Charles, 166
Glyn, Charles, 170–171

INDEX

"Golden Apples, The" (folk legend), 129
Golding, Arthur, 89
Goncourt, Edmond de, 7, 27, 188n35
Gosse, Edmund, 1–6, 17
Government of National Defense, 47, 54
Grant, Maria M., 13, 53, 176
Graphic, 32, 50, 99, 151, 158, 169
Great Exhibition of 1878, 70, 77–78
Gribble, Francis Henry, 13, 76–77, 176
Grousset, Paschal, 10
Guide to Historical Fiction (Baker), 13
Guiron, Henry, 179
Gullickson, Gay L., xi, 6, 47–48, 49

Hall, Sydney, *24, 26*
Hamnett, Brian, 68
Hanson, Ingrid, 133
Harrison, Austin, 80
Harrison, Frederic, ix, x, 10, 20, 38, 40, 80, 154
Harrison, Nell, 89, 91
Harrow Liberal Society, 85
Harvey, David, 172
Haupt, Georges, 131–132, 139, 141, 165
Haussman, Georges-Eugène (Baron Haussman), 29, 110, 161, 171
Hay, William Delisle, 23
Hayens, Herbert, 13, 14
Headingley, Adolphe S. (Adolphe Smith), 40, 90, 201n12
Healey, Elizabeth, 157, 163
Hegel, Friedrich, 130, 218n51
Heine, Heinrich, 133
Heinemann, William, 5
Hemyng, Samuel Bracebridge, 166
Henderson, Fred, 133, 137–138, 140
Henning, Millicent, 108
Henri V, Comte du Chambord, 34, 35
Henty, George Alfred, 13–14, 16, 21, 57, 177
Heraclitus, 158
"Herbert George Wells and His Work" (Bennett), 151
Hercules, 129
heroism, 125–131, 136–138, 140–141, 164
Her Two Millions (Westall), 13
Herwegh, Georg, 133
Histoire de la Commune de Paris 1871 (Laronze), 22
Histoire de la Commune de Paris en 1871 (Brugere), 177
Historical Basis of Socialism in England, The (Hyndman), 143
historical determinism, 18
Historical Novel, The (Lukács), 76

History of the Paris Commune of 1871 (Lissagaray), 11, 58, 139
History of the Paris Commune of 1871, The (March), 177
Hobsbawm, Eric, 3, 143
Holub, Robert C., 187n16
Homer, 129
"Hopes of Civilization, The" (Morris), 126, 131
Hopkins, Gerard Manley, 115
Houghton, Arthur Boyd, 50, *51*
House of Bourbon, 35
Howard, George, 10
Howard, George, 9th Earl of Carlisle, 41
"How Paris Mourns" (unknown), 174
"How the Paris Commune Made the Republic" (Grousset), 10
"How We Live and How We Might Live" (Morris), 160
Hugo, Victor, 10, 135
Human Tragedy, The (Austin), 119–120, 120–125, 127–128, 130, 169
Hyndman, Henry Mayers, 142–145, 146–148, 151

ideological polarization, 102
"Ideology of Modernism, The" (Lukács), 18
Illustrated London News, 10–11, 41, *42–44*, 48, *75*
Illustration, L', 22
Impressionism, 95–96
Impressions of Theophrastus Such (Eliot), 50–52, *52*
"In a Cellar in Soho," 99
incendiaries, 68. See also *pétroleuses*
"Industry under Socialism" (Shaw), 145
"Influence of Democracy on Literature, The" (Gosse), 2, 5
In Full Sunlight (Tissot), 41
"In Memory of the Commune of Paris" (Crane), viii, 133, *134*, 147
Insurgé, L' (Valles), 60, 174
"International, and Its Influence on English Politics, The" (Bagenal), 120
International School, 90
International School Conducted by Louise Michel: Prospectus (Crane), 91
International Workingmen's Association, 23–27
In the Days of the Comet (Wells), 163, 165
In the Year of the Jubilee (Gissing), 94
Iron Flail, The (Oxenham), 33
Island of Doctor Moreau, The (Wells), 166
Italian unification, 121

Jacobson, Marcia, 108, 115
Jacques Vingtras trilogy (Vallès), 60
James, Henry: and conspiracy narratives, 26–28; and context of study, x; and context of *The Princess Casamassima*, 98–101; extrication of protagonists from revolutionary commitment, 175; and ghost story genre, 72; and historical novel genre, 179–180; and overview of study, 15, 17; and politics of *ressentiment*, ix, 7, 106–112; and politics of topography, 96; and repetition/cyclicality, 112–118; subterranean settings in *The Princess Casamassima*, 101–106
James, Simon, 87, 97
Jameson, Fredric: on aesthetics of ideology, 115–116; and eternal return, 159–160; and historical novel genre, 76, 178–180; and overview of study, 15; and politics of *ressentiment*, 84, 92, 111–112; and politics of topography, 93–94
Janowitz, Anne, 127, 129
Jay, Elisabeth, 49
Jewett, Sarah Orne, 179
Johnson, Martin Phillip, xi
Joll, James, 77
Jones, Gareth Stedman, 143
Jones, Richard Sainthill, 176
Jones, Thomas, 89
Joshua Davidson: Christian and Communist (Linton), 9, 38, 45–46, 56
journalists, 27, 40, 47, 54–55, 60, 98, 105, 133, 138, 145
Joyce, Patrick, 147
Joynes, James Leigh, 133
Jude the Obscure, 118
July Monarchy, 23
Jungle Book, The (Kipling), 156
juvenile adventure fiction, 14

Katz, Philip M., xi
Kautsky, Karl, 132
Keating, Peter, 14
Keenan, Henry F., 13
Kenelm Chillingly (Bulwer-Lytton), 30–31
Kimmey, John, 114
King, Edward, 13, 14, 57, 66
King Lazarus (Derwent), 13
Kingsley, Charles, 37, 38, 45
Kingsley, Henry, 177
Kipling, Rudyard, 1–2, 156
Klee, Paul, 133–135
Kropotkin, Peter, 4, 145
Kugelman, Ludwig, 173

labor activism, 11, 145, 153
Labouchère, Henry, 27
"La Commune de Paris" (exhibition), 22
Lady Audley's Secret (Braddon), 54
Lafargue, Laura, 133
Lanos, H., 151
Laronze, Georges, 22
Lassassie, F., 90
"Last Barricade of the Commune, The" (Beatty), 135
Le Bon, Gustave, 157
Lecamus, Paul, 73, 74, 75
Lecomte, Claude, vii, 47, 136
Le Fanu, Sheridan, 70
Lefebvre, Henri, 74, 124, 168–169
Legitimism, 28, 35
Legros, Alphonse, 41
Lenin, Vladimir, 132
Léo, Andre, 64
Lescar, the Universalist (Grant), 13, 53, 176
Lesjak, Carolyn, 45
Leslie, Esther, 162
"Letters to John Bull, Esq." (Bulwer-Lytton), 31
Leverdays, Émile, 9, 189n44
Levine, George, 19
Librairie Parisienne, 90
Life and Labour of the People in London (Booth), 99
Linton, Eliza Lynn, x, 9, 37–40, 45–46, 53, 56
Linton, James Dromgole, 170
Linton, William James, 39
Lissagaray, Prosper-Olivier, 11, 47, 58, 74–75, 101, 139
Literary Club, 33
Literature and Revolution (Trotsky), 168–169
Local Government Act, 145–146
Lodge, David, 196n100
Lomax, J. Harvey, 159
London County Council (LCC), 144–145, 146–147
"London County Council I. Towards a Commune, The" (Burns), 145
London Dock Strike, 145
London in the Nineteenth Century, 40
London Labour and the London Poor (Mayhew), 99
Longfellow, Henry Wadsworth, 70
Long Revolution, The (Williams), vii
Looking Backward (Bellamy), 146, 153
Lothair (Disraeli), 26
Louis Napoleon, 114
Louvre Museum, 3, 6–7, 169, 177, 188n35

INDEX

Love and Mr. Lewisham (Wells), 163
Lovell, Terry, 83
Löwith, Karl, 158, 159, 164, 214n56, 216n90
Lucas, John, 105
Lukács, Georg, 18, 76
Lytton, Edward Bulwer Lytton, Baron: *The Coming Race*, 23, 28–31, 35, 152; and context of study, x; failure to complete *The Parisians*, 173; and overview of study, 13; *The Parisians*, 13–14, 21–33, 24, 26, 35, 37, 67, 86, 153, 173; Ritchie compared with, 67; and scope of responses to Paris Commune, 46
Lytton, Edward Robert Bulwer Lytton, Earl of, 21–22, 36

"Machine Stops, The" (Forster), 23
MacKay, Carol Hanbery, 64, 78
MacKenzie, Jeanne, 157
MacKenzie, Norman, 157
MacMahon, Patrice de, 177
Macmillan's Magazine, 61
Magazine of Commerce, 163
Magnus, Bernd, 164
Maguire, Tom, 133
Maillard, Stanislas-Marie, 19
Man and Superman (Shaw), 153
Manet, Édouard, 95, 96
Mankind in the Making, 167
"Man with the Hoe, The" (Markham), 136
March, Thomas, 177–178
Marguerite, Paul, 13
Marguerite, Victor, 13
Markham, Charles Edwin, 135–136, 137, 140
Markovitz, Stephanie, 112–113
martyrdom and martyrology, x, 15–16, 65, 125–126, 129, 131–141
Marx, Eleanor, 4, 11, 139
Marx, Karl: on anti-Commune reactionaries, 74; characterization of the Commune, 30; and disputes over the Commune's legacy, 132; and eternal return, 160–161; and fears of social revolution, 5; and "feudal socialist" characters, 26; and legacy of the Commune, 173; and poetics of martyrdom, 139–140; and political influence of the Commune, 2; and politics of *ressentiment*, 85; on responses to physical destruction, 7
Marxism, 54–55
Mary Barton (Gaskell), 45
Maxwell, Richard, 176, 218n51
Mayhew, Henry, 98–99
McCarthy, Justin, 9
McCracken, Scott, xi, 96–97, 98, 110, 144

melodrama genre, 16, 53, 54, 56, 87, 153, 178
Memoir of the Life of Laurence Oliphant (Oliphant), 70
mental illness, 83–84, 86
Meredith, Owen (Robert Bulwer-Lytton pen name), 22
Merriman, John M., xi, 32, 188n35
Michel, Louise, 11, 47, 90–92, 133
Miller, Elizabeth, 132
Millet, Jean-François, 136
Milner, John, xi, 174
Mink, Paule, 64
Minto, William, 10
Mistletoe Bough, 54
Mitchell, Leslie, 21, 30–31
mob rule and violence, 33, 55, 63–64, 66, 73, 155, 199n57
Modern Tragedy (Williams), 123–124
Modern Utopia, A (Wells), 159, 167
Monet, Claude, 95, 96
Montbard, George, 11, 99, *100*
Montmajour Abbey, 109
Moore, George, 3
More, Thomas, 36–37
Moretti, Franco, 180
Morris, William: and epic genre, 120; on fears of social revolution, 4; and fin-de-siècle socialism, 37; on legacy of the Commune, 142; and Legitimist politics, 34; on municipal socialism, 143–144; and overview of study, 17; and poetics of martyrdom, x, 125–133, 135–138, 140–141; and relationship between tragedy and revolution, 119–120, 121; and socialist revival in Britain, 11–12
Mot d'Ordre, 54
Mrs Dymond (Ritchie), 13, 40–41, 49–50, 53, 61–69, 71, 76, 176
municipal socialism, 143–149
Mysteries of Modern London, The (Sims), 98

Napoleonic Wars, 19, 31
Napoleon of Notting Hill, The (Chesterton), 150–151, 213n31
Napoleon III, 25, 28, 33, 110, 155
National Reformer, 83
National Review, 119–120
naturalism, 16, 95, 96, 204n59
Nead, Lynda, 142
Nether World, The (Gissing), 79–80
New Grub Street (Gissing), 87
New London: Her Parliament and Its Works (*Daily Chronicle* booklet), 147
Newman Passage, 99

New Quarterly Magazine, 70
New Review, 1
News from Nowhere (Morris), 17, 127, 143–145, 147, 157
newspapers. *See* journalists; *specific publications*
"new woman" fiction, 64
Nicholls, Julia, xi, 12, 140
Nicoll, David, 133
Nield, Jonathan, 13
Nietzsche, Friedrich: and anti-Communard sentiment, 3, 111, 153, 187n16, 214n41; on Enlightenment optimism, 122–123; eternal return, 157–158, 158–162, 162–164, 175, 214n56, 216n90; influence on Wells's work, 153, 155, 157–162; and politics of *ressentiment*, ix, 7, 84–85, 92, 106–112, 113, 115–116, 159–160, 173, 176
Nineteenth Century, 145
Norman, Helen, 108
Norton, Charles Eliot, 115
"Notes of Social Democracy" (Gissing), 90
Notes pour Servir à l'Histoire de la Commune de Paris en 1871 (Brown), 10

objectivity, 58
Ó Donghaile, Deaglán, 115, 118, 185n5
Odyssey (Homer), 129
Old Wives' Tale, The (Bennett), 198n41
Oliphant, Laurence, 48, 70, 199n71
Oliphant, Margaret, x, 69–78
O'Neill, Morna, 147–148
One Life, One Love (Braddon), 29, 98–100
On the Genealogy of Morals (Nietzsche), 3
"On the Position and Prospects of Poetry" (Austin), 120
ontology, 102
Orléans, Louis Philippe Joseph, duc d', 23, 34
Orpheus, 108
Orr, Alexandra, 13, 53, 57, 59, 64, 66, 169, 171
Osterhammel, Jurgen, 2
"Our Paris Letter" (column), 48–49
Oxenham, John, 13–15, 33, 70, 170–171, 173
Oxford English Dictionary, 144

Pall Mall Gazette, 9
Paris, siege of, vii, 7, 21, 27, 31, 59–60, 76–77, 96, 143
"Paris, Capital of the Nineteenth Century" (Benjamin), 155, 161
Paris at Bay (Hayens), 13
Paris Commune, The (Linton), 38

"Paris Commune of 1871: Its Origin, Legitimacy, Tendency, and Aim, The" (Cluseret), 10
parishes, 143
Parisian National Guard, 47
Parisians, The (Bulwer-Lytton), 13–14, 21–33, 24, 35, 37, 67, 86, 153, 173
Paris Municipal Council, 11
Paris workers' uprising of 1871, 79
Parsons, Deborah, 96, 204n59
Party of Order, 39
Past and Present (Carlyle), 29
patriarchal gender relations, 69
Pattison, A. Seth Pringle, 158
Pennell, Joseph, 147
Perfect Wagnerite, The (Shaw), 153
periodical press, 10, 50. *See also* journalists; *specific publications*
Perseus, 128–129
pétroleuses, 38–39, 47–48, 48–54, 56, 63, 143, 176
Pfau, Ludwig, 133
"physical metaphysics," 164
Pike, David L., 22–23, 28
Pilgrims of Hope, The (Morris), 120–121, 125–133, 136–138, 153–154; identity of protagonist and narrator, 209n39
Poetry of the Period, The (Austin), 126
polemical literature, 106
political cartoons, 106–107, 147–148, 156
political pamphlets, 85, 189n44
Political Unconscious, The (Jameson), 15, 92
politics of envy, 113
Poole, Adrian, 96
Porter, Bernard, 98–99
Portico of the National Gallery, The (Tissot), 41
Positivism, ix, 10, 20, 38, 40, 80, 96, 154
Pottier, Eugène, 133
Pound, Ezra, 1
Poupin, Eustache, 101, 103–105
Praeterita (Ruskin), 36
Pre-Raphael Brotherhood, 9, 11–12, 41
Princess Casamassima, The (James): concern with observation and surveillance, 205n18; and conspiracy narratives, 28; context of, 100–101; and eternal return, 160, 175; and historical novel genre, 180–181; and overview of study, 15, 17; and politics of *ressentiment*, 109–110; and repetition/cyclicality, 112–118; and subterranean imagery, 101–106, 107, 109, 152, 169
Private Papers of Henry Ryecroft, The (Gissing), 94

INDEX

private property, 14, 23, 31, 37, 94, 155, 162, 165–166, 191n76
Proclamation de la Commune, La, 26 Mars 1871 (Lefebvre), 124
propaganda, 60, 85, 156
Prothero, R. E., 145
Przyblyski, Jeannene, 136
Psychology of Revolution, The (Le Bon), 157
psychology of revolutionary sentiment, 104
publishing business, 65–66
Pythagoreans, 158

quarante-huitard refugees, 41, 89–90, 114
Quarterly Review, 13, 27, 28, 85
Quatrevingt-Treize (Hugo), 10
Quentin, Charles, 13
Quin, Clara, 74
Quintessence of Ibsenism, The (Shaw), 139–140

Radical Working Men's Club, 81, 93
Railton, Herbert, 147
Rancière, Jacques, x, 3
Reclus, Élisée, 145
Records of Tennyson, Ruskin and Browning (Ritchie), 66
Red Republic, The (Chambers), 13
Red Spell, The (Gribble), 13, 76–77, 176
Red Terror, The (King), 13, 57, 66
reformist politics, 81, 130, 147, 154, 164, 166–167, 203n37. *See also* Fabian Society
Régamey, Félix, 41, 42, 42–44
Reminiscences (McCarthy), 9
Renoir, Auguste, 95
repetition, 114, 175. *See also* cyclicality; eternal return
Republicanism, 82
ressentiment, ix, 7, 84–85, 92, 106–112, 113, 115–116, 159–160, 173, 176
revenge and retribution, 80–86. See also *ressentiment*
Revolutionary Commune Group, 85
revolutionary ideologies, 133–135
revolutionary romanticism, 126
Richard, Victor, 90
Riddell, Charlotte, 70
Rifkin, Adrian, xi
Rigault, Raoul, 55
Rimbaud, Arthur, 154
Ring Cycle (Wagner), 123
Ritchie, Anne Thackeray: on Communard refugees in Britain, 40–41, 44; and context of study, x; and emergence of *pétroleuse* characters, 49–50; extrication of protagonists from revolutionary commitment, 175; gender panic provoked by the Commune, 46; and ideological polarization during Commune era, 21; James's characters compared to, 103; *Mrs Dymond*, 61–69; and Oliphant, 69–70, 78, 199n71; and overview of study, 13, 16; and politics of *ressentiment*, 112
Ritchie, C. T., 145–146
Robins, Elizabeth, 64
Robson, Catherine, 132
Rochefort, Henri, 54, 205n9
"Role des Femmes dans l'Humanite, Le," 91–92
Romulus, 129
Ross, Kristin: on anti-Commune propaganda, 156; on ascertaining lessons of the Commune, 141; on battle over Commune's legacy, 12; on Commune's occupation of Paris, 171; and context of study, xi; on fears of social revolution, 4; on Legitimist politics, 35; on Morris's vision of social transformation, 145; on origins of the Commune, 21; on Parisian barricades, 151; on perceptions of Communard equality, 17; on politicized public spaces, 71; on politics of topography, 95
Rossetti, Dante Gabriel, 9, 41, 101, 189n46
Rossetti, William Michael, 6
Rougerie, Jacques, xi
Rowe, John Carlos, 207n63
Ruskin, John, x, 12–13, 36–38, 41, 46, 60, 66, 69, 115, 173

Saint Paul's Second Epistle to the Thessalonians, 37
Salisbury, Robert Gascoyne-Cecil, Marquess of, 13, 28, 33, 120, 173
Sánchez, Gonzalo J., xi
Sarcey, Francisque, 59
Saunders, Max, 94
Savidge, Eugene C., 13
Scanlan, Margaret, 113
Schor, Esther, 72, 78
Schramm, Jan-Melissa, 39
Schreiner, Olive, 64
Schulkind, Eugene, viii, xi
Schwartz-McKinzie, Esther, 68–69
Scott, Walter, 76, 176
Scott, William Bell, 9
Second Empire, 21, 23–26, 29, 33, 34, 49, 55–56, 111, 161
Secret Agent, The (Conrad), 102
self-sacrifice, 123, 155, 164
Seltzer, Mark, 99–100, 105, 117

Semur (commune), 71–75, 77–78
Sérizier, Jean-Baptiste, 55, 56, 58, 176
sexual awakening, 69
sexual love, 121–122
Shape of Things to Come, The (Wells), 167
Shaw, George Bernard, x, 135, 139–140, 145, 153–154, 158
Sherard, Robert, viii
Sichel, Edith, 80
siege of Paris, 7, 21, 27, 31, 59–60, 76–77, 96, 143
Sigurd the Volsung (Morris), 128
Sims, George R., 98, 99–100, 205n9
Singer, I., 166
Sloan, John, 97
Smith, Adolphe (Adolphe S. Headingley), 40, 90, 201n12
Social Democratic Federation (SDF), 140, 142, 144
socialist-feminism, 128
Socialist League, 11, 131–133, 137, 140, 144–145, 147, 157, 165, 173
socialist periodicals, x
socialist press, 133–135
"social problem" novels, 45
Socratic Christianity, 123
Socratic optimism, 123
Soho, 99
"Song for To-Day, A" (Henderson), 137–138
"Song of the Workers, The" (Markham), 136
Sophocles, 124
spectral allegory, x, 69–78
Standard, The, 48, 119
Star, The, 138
Starr, Peter, xi, 168–169
St Guy's Hospital, 9
Stigand, William, 20–21, 27, 28, 32, 46
Stoddart, Judith, 37
stoicism, 121
Story of My Dictatorship, The (Berens), 166
"Story of the Days to Come, A" (Wells), 151
Street Life in London (Thomson), 40
Strike, The (Michel), 11
subterranean settings and imagery, 7, 22–23, 28–30, 35, 101–107, 109, 152
suicide, 108, 175
Susbielle, Adolphe Roger de, 47
Swinburne, Algernon Charles, x, 5–8, 9, 12–13
Sypher, Eileen, 102–103, 207n64

Tableaux de Siège: Paris 1870–1871 (Gautier), 6–7
Taine, Hippolyte, 84–85

Tale of Two Cities, A (Dickens), 63
teleology, 15
temperance, 87
Temple Bar, 126
Tendenz-Roman novels, 79
Tennyson, Alfred, 1–2, 5, 120
Thiers, Adolphe: and Basilica of Sacre-Coeur project, 172; and fictional pardon of Henry Guiron, 179; in *Pilgrims of Hope*, 138; and Legitimist politics, 34–35; and political mobilization in Paris, vii; in *The Princess Casamassima*, 101; quoted by Austin, 120; seizure of Parisian National Guard cannons, 47, 48; and Shaw's anti-Commune sentiment, 154; and violent suppression of the Commune, 32
Thiesz, Albert, 90
Third Republic, 23, 34, 36, 49, 82, 95, 103, 111, 157
Thomson, James, 128
Thomson, John, 40
"Three Days in Paris" (Oliphant), 70
Three Hundred Years Hence (Hay), 23
Through the Storm (Quentin), 13, 74
Thus Spake Zarathustra (Nietzsche), 158, 164
Tille, Alexander, 158
Tilley, Wesley H., 103
Tillier, Bertrand, xi
Time (literary journal), 10
Time Machine, The (Wells), 23, 152, 166
Times (London), 48
Tissot, James, 41
To-Day: Monthly Magazine of Scientific Socialism, x, 60, 135
Tolstoy, Leo, 68, 76
Tomba, Massimiliano, 218n51
Tombs, Robert, xi, 32, 89, 194nn50–51
"Towards a Theory of the Artwork" (Adorno), 18
tragedy, 119–120, 121, 125. See also *Human Tragedy, The* (Austin); *Pilgrims of Hope, The* (Morris)
Trajan: The History of a Sentimental Young Man (Keenan), 13
Traverso, Enzo, 140
Trela, D. J., 78
Trilling, Lionel, 105
triumphalist teleology, 125
Trollope, Anthony, 10
Trotsky, Leon, 168–169
True History of Joshua Davidson, The (Linton), 37–39, 40, 44–46, 53
Tucker, Herbert, 120, 126, 127

INDEX

Tuileries Palace, viii, 74, 75, 96, 169
Tupper, Lucas, 9
Turn of the Screw, The (James), 72
Twins of Saint Marcel, The (Orr), 13, 53, 57, 64, 169, 171

Unclassed, The (Gissing), 101–102
Under the Iron Flail (Oxenham), 13, 15, 170–171
Under the Red Flag (Braddon): American printing, 198n30; compared with Linton's *Joshua Davidson,* 40; and conspiracy narratives, 26, 28; and cross-fertilization between history and fiction, 176–177; on Fall of the Commune, 172; and overview of study, 13, 17; and Paris as "beleaguered city," 70; and *pétroleuse* characters, 47–48, 48–54, 49, 53, 56, 63; and scope of Braddon's writings, 98; vengeance in, 54–61
Under the Red Flag and Other Tales (Braddon), 54
underworld myths, 108. *See also* subterranean settings and imagery
Une Epoque (Marguerite and Marguerite), 13
"Unification of London: A Suggestion for the Lord Mayor's Show under the London County Council" (Crane), 147, 148
Universalist, The (Grant), 176
Utopia (More), 36–37
utopianism, 67, 126–127, 147, 159, 165–167

Vaillant, Édouard, 11, 140–141, 173–174
Vallès, Jules, 10, 174
Vanden Bossche, Chris, 19
Vargish, Thomas, 57
Varley, Karin, 194n50
Varlin, Eugène, 101
Verlaine, Paul, 11
Vermersch, Eugène, 11
Victorian gender politics, 64
Victorian ghost stories, 70
Virgil, 129
virtue ethics, 126
"Vive la Commune!" (Crane), 147, 149
"Vive la Commune!" (Régamey), 41–42, 42
"Vive la Commune!" (Vaillant), 11
Vizetelly, Henry, 48
Voix de Peuple, La, 11
Vril-ya, 28, 35, 152

Wagner, Richard, 123
"Waiting for the End—A Sketch on the Terrace of St. Germain" (Dromgole Linton), 170

Wallace, W., 158
Waste Land, The (Eliot), 108
Waters, Mrs. John, 13, 53, 57, 64
Watson, William, 1–2
We (Zamyatin), 155
Wegner, Phillip E., 155
Wells, H. G.: and context of study, x; and eternal return, 158–160, 175; and historical novel genre, 181; and overview of study, 15–16; and politics of *ressentiment,* ix, 7; and subterranean imagery, 23; *When the Sleeper Wakes,* 150–155, 155–158, 162–167
Westall, William, 13, 177
When All Men Starve (Gleig), 166
When the Sleeper Wakes (Wells), 15, 23, 151–155, 158, 163–167, 175, 181
White, Hayden, 58
White, Richard J., 123
Whitman, Walt, 189n46
"Why We Celebrate the Commune Paris" (Morris), 125, 142
Wilde, Oscar, viii
Williams, Raymond, vii, 35, 79, 123–125, 126, 129, 173
Will to Power, The (Nietzsche), 161
Wilson, Colette E., xi, 58
Wilson, John, 85–86
Wisnicki, Adrian, 105
Wolff, Robert Lee, 54, 60, 78
Woman in White, The (Collins), 26
Woman of the Commune, A (Henty), 13, 57
Women of Trachis (Sophocles), 124
Workers in the Dawn (Gissing): context of, 79–80; extrication of protagonists from revolutionary commitment, 175; motivations of characters, 80–86; and overview of study, 15; and pathologization of political dissent, 86–93; and pessimism in Gissing's writings, 166; and politics of topography, 93–97; and repetition/cyclicality, 112, 160; and self-sacrifice theme, 155
Workman and Soldier (Cobb), 13, 14, 33
World Set Free, The (Wells), 167

Yates, Edmund, 10
Yeats, William Butler, 158
Young Girl's Adventures in Paris during the Commune, A (Waters), 13, 53, 57, 64

Zamyatin, Yevgeny, 155
Zethus, 129
Zola, Émile, 13, 54, 60, 158, 180

About the Author

Owen Holland is associate professor in the Department of Literature at Xi'an Jiaotong-Liverpool University. He has previously taught nineteenth-century literature at Jesus College, Oxford, and in the English department at University College London. His first monograph, *William Morris's Utopianism: Propaganda, Politics and Prefiguration*, was published in 2017, and he has also edited a selection of Morris's political writings.

Printed in the United States
by Baker & Taylor Publisher Services